The Satan

THE SATAN

How God's Executioner Became the Enemy

Ryan E. Stokes

William B. Eerdmans Publishing Company
Grand Rapids, Michigan

Wm. B. Eerdmans Publishing Co.
4035 Park East Court SE, Grand Rapids, Michigan 49546
www.eerdmans.com

Published 2019
Printed in the United States of America

25 24 23 22 3 4 5 6 7

ISBN 978-0-8028-7250-0

Library of Congress Cataloging-in-Publication Data

Names: Stokes, Ryan E., 1977– author.
Title: The Satan : how God's executioner became the enemy / Ryan E. Stokes.
Description: Grand Rapids, Michigan : William B. Eerdmans Publishing Company, 2019. | Includes bibliographical references and index.
Identifiers: LCCN 2018056929 | ISBN 9780802872500 (pbk. : alk. paper)
Subjects: LCSH: Devil—History of doctrines. | Devil—Biblical teaching.
Classification: LCC BT982 .S76 2019 | DDC 235/.47—dc23
LC record available at https://lccn.loc.gov/2018056929

To the one who shared our flesh and blood
so that through death he might destroy
the one who has the power of death

Contents

Foreword *by John J. Collins* xi
Preface xv
Abbreviations xxiv

1. THE ORIGIN OF THE SATAN 1
The Satan Tradition in the Hebrew Scriptures 3
What Is a Satan? 6
The Angel of Yahweh as a Satan in Numbers 22 10
The Satan Rebuked by the Angel of Yahweh in Zechariah 3 12
The Satan Who Stands against Israel in 1 Chronicles 21 17
What Kind of Satan Stands against Israel? 18
Reading the Census Story in Light of the Balaam Narrative 21
Early Notions of God's Executioner 26

2. THE SATAN AND THE INNOCENT JOB 29
The Composition of the Job Story 30
The Satan as Attacker/Executioner 40
The Satan Attacks an Innocent Person 43
Is the Satan an "Accuser" in Job? 45
The Contributions of Job to the Satan Tradition 46

3. **Demons, Evil Spirits, Fallen Angels, and Human Sin** 48
Taxonomies and Terminology for Harmful Superhuman Beings 48
Demons, Evil Spirits, and the Sons of God in the Hebrew Scriptures 50
Šēdîm, *"Demons"* 51
Evil Spirits 52
Sons of God 59
Demons, Evil Spirits, and the Sons of Heaven in the Book of the Watchers 61
The Watchers and Forbidden Knowledge 62
The Origin and Activity of Evil Spirits 63
Demons, Evil Spirits, Fallen Angels, and the Worship of False Gods 69
Superhuman Beings and Human Sin 73

4. **The Prince of Mastema and His Deceptive Spirits** 75
Interpreting Jubilees 75
Taxonomy, Terminology, and Titles for Harmful Superhuman Beings 79
Satanic Titles and Terminology 81
Designations for Demons and Evil Spirits 87
The Prince of Mastema, Deceptive Spirits, and the Nations 88
The Danger of Deceptive Spirits 88
The Prince of Mastema, Chief of the Deceptive Spirits 90
Evil Spirits and the Election of Israel 94
The Satan and the Deception of the Nations 98

5. **The Prince of Mastema, Enemy of God's People** 100
The Prince of Mastema Attempts to Harm God's People 100
The Prince of Mastema Causes a Famine 101
The Prince of Mastema Tests Abraham 101
The Prince of Mastema Assists the Egyptians 105

Two Perspectives on the Prince of Mastema 109

The Prince of Mastema as "Accuser" 111

Jubilees on the Origin of Evil 115

Unity and Diversity in the Portrayal of the Satan in Jubilees 118

6. Demons, Evil Spirits, the Satan, and Human Responsibility for Sin 120

Human Responsibility for Sin according to the Wisdom of Ben Sira 121

Demons, Evil Spirits, and Human Responsibility for Sin in the Epistle of Enoch 126

Lawlessness Was Not Sent upon the Earth 128

Demons and Evil Spirits as Mere Objects of Worship 134

"Evil Inclination" instead of the Satan in Barkhi Nafshi? 138

The Satan and Human Responsibility for Sin in the Epistle of James 139

Superhuman Beings and Human Responsibility for Sin in Early Jewish Literature 141

7. Belial, Sin, and Sectarianism 142

The Corpus of the Dead Sea Scrolls 142

Taxonomies, Terminology, and Titles for Harmful Superhuman Beings 143

Demons 144

Spirits 145

Satans 146

Other Harmful Superhuman Beings 148

Melchiresha in the Visions of Amram 149

Belial in the Damascus Document 152

Are Belial and the Prince/Angel of Mastema the Same Person? 160

Belial in the Rule of the Community 163

The Dead Sea Scrolls, the Satan, and Sin 165

8. **Belial and the Powers of Darkness** 167

The Angel of Darkness in the Treatise on the Two Spirits 167

The Two Spirits 168

The Angel of Darkness 173

Belial, the Enemy, in the War Rule 181

Belial, Sin, and Punishment 183

Belial and the Sons of Darkness versus Israel 185

Belial versus God 189

Etiologies of Maleficent Superhuman Beings 190

The Question of Zoroastrian Influence 191

The Satan as Leader of the Forces of Darkness 194

9. **The Satan in the New Testament** 195

Taxonomies, Terminology, and Titles for Harmful Superhuman Beings 196

Ho satanas, *"(the) Satan"* 198

Ho diabolos, *"the Adversary"* 201

The Activity of the Satan 202

The Satan and Sin 204

The Satan as Attacker 205

The Satan as God's Agent and as God's Enemy 208

The Accuser of the Comrades 210

Excursus: Satans in the Book of Parables 214

The Ancient Serpent 216

10. **Conclusion** 221

Bibliography 227

Index of Authors 255

Index of Subjects 260

Index of Ancient Sources 264

Foreword

The great dragon was thrown down, that ancient serpent, who is called the Devil and Satan, the deceiver of the whole world—he was thrown down to the earth, and his angels were thrown down with him" (Rev 12:9).

So says the book of Revelation, narrating a vision of John of Patmos. In John's vision, Satan was thrown down from heaven because the followers of Jesus had defeated him "by the blood of the Lamb and by the word of their testimony, for they did not cling to life even in the face of death" (12:11). This casting down, however, was not the final demise of Satan. Later we read that after Christ appears from heaven as a warrior riding a white horse, an angel seizes "the dragon, that ancient serpent, who is the Devil and Satan," binds him for a thousand years, and throws him into the pit (20:2–3). Even then he is not finished. After the thousand years are ended, Satan is released from his prison and comes out to deceive the nations and gather them for battle. His host is destroyed, however, by fire from heaven, and Satan himself is finally thrown into the lake of fire and sulfur, to "be tormented day and night forever" (20:10).

The book of Revelation does not describe the full history of Satan, but it provides hints to show that he has a history. His role in this world is said to escalate in the latter days when he is cast down from heaven. That he is variously known as the dragon, the ancient serpent, and the Devil hints that the figure we know as Satan has a complex history and various identities. Even Revelation does not yet assign to him the role for which he is best known in modern times, that of torturer of the damned in hell.

Satan as he appears in the book of Revelation is a prince of evil, the main adversary of God and Christ in the end time. It may come as a surprise to Christian readers that no such figure is known in the Hebrew Bible.

The closest analogue, perhaps, is the figure to which Revelation refers as the dragon. In many ancient Near Eastern cultures, the process of creation is thought to have involved a battle between the creator god and a sea monster—Tiamat in the Babylonian Enuma Elish, Yamm (Sea) in the Canaanite Baal myth known from texts found at Ugarit in northern Syria. We find allusions to similar creation stories in the poetic books of the Hebrew Bible. So Job 26:12: "By his power he stilled the Sea; by his understanding he struck down Rahab." Or again, in Isa 51:9: "Awake, awake, put on strength, O arm of the Lord! Awake as in days of old, the generations of long ago! Was it not you who cut Rahab in pieces, who pierced the dragon?" In Isa 27:1, the battle with the monster is projected into the future: "On that day, the Lord with his cruel and great and strong sword will punish Leviathan the fleeing serpent, Leviathan the twisting serpent, and he will kill the dragon that is in the sea." When Daniel sees the four winds of heaven stirring up the great sea, and four great beasts coming up out of it (Dan 7), this too is a reflection of the same mythic tradition, as indeed is the beast from the sea in the book of Revelation.

But while the dragon is an eschatological adversary of God, it is not a force of moral evil. It rather represents chaos—all the forces that threaten life and flourishing. It can represent natural forces or political entities, but it is not usually concerned with individuals. It is not a tempter, nor one who leads people astray.

The idea of the tempter is associated in popular imagination especially with the snake in the garden of Eden, the "ancient serpent" of Revelation. But the snake in Genesis is not a supernatural agent. Rather the story in Genesis is a fable that expresses the lure of temptation in a literary way. It was not until the first century CE that the snake was identified with the devil (in Wis 2:24, written in Alexandria about the time of Christ).

The figure of Satan does appear in the Hebrew Bible. Best known is his appearance in the book of Job, where he serves Yahweh by going to and fro upon the earth and testing people. Here he is clearly God's agent and has not yet been expelled from the heavenly council. Ryan Stokes makes the case that originally "the satan" was God's executioner. The expression "the satan" is not a proper name but refers to a role. In the story of Balaam in Num 22, it can even be played by the angel of Yahweh. In Job, however, this figure is transformed into one who also attacks the righteous. The book of Job, then, is pivotal in the development of the figure of Satan, even though he is still far from the character described in the book of Revelation.

The crucial period for the development of the figure of Satan, however, was the Hellenistic age, especially the last two centuries before the Common Era. The Book of the Watchers, in 1 En. 1–36, tells the story of the fallen angels, or watchers, who beget evil spirits on the earth. These evil spirits have much in common with the demons of Mesopotamian incantation texts. Unlike the evil spirit that troubled Saul in 1 Samuel, these spirits are not affiliated with God. Unlike the Mesopotamian demons, they not only afflict people with illness but become instigators of sin.

In the book of Jubilees, the leader of these evil spirits is called Mastema, but his character is that traditionally associated with Satan. When Noah's sons beseech God to banish these spirits, Mastema lodges an appeal, asking God to let some of them remain: "For if some are not left me, I shall not be able to exercise over men the authority I want; for these are destined for corruption and to be led astray" (Jub. 10:7–8). Remarkably, God agrees. One-tenth of the evil spirits are allowed to remain on earth, while nine-tenths descend to the place of punishment.

The mythology of evil spirits underwent further development in the Dead Sea Scrolls. Here the leader of evil spirits is given other names, most prominently Belial. (The word is used in the Hebrew Bible, but not as a proper name. "Sons of Belial" is a designation for "evil people.") Most significant is the Treatise on the Two Spirits in the Community Rule (1QS 3–4). Here we are told that when God created human beings, he gave them two spirits, one of light and one of darkness. These struggle within the hearts of individuals and incline them toward good or evil. God has assigned them equal measure until the final judgment. Another text from the scrolls, the War Rule, describes a final battle between the children of Light, led by the archangel Michael, and the children of Darkness, led by Belial. The battle is divided into seven phases. The forces of Light and the forces of Darkness each prevail in three phases until God intervenes decisively in the final phase.

The mythology of evil in the Dead Sea Scrolls is distinctive in ancient Judaism in two respects. First, the Treatise on the Two Spirits is unambiguous in claiming that God created the spirit of Darkness as well as the spirit of Light. In the older mythology, the dragon and the Sea seem to have an existence independent of God. The fallen angels of Enoch and Jubilees are created, but their intervention on earth is originally a rebellion. Nonetheless, the rebellion is qualified in Jubilees, where the evil spirits receive divine permission to continue to lead human beings astray. In the scrolls, however, Belial and the Angel of Darkness (who are presumably the same figure) do the will of God, mysterious though it may be, although they are not less evil for that reason.

Second, the dualism of the scrolls is evenly balanced between the forces of good and evil. In Enoch and Jubilees, the fallen angels and their progeny are agents of disruption in a good creation. In the scrolls the world is divided evenly until the time of judgment. There can be little doubt that the distinctive dualism of the scrolls is influenced to a degree by Zoroastrianism, which also divided the world between Light and Darkness, although the channels of influence are obscure. This is not to say that the scrolls reproduce the Zoroastrian system. On the contrary, they adapt it to reconcile it with Judaism. One of the notable differences between the scrolls and Zoroastrianism is that people are predestined to good or evil in the scrolls, whereas the Persian system insisted on freedom of choice.

The Satan of the NT, then, was heir to complex traditions, and was indeed a complex personality. Passages that speak of Satan draw on different traditions, and these are not fully reconciled. Satan continued to evolve after the NT period. He appears as a prominent figure in two of the classic works of Western literature, Dante's *Inferno* and Milton's *Paradise Lost*. Dante's Satan is a grotesque giant lacking in personality. Milton's Satan is a proud rebel, who thinks it better to reign in hell than to serve in heaven. Satan (Shaitan) is also a major figure in Islam, where he is granted divine permission to mislead Adam and his descendants.

Ryan Stokes has done a masterful job in showing how the understanding of Satan developed in the biblical tradition. In so doing, he uncovers different nuances in the phenomena of temptation, sin, and life-threatening evil that have beset humanity since ancient times and are still very much with us today.

John J. Collins
Holmes Professor of Old Testament
Yale Divinity School

Preface

Writing in the latter part of the first century CE, a prophet named John gives his visionary account of a heavenly struggle. The central figure in this conflict is the dragon who leads an army of evil angels. At the end of the war, this dragon and his angels are defeated and thrown down to the earth. To ensure that his readers comprehend the significance of the dragon's defeat, John clarifies just who it is that has been cast out of heaven.

> The great dragon was thrown down, that ancient serpent, who is called the Devil and Satan, the deceiver of the whole world—he was thrown down to the earth, and his angels were thrown down with him. . . . "The accuser of our comrades has been thrown down, who accuses them day and night before our God." (Rev 12:9–10)[1]

Employing various titles and alluding to a number of earlier traditions, John tells his readers that this dragon is responsible for leading the whole world astray and is the one behind the suffering that they are experiencing. The churches to whom John writes are participants in a cosmic conflict, and their enemy is an ancient and terrible serpent, who accuses, deceives, and makes war.

Since modern conceptions of the devil have been heavily influenced by John's depiction of the dragon, modern readers overlook much of its peculiarity. It seems only natural that John would refer to this great dragon, the accuser and deceiver, as "Satan," who, of course, is the Accuser and

1. Unless otherwise indicated, all biblical quotations in this book (including quotations from the Apocrypha/deuterocanonical writings) follow the NRSV.

the Deceiver according to centuries of theology and popular imagination. There is, nonetheless, an oddity in John's use of the title "Satan" when one compares what he says about this figure with the Satan who appears in the Hebrew scriptures.

Calling this enemy "(the) Satan" or "the Devil," John associates the commander of the evil angelic forces in his vision with the individual who long ago approached God and created problems for the righteous Job (Job 1–2). John also calls to mind the superhuman adversary whom the prophet Zechariah saw in his vision of the high priest Joshua standing before the angel of Yahweh (Zech 3). John no doubt intends to speak of the same figure whom one encounters in these earlier Hebrew texts. When one compares John's depiction of the Satan with those of the Hebrew scriptures, however, one finds that John's Satan has surprisingly little in common with those of Job and Zechariah. The satans of Job and Zechariah are not serpents or dragons. They command no army of evil angels. They do not deceive the world, or anyone for that matter. They do not engage in battle either in heaven or on earth. These satans are not the rebellious enemies of God and of God's people, but are agents of God, executing the divine will among humankind. When one compares John's Satan to the satans of the Hebrew scriptures, it quickly becomes apparent that John is not simply deriving his ideas about this figure directly from the Hebrew scriptures, but that John is the recipient of a tradition that has passed for centuries through the hands of creative theologians and interpreters. These religious thinkers reshaped the Satan tradition in various ways to meet the needs of their own communities, transforming this modest functionary of Yahweh into the great enemy of God and God's people.

This book is a history of the origin, shaping, and reshaping of beliefs about satan figures and about the Satan.[2] It traces the development of ideas pertaining to these figures from their earliest literary manifestations in the Hebrew scriptures to the varied depictions of the Satan and his evil forces in the Jewish and Christian literature of the late Second Temple period. It explains the genesis of this tradition as evidenced in the Hebrew scriptures and describes the interpretive and creative process that transformed an agent of Yahweh into the preeminent antagonist and archenemy of good

2. As I will discuss below, the Hebrew noun שטן, "satan," is used with reference to several different individuals, as well as to one particular figure called "Satan" or "the Satan." In this book when I refer to a "satan" or "satans" generically, a lowercase *s* will be used. "Satan" with an uppercase *S* refers to the particular figure called "the Satan" or "Satan."

about whom one reads in works such as Revelation. In particular, it follows the evolution of the tradition as the idea of a heavenly satan figure is brought into conversation with different aspects of the problem of evil and as this figure little by little receives the blame for all that is wrong in the world.

The historiographic nature of this study distinguishes it methodologically from other sorts of inquiries into ancient religious texts. It is not my objective in the present work to construct a theology of Satan or of evil. Nor is it my purpose even to evaluate the merit of the theologies of ancient writers. The goal of this investigation is simply to describe the religious thought to which the ancient literature attests.[3] I will not ask questions such as, Does Satan exist? or, What can one know about Satan's nature or origin? Neither will I attempt to construct any sort of "canonical" or "biblical" perspective on evil or on the superhuman. Although such theological work is valuable, and I hope that this book will contribute to the theological enterprise, this is not my pursuit in the present historical inquiry. The primary questions I ask will be, What did ancient writers say and believe about the Satan and related figures? What can one learn of the ancient literary and theological processes that gave rise to later conceptions of the Satan?

Correspondingly, the present study is necessarily diachronic rather than synchronic in nature. Although thematic considerations bear upon certain aspects of this book's structure, the chapters are generally arranged chronologically, beginning with the literature of the Hebrew scriptures and concluding with the literature from around the first century CE. In the cases of some complex texts, it will even be necessary to distinguish between portions of them that were composed at different times and that may not be entirely uniform in how they present the Satan figure.

Another aspect of this study is attention to the terminology and categories that ancient texts employ for the purpose of describing the superhuman realm. The terminology and taxonomies for superhuman beings found in ancient texts can reveal much about their authors' conceptions of these figures. What does the word *śāṭān*, "satan," mean? How do the categories "demon," "evil spirit," and "fallen angel" relate to one another? Ancient authors did not necessarily employ these designations and conceive of these categories in the same way that modern religious thinkers

3. Although here I refer to historiography as a "descriptive" task, this should not be construed as a denial that history writing is also in a very real sense "constructive."

do. Nor does ancient literature even reflect a single conception of these beings and their relationships to one another. Rather, different texts depict the superhuman realm in different ways. While the imposition of modern categories on ancient texts to some degree is unavoidable, I hope that this book advances the accuracy and clarity with which modern scholars represent ancient beliefs about the Satan and related figures.

I will generally employ the designation "the Satan" rather than the name Satan for the Satan figure. The earliest texts that speak of this particular figure refer to him as *haśśāṭān*, which is probably to be translated as the title "the Satan" rather than as the name Satan. Though early Jewish literature would eventually apply other designations to this figure (e.g., Belial, the Prince of Mastema), the title "the Satan" continued to be used throughout the period under consideration in this book. It is not as clear, conversely, precisely when and to what extent in the Second Temple era the name Satan came to be used with reference to this figure. Another potential drawback of using the name Satan for our purposes is the theological connotations that this name carries. Since the name Satan evokes for many people notions of the Evil One that arose only late in the Second Temple period or even subsequent to this era, in this study I will generally avoid using the name, except in those instances in which the particular text under consideration appears to make use of it.

The topic of the Satan has experienced a notable surge in popularity among biblical scholars in recent years. Several collections of essays devoted to the Satan and evil superhuman beings have appeared, as well as numerous stand-alone essays on the subject.[4] It is difficult to know exactly to what to attribute the recent increase in curiosity about these evil beings. It no doubt stems in part, however, from the growing interest among schol-

4. See, e.g., Stefan Schreiber, "The Great Opponent: The Devil in Early Jewish and Formative Christian Literature," in *Angels: The Concept of Celestial Beings*, ed. Friedrich V. Reiterer, Tobias Nicklas, and Karin Schöpfin, *DCLY* (Berlin: de Gruyter, 2007), 437–57; Gerd Theissen, "Monotheismus und Teufelsglaube: Entstehung und Psychologie des biblischen Satansmythos," in *Demons and the Devil in Ancient and Medieval Christianity*, ed. Nienke Vos and Willemien Otten, VCSup 108 (Leiden: Brill, 2011), 37–70; Ida Fröhlich and Erkki Koskenniemi, eds., *Evil and the Devil*, LNTS 481 (London: Bloomsbury, 2013); Anne-Sarah Schmidt, "Die biblische Satansvorstellung—eine Entwicklungsgeschichte: Altes Testament und zwischentestamentliche Texte," *BN* 166 (2015): 109–41; Jan Dochhorn, Susanne Rudnig-Zelt, and Benjamin Wold, eds., *Das Böse, der Teufel und Dämonen—Evil, the Devil, and Demons*, WUNT 2/412 (Tübingen: Mohr Siebeck, 2016); Chris Keith and Loren T. Stuckenbruck, eds., *Evil in Second Temple Judaism and Early Christianity*, WUNT 2/417 (Tübingen: Mohr Siebeck, 2016).

ars in the literature of early Judaism, which has provided us with much to consider regarding ancient beliefs about the superhuman realm. Also, several works in which rebellious superhuman beings feature prominently, such as 1 Enoch, Jubilees, and some of the Dead Sea Scrolls, have come to figure fundamentally into discussions of early Jewish thought. As a result, scholars are rethinking old paradigms about the Satan and related figures and their place in Jewish and Christian belief and practice in the centuries surrounding the turn of the era.

Given the scope of the present study and the variety of texts and issues to which it pertains, I will reserve the majority of interaction with previous scholarship for the individual chapters to which the different scholarly discussions are relevant. A few preliminary remarks about previous scholarship, however, are in order at the outset.

Many books have been written about the Satan that are much broader in scope than the present work, tracing this tradition from the ancient period well into the Middle Ages or even into the modern era.[5] While these studies helpfully describe the general trajectory of the Satan tradition from ancient to more recent times, they contribute little to the discussion about the Satan tradition prior to the rise of Christianity. The authors of these volumes, who are in many cases specialists in later literature or theology rather than the literature of early Judaism, are typically more concerned with the subsequent history of the tradition than with its origin and early development. This assessment is not so much a criticism of these books as it is an observation regarding the nature of their contributions.

Exceptional among these broader studies is Neil Forsyth's *The Old Enemy: Satan and the Combat Myth*, which deals quite competently and illuminatingly with the early Satan tradition and how it developed in relation to ancient combat mythology.[6] Even so, the breadth of Forsyth's work, which

5. Examples of such works include Henry Ansgar Kelly, *Satan: A Biography* (Cambridge: Cambridge University Press, 2006); Miguel A. De La Torre and Albert Hernández, *The Quest for the Historical Satan* (Minneapolis: Fortress, 2011). I would also classify the four-book series by Jeffrey Burton Russell among these broader studies, although the first volume (*The Devil: Perceptions of Evil from Antiquity to Primitive Christianity* [Ithaca, NY: Cornell University Press, 1977]) is devoted to the earlier period. The other three books are *Satan: The Early Christian Tradition* (Ithaca, NY: Cornell University Press, 1981); *Lucifer: The Devil in the Middle Ages* (Ithaca, NY: Cornell University Press, 1984); *Mephistopheles: The Devil in the Modern World* (Ithaca, NY: Cornell University Press, 1986).

6. Neil Forsyth, *The Old Enemy: Satan and the Combat Myth* (Princeton: Princeton University Press, 1987).

deals with a wide range of texts and topics from the Sumerian Gilgamesh and Huwawa to the writings of Augustine, limits the extent to which Forsyth can consider the earliest texts pertaining more directly to the Satan. And, although elements of the combat myth eventually merged with the Satan tradition, this merger began to take place only very late in the period under consideration in the present work. Beliefs about the Satan arose and underwent considerable development long before their integration with the sorts of myths with which Forsyth's work is primarily concerned.

The only monograph to deal exclusively with the topic of ideas about the Satan prior to the advent of Christianity is Peggy Day's useful study, *An Adversary in Heaven.*[7] In this work, Day first considers the meaning of the Hebrew noun *śāṭān,* which she argues can mean either "adversary" or "accuser." She then analyzes each of the texts in the Hebrew scriptures in which this word is used to refer to a superhuman adversary or accuser, concluding that there is no single celestial satan in this literature, but various satans. In ch. 1 of the present study I engage Day's work more closely, benefiting from her insights but also parting ways with her conclusions in significant respects.

Two additional important studies should be mentioned. The first is Elaine Pagels's *The Origin of Satan.*[8] Pagels's "social history" of Satan demonstrates how various Jews, particularly those who authored NT Gospels, appropriated the idea of Satan in an effort to characterize their fellow Jewish opponents. The other study is Miryam Brand's *Evil Within and Without,* a perceptive analysis of how early Jewish literature deals with the problem of sin.[9] A large portion of Brand's study discusses the various ways in which early Jewish texts describe the relationship between superhuman beings and human moral failing. Both Pagels and Brand make important contributions to our understanding of the Satan and other evil superhuman beings. In the present study, however, rather than limiting discussion to the social implications of certain depictions of the Satan or to the relationship between the Satan and human sin, I describe the origin and development of ideas about the Satan more generally.

7. Peggy L. Day, *An Adversary in Heaven: śāṭān in the Hebrew Bible*, HSM 43 (Atlanta: Scholars Press, 1988).

8. Elaine Pagels, *The Origin of Satan* (New York: Vintage, 1995). See also her discussion of the Satan and related figures in the literature of Israel and Judaism in "The Social History of Satan, the 'Intimate Enemy': A Preliminary Sketch," *HTR* 84.2 (1991): 105–28.

9. Miryam T. Brand, *Evil Within and Without: The Source of Sin and Its Nature as Portrayed in Second Temple Literature*, JAJSup 9 (Göttingen: Vandenhoeck & Ruprecht, 2013).

In the first two chapters I discuss the Satan tradition in the Hebrew scriptures, which are the earliest writings that mention a superhuman "satan" figure. Chapter 1 locates the origin of the Satan tradition among other traditions in the Hebrew scriptures pertaining to superhuman bringers of death. It demonstrates that the superhuman satans of these texts were believed to be divine executioners of the wicked. In ch. 2 I contend that the latest manifestation of the Satan tradition in this literature is found in the book of Job. In the Hebrew scriptures, it is the book of Job that reflects the most developed understanding of the Satan, whom this work credits with attacking a righteous person.

In ch. 3 I take up the matter of early conceptions of demons, evil spirits, and those divine beings called "sons of God," since early Jewish thinking about these beings would have a significant and lasting impact on beliefs about the Satan. Although the Hebrew scriptures do not associate demons, evil spirits, and the Gen 6 "sons of God" with one another, the third-century BCE Book of the Watchers (1 En. 1–36) brings these three traditions together in an effort to account for many of the world's problems. Most importantly for the present study, as I show in ch. 3, the Book of the Watchers teaches that evil spirits are in league with sinful angels and that they lead humans to worship false gods. Evil spirits in the earlier literature are not engaged in this sort of activity, so this novelty marks a major development in the discussion of the relationship between superhuman beings and human sin. This development would influence early Jewish thinking about the Satan considerably.

In chs. 4 and 5 I consider how the second-century BCE book of Jubilees depicts the Prince of Mastema and the evil spirits under his authority. In these chapters I demonstrate that Jubilees' portrait of the Satan is complex. On the one hand, it characterizes the Prince of Mastema as one who functions within God's design for humankind, deceiving and punishing the idolatrous nations through the agency of harmful spirits. On the other hand, Jubilees portrays the Prince of Mastema as the enemy of God's people who opposes God's plan for them. This combination of disparate traditions paves the way for later depictions of Satan as deceiver of the world and enemy of God's people.

In ch. 6 I analyze what the Epistle of Enoch (roughly 1 En. 91–108) and other early Jewish works say concerning human responsibility for evil. Several texts from the second century BCE and afterward express disagreement with explanations for human sin that blame God or other powers external to humans themselves for this evil. Although the Epistle does not typically figure into discussions of Satan and evil spirits, a careful look at statements in this work concerning the origin of evil suggests that its teaching responds, at least in part, to developing notions of Satan and evil spirits. In ch. 6 I argue that the Epistle takes issue, in particular, with the teachings of Jubilees that the Prince of Mastema and evil spirits lead human beings into sin. In this chapter I also consider the NT Epistle of James, the Dead Sea text Barkhi Nafshi, and how these works' teachings on human responsibility relate to developing notions of the Satan.

The Dead Sea Scrolls' teachings about Belial and the superhuman forces of evil are the foci of chs. 7 and 8. I maintain that the Satan of these documents is foremost a wicked figure who leads humankind into sin. The Damascus Document adapts the theology of Jubilees to meet the needs of the Damascus group's sectarian context. In the Damascus Document, Belial misleads not only the gentile nations but also those Jews whose observance of Mosaic Torah differs from that of the Damascus sect. The Treatise on the Two Spirits and the War Rule (or War Scroll) conceive of reality in terms of a cosmic conflict between light and darkness and divide humankind into two camps: the Sons of Light and the Sons of Darkness. The Treatise provides a comprehensive explanation for the existence of sin and blames the Angel of Darkness even for the errors of the Sons of Light. The War Rule combines a number of earlier traditions about the Satan, depicting Belial as the enemy of Israel and of God.

In the ninth chapter I address beliefs about the Satan that are found in the NT. The Satan has a prominent place in the theology of the NT authors. In the NT, as in those Dead Sea Scrolls considered in the previous chapters, the Satan appears frequently as a wicked figure. The NT writings credit this figure with leading humans into sin and blame him for opposition to Christ and the churches. Some NT authors, however, preserve the more ancient conception of the Satan as one who physically attacks sinners on behalf of God. In this chapter I also devote some attention to the notion that the Satan is an "accuser" and the association of the Satan with the serpent of Gen 3, which are reflected in some NT passages, most explicitly in Rev 12.

The Satan tradition is one whose origins have been obscured by its evolution. The Satan has not always been what he eventually came to be in the minds of religious thinkers. Nevertheless, one can discern in the literature of ancient Judaism and Christianity much about the process that gave rise to this principal antagonist. The Satan tradition attested in ancient literature is multifaceted and dynamic. The Satan is a figure who has inspired intrigue among ancient and modern interpreters alike; and, fittingly, the history of beliefs about the Satan is a fascinating one.

* * *

I am indebted to a number of organizations and individuals who contributed to the completion of this volume. Several portions of the study have improved as the result of feedback I received from scholars to whom I had the privilege of presenting preliminary versions of chapters. Particularly helpful were the comments of James Kugel, Miryam Brand, Michael Segal, and others who attended the Jonas C. Greenfield Scholars Seminar graciously hosted in 2013 by the Orion Center for the Study of the Dead Sea Scrolls and Associated Literature. Thomas Farrar and Eibert Tigchelaar kindly shared with me some of their not-yet-published research, which proved useful to my investigation.

John Collins supervised my dissertation, steering me clear of many errors in the early stages of my research. I am deeply honored that he has written the foreword for the book. Less formally, but no less importantly, the input of friends and colleagues who have suffered through many conversations with me about the Satan and other evil figures has honed my thinking. These include Samuel Adams, David Eastman, Madison Grace, and Joshua Williams. Adam Dodd shouldered the majority of the responsibility for compiling the indexes for the volume. A research sabbatical granted to me by Southwestern Baptist Theological Seminary in 2017 and a Junior Scholar Grant from the Southwest Commission on Religious Studies the same year allowed me to complete the project.

Most significantly, this study would not have been possible without the patience, encouragement, and support of my wife, Robyn, and my sons, Seth and Sam.

Abbreviations

AB	Anchor Bible
ABD	*Anchor Bible Dictionary*. Edited by David Noel Freedman. 6 vols. New York: Doubleday, 1992
AfOB	Archiv für Orientforschung: Beiheft
AJEC	Ancient Judaism and Early Christianity
AnBib	Analecta Biblica
AOAT	Alter Orient und Altes Testament
AOTC	Abingdon Old Testament Commentaries
APOT	*The Apocrypha and Pseudepigrapha of the Old Testament*. Edited by Robert H. Charles. 2 vols. Oxford: Clarendon, 1913
AYB	Anchor Yale Bible
AYBRL	Anchor Yale Bible Reference Library
b.	Babylonian Talmud
BDAG	Danker, Frederick W., Walter Bauer, William F. Arndt, and F. Wilbur Gingrich. *Greek-English Lexicon of the New Testament and Other Early Christian Literature*. 3rd ed. Chicago: University of Chicago Press, 2000
BEATAJ	Beiträge zur Erforschung des Alten Testaments und des antiken Judentum
BHHB	Baylor Handbook on the Hebrew Bible
Bib	*Biblica*
BibOr	Biblica et Orientalia
BibSem	Biblical Seminar
BJS	Brown Judaic Studies
BKAT	Biblischer Kommentar, Altes Testament
BN	*Biblische Notizen*

BSRLL	*Bulletin de la Société Royale des Lettres de Lund 1944–1945*
BZ	*Biblische Zeitschrift*
BZAW	Beihefte zur Zeitschrift für die alttestamentliche Wissenschaft
CahRB	Cahiers de la Revue biblique
CAT	Commentaire de l'Ancien Testament
CBQ	*Catholic Biblical Quarterly*
CBQMS	Catholic Biblical Quarterly Monograph Series
CCWJCW	Cambridge Commentaries on Writings of the Jewish and Christian World, 200 B.C. to A.D. 200
CEJL	Commentaries on Early Jewish Literature
ConBOT	Coniectanea Biblica: Old Testament Series
CRINT	Compendia Rerum Iudaicarum ad Novum Testamentum
CSCO	Corpus Scriptorum Christianorum Orientalium
CurBR	*Currents in Biblical Research*
DCLY	*Deuterocanonical and Cognate Literature Yearbook*
DDD	*Dictionary of Deities and Demons in the Bible.* Edited by Karel van der Toorn, Bob Becking, and Pieter W. van der Horst. 2nd ed. Leiden: Brill; Grand Rapids: Eerdmans, 1999
DJD	Discoveries in the Judaean Desert
DSB	Daily Study Bible
DSD	*Dead Sea Discoveries*
DSSR	*The Dead Sea Scrolls Reader.* Edited by Donald W. Parry and Emmanuel Tov. 2nd ed. 2 vols. Leiden: Brill, 2014
DSSSE	*The Dead Sea Scrolls: Study Edition.* 2 vols. Edited by Florentino García Martínez and Eibert J. C. Tigchelaar. Leiden: Brill; Grand Rapids: Eerdmans, 1997–1998
EDEJ	*Eerdmans Dictionary of Early Judaism.* Edited by John J. Collins and Daniel C. Harlow. Grand Rapids: Eerdmans, 2010
EDSS	*Encyclopedia of the Dead Sea Scrolls.* Edited by Lawrence H. Schiffman and James C. VanderKam. 2 vols. New York: Oxford University Press, 2000
EJL	Early Judaism and Its Literature
FAT	Forschungen zum Alten Testament
HALOT	*The Hebrew and Aramaic Lexicon of the Old Testament.* Ludwig Koehler, Walter Baumgartner, and Johann J. Stamm. Translated and edited under the supervision of Mervyn E. J. Richardson. 5 vols. Leiden: Brill, 1994–2000
HB	Hebrew Bible
HBT	*Horizons in Biblical Theology*

HCOT	Historical Commentary on the Old Testament
Hen	*Henoch*
HSM	Harvard Semitic Monographs
HThKAT	Herders theologischer Kommentar zum Alten Testament
HTR	*Harvard Theological Review*
IB	*Interpreter's Bible.* Edited by George A. Buttrick. 12 vols. New York: Abingdon, 1951–1957
ICC	International Critical Commentary
IDB	*The Interpreter's Dictionary of the Bible.* Edited by George A. Buttrick. 4 vols. New York: Abingdon, 1962
ISCO	International Studies on Christian Origins
JAAR	*Journal of the American Academy of Religion*
JAJSup	Journal of Ancient Judaism Supplements
JAOS	*Journal of the American Oriental Society*
JB	Jerusalem Bible
JBL	*Journal of Biblical Literature*
JECS	*Journal of Early Christian Studies*
JJS	*Journal of Jewish Studies*
JPSTC	Jewish Publication Society Torah Commentary
JSHRZ	Jüdische Schriften aus hellenistisch-römischer Zeit
JSJ	*Journal for the Study of Judaism in the Persian, Hellenistic, and Roman Periods*
JSJSup	Supplements to the Journal for the Study of Judaism
JSNT	*Journal for the Study of the New Testament*
JSOT	*Journal for the Study of the Old Testament*
JSOTSup	Journal for the Study of the Old Testament Supplement Series
JSP	*Journal for the Study of the Pseudepigrapha*
JSPSup	Journal for the Study of the Pseudepigrapha Supplement Series
JSS	*Journal of Semitic Studies*
JTS	*Journal of Theological Studies*
KJV	King James Version
LCL	Loeb Classical Library
LHBOTS	Library of Hebrew Bible/Old Testament Studies
LNTS	Library of New Testament Studies
LSJ	Liddell, Henry George, Robert Scott, Henry Stuart Jones. *A Greek-English Lexicon.* 9th ed. with revised supplement. Oxford: Clarendon, 1996
LSTS	Library of Second Temple Studies

LXX	Septuagint
m.	Mishnah
MS(S)	manuscript(s)
MT	Masoretic Text
NAB	New American Bible
NASB	New American Standard Bible
NIB	*New Interpreter's Bible*. Edited by Leander E. Keck. 12 vols. Nashville: Abingdon, 1994–2004
NICOT	New International Commentary on the Old Testament
NIDB	*New Interpreter's Dictionary of the Bible*. Edited by Katharine Doob Sakenfeld. 5 vols. Nashville: Abingdon, 2006–2009
NIDOTTE	*New International Dictionary of Old Testament Theology and Exegesis*. Edited by Willem A. VanGemeren. 5 vols. Grand Rapids: Zondervan, 1997
NIGTC	New International Greek Testament Commentary
NIV	New International Version
NJB	New Jerusalem Bible
NKJV	New King James Version
NRSV	New Revised Standard Version
NTM	New Testament Message
NTOA	Novum Testamentum et Orbis Antiquus
NTS	*New Testament Studies*
OBO	Orbis Biblicus et Orientalis
OED	*Oxford English Dictionary*. Online ed. Oxford University Press, 2018
OTL	Old Testament Library
OTP	*Old Testament Pseudepigrapha*. Edited by James H. Charlesworth. 2 vols. New York: Doubleday, 1983–1985
OTS	Old Testament Studies
PAAJR	*Proceedings of the American Academy of Jewish Research*
PTSDSSP	Princeton Theological Seminary Dead Sea Scrolls Project
RB	*Revue biblique*
RevExp	*Review and Expositor*
RevQ	*Revue de Qumran*
RHR	*Revue de l'histoire des religions*
RNBC	Readings: A New Biblical Commentary
RSV	Revised Standard Version
SAACT	State Archives of Assyria Cuneiform Texts
SBLDS	Society of Biblical Literature Dissertation Series

SBLSP	Society of Biblical Literature Seminar Papers
StBibLit	Studies in Biblical Literature
STDJ	Studies on the Texts of the Desert of Judah
StPB	Studia Post-biblica
SUNT	Studien zur Umwelt des Neuen Testaments
SVTP	Studia in Veteris Testamenti Pseudepigraphica
SymS	Symposium Series
t.	Tosefta
TBN	Themes in Biblical Narrative
TDNT	*Theological Dictionary of the New Testament.* Edited by Gerhard Kittel and Gerhard Friedrich. Translated by Geoffrey W. Bromiley. 10 vols. Grand Rapids: Eerdmans, 1964–1976
TDOT	*Theological Dictionary of the Old Testament.* Edited by G. Johannes Botterweck, Helmer Ringgren, and Heinz-Josef Fabry. Translated by John T. Willis et al. 15 vols. Grand Rapids: Eerdmans, 1974–2006
ThWQ	*Theologisches Wörterbuch zu den Qumrantexten.* Edited by Heinz-Josef Fabry and Ulrich Dahmen. 3 vols. Stuttgart: Kohlhammer, 2011
TJ	*Trinity Journal*
TLOT	*Theological Lexicon of the Old Testament.* Edited by Ernst Jenni, with assistance from Claus Westermann. Translated by Mark E. Biddle. 3 vols. Peabody, MA: Hendrickson, 1997
TOTC	Tyndale Old Testament Commentaries
TSAJ	Texte und Studien zum antiken Judentum
TT	Texts and Translations
VCSup	Vigiliae Christianae, Supplements
VT	*Vetus Testamentum*
WBC	Word Biblical Commentary
WUNT	Wissenschaftliche Untersuchungen zum Neuen Testament
ZAW	*Zeitschrift für die alttestamentliche Wissenschaft*
ZTK	*Zeitschrift für Theologie und Kirche*

CHAPTER 1

The Origin of the Satan

In ancient religious thought, the world abounded with deities and other superhuman entities. These invisible beings were at work in the world, shaping history and influencing humankind. Unseen powers controlled the fortunes of individuals, sometimes for a person's benefit and sometimes for a person's harm. The rise and fall of nations were subject to decisions made and actions taken by deities. The writers of the Hebrew scriptures shared this understanding of the world.

The literature of the Hebrew scriptures centers on the activity of Yahweh, the God of Israel, in the world, especially as it pertains to the people of Israel. While numerous passages acknowledge the existence of other divine beings, only a small number of passages suggest that a foreign deity or a god other than Yahweh either blesses or creates problems for Israel. In 2 Kgs 3, the army of Israel is forced to retreat when King Mesha of Moab sacrifices his firstborn son—presumably to the Moabite god Chemosh—and receives divine assistance against the Israelites.[1] Jeremiah 44 narrates a dispute between the prophet Jeremiah and the people of Judah, in which the men and women of Judah tell the prophet that hardship has come upon them because they have ceased making offerings to the "queen of heaven." This view is not shared by Jeremiah, who contends

1. That it was the wrath of the foreign deity Chemosh that forced the Israelite armies to retreat is a point of disagreement among scholars, primarily because ascribing this sort of potency to a god other than Yahweh is unparalleled in the biblical literature. That it was indeed supposed to be the god Chemosh who repelled the Israelite forces, nevertheless, seems the most natural reading of the passage. For a review of the various interpretations of this story and a bibliography, see John Barclay Burns, "Why Did the Besieging Army Withdraw?," *ZAW* 102.2 (1990): 187–94.

rather that the people's unfaithfulness to Yahweh is the source of their problems. In Daniel, one reads of superhuman "princes" of nations, with the princes of Persia and Greece engaged in combat with Michael, Israel's prince (Dan 10:13, 20–21).[2] Israel's subjugation to foreign powers is not merely a matter of wars between human armies, but is connected to conflicts taking place in the divine realm. And Israel's eventual deliverance is tied to Michael's ascendancy above the superhuman princes of the other nations (12:1).

Although deities other than the God of Israel at times make their presence felt in the Hebrew scriptures, more typically it is Yahweh alone who is said to control Israel's fate. Even in the example of Daniel mentioned above, the reader is assured that the outcome of the battles between the superhuman princes has been determined in advance by Yahweh. If Yahweh alone controls the destiny of the children of Israel, then Yahweh receives the credit when things go well for them. The reverse is also true, however. Misfortune, when it occurs, is thought to come from Israel's one true God. "I am the LORD, and there is no other. I form light and create darkness, I make weal and create woe; I the LORD do all these things" (Isa 45:6b–7). "Does disaster befall a city, unless the LORD has done it?" (Amos 3:6b). The Hebrew scriptures are largely monistic in outlook, in that both good and evil are believed to come ultimately from one and the same God.

Frequently, nevertheless, the Hebrew scriptures speak of various superhuman beings who serve as divine agents for accomplishing God's purposes among humankind. While some of these beings are God's agents for blessing the righteous, some of them are God's agents for bringing judgment upon the wicked. These agents of judgment include "angelic" beings who bring death to God's enemies, and "spirits" who variously afflict and mislead the wicked. The most notorious of these divine emissaries of judgment in the Hebrew scriptures is the Satan.[3]

2. In the discussion that follows, the gods of nations are credited with bringing trouble upon their own peoples also in Ps 82, in which the "sons of the Most High" are condemned for having governed their nations unjustly.

3. I occasionally substitute "satan" for the NRSV's translation of *śāṭān*. Similarly, I use "the Satan" to translate *haśśāṭān*. Any other deviations from the NRSV will be noted as they occur.

The Satan Tradition in the Hebrew Scriptures

Early discussions of the Satan tradition were predominantly theological in their approach. Interpreters took for granted that the canonical texts bore witness to a uniform doctrine. In particular, they assumed that the authors of the Hebrew scriptures conceived of Satan in the same way as the authors of the NT. Such theological presuppositions characterized treatments of the topic well into the modern era. More historically minded scholars, on the other hand, were reluctant to take up the topic of Satan and evil spirits, perhaps in part because they did not consider such doctrines of invisible evil forces to be appropriate to critical historical inquiry.[4] In the late nineteenth century, critical scholars finally entered the discussion of Satan.[5] These interpreters were more attuned to diversity among the biblical writings than their less critical predecessors had been. These scholars were unwilling to assume that the authors of the Hebrew scriptures had the same beliefs regarding Satan as did later Jewish and Christian writers. Nor did they assume that the Hebrew Scriptures were themselves completely uniform in their depictions of this figure, but they discerned diversity and development even among these early biblical writings.

Eventually, biblical scholars arrived at a general consensus about the origin and evolution of the Satan tradition. They hypothesized that this development took place in three stages. The earliest text to speak of a heavenly satan figure, according to this scholarly consensus, was the story of Balaam's encounter with the angel of Yahweh found in Num 22. Although this passage uses the Hebrew noun *śāṭān* (שָׂטָן), it is not the name Satan as it would later become. It is merely a common noun meaning "adversary" or perhaps "obstacle." This satan was not God's enemy, but was none other

4. Derek Brown, "The Devil in the Details: A Survey of Research on Satan in Biblical Studies," *CurBR* 9.2 (2011): 200–202, hypothesizes that more historically oriented scholars were not eager to enter discussions about Satan since this topic was thought to be more a matter of "doctrinal speculation" than of historical study and since a skepticism with regard to the supernatural prevailed in modern scholarship. Richard H. Bell, *Deliver Us from Evil: Interpreting the Redemption from the Power of Satan in New Testament Theology*, WUNT 216 (Tübingen: Mohr Siebeck, 2007), 4–6, similarly refers to the embarrassment on the part of scholars since the eighteenth century to speak of the devil.

5. In Brown's survey of the history of research on Satan, Otto Everling, *Die paulinische Angelologie and Dämonologie: Ein biblisch-theologischer Versuch* (Göttingen: Vandenhoeck & Ruprecht, 1888), appears to be the earliest treatment of the topic that deals with the particulars of a biblical author's demonology (in this case, that of Paul), which Everling also situated within the context of early Jewish beliefs about demons.

than the angel of Yahweh himself, who happened on this occasion to be functioning as an "adversary" to Balaam.

The next phase in the development of the tradition, scholars argued, appears in Job 1–2 and Zech 3. In these passages, one encounters not merely *a* satan, as in Num 22, but *the* Satan (*haśśāṭān*, השטן). Although "satan" has not yet become a name, these texts mark a significant step for the tradition in that direction, in that the word *śāṭān* is used not simply as a common noun but as a title for an officer in God's court. Translating the noun *śāṭān* as "accuser," scholars concluded that the Satan in this phase of the tradition was the divine "Accuser" or "Prosecutor" of the wicked in God's heavenly courtroom.

The final phase in the evolution of the Satan tradition, according to the scholarly consensus, is attested by the census story of 1 Chr 21, which uses the noun *śāṭān* without the definite article. In this late text, the Chronicler did not speak of "*a* satan" (as in Num 22), or of "the Satan" (as in Job and Zechariah), but of one named "Satan." The Chronicler alleviated the theological problem created by 2 Sam 24, in which Yahweh incites David to take a disastrous census of Israel, by substituting Satan for Yahweh as the instigator of the census. Finally, in the latest of these biblical texts to speak of a superhuman satan, one reads of a figure resembling the Satan of later Jewish and Christian literature. By the time of Chronicles, "Satan" was apparently the name of an evil heavenly being who leads humans into sin.

This standard critical explanation of the history of the Satan tradition was attractive in its simplicity. Moving from the earlier biblical texts to the later ones (as commonly dated by scholars), it was easy to see how the belief that a superhuman being might serve as *a* satan was transformed into the belief that there was a particular malevolent superhuman being named Satan. The simplicity of this developmental hypothesis, however, would eventually lead to its rejection, as scholars began to call into question whether the biblical texts did attest such an uncomplicated linear trajectory for this tradition and, moreover, whether these texts even pertained to the same satan figure.

Sara Japhet was the first to deal a blow to the standard developmental hypothesis. In her work on Chronicles, Japhet argued that *śāṭān* in 1 Chr 21 is not a name but a common noun as it is used elsewhere in the Hebrew scriptures, meaning "adversary."[6] Further, she contended that the

6. Sara Japhet, *The Ideology of the Book of Chronicles and Its Place in Biblical Thought*, 2nd ed., BEATAJ 9 (Frankfurt am Main: Peter Lang, 1989), 145–49 (Hebrew original 1977).

Chronicler does not speak of a superhuman adversary at all, but merely of a mundane, human adversary, no more than one of the king's counselors who, against Israel's interests, advised the king to number the people. First Chronicles 21, then, does not represent the final stage in the development of beliefs about Satan, nor any stage in such a tradition.

The next challenge to the consensus was posed by Peggy Day in her monograph on the concept of a heavenly satan in the Hebrew scriptures.[7] Although Day identified the Chronicler's satan as a heavenly being, she agreed with Japhet that this figure was not named "Satan." Rather this satan was an anonymous "accuser" in God's court. Day called the scholarly consensus further into question in her analysis of Job and Zechariah. She translated *haśśāṭān* in these books not as a title, "the Accuser," but as "*a certain* accuser." Job and Zechariah speak not of a permanent prosecutor in God's court, but of heavenly beings who merely happen on these occasions to serve as prosecutors. According to Day's analysis, the Hebrew scriptures reveal no development from the belief that heavenly beings may on occasion serve as satans to the belief in one particular satan.

The discussions of individual passages below will engage more closely the various interpretations and arguments that scholars have offered, but this preliminary survey of scholarship on the satan tradition in the Hebrew scriptures sufficiently highlights several questions that I will answer in the first two chapters of the present study. To what extent can one speak of a satan tradition in the Hebrew scriptures, or can one speak only of various unrelated satans? If there is a common tradition behind some of the passages that mention superhuman satans, can one discern the history of its development? Do the biblical texts exhibit a simple linear evolution of thinking on this topic, or was the process more complex? What sort of satan did the biblical authors eventually come to describe? Does any passage in the Hebrew scriptures speak of a person named Satan or of a figure resembling the Satan of later Jewish and Christian theology?

Here I will summarize my own position on these matters. There is a satan tradition in the Hebrew scriptures. Although it is undeniable that the biblical authors portray heavenly satan figures in differing ways, some common notions underlie their portrayals. The interrelatedness of these texts is also apparent in that later passages containing satan figures reinterpret and reapply earlier passages that mention such figures.

7. Peggy L. Day, *An Adversary in Heaven: śāṭān in the Hebrew Bible*, HSM 43 (Atlanta: Scholars Press, 1988).

Furthermore, one can discern much of the process by which the tradition developed. The trajectory of this tradition's evolution, however, is different from what interpreters up to this point have surmised. I also diverge fundamentally from most of previous scholarship, arguing that the Satan is not primarily an "adversary" or "accuser," but an "attacker" or "executioner."

What Is a Satan?

In order to comprehend the origin and early development of the Satan tradition, it is necessary to begin in the proper place. For most readers of the Hebrew scriptures, even for many biblical scholars, their understanding of the Satan figure derives largely from the book of Job. The story of Job is a familiar one, and the Satan plays a prominent and fascinating role in that story.

As I contend in ch. 2, the book of Job's Satan marks a pivotal moment in the development of the Satan tradition. Nonetheless, the story of Job is not the place to begin an investigation of the Satan tradition. The take on the Satan figure in the book of Job, I argue, is the most developed of the Hebrew scriptures, and its depiction of the Satan is not in every respect representative of the tradition to which it is the heir. With its literary and theological sophistication, the book of Job is also the most challenging text to make sense of with regard to a history of beliefs about the Satan. It is a story into which it is very easy even for careful interpreters to read their own ideas. In order to comprehend the early Satan tradition and the book of Job's contribution to it, one must correctly discern the origins and basic elements of the tradition. Then one will be in a position to evaluate its development and more complex manifestations.

We begin with the definition of the noun *śāṭān*, "satan," considering first those texts in which the meaning of the word is clear and then those texts that are more ambiguous. Once we have defined *śāṭān*, then we may evaluate those texts in which a superhuman satan appears.

With the possible exception of 1 Chr 21, the Hebrew scriptures do not use the word *śāṭān* as a name, but simply as a common noun. (That the word occurs as a name even in Chronicles is doubtful, as will be shown below.) While scholars have suggested various translations for *śāṭān*, until recently the overwhelming majority have agreed that it should be translated as "adversary," and more specifically, in legal contexts, as "accuser."[8] The result of this translation is the widely held belief among scholars that the Satan one encounters in the Hebrew scriptures is "the Adversary" or, more specifically, "the Accuser."

It is clear that at some point in the history of the tradition, Satan came to be understood as a divine accuser, a sort of prosecuting attorney in the divine court. At the conclusion of the heavenly battle described in Rev 12, in which Satan and his angels are defeated and thrown out of heaven, John hears a loud voice proclaiming, "Now have come the salvation and the power and the kingdom of our God and the authority of his Messiah, for the accuser [*ho katēgōr*] of our comrades has been thrown down, who accuses [*ho katēgorōn*] them day and night before our God" (Rev 12:10). By the latter part of the first century CE, Satan had come to be regarded as "the accuser of the comrades," but precisely when and how the notion of Satan as "the accuser" arose is not as simple a matter as scholars have thought. For those who translate *śāṭān* as "accuser," this understanding of (the) Satan was part of the tradition from the very beginning. The Satan one encounters in the Hebrew scriptures is already, by definition, an accuser. When one examines the uses of *śāṭān* and its cognates in this literature, however, one finds meager evidence that the word means "accuser." Rather, interpreters have inadvertently and incorrectly imposed this translation and, along with it, a later notion of the Satan on earlier texts.[9]

The noun *śāṭān* is used to describe several different individuals in the Hebrew scriptures. Although the satans who are most familiar to students of the Bible are the superhuman satans of Job, Zechariah, and Chronicles,

8. See, e.g., T. H. Gaster, "Satan," *IDB* 4:224–25; G. von Rad, "The OT View of Satan," *TDNT* 2:73–75; Day, *Adversary in Heaven*, 25–43; Victor P. Hamilton, "Satan," *ABD* 5:985–86; Cilliers Breytenbach and Peggy L. Day, "Satan שׂטן Σατάν, Σατανᾶς," *DDD* 726–32; John H. Walton, "Satan," *Dictionary of the Old Testament Wisdom Poetry and Writings*, ed. Tremper Longman III and Peter Enns (Downers Grove, IL: InterVarsity Press, 2008), 714–15; Chad T. Pierce, "Satan and Related Figures," *EDEJ* 1196–97; Bruce Baloian, "שָׂטָן," *NIDOTTE* 3:1231. Only a small number of scholars question the translation "accuser." G. Wanke says that *śāṭān* does not refer to "accusers" but merely to "opponents in legal matters" ("שָׂטָן *śāṭān* adversary," *TLOT* 3:1268–69). Similarly, although K. Nielsen acknowledges that *śāṭān* can denote a specifically legal kind of opposition, he stops short of saying that the word can mean "accuser" ("שָׂטָן *śāṭān*; שָׂטַן *śāṭan*; שָׂטַם *śāṭam*," *TDOT* 14:73–77). Friedrich Horst, *Hiob 1–19*, BKAT 16.1 (Neukirchen-Vluyn: Neukirchener Verlag, 1968), 13–14, argues that the idea of Satan as "the Accuser" does not appear in the Hebrew scriptures but arises in the postbiblical period.

9. The following analysis of the meaning of *śāṭān* can be found in fuller form in Ryan E. Stokes, "Satan, YHWH's Executioner," *JBL* 133.2 (2014): 251–70.

most of the persons referred to as satans in the Hebrew scriptures are human beings. And while it is not entirely incorrect to characterize these persons as "adversaries," this characterization fails to convey the precise nature of these adversaries' activity. A satan is not merely an opponent or an adversary in a generic sense, but is an "attacker" who intends to harm another person physically. Usually, if not always, the purpose of the attack is to kill a person.

A satan may be of a national, military kind. For example, in 1 Sam 29:4 David, on the run from King Saul, has aligned himself temporarily with the Philistines for protection. As the Philistines prepare to go to battle against Saul and Israel, however, their leaders send David away. They fear that the Israelite warrior would betray them in battle, killing Philistine soldiers in order to win back Saul's favor: "The commanders of the Philistines said to [Achish], 'Send the man back, so that he may return to the place that you have assigned to him; he shall not go down with us to battle, or else he may become a satan to us in the battle. For how could this fellow reconcile himself to his lord? Would it not be with the heads of the men here?'"

This sort of national, military attacker is also likely in mind in 1 Kgs 5, which describes the early part of Solomon's reign as a period of peace in which there is "neither satan nor misfortune" (1 Kgs 5:18 [Eng. 4]). David's reign is occupied with securing the land, but Solomon, unencumbered by attacks from neighboring nations, could devote his attention and resources to building a house for God. Later, however, on account of Solomon's involvement with the worship of foreign gods, Yahweh raises up Hadad the Edomite and a marauder by the name of Rezon as satans, foreign enemies who attack Solomon and Israel (1 Kgs 11:14, 23, 25).[10]

A slightly different type of satan can be observed in 2 Sam 19. As David returns to Jerusalem after Absalom's rebellion has been quashed, he encounters the Benjaminite Shimei, who earlier cursed the king and hurled rocks at him when David was fleeing from Absalom. Shimei, fearful for his life now that the king he cursed is being reinstated, hurries to meet David in order to beg for pardon. Abishai, one of the sons of Zeruiah, zealous to protect his king, calls for the rebel's death: "Shall not Shimei be put to death for this, because he cursed the LORD's anointed?" (19:22 [Eng. 21]). David responds to Abishai's suggestion with a rebuke: "What have

10. Gerhard von Rad, "διαβάλλω, διάβολος: The OT View of Satan," *TDNT* 2:73, argues unpersuasively that Hadad and Rezon are "accusers" of Israel.

I to do with you, you sons of Zeruiah, that you should today become my satan? Shall anyone be put to death in Israel this day?" (19:23 [Eng. 22]).[11] As in the passages considered above, the satan in this passage is someone who would attack and kill another person. Second Samuel 19 differs from the passages considered above in that this attack is supposed (at least by Abishai) to be justified by Shimei's crime. Abishai suggests that Shimei be punished capitally for his crime, so the satan in this passage would be an "executioner."[12]

Another word that has bearing on this discussion is the verb *śṭn*, which occurs in a few psalms (Pss 38:21 [Eng. 20]; 71:13; 109:4, 20, 29). Although translators often render this verb as "to accuse," this word, like its cognate noun *śāṭān*, more likely denotes lethal, physical attack. The psalmist prays in 71:13, "Let those who attack me [*śōṭnê napšî*] be put to shame and consumed; let those who seek to hurt me be covered with scorn and disgrace." Psalm 109:29 uses the verb similarly: "May my attackers [*śôṭnay*] be clothed with dishonor; may they be wrapped in their own shame as in a mantle."[13] In each of these texts, the psalmist asks for God's support against human attackers who seek his life.

Three passages in the Hebrew scriptures speak unambiguously of superhuman satans. In Num 22, the angel of Yahweh comes as a "satan" against the seer Balaam, to strike him with a sword if he does not obey God. Job 1–2 and Zech 3 speak of a member of the divine court called

11. The words "that you should today become my satan" in this verse translate *kî tihyû lî hayyôm ləśāṭān*. The NRSV renders this phrase "that you should today become an adversary to me." Peggy L. Day, "Abishai the *śāṭān* in 2 Sam 19:17–24," *CBQ* 49.4 (1987): 543–47, correctly contends that Abishai is proposing that he serve not as a "satan" against David but on David's behalf, though she mistakenly assumes that "satan" means "accuser."

12. Although Day ("Abishai the *śāṭān*") regards Abishai in 2 Sam 19:23 (Eng. 22) as an "accuser," I argue in "Satan, YHWH's Executioner," 253–55, that "executioner" is much more likely the meaning of *śāṭān* in this passage. What is clearly in question here is not whether David will allow Abishai to serve as an accuser, but whether David will allow Abishai to put Shimei to death. David also curses not Abishai alone but the "sons of Zeruiah." Abishai's brother Joab, who does not even speak in the present passage, cannot be said to be an "accuser." On the other hand, Joab has certainly earned David's disapproval for executing the king's enemies against David's more magnanimous wishes (2 Sam 3:17–39; 18:5–33; 20:4–10; 1 Kgs 2:5–6). Abishai too has earned the king's disapproval on more than one occasion by offering David his services as an executioner (1 Sam 26:7–11; 2 Sam 16:9).

13. The NRSV has "my accusers" both for *śōṭnê napšî* in Ps 71:13 and for *śôṭnay* in 109:29. For arguments that these should be translated in terms of "attack," see Stokes, "Satan, YHWH's Executioner," 256–61.

haśśāṭān, usually understood as "the Satan." A fourth passage, the much-debated 1 Chr 21:1, is also typically taken to refer to a superhuman satan who incites David to take a disastrous census of Israel. Scholars commonly understand these satans as accusers. As demonstrated below, however, there is little evidence for understanding these satans in this way. Like their human counterparts discussed above, each of these satans is presumed to be an attacker. More specifically, these satans are portrayed as divine executioners of the guilty.[14]

The Angel of Yahweh as a Satan in Numbers 22

The earliest text that refers to a superhuman being as a "satan" is Num 22. In this passage, the Israelites set up camp on the plains of Moab on their way to the promised land. When Balak king of Moab learns of the Israelites' presence, he worries that the encroaching multitude will sap the territory's resources, so he summons the prophet Balaam to curse the Israelites. Although Balaam initially refuses the king's invitation, he eventually accedes and sets out by donkey for Moab.[15]

At this point in the story, "God's anger was kindled because [Balaam] was going, and the angel of the LORD took his stand in the road as his satan" (Num 22:22).[16] In the irony-laden encounter that ensues, the sword-wielding angel, who is invisible to Balaam, positions himself three times in Balaam's path. The first two times, Balaam's donkey, who can see what

14. The case of Job, which I address in the next chapter, is more complex than the other three that speak of superhuman satans. Job's narrative appears to presume the notion of the Satan as the attacker or executioner, but further develops this idea and presents the Satan also as one who incites God to test the innocent Job with adversity.

15. This summary of the story in Num 22 smooths over certain tensions in the Balaam story, which most commentators cite as evidence that the pericope involving Balaam, his donkey, and the angel (Num 22:22–35) is not of one piece with the surrounding narrative. The most glaring of these tensions is that God condones Balaam's journey in 22:20, but becomes angry when Balaam embarks in 22:22. Several commentators deem this pericope to be an interpolation from a later tradition, a tradition that casts Balaam in a more negative light than does the surrounding narrative. See, e.g., the discussions of this passage in Day, *Adversary in Heaven*, 45–67; Jacob Milgrom, *Numbers*, JPSTC (Philadelphia: Jewish Publication Society, 1990), 468–69; Baruch A. Levine, *Numbers 21–36: A New Translation with Introduction and Commentary*, AB 4A (New York: Doubleday, 2000), 154–59.

16. Both in this verse and in v. 32, the NRSV has "adversary" for satan. The LXX renders *lśṭn* in v. 22 not as a noun but as an infinitive, *endiaballein*.

Balaam cannot, averts Balaam's execution by steering clear of the angelic adversary. The third time, however, the donkey, unable to get around the angel, simply crouches beneath Balaam and refuses to move forward. Each time the donkey takes action to save its master, it receives a beating from Balaam. Finally, Balaam's eyes are opened so that he becomes aware of the threat to his life. Though at this point Balaam offers to turn around and return home, the angel instructs him to continue on his way to Moab, but to speak only what God instructs. When Balaam arrives in Moab, he obediently speaks only what Yahweh permits. To King Balak's frustration, rather than cursing Israel, Balaam blesses them three times.

In the story of Balaam, *śāṭān* is a common noun. The individual called a satan in this story is not one who is at cross-purposes with God, but is the very angel of Yahweh.[17] The angel of Yahweh has come to bring divine judgment on Balaam because he has set out on a journey that is inconsistent with God's plan for Israel. "The angel of the Lord said to him, 'Why have you struck your donkey these three times? I have come out as a satan, because your way is perverse before me. The donkey saw me, and turned away from me these three times. If it had not turned away from me, surely just now I would have killed you and let it live'" (Num 22:32–33). The angel of Yahweh has come against Balaam as a satan, that is, as an executioner, to put Balaam to death for his plan to curse God's people. In this regard, the angel of Yahweh in the Balaam story may be compared with Abishai, who in 2 Sam 19 intends to put Shimei to death for cursing David.

While Num 22 does not speak of an individual who occupies a permanent position as a satan in the divine court, this story does attest the belief that a superhuman being might on occasion serve as a satan. Beyond this idea, one cannot speak of a developed satan tradition in Numbers. The belief that a superhuman being such as the angel of Yahweh might at times act as an executioner of the wicked, however, is likely the idea from which (and in response to which) there arose the conception of one particular superhuman being whose primary task it was to serve God as an executioner.[18]

17. On the ambiguous relationship between the angel of Yahweh and God, see the discussion and bibliography in S. A. Meier, "Angel of Yahweh," *DDD* 53–59. The relationship between Yahweh and the angel of Yahweh is at times blurred in the Hebrew scriptures, as it is in this passage (Num 22:35; cf. 22:20). Rivkah Schärf Kluger, *Satan in the Old Testament*, trans. Hildegard Nagel, Studies in Jungian Thought (Evanston, IL: Northwestern University Press, 1967), 72, goes so far as to say, "it is God himself who stands as an adversary in Balaam's path."

18. Perhaps some will object to identifying the satan of Num 22 as an executioner on the

The Satan Rebuked by the Angel of Yahweh in Zechariah 3

The next text, chronologically, that mentions a superhuman satan in the Hebrew scriptures is Zech 3.[19] Until recently, scholars have generally agreed that the Satan in this passage is "the Accuser," who accuses the high priest Joshua before the angel of Yahweh. Some scholars (including me), however, understand the Satan in this text not as an accuser but as one who would attack and kill Joshua.[20] Since our discussion of this passage will require familiarity with the first seven verses of Zech 3, I quote them in full at this point. In that it represents what has until recently been the scholarly consensus on how the satan in these verses is to be understood, the NRSV translation will serve as a suitable starting point.

> Then he showed me the high priest Joshua standing before the angel of the LORD, and the Satan [*haśśāṭān*] standing at his right hand to accuse him [*ləśiṭnô*]. And the LORD said to the Satan [*haśśāṭān*], "The LORD rebuke you, O Satan [*haśśāṭān*]! The LORD who has chosen Jerusalem rebuke you! Is not this man a brand plucked from the fire?" Now Joshua was dressed with filthy clothes as he stood before the angel. The angel

---

grounds that this satan does not in the end carry out Balaam's execution. Nevertheless, the angel of Yahweh makes it clear that his purpose as a satan is to put Balaam to death for his rebellion (vv. 32-33). As with the human satans in the passages discussed above, the threat that this satan poses to his victim is a mortal one. Further, as I will argue below, the satan of 1 Chr 21 is probably to be identified with the angel of Yahweh, who does indeed carry out the execution of 70,000 Israelites.

19. The place of Zech 3 within the book of Zechariah is a matter of debate. Some scholars treat it as a unified vision that belongs in its present context (e.g., Carol L. Meyers and Eric M. Meyers, *Haggai, Zechariah 1–8*, AB 25B [Garden City, NY: Doubleday, 1987], 178–227). Others regard it as composite (e.g., David L. Petersen, *Haggai and Zechariah 1–8: A Commentary,* OTL [Philadelphia: Westminster, 1984], 202) and/or from a different hand from the visions that surround it (e.g., Christian Jeremias, *Die Nachtgesichte des Sacharja* [Göttingen: Vandenhoeck & Ruprecht, 1977], 201–3; Day, *Adversary in Heaven,* 107–26).

20. See Edgar W. Conrad, *Zechariah*, RNBC (Sheffield: Sheffield Academic Press, 1999), 89–90; Stokes, "Satan, YHWH's Executioner," 262–66; Max Rogland, *Haggai and Zechariah 1–8: A Handbook on the Hebrew Text*, BHHB (Waco, TX: Baylor University Press, 2016), 112; Ryan E. Stokes, "Airing the High Priest's Dirty Laundry: Understanding the Imagery and Message of Zechariah 3:1–7," in *Sibyls, Scriptures, and Scrolls: John Collins at Seventy*, ed. Joel Baden, Hindy Najman, and Eibert Tigchelaar; JSJSup 175, 2 vols. (Leiden: Brill, 2017), 2:1247–64, who regard the Satan of Zech 3 as one who would harm Joshua.

> said to those who were standing before him, "Take off his filthy clothes." And to him he said, "See, I have taken your guilt away from you, and I will clothe you with festal apparel." And I said, "Let them put a clean turban on his head." So they put a clean turban on his head and clothed him with the apparel; and the angel of the LORD was standing by.
>
> Then the angel of the LORD assured Joshua, saying "Thus says the LORD of hosts: If you will walk in my ways and keep my requirements, then you shall rule my house and have charge of my courts, and I will give you the right of access among those who are standing here."

Modern interpreters agree that this passage does not contain the name Satan.[21] Rather, *haśśāṭān* is a title, "the Satan." Zechariah's satan, understood in this way, is not simply a superhuman being who happens on this occasion to be serving as a satan, as in Num 22, but is an officer in the divine court whose title is "the Satan."[22]

21. Samuel Rolles Driver and George Buchanan Gray, *A Critical and Exegetical Commentary on the Book of Job*, 2 vols., ICC (New York: Scribner's Sons, 1921), 1:10–11; Edward Langton, *Satan, A Portrait: A Study of the Character of Satan through All the Ages* (London: Skeffington, 1946), 9; Marvin H. Pope, *Job: Introduction, Translation, and Notes*, AB 15 (Garden City, NY: Doubleday, 1965), 10–11; Ralph L. Smith, *Micah–Malachi*, WBC 32 (Waco, TX: Word, 1984), 199; Norman C. Habel, *The Book of Job: A Commentary*, OTL (Philadelphia: Westminster, 1985), 89; Neil Forsyth, *The Old Enemy: Satan and the Combat Myth* (Princeton: Princeton University Press, 1987), 110, 115; Meyers and Meyers, *Haggai, Zechariah 1–8*, 183; John E. Hartley, *The Book of Job*, NICOT (Grand Rapids: Eerdmans, 1988), 71; Marvin E. Tate, "Satan in the Old Testament," *RevExp* 89.4 (1992): 462; Sydney H. T. Page, *Powers of Evil: A Biblical Study of Satan and Demons* (Grand Rapids: Baker, 1995), 24, 32. Although many modern translations of Zech 3:1–2 and Job 1–2 continue to render *haśśāṭān* traditionally as "Satan," several, such as the NRSV, contain an explanatory note, defining the term as "the Adversary" or "the Accuser."

22. As already noted, Day, *Adversary in Heaven*, 43, has challenged the consensus understanding of *haśśāṭān* as the title "the Satan." She contends that *haśśāṭān* should instead be translated as "*a certain* satan" (emphasis mine). See also Gaster, "Satan," 224–25, who takes *haśśāṭān* in Zechariah and Job as "an *ad hoc* accuser." According to Day, Job and Zechariah do not speak of an individual in God's court who holds the office of "satan," but simply of superhuman beings who happen on these occasions to serve as ad hoc satans.

Day's argument that the article should be understood in this atypical fashion, however, is tenuous. Day bases her translation not on any contextual evidence in Zechariah or Job, but on the fact that she is unable to find reference to a professional "accuser" in Canaanite or Mesopotamian literature. In addition to Day's case being built upon an argument from silence, there is no compelling reason to translate the definite article in *haśśāṭān* in any way other than its usual fashion. Indeed, in the case of Job, that the Satan appears before God and reports that he has been patrolling the earth suggests that "Satan" was an office held by

According to most commentators and translators, the Satan is "the Accuser," and he stands on Joshua's right "to accuse" the high priest.[23] The Satan is depicted in this passage as a heavenly prosecuting attorney, who has set his sights on eliciting a guilty verdict against Joshua in the divine courtroom. What is somewhat surprising, given the widespread acceptance of this interpretation, is that nothing in Zech 3 indicates that the Satan is an "accuser" or that the Satan is "accusing" Joshua. The scene does appear to involve a sort of legal procedure, but the passage merely states that the satan is standing on Joshua's right in order to *satan* him. Translators and commentators have mistakenly supposed that *śāṭān* and *śāṭan* refer to accusation and have interpreted the passage accordingly.

Based on the meaning of these words as they are used outside Zechariah, however, one would expect them to denote not accusation but lethal, physical attack. Psalm 109:6 is commonly thought to describe a legal procedure similar to that of Zech 3 (though the particular scenario to which Ps 109:6 refers is difficult to pinpoint with certainty). And like Zech 3, this verse speaks of a satan standing on someone's right.

> Appoint a wicked man against him;
> let a satan stand on his right.
> When he disputes, let wickedness transpire;
> let his prayer result (only) in sin.
> May his days be few;

---

this figure, not just an activity that he happened to be engaged in at that particular moment. The majority of scholars have correctly understood *haśśāṭān* as the title "the Satan."

23. E.g., Hinckley G. Mitchell, John Merlin Powis Smith, and Julius A. Bewer, *A Critical and Exegetical Commentary on Haggai, Zechariah, Malachi and Jonah*, ICC (Edinburgh: T&T Clark, 1912), 147–49; Petersen, *Haggai and Zechariah 1–8*, 189–90; R. Smith, *Micah–Malachi*, 199; Meyers and Meyers, *Haggai, Zechariah 1–8*, 183–86; Karin Schöpflin, "YHWH's Agents of Doom: The Punishing Function of Angels in Post-Exilic Writings of the Old Testament," in *Angels: The Concept of Celestial Beings—Origins, Development and Reception*, ed. Friedrich V. Reiterer, Tobias Nicklas, and Karin Schöpflin; *DCLY* (Berlin: de Gruyter, 2007), 135; Dominic Rudman, "Zechariah and the Satan Tradition in the Hebrew Bible," in *Tradition in Transition: Haggai and Zechariah 1–8 in the Trajectory of Hebrew Theology*, ed. Mark J. Boda and Michael H. Floyd, LHBOTS 475 (New York: T&T Clark, 2008), 191. Interestingly, the LXX translator did not understand the activity of the Satan in this way, but rendered the verb *śāṭān* with *antikeimai*. The verb *antikeimai* can denote adversarial activity of various sorts, often of a military kind (e.g., Exod 23:22; 2 Sam 8:10; Esth 8:11). It does not mean "to accuse."

> may another seize his position.
> May his children be orphans,
> and his wife a widow. (Ps 109:6–9, my trans.)

Although translators typically understand the satan of Ps 109:6 as an accuser, I have argued that the satan in this verse is an attacker or executioner.[24] That the satan is supposed to kill the speaker's enemy is indicated unambiguously in vv. 8–9: "May his days be few. . . . May his children be orphans, and his wife a widow." "Attack" or, more specifically, "execution" is likely the idea to which *śāṭan* (verb) and *śāṭān* (noun) refer in Zech 3 as well.

Not only does the usage of *śāṭan* and *śāṭān* elsewhere in the Hebrew scriptures lead one to expect these words to pertain to some sort of attack in Zech 3, but the translations "execute" and "executioner," respectively, are supported contextually within Zech 3. Zechariah sees the Satan standing on Joshua's right to attack him. Joshua is no innocent victim, however, since he stands guilty before the angel of Yahweh. This guilt (*ʿāwōn*) is somehow associated with the high priest's filthy clothes, but Zechariah does not state precisely how Joshua came to be guilty. At the conclusion of instructions given to Moses regarding the priestly vestments to be worn by Aaron and his descendants, Exod 28:43 contains the following warning: "Aaron and his sons shall wear them when they go into the tent of meeting, or when they come near the altar to minister in the holy place; or they will bring guilt [*ʿāwōn*] on themselves and die. This shall be a perpetual ordinance for him and for his descendants after him." Perhaps Zechariah envisions a scenario similar to this one. Since the Satan's attack on Joshua's life seems to be justified, the Satan here should be understood as a divine executioner, similar to the one whom Balaam encountered on his way to Moab in Num 22.

Parallels between this passage and others further supplement our understanding of what Zechariah observes taking place in the divine court. The interaction between the angel of Yahweh, Joshua, and the Satan closely resembles that which took place between David, Shimei, and Abishai in 2 Sam 19. In the Samuel text, the criminal Shimei appears before the king, and Abishai stands ready to execute him. David, nevertheless, rebukes Abishai and informs Shimei that he will not die

24. See Stokes, "Satan, YHWH's Executioner," 257–61; Stokes, "Airing the High Priest's Dirty Laundry," 1256–57.

for his crime. In the same way, Joshua appears guilty before the angel of Yahweh, and the Satan intends to execute him. The angel of Yahweh, however, rebukes the Satan and informs Joshua that his guilt has been removed.

The prophet Isaiah's vision of God and prophetic commission in Isa 6 are also instructive. Isaiah sees the Lord enthroned in the temple, surrounded by divine attendants. Having caught a glimpse of Yahweh of hosts, Isaiah fears for his life, being a person of unclean lips. Rather than allow Isaiah to die, one of the divine attendants takes a burning coal from the altar and touches Isaiah's mouth. The seraph then declares to Isaiah, "your guilt [*ʿāwōn*] has departed and your sin is blotted out" (Isa 6:7). At this point, Isaiah receives his commission to prophesy to the people.

Zechariah 3 follows this same sequence of events. Both Isaiah and Joshua find themselves in the presence of (the angel of) Yahweh. And just as Isaiah's life is in danger on account of his unclean lips, Joshua's life is in peril on account of his filthy clothes. Nevertheless, as one of the seraphs touches Isaiah's lips with a coal and declares that his guilt (*ʿāwōn*) has been taken care of, the angel of Yahweh in Zechariah has his divine attendants remove Joshua's filthy garments and declares to him, "See, I have taken your guilt [*ʿāwōn*] away from you" (Zech 3:4). That Isaiah's lips must be cleansed and Joshua's garments must be changed portrays the removal of their guilt with imagery befitting their roles as prophet and priest, respectively. Finally, Joshua, having been clothed with clean garments, is in a position to receive his commission as priest, as Isaiah, once his lips have been purified, is able to receive his prophetic commission.

Although the Satan of Zech 3 is an executioner similar to the satan of Num 22, the Satan who threatens Joshua differs from the one who threatens Balaam in two notable respects. First, the Satan of Zech 3 appears to be an officer in the divine court, "the Attacker" or "the Executioner." The Satan of Zechariah is not simply an angelic being who happens on this occasion to serve as an executioner, as is the angel of Yahweh in Num 22. Second, in Num 22 the angel of Yahweh *is* the satan, whereas in Zech 3 these two individuals are not only distinct but opposed to each other. The Satan intends to execute Joshua, but the angel of Yahweh rebukes the Satan and pardons Joshua. Apparently, the angel of Yahweh outranks the Satan and speaks with Yahweh's authority: "The LORD rebuke you, O Satan! The LORD who has chosen Jerusalem rebuke you!" (3:2).[25] This rebuke effectively prevents the Satan from executing Joshua.[26]

Zechariah does not explain his theological motivation for distinguishing the angel of Yahweh and the Satan the way that he does, though it may pertain to his understanding of God's transcendence. Writers of the postexilic period increasingly emphasized God's transcendence, and, correspondingly, angelic beings increasingly occupied positions as intermediaries between God and humans in the literature of the period.[27] In Zech 3, the prophet sees Joshua standing before the angel of Yahweh, who is perhaps to be distinguished from Yahweh. The Satan, who intends to harm the high priest, is yet another heavenly figure, distinct from both Yahweh and the Deity's representative, the angel of Yahweh. By means of this diverse cast of characters, this scene serves to distance God, who has chosen Jerusalem, from that superhuman being who intends to execute the city's high priest. Whether the distancing of Jerusalem's benevolent God from this sort of harmful activity was the intent of Zechariah in describing Joshua's commission as he did is not certain. Regardless of the prophet's intent, this depiction would allow later readers to imagine a great deal of distance between God's activity and that of the Satan.

The Satan Who Stands against Israel in 1 Chronicles 21

First Chronicles 21:1 is the most debated of the satan passages in the Hebrew scriptures. This verse introduces the Chronicler's version of the story of David's census, the earlier account of which is found in 2 Sam 24. In

25. The nature of the relationship between Yahweh and the angel of Yahweh in Zech 3 is obfuscated by textual disagreement. Although the MT has Yahweh speaking in 3:2, the Peshitta has the angel of Yahweh speaking. The tradition attested by the Syriac makes good sense given that Yahweh has not been mentioned up to this point in the vision account and the speech refers to Yahweh in the third person. That it is the angel of Yahweh who speaks may receive further support from Jude 9, which refers to an early interpretation of Zech 3 in which Michael is the one who proclaims the Deity's rebuke. In Zech 3, as elsewhere in the Hebrew scriptures, the relationship between Yahweh and the angel of Yahweh is not clearly delineated.

26. Later interpreters would regard the rebuke that the angel of Yahweh issues to the Satan in Zech 3:2 as an effective means of repelling harmful spirits. Jewish exorcists would quote it in order to drive out an evil presence. See, e.g., Amulet 1, lines 5–6; and Bowl 11, lines 5–6 in Joseph Naveh and Shaul Shaked, *Amulets and Magic Bowls: Aramaic Incantations of Late Antiquity*, 3rd ed. (Jerusalem: Magnes, 1998).

27. The next passage to be discussed, 1 Chr 21:1, is an example of this phenomenon.

the Deuteronomistic telling of this story, Yahweh is angry with Israel and moves David, Israel's king, to take a census of the people. Then the angel of Yahweh strikes Israel with a deadly plague, taking some 70,000 lives.[28] The Chronicler's account deviates somewhat from the story as we have it in 2 Samuel, most remarkably in the very first line. Second Samuel 24:1 introduces the story as follows:

> Again the anger of the LORD was kindled against Israel, and he incited David against them, saying, "Go, count the people of Israel and Judah."

In an intriguing interpretive move, the Chronicler's story begins differently:

> A satan [NRSV Satan] stood up against Israel, and incited David to count the people of Israel. (1 Chr 21:1)

In the Chronicler's account, the immediate cause of David's misstep is not Yahweh or Yahweh's anger, as in 2 Samuel, but a satan. It has proved difficult for interpreters to determine, however, just who this satan is supposed to be. A related question: Why would an editor have substituted this satan for God as the one who incited David to take the census?

What Kind of Satan Stands against Israel?

Some of the ambiguity in this verse is due to the fact that the noun שטן may be translated either as a common noun, "a satan," or as the name Satan. The traditional reading of 1 Chr 21:1 holds that the satan in this verse is Satan, God's archnemesis, as in later Jewish and Christian tradition. The redactor substituted Satan for God in order to resolve the theological difficulty of attributing David's sin and the resulting calamity to the work of God. While this interpretation would explain the Chronicler's editorial adjustment, Jewish writings from long after the time of Chronicles continue to speak of the Satan figure as an agent of God, not as God's adversary (e.g., Jub. 10). By all indications outside this passage, Jews did not arrive at the belief

28. Although both versions of this incident describe the plague as punishment for David's sin (2 Sam 24:10, 17; 1 Chr 21:8, 17), the plague that follows the census, from a tradition-historical perspective, is likely related to the ancient cultic taboo of census taking (Exod 30:12–16).

that Satan was God's rival until a much later period. To assume that such an idea would be found in Chronicles runs the risk of anachronism.

More recently, some scholars have become aware of the problem with assuming that this passage, or any other in the Hebrew scriptures for that matter, speaks of Satan in the way that later literature does.[29] Nevertheless, many, if not most, continue to translate *śāṭān* in 1 Chr 21:1 as the name Satan.[30] Although they recognize that this figure is not to be equated with the Satan of later tradition, they take the Chronicles passage to be the latest stage in the development of the superhuman satan tradition in the Hebrew scriptures. Zechariah and Job speak of an individual who goes by the title "the Satan," but finally in Chronicles, they conclude, one finds an adversary named Satan. Others, however, have questioned this interpretation of the text. Day has argued that the satan of this verse should be regarded as an unnamed heavenly accuser.[31] Some have proposed that this satan is not a heavenly being at all but a terrestrial opponent. This human satan, according to some, could be a military opponent like those who trouble Solomon in 1 Kgs 11.[32] Japhet has argued that this satan is merely one of

29. See, however, Rudman, "Zechariah and the Satan Tradition," who argues that the satan of Job, Zechariah, and 1 Chronicles represents the forces of chaos and is the enemy of God's people and perhaps even of God.

30. These include Hans Duhm, *Die Bösen Geister im Alten Testament* (Tübingen: Mohr Siebeck, 1904), 61; Edward Lewis Curtis and Albert Alonzo Madsen, *A Critical and Exegetical Commentary on the Books of Chronicles*, ICC (New York: Scribner's Sons, 1910), 246–47; Langton, *Satan: A Portrait*, 10; Kluger, *Satan in the Old Testament*, 155; J. G. McConville, *I & II Chronicles*, DSB (Philadelphia: Westminster, 1984), 69–70; Roddy Braun, *1 Chronicles*, WBC 14 (Waco, TX: Word, 1986), 216–17; Forsyth, *Old Enemy*, 119–21; Page, *Powers of Evil*, 33–37; Kirsten Nielsen, *Satan: The Prodigal Son? A Family Problem in the Bible*, BibSem 50 (Sheffield: Sheffield Academic Press, 1998), 100–105; Peter B. Dirksen, *1 Chronicles*, HCOT (Leuven-Dudley: Peeters, 2005), 257; T. J. Wray and Gregory Mobley, *The Birth of Satan: Tracing the Devil's Biblical Roots* (New York: Palgrave Macmillan, 2005), 67; Ralph W. Klein, *1 Chronicles: A Commentary*, Hermeneia (Minneapolis: Fortress, 2006), 418–19; Stefan Schreiber, "The Great Opponent: The Devil in Early Jewish and Formative Christian Literature," in *Angels*, ed. Reiterer, Nicklas, and Schöpflin, 430–40. See also the following English translations: JB, KJV, NKJV, NASB, NIV, NJB, NRSV, and RSV. The NAB is exceptional in that it has "a satan."

31. Day, *Adversary in Heaven*, 127–45; Tate, "Satan in the Old Testament," 464–66. Klein, *1 Chronicles*, 418, and Schreiber, "Great Opponent," 440, also regard this satan as an accuser, though they take *śāṭān* as the name Satan.

32. John H. Sailhamer, "1 Chronicles 21:1—A Study in Inter-Biblical Interpretation," *TJ* n.s. 10.1 (1989): 33–48; John W. Wright, "The Innocence of David in 1 Chronicles 21," *JSOT* 60 (1993): 92–93; Gary N. Knoppers, *1 Chronicles 10–29: A New Translation with Introduction and Commentary*, AB 12A (New York: Doubleday, 2004), 751–52; Steven L. McKenzie,

David's court advisers who, pretending to be David's ally, gives the king adverse counsel.[33]

That the satan of 1 Chr 21 is of a terrestrial, military kind would fit the context of the census in this passage.[34] With the possibility of war looming, a king might find it necessary to take inventory of his fighting force. The problem with this interpretation, however, is that it would be strange for a military opponent to "incite" (*swt*) David to take a census. This word normally denotes an act of persuasion or (in a negative context) seduction.[35] It would not likely be used to describe a military threat to which someone responds by numbering his troops.[36] Thus some scholars have suggested that the satan is one of David's advisers who encouraged him to take the fateful census.

Taking the satan in this verse as a terrestrial opponent, nonetheless, does not seem the most plausible reading of the passage. That a human

---

1–2 Chronicles, AOTC (Nashville: Abingdon, 2004), 170–71. Pancratius C. Beentjes, "Satan, God, and the Angel[s] in 1 Chronicles 21," in *Angels,* ed. Reiterer, Nicklas, and Schöpflin, 140, says, "one should at least reckon with the possibility that 1 Chr 21:1 refers to an unknown (military) adversary."

33. Japhet, *Ideology,* 145–49; Japhet, *I & II Chronicles: A Commentary,* OTL (Louisville: Westminster John Knox, 1993), 373–75; Japhet, *1 Chronik,* HThKAT (Freiburg: Herder, 2002), 346–48. John Jarick, *1 Chronicles,* RNBC (London: Sheffield Academic Press, 2002), 125, seems to prefer the human understanding of the satan in this verse. He rules out the possibility of translating *śāṭān* as Satan. Instead, says Jarick, the Chronicler here "may be saying no more than that the king received adverse counsel (that is to say, advice which ran counter to the best interest of the nation) upon which he was persuaded to undertake a census of the people." N. H. Tur-Sinai (Torczyner), *The Book of Job: A New Commentary* (Jerusalem: Kiryath Sepher, 1957), 44, proposes that the satan of this passage is a false prophet.

34. The discussion that follows resembles the argument in my article, "The Devil Made David Do It . . . or Did He? The Nature, Identity, and Literary Origins of the Satan in 1 Chronicles 21:1," *JBL* 128.1 (2009): 91–106. The analysis in the present chapter, however, differs from that of the earlier article in certain respects. First, while I argued in the earlier study that the satan of 1 Chr 21:1 is an anonymous heavenly punisher, I specify in this chapter that this figure is an "attacker" or "executioner." Second, I no longer assume that the satan material in Job predated Chronicles (see ch. 2 below). There are additional minor differences between the discussion in this chapter and the earlier study.

35. In addition to 2 Sam 24:1 and 1 Chr 21:1, see also this verb in Deut 13:7 (Eng. 6); Josh 15:18; Judg 1:14; 1 Sam 26:19; 1 Kgs 21:25; 2 Kgs 18:32; 2 Chr 18:2, 31; 32:11, 15; Job 2:3; 36:16, 18; Isa 36:18; Jer 38:22; 43:3.

36. Knoppers, *I Chronicles 10–29,* 751–52, seems to argue that the satan is one of the surrounding nations who sets out to attack Israel not directly but indirectly by seducing David into taking a census, thus bringing God's wrath upon Israel. This interpretation reconciles the verb סות with the notion of a foreign military opponent, but the complexity of this hypothesized scenario diminishes its probability.

adversary, rather than God, would stir up trouble for Israel creates more questions than it answers. If the adversary were a military opponent, whatever came of this threat to Israel's safety? If one of David's advisers, then why did this person counsel the king in this way? Parallels with other stories in the Hebrew scriptures also suggest that this satan is more likely to be celestial than terrestrial. For instance, in 1 Kgs 22 (// 2 Chr 18) God entices Ahab to his death through the agency of a deceptive spirit. Moreover, that 1 Chr 21:1 speaks of a heavenly opponent in the service of God makes perfect sense as an interpretation of 2 Sam 24. The Chronicler clarifies that God did not incite David directly, but did so through the agency of a superhuman intermediary. If the satan is human, however, then a much more drastic and less easily explicable interpretive maneuver has taken place.

Reading the Census Story in Light of the Balaam Narrative

The satan of 1 Chr 21 is very likely a divine attacker or executioner like the one who comes against Balaam in Num 22. Several impressive similarities between the Chronicles and Numbers pericopes make this by far the most plausible interpretation of the Chronicles passage.

With regard to parallels between this passage and other passages that mention satans, it is not unusual for scholars to note the resemblance between 1 Chr 21 and Zech 3 or between 1 Chr 21 and Job 1–2. In Zech 3:1, "the Satan" "stands to the right" (*ʿōmēd ʿal yəmînô*) of Joshua, and the satan of Chronicles "stands against" (*wayyaʿămōd ʿal*) Israel. Also, "the Satan" in Job "incites" (*swt*) God to strike Job, and the satan of Chronicles "incites" (*swt*) David to take a census. These similarities between 1 Chr 21 and the satan passages of Zechariah and Job have led some commentators to conclude that the Chronicler is making use of either or both of these passages and that the Chronicler has this same individual in mind.[37]

These correspondences, however, are not as significant as they might at first appear. With regard to the similarity between Zech 3 and 1 Chr 21, one can argue that "stands to the right" and "stands against" are roughly synonymous on the basis of Ps 109:6: "Appoint a wicked person against [*ʿal*] him;

37. Those who adduce these parallels with Job and/or Zechariah as evidence that the Chronicler intends *śāṭān* as the name Satan include Nielsen, *Satan: The Prodigal Son?*, 102; Paul Evans, "Divine Intermediaries in 1 Chronicles 21," *Bib* 85.4 (2004): 553–54; Dirksen, *1 Chronicles*, 257; and Klein, *1 Chronicles*, 418–19.

let a satan stand on his right [*yaʿămōd ʿal yəmînô*]."[38] On the other hand, since this sort of terminology with reference to a satan occurs not only in 1 Chronicles and Zechariah but also in Ps 109, one cannot jump to the conclusion that Chronicles necessarily depends on Zechariah. That Ps 109 uses this language may indicate that "standing against" or "standing on the right" was simply the way one would speak of a satan's activity. Likewise, the similarity between Chronicles and Job can be easily explained without positing that the Chronicler depended on Job. The verb *swt* in 1 Chr 21:1, the only connection between this verse and Job 1–2 (aside from the satan), is more obviously derived from the census story of 2 Sam 24, where God "incites" (*swt*) David to take the census. It does not constitute compelling evidence that the Chronicler had the story of Job in mind. And, as I argue in the next chapter, it is more likely that Job derived this idea from the Chronicles census story than the reverse.

In contrast, the parallels between the census story and Num 22 are abundant and significant. Before the Chronicles account was composed, several similarities existed already between Num 22 and the earlier version of the census story in 2 Sam 24. These links likely prompted the editor to read the account of David's census in light of the Balaam narrative. These parallels include the following:

1. Both accounts begin in a like fashion, declaring that God is angry.
   Num 22:22: *wayyiḥar ʾap ʾĕlōhîm*, "God's anger was kindled"
   2 Sam 24:1: *wayyōsep ʾap yhwh laḥărôt*, "Again the anger of the LORD was kindled"
2. In both stories the angel of Yahweh goes forth as an executioner to punish the guilty (Num 22:22–30; 2 Sam 24:15–16).
3. When Balaam and David see the angel of Yahweh, they confess their sin.
   Num 22:34: *wayyōʾmer Bilʿām ʾel malʾak yhwh ḥāṭāʾtî*, "Then Balaam said to the angel of the LORD, 'I have sinned'"
   2 Sam 24:17: *wayyōʾmer hinnê ʾānōkî ḥāṭāʾtî*, "He said, 'It is I who have sinned'"[39]

38. Japhet, *Ideology*, 147–48, argues that to "stand to a person's right" (*ʿmd ʿal yāmîn*), as in Zech 3 (and Ps 109:6), is not necessarily the same thing as to "stand against" (*ʿmd ʿal*) someone. So also Stokes ("Devil Made David Do It," 100), though here I revise my position on this matter somewhat.

39. My translation. The NRSV translates this phrase in context, "he said to the LORD, 'I alone have sinned.'"

4. God instructs both Balaam and David as to how they can avoid (further) disaster. Balaam will not be killed if he speaks only what Yahweh commands him when he arrives in Moab (Num 22:35). The plague will be stopped and Jerusalem spared if David builds an altar and makes an offering on the threshing floor of Araunah the Jebusite (2 Sam 24:18–25). Both men obey their orders.
5. A further and very important correlation is the perplexing theological paradox in both passages: God brings disaster upon an individual or group for a decision that is instigated by God. In the Balaam story, God grants Balaam permission to undertake his journey, but then responds in anger when the prophet sets out on it (Num 22:20–22). Likewise, God incites David to take the census of Israel, but then sends a plague against the people in response (2 Sam 24:1).

With such an impressive list of commonalities between the two stories, it would have made sense to a postexilic interpreter to associate the narratives and borrow ideas and language from one to clarify the other.

Further support for this explanation of the Chronicler's version of the census story is found in a manuscript of Samuel discovered among the Dead Sea Scrolls. The account of David's census in 4QSam^a contains lines that are not found in the MT of 2 Sam 24. In language reminiscent of Num 22:31, these lines describe the angel of Yahweh and David's reaction when he sees this figure.

Num 22:31

ויגל יהוה את עיני בלעם וירא את מלאך
יהוה נצב בדרך וחרבו שלפה בידו ויקד
וישתחו לאפיו

Then the Lord opened the eyes of Balaam, and he saw the angel of the Lord standing in the road, with his drawn sword in his hand; and he bowed down, falling on his face.

1 Chr 21:16 (//4QSam^a, frag. 164, 1–3)

וישא דויד את עיניו וירא את מלאך
יהוה עמד בין הארץ ובין השמים וחרבו
שלופה בידו נטויה על ירושלם ויפל דויד
והזקנים מכסים בשקים על פניהם

David looked up and saw the angel of the Lord standing between earth and heaven, and in his hand a drawn sword stretched out over Jerusalem. Then David and the elders, clothed in sackcloth, fell on their faces.

Most scholars speculate that these lines were lost from the MT of 2 Sam 24 by haplography.[40] The Chronicler, however, had access to the longer version of the text represented by 4QSam[a] and made use of it in composing his history of Judah.[41] This substantial parallel, in addition to the many other points of contact between the Balaam and census stories listed above, increased the potential for an interpreter such as the Chronicler to associate the two stories.

Furthermore, the Chronicler's version of the story seems to have been edited so that it even more closely aligns with the Balaam story. In 2 Sam 24:18–19, the seer Gad instructs David to build an altar on the threshing floor of Araunah the Jebusite in order to put an end to the plague and save Jerusalem. David follows his orders "as the LORD had commanded" (2 Sam 24:19). A subtle change in 1 Chronicles has not Yahweh but the angel of Yahweh communicate with Gad (21:18–19). That the angel com-

40. It is also possible in theory that these lines were added by an editor who had observed the other points of contact between the Balaam narrative and the census story. In this case, it could have been this editor, rather than the Chronicler, as is usually presumed, who altered the opening line of the account so that a satan incited David to take the census instead of God. Unfortunately, the portion of 4QSam[a] that would have mentioned the satan has not been preserved, so it is impossible to know for sure at what point this figure entered the text. For text-critical analyses of this passage, see, e.g., Eugene Charles Ulrich, *The Qumran Text of Samuel and Josephus*, HSM 19 (Missoula, MT: Scholars Press, 1978), 157; Steven L. McKenzie, *The Chronicler's Use of the Deuteronomistic History*, HSM 33 (Atlanta: Scholars Press, 1985), 56; F. M. Cross, D. W. Parry, and R. J. Saley, "4QSam[a]," in *Qumran Cave 4, XII: 1–2 Samuel*, by Frank Moore Cross, Donald W. Parry, Richard J. Saley, and Eugene Ulrich; DJD 17 (Oxford: Clarendon, 2005), 193; Knoppers, *1 Chronicles 10–29*, 747; Klein, *1 Chronicles*, 415–16n30. Cf. Paul E. Dion, "The Angel with the Drawn Sword (II Chr 21, 16): An Exercise in Restoring the Balance of Text Criticism *and* Attention to Context," *ZAW* 97.1 (1985): 114–17, who draws attention to the way the Chronicler makes use of this tradition found in his *Vorlage*. Werner E. Lemke, "Synoptic Studies in the Chronicler's History" (ThD thesis, Harvard University, 1963), 3–6, and McKenzie, *Chronicler's Use*, 34, urge redaction critics to approach the text of Chronicles with restraint. According to these scholars, two criteria must be met in order for one to be confident that the Chronicler's text is a tendentious reworking: (1) the reading in Chronicles can be attested by no major version of Samuel; and (2) the reading must reflect an agenda of the Chronicler that can be discerned throughout the work.

41. The texts of 4QSam[a], frag. 164, 1–3 and 1 Chr 21:16 are not completely identical, but the differences are inconsequential as far as the present discussion is concerned. For a reconstruction of the Qumran text and a list of the differences with the Chronicles version, see Cross, Parry, and Saley, "4QSam[a]," 192–93. One should note, additionally, that a similar passage also appears in Josh 5:13–15, where Joshua encounters the commander of the army of Yahweh.

municates with Gad resembles the Balaam narrative, in which the angel of Yahweh instructs the prophet Balaam as to how he might save his life (Num 22:32–35). Finally, that Chronicles does not speak of *haśśāṭān* ("the Satan"), as in Zechariah and Job, but only of *śāṭān* (without the definite article), as in Num 22, should not be discounted. Outside 1 Chr 21, the only passage in all of the Hebrew scriptures that speaks of a superhuman satan simply as "a satan" (*śāṭān*) as opposed to "the Satan" (*haśśāṭān*) is Num 22.

Given the numerous ways in which the census story, especially the version in Chronicles, mirrors the Balaam narrative, the satan of 1 Chr 21 should be understood similarly to that of Num 22, as a superhuman attacker or, more specifically, as God's executioner. Nothing in the story suggests that this satan is an "accuser." There is no courtroom scene, and this satan does not bring charges against anyone. Nor does the satan of 1 Chronicles appear to be a "tempter," such as the Satan of later tradition. Granted, the satan in this passage incites David to sin, but this is not merely for the sake of encouraging sin, let alone in an act of rebellion against God. It is because this satan, as God's agent of death, intends to slay thousands of people in Israel. The opening statement says, "a satan stood up against Israel." Israel, not David, is the real object of this satan's attack. Although the activity of the satan in Chronicles is not limited to the simple physical act of attacking Israel, inciting David to sin is merely the means to that end in this particular instance. Furthermore, though it is not impossible that the noun *śāṭān* has come to be the name Satan by the time of the Chronicler, nothing in the passage suggests this. In the absence of compelling evidence to the contrary, one should assume that the Chronicler employs the noun in the same manner as does Numbers, to mean simply an "attacker" or "executioner."

We have yet to address the question of what motivated the Chronicler to make this adjustment of the story. Although it is possible that this editorial move stemmed from an attempt to deal with the "problem" of having God act against Israel, this is far from clear. The satan who incites David, according to our interpretation, acts on God's behalf, so any distance that this intermediary creates between Yahweh and David's sin or between Yahweh and Israel's suffering is very slight. God is still responsible for the events that transpire in this story at the end of the day. As in Numbers, the satan in 1 Chr 21 is probably to be identified with the sword-wielding "destroying angel" (*hammal'āk hammašḥît*) of Yahweh.[42] While one cannot

42. That the satan and the angel of Yahweh are to be identified in this passage is sug-

rule out the possibility that the Chronicler is diminishing God's involvement with sin and suffering, there is little evidence that this is the case.

In all probability, the substitution of a satan for Yahweh is part of a more general trend observable in Chronicles and other literature from the postexilic period to attribute God's work among human beings, both for weal and woe, to angelic intermediaries. For instance, although the distinction between Yahweh and the angel of Yahweh is often blurred in earlier literature, the Chronicler more clearly distinguishes the two.[43] In Chronicles, the angel of Yahweh appears to be simply an angel sent by Yahweh.[44] Similarly, we have already noted the difference between 1 Chr 21:18 and its counterpart in 2 Sam 24:18–19. In the Chronicles passage, the angel tells Gad how to instruct David. In 2 Sam 24, the angel does not speak to Gad. David is said to follow Gad's instructions, "as Yahweh commanded."[45] There was no matter of theodicy that motivated the Chronicler to have the angel, rather than Yahweh, speak with Gad. So also the use of a satan in 1 Chr 21 is not obviously rooted in any perceived problem with God's involvement in evil, but likely stems from the belief that God's dealings on the earth, both good and evil, were often carried out through the agency of angelic emissaries. God's transcendence, not the problem of evil, is more likely the concern.

Early Notions of God's Executioner

The origin of the satan tradition should be understood in the context of other traditions pertaining to superhuman agents of death in the Hebrew scriptures. Such divine bringers of death include "the destroyer" (*ham-*

gested by the symmetry with Num 22, but also by the fact that, as the satan stands in place of Yahweh or Yahweh's anger in 1 Chr 21:1 (cf. 2 Sam 24:1), the angel of Yahweh later replaces God as the one who speaks to Gad in 1 Chr 21:18 (cf. 2 Sam 24:19).

43. E.g., Gen 16:7–14; 22:11–12; Judg 13:2–23.

44. The angel of Yahweh who appears in 2 Kgs 19:35 is referred to in 2 Chr 32:21 simply as "an angel." Similarly, the angel of Yahweh who appears in 1 Chr 21 is introduced only as "an angel" in 21:15. So also observes S. A. Meier, "Angel of Yahweh," *DDD* 54.

45. Cf. 21:9, however, where God speaks directly to Gad. On the complexity of the "transcendence" and "immanence" of God in Chronicles, see John W. Wright, "Beyond Transcendence and Immanence: The Characterization of the Presence and Activity of God in the Book of Chronicles," in *The Chronicler as Theologian: Essays in Honor of Ralph W. Klein*, ed. M. Patrick Graham, Steven L. McKenzie, and Gary N. Knoppers; JSOTSup 371 (London: T&T Clark International, 2003), 240–67.

mašḥît) who kills the firstborn children of Egypt on the eve of the exodus (Exod 12:23). Ezekiel 9 speaks of superhuman executioners as well. The angel of Yahweh also serves in the capacity of executioner in several passages. It is the angel of Yahweh who, in response to the prayer of Hezekiah, strikes down 185,000 Assyrians who have marched on Judah (2 Kgs 19:35 // Isa 37:36). It is also the angel of Yahweh who kills 70,000 Israelites as a result of David's census in 2 Sam 24. In Num 22, the angel of Yahweh comes against Balaam as a satan, an executioner ready to strike the seer down on his way to Moab. First Chronicles 21 combines the descriptions of the executing angel of Yahweh found in the Balaam and census stories, explaining that an unnamed satan incited David to take the census.

Zechariah 3 likely responds to and modifies the notion of the angel of Yahweh as an executioner. Zechariah sees the high priest Joshua standing before the angel of Yahweh, with the Satan standing on the priest's right to execute him. In this passage, rather than being one and the same person, the angel of Yahweh and the Satan are distinct and are at odds with each other. The angel of Yahweh, representing Yahweh's wishes, does not execute Joshua, but rebukes Joshua's would-be executioner and spares Joshua's life. This idea of a division of labor and even disagreement among God's superhuman functionaries would manifest itself in various ways in Jewish and Christian literature, which would eventually speak of cosmic combat between good and evil angels. The Satan of Zechariah is not yet this sort of rebel. Like the satans of Numbers and Chronicles, the Satan in Zechariah, under the employ of God, is an executioner of sinners.[46] He is an employee whom God keeps in check, at least in this one instance, when it comes to Israel.

While the satan tradition likely developed from the idea that the angel of Yahweh would at times serve as an executioner of the wicked into the idea that there was a particular satanic attacker distinct from the angel of Yahweh, it is not the case that this tradition exhibits a simple linear progression corresponding to a chronological arrangement of the biblical texts. Although it was written after Zechariah, 1 Chronicles does not speak of "the Satan," as does Zechariah. Nor does it speak of "Satan." Rather,

46. Christopher A. Rollston, "An Ur-History of the New Testament Devil: The Celestial שטן (*śāṭān*) in Zechariah and Job," in *Evil in Second Temple Judaism and Early Christianity*, ed. Chris Keith and Loren T. Stuckenbruck, WUNT 2/417 (Tübingen: Mohr Siebeck, 2016), 6–16, goes as far as to characterize the work of the Satan in Zechariah (and Job) as "useful" and "good."

drawing on the even earlier book of Numbers, 1 Chr 21 speaks of an unnamed superhuman satan such as the one whom Balaam encountered. While the Chronicler's satan is distinct from God (similar to Zechariah's), this satan is likely to be identified with the angel of Yahweh (similar to the satan of Numbers). Finally, while both Chronicles and Zechariah appear to make use of satan figures in an effort to deal with God's transcendence, there is little evidence that the Chronicler was uncomfortable, in particular, with God's involvement with David's sin and Israel's suffering. The texts discussed in this chapter bear witness to theological development, but not a simple one. Rather, they attest to the simultaneous existence of differing notions of satans.

CHAPTER 2

The Satan and the Innocent Job

Job was a blameless and upright man who feared God and kept himself from wrongdoing. And Job prospered accordingly with the blessing and protection of the God he served so faithfully. So begins the story of Job.[1] Suddenly and drastically, however, Job's situation changed. God withdrew divine favor, and the righteous man suffered the loss of all he had. This turn of events sets the stage in the book of Job for a dialogue on the problem of human suffering as Job defends his integrity to his friends, who suspect that he has by his own wrongdoing brought calamity upon himself. The reader, of course, knows that Job is innocent; he has not offended God, thus he has not incurred the Deity's wrath. What neither Job nor his friends know, however, is that the quality of Job's piety is undergoing a rigorous examination by God at the instigation of a figure called "the Satan."

Job's trouble begins on a day when divine beings, including the Satan, assemble before God. At this gathering, God asks the Satan if he has taken notice of Job's exceptional character. In response, the Satan questions God's assessment of Job, expressing doubt that Job's integrity would remain intact were God to withdraw the divine favor that Job had come to expect in return for his loyalty. God grants the Satan permission to test his hypothesis, and Job incurs the loss of all his property and the death

1. The book of Job in its present form is difficult to date, and proposals range from the eleventh or tenth century to the second century BCE. For a discussion of Job's date and bibliography, see C. L. Seow, *Job 1–21: Interpretation and Commentary*, Illuminations (Grand Rapids: Eerdmans, 2013), 39–46. On the difficulties of locating Job in a precise historical context, see J. J. M. Roberts, "Job and the Israelite Religious Tradition," *ZAW* 89.1 (1977): 107–14.

of his children. Despite these catastrophes, Job remains steadfast in his devotion to God, thus proving the Satan incorrect. On a second occasion when the divine beings are gathered before God, God again asks the Satan if he has observed Job's righteousness, even in spite of the unwarranted loss of all that he possessed. The Satan replies that, although he may have underestimated Job's resolve, he was correct in principle that Job would curse God—given sufficient adversity. God needs only to apply a bit more pressure, the Satan argues, and afflict Job's flesh for the man's true quality to be revealed. God agrees to test the Satan's slightly modified hypothesis, allowing the Satan to attack Job's body. Only Job's life itself is to be spared. The Satan then strikes Job's body with loathsome sores and disappears from the story.

The Composition of the Job Story

Generations of readers have found Job to be a literary masterpiece of the ancient world. While reading the work as a unified whole is an undeniably legitimate enterprise, it is important here to examine the debated issue of just how this piece of literature came to be in its present form. Scholars generally divide the book of Job into three major sections: a prologue (1:1–2:13), the dialogues (3:1–42:6), and an epilogue (42:7–17). The prologue and epilogue are written in prose and serve as the narrative framework for the much lengthier poetic dialogues addressing Job's suffering, the nature of wisdom, and other matters.

Although a number of scholars regard Job as a unity composed by a single author, many have suggested that a more complex process of composition and editing has given Job its present shape.[2] It has become standard for commentators to distinguish between the book's narrative framework (1:1–2:13 and 42:7–17), which portrays Job as one who dutifully accepts suffering from the hand of his God, and the dialogues, in which Job more audaciously vents his frustration with the quality of God's

2. For a bibliography as well as a summary of the discussion of Job's composition, see Seow, *Job 1–21*, 26–39. Seow himself is among those recent scholars who read Job as a unity. Also among recent treatments of Job as a largely unified work is Carol A. Newsom, *The Book of Job: A Contest of Moral Imaginations* (Oxford: Oxford University Press, 2003). Newsom, however, does not make a historical-critical case for Job's unity, but employs the "heuristic fiction" that a single author composed the book, except for the Elihu speeches (16).

governance of human affairs. Opinions vary as to whether the narrative or the dialogues are to be regarded as the earlier of the two. Within the dialogues, it is common to regard the speech of Elihu as secondary (chs. 32–37), since, among other reasons, Elihu is nowhere else mentioned in the book. Commentators have also suggested that the divine responses to Job (38:1–42:6) and the praise of wisdom (ch. 28) have been inserted into the work by an editor. Fewer scholars have called into question the unity of the narrative framework.[3] While this is not the place for a comprehensive treatment of Job's composition, the relationship between those portions of the work pertaining to the Satan and the rest of the work requires some attention.

With regard to Job's narrative prologue, several scholars in the early to mid-twentieth century suggested that the two heavenly court scenes in which the Satan makes an appearance (1:6–12; 2:1–6) are secondary.[4] Their basic argument was that the explanation of Job's suffering as stemming from the Satan's challenge in the divine court is incompatible with the rest of the book, which does not mention any such adversarial figure. This hypothesis did not gain much traction among scholars, however, and many recent discussions of Job's composition do not even mention the possibility.[5] Even those scholars who are happy to posit a complex composition process for Job in other respects do not consider this hypothesis.[6] The Satan's absence outside the prologue is not so conspicu-

3. For an overview of hypotheses concerning the composition of Job's prologue and epilogue, see Yair Hoffman, *A Blemished Perfection: The Book of Job in Context*, JSOTSup 213 (Sheffield: Sheffield Academic Press, 1996), 269–70.

4. E.g., Eduard König, *Einleitung in das Alte Testament mit Einschluss der Apokryphen und der Pseudepigraphen Alten Testaments* (Bonn: Weber, 1893), 415; Louis Finkelstein, *The Pharisees: The Sociological Background of Their Faith*, 2 vols. (Philadelphia: Jewish Publication Society of America, 1938), 1:235; Robert H. Pfeiffer, *Introduction to the Old Testament* (New York: Harper & Brothers, 1941), 668–70. See further bibliography in G. Fohrer, "Zur Vorgeschichte und Komposition des Buches Hiob," *VT* 6.3 (1956): 262–63n3.

5. This statement is more accurate of English-speaking scholarship than German scholarship, in which literary-critical hypotheses with regard to Job's prose framework continue to receive attention. See, e.g., the discussion in Raik Heckl, *Hiob—vom Gottesfürchtigen zum Repräsentanten Israel: Studien zur Buchwerdung des Hiobbuches und zu seinen Quellen*, FAT 70 (Tübingen: Mohr Siebeck, 2010), 324–37.

6. E.g., Marvin H. Pope, *Job*, AB 15 (Garden City, NY: Doubleday, 1965), xxi–xxviii; David J. A. Clines, *Job 1–20*, WBC 17 (Dallas: Word, 1989), lvii–lix. See, however, Heinz-Josef Fabry, "'Satan'—Begriff und Wirklichkeit: Untersuchungen zur Dämonologie der alttestamentlichen Weisheitsliteratur," in *Die Dämonen: Die Dämonologie der israelitisch-*

ous as to warrant such a compositional hypothesis in the minds of most interpreters.[7] Another weakness of supposing that 2:1–6 is an editorial addition is that it requires one to emend the text of 2:7, where the Satan afflicts Job with loathsome sores.[8] Only a minority of commentators still hold that the material in the prologue pertaining to the Satan is a later addition to the text.[9]

Nevertheless, there are good reasons for taking this viewpoint seriously, though perhaps in slightly modified form from how it is normally stated. Older versions of the hypothesis were weak in that they typically supposed that only 1:6–12 and 2:1–6 belonged to the redactional stratum of the prologue.[10] If one also includes 2:7–8 in the editorial layer, then the need to emend 2:7 is obviated, and a much stronger case can be made that the Satan material in Job's prologue was indeed added by a later editor.[11]

---

jüdischen und frühchristlichen Literatur im Kontext ihrer Umwelt = Demons: The Demonology of Israelite-Jewish and Early Christian Literature in Context of Their Environment, ed. Armin Lange, Hermann Lichtenberger, and K. F. Diethard Römheld (Tübingen: Mohr Siebeck, 2003), 282–83, who expresses the view that the Satan material is secondary. According to his reconstruction, an initial editor added 1:6–12 and 2:1–7 to the story, and a second editor supplied 2:11–13 and 42:7–9a, 10aα.

7. E.g., G. Fohrer, "Zur Vorgeschichte und Komposition," 262–65; Hoffman, *Blemished Perfection*, 270.

8. Karl Kautzsch, *Das sogenannte Volksbuch von Hiob und der Ursprung von Hiob Cap I. II. XLII, 7–17: Ein Beitrag zur Frage nach der Integrität des Buches Hiob* (Leipzig: Drugulin, 1900), 58; Samuel Terrien, "The Book of Job," *IB* 3:884n68.

9. E.g., Fabry, "'Satan'—Begriff und Wirklichkeit," 282–83, whose view is summarized in n6 above. Ludger Schwienhorst-Schönberger and Georg Steins, "Zur Entstehung, Gestalt und Bedeutung der Ijob-Erzählung (Ijob 1f; 42)," *BZ* 33 (1989): 4-7, argue that an original Job narrative consisting of 1:1-5, 13-22 and 42:2-17 was updated in two stages. According to their analysis an initial editor added 1:6-12. On the basis of certain differences between 1:6-12 and 2:1-7a (or perhaps 2:1-10), Schwienhorst-Schönberger and Steins conclude that a second editor was responsible for the latter passage.

10. Two exceptions should be noted in this regard. One is Johannes Lindblom, *La composition du livre de Job* (Lund: Gleerup, 1945), 3–35, who considered 1:1–5, 13–22, and 2:11–13 to correspond to an early Edomite tale. A second and more recent is Fabry, "'Satan'—Begriff und Wirklichkeit," 282–83, whose reconstruction of the text's history is summarized in n6 above.

11. So also Fabry, "'Satan'—Begriff und Wirklichkeit," 282–83.

Early Job Narrative

1:1 There was once a man in the land of Uz whose name was Job. That man was blameless and upright, one who feared God and turned away from evil. 2 There were born to him seven sons and three daughters. 3 He had seven thousand sheep, three thousand camels, five hundred yoke of oxen, five hundred donkeys, and very many servants; so that this man was the greatest of all the people of the east. 4 His sons used to go and hold feasts in one another's houses in turn; and they would send and invite their three sisters to eat and drink with them. 5 And when the feast days had run their course, Job would send and sanctify them, and he would rise early in the morning and offer burnt offerings according to the number of them all; for Job said, "It may be that my children have sinned, and cursed God in their hearts." This is what Job always did.

Supplemental Satan Material

6 One day the heavenly beings came to present themselves before the LORD, and the Satan also came among them. 7 The LORD said to the Satan, "Where have you come from?" The Satan answered the LORD, "From going to and fro on the earth, and from walking up and down on it." 8 The LORD said to the Satan, "Have you considered my servant Job? There is no one like him on the earth, a blameless and upright man who fears God and turns away from evil." 9 Then the Satan answered the LORD, "Does Job fear God for nothing? 10 Have you not put a fence around him and his house and all that he has, on every side? You have blessed the work of his hands, and his possessions have increased in the land. 11 But stretch out your hand now, and touch all that he has, and he will curse you to your face." 12 The LORD said to the Satan, "Very well, all that he has is in your power; only do not stretch out your hand against him!" So the Satan went out from the presence of the LORD.

Early Job Narrative

13 One day when his sons and daughters
were eating and drinking wine in the
eldest brother's house, 14 a messenger
came to Job and said, "The oxen were
plowing and the donkeys were feed-
ing beside them, 15 and the Sabeans
fell on them and carried them off, and
killed the servants with the edge of the
sword; I alone have escaped to tell you."
16 While he was still speaking, another
came and said, "The fire of God fell
from heaven and burned up the sheep
and the servants, and consumed them;
I alone have escaped to tell you." 17
While he was still speaking, another
came and said, "The Chaldeans formed
three columns, made a raid on the camels and carried them off, and killed the
servants with the edge of the sword; I
alone have escaped to tell you." 18 While
he was still speaking, another came and
said, "Your sons and daughters were
eating and drinking wine in their eldest
brother's house, 19 and suddenly a great
wind came across the desert, struck the
four corners of the house, and it fell on
the young people, and they are dead; I
alone have escaped to tell you."

20 Then Job arose, tore his robe,
shaved his head, and fell on the ground
and worshiped. 21 He said, "Naked I
came from my mother's womb, and naked shall I return there; the LORD gave,
and the LORD has taken away; blessed
be the name of the LORD."
22 In all this Job did not sin or charge
God with wrongdoing.

Supplemental Satan Material

2:1 One day the heavenly beings came
to present themselves before the LORD,
and the Satan also came among them to
present himself before the LORD. 2 The
LORD said to the Satan, "Where have
you come from?" The Satan answered
the LORD, "From going to and fro on the
earth, and from walking up and down
on it." 3 The LORD said to the Satan,
"Have you considered my servant Job?
There is no one like him on the earth,

Early Job Narrative

Supplemental Satan Material

a blameless and upright man who fears
God and turns away from evil. He still
persists in his integrity, although you incited me against him, to destroy him for
no reason." 4 Then the Satan answered
the LORD, "Skin for skin! All that people have they will give to save their
lives. 5 But stretch out your hand now
and touch his bone and his flesh, and
he will curse you to your face." 6 The
LORD said to the Satan, "Very well, he
is in your power; only spare his life."
7 So the Satan went out from the
presence of the LORD, and inflicted
loathsome sores on Job from the sole of
his foot to the crown of his head. 8 Job
took a potsherd with which to scrape
himself, and sat among the ashes.

9 Then his wife said to him, "Do you
still persist in your integrity? Curse
God, and die." 10 But he said to her,
"You speak as any foolish woman would
speak. Shall we receive the good at the
hand of God, and not receive the bad?"
In all this Job did not sin with his lips.
11 Now when Job's three friends heard
of all these troubles that had come
upon him, each of them set out from
his home—Eliphaz the Temanite,
Bildad the Shuhite, and Zophar the
Naamathite. They met together to go
and console and comfort him. 12 When
they saw him from a distance, they did
not recognize him, and they raised their
voices and wept aloud; they tore their
robes and threw dust in the air upon
their heads. 13 They sat with him on the
ground seven days and seven nights, and
no one spoke a word to him, for they
saw that his suffering was very great.

As one can see, the prologue of Job is more than adequately coherent without the Satan material (the right column). In this version of the narrative, Job is a righteous man who in one day loses all that he owns. There is no Satan, and there are no scenes in heaven. Nor does there remain a two-phase test. Job's ordeal consists of a single series of events that in one day bereaves him of all that he has. There is no mention of Job suffering any bodily affliction.[12] The earlier narrative prologue comes to a close as Job's friends arrive to comfort him and sit silently beside him. The conclusion to Job's story, in both its earlier form and in the present expanded version of the prologue, is to be found outside these verses.

Aside from the coherence of the early narrative posited above, the merits of supposing that an earlier form of Job did not contain the Satan material are many.

1. Job 1:1–5, which sets the stage for the story that follows, describes Job as a wealthy man who possesses a great number of sheep, camels, oxen, donkeys, servants, and children. These verses contain an itemized list of all the things that Job loses in 1:13–19. Nothing, however, is said of Job's flesh in these introductory verses. These verses provide in systematic fashion the background information necessary for comprehending Job's first trial, the loss of all that belongs to him, the most valuable of which are his children. In contrast, absolutely nothing in these verses prepares the reader for Job's second test, the sores on his body. This observation is all the more astounding since this second test is supposed to be the more significant of the two trials (2:4–5).

2. If we look for the moment at the concluding narrative in 42:7–17, even more compelling is that when Job's fortunes are finally restored, nothing at all is said of Job's sores being healed.[13] The conclusion of the story relates only that Job acquires new property and children to replace those he had lost. It would be very surprising for the single author of a unified narrative to fail to mention the restoration of Job's health, the loss of which was supposed to be his most severe ordeal.[14]

12. Interpreters typically explain that Job's three friends do not "recognize him" (*hikkîrūhû*) on account of Job's skin disease (e.g., Samuel Rolles Driver and George Buchanan Gray, *A Critical and Exegetical Commentary on the Book of Job*, ICC, 2 vols. [New York: Scribner's Sons, 1921], 27; Pope, *Job*, 25). Clines, *Job 1–20*, 59–62, however, is probably correct to translate this expression as, "they did not acknowledge him." That is, they did not speak to him. Instead, they wept and sat silently with him. Even if one prefers the traditional translation "recognize," the three friends' inability to do this can be accounted for by Job's having torn his garment, shaven his head, and fallen on the ground. This would not have been how Job's friends were accustomed to seeing him.

13. Lindblom, *Composition du livre de Job*, 26–27, also notices this glaring omission in the epilogue.

14. Noting that 42:12–17 reveals an awareness neither of Job's illness nor of Job's three friends, Albrecht Alt, "Zur Vorgeschichte des Buches Hiob," *ZAW* 55.3–4 (1937): 265–68,

Given these peculiar lacunae in the Job story, one has reason to look for other indicators that a redactor has added the passages about the Satan and Job's bodily affliction. There are several.

3. In the earlier version of the narrative proposed above, 1:13 follows directly on 1:4–5. The narrative moves without interruption from introducing the custom of Job's children gathering together for meals to speaking of an occasion when they were doing that very thing.

4. Job 1:13 begins with the expression, "One day" (*wayyəhî hayyôm*), which is odd if the canonical form of the prologue was composed by a single author. In the present form of the narrative, the expression "one day" also occurs in 1:6 and 2:1, each of which introduces one of Job's two trials. Following the second conversation between God and the Satan, 2:7 says simply that the Satan goes out from God's presence and strikes Job. There is no indication that any time has passed between the second meeting in heaven and the Satan's second attack. In contrast, the initial meeting of the Satan with God and Job's first trial inexplicably occur on two separate occasions, being separated by the temporal marker "one day" in 1:13. This marker in 1:13 is perfectly understandable, however, if this verse immediately follows 1:5.

5. Job 1:13 continues, "when *his* sons and daughters were eating and drinking" (italics mine). The pronoun "his" here is awkward in the current form of the prologue, since "the Satan" is the subject of the previous sentence in 1:12: "the Satan went out from the presence of the LORD." This awkwardness is eliminated, however, if 1:13 follows immediately upon 1:5, where Job is the subject of the final sentence.[15]

---

posited that an earlier version of the story contained only Job 1 and 42:12–17, to which ch. 2 and 42:7–9 were later added. See the similar views of Friedrich Horst, *Hiob 1–19,* BKAT 16.1 (Neukirchen-Vluyn: Neukirchener Verlag, 1968), ix; and Paul Kang-Kul Cho, "The Integrity of Job 1 and 42:11–17," *CBQ* 76.2 (2014): 230–51.

Although one might construe a few statements in Job 42 to imply that Job's health was restored, it is unlikely that these statements imply this. Job 42:10a says that God "restored Job's fortunes" (*šāb 'et šəbût*), but the elaboration of Job's restoration in 42:10b–17 clarifies that Job receives property and children to replace those taken from him in ch. 1 with no mention of his fleshly affliction. (Cf. the expression *šwb 'et šəbût* in Jer 32:42–44 and Amos 9:14.) Heckl, *Hiob*, 308, 331, argues that Job's social restoration in Job 42 presupposes his physical healing. On the contrary, although Job's social restoration may presume his health, it does not necessarily presuppose that he had lost his health and regained it. Also, that the final verses of the book note Job's longevity (42:16–17) does not imply the restoration of Job's health. Job's life was never in jeopardy, even in the Satan material (2:6). The remark about Job's lifespan attests to God's blessing, but does not presume that Job suffered from sores on his body.

15. Augustus Heiligstedt, *Commentarius Grammaticus Historicus Criticus in Jobum*

6. When Job hears the news of his children's death, he tears his robe, shaves his head, and falls on the ground (1:20). In a similar fashion, when Job's friends arrive and see his misery, they tear their robes, throw dust on their heads, and sit on the ground (2:12). The friends' actions are intended to correspond to Job's, but the symmetry between Job and his friends' actions is broken up if there is a narrative between these passages saying simply that Job sat among the ashes (2:8).

7. In 2:9, Job's wife asks him, "Do you still persist in your integrity?" According to the canonical form of the narrative, this question follows the statement that Job sat among the ashes and scraped himself with a potsherd. Sitting among ashes was an extreme act of mourning.[16] Job's scraping himself with a potsherd is more difficult to interpret, though it is often understood as a means of relieving the discomfort (itching?) caused by his sores. Although these are appropriate activities for Job given his situation, they are not especially virtuous. If 2:9 comes right after 1:20–22, which says that Job fell on the ground, worshiped, and blessed God's name, then the words of Job's wife fit their context much better.

8. Job's loss of property in 1:13–19 is not attributed to the Satan. It is certainly presumed to be an "act of God," but the Satan is not explicitly involved. This stands in contrast to 2:7, which says that the Satan inflicted sores on Job. That 1:13–19 originally described disasters that were not attributed to the Satan accounts for this difference.

9. The Satan is not mentioned in the resolution of the story in the epilogue. Granted, it is not necessary for the Satan to reappear at the end of the story for the plot's conflict to be resolved. Nevertheless, the absence of this villain, the one who caused all of Job's woes to begin with, is striking.

While some of the items cited above do not independently constitute proof that an editor added the Satan to the Job story, several of them are quite significant. The cumulative import of the list is difficult to deny. To be sure, there is room to disagree over some of the details in the division of the text laid out in the preceding pages.[17] Particulars aside, the basic

---

(Leipzig: Sumptibus Librariae Rengerianae, 1847), xix, also points to this as evidence that vv. 6–12 are secondary.

16. E.g., Isa 47:1; 58:5; Jer 6:26; Ezek 27:30; Jonah 3:6. See Morris Jastrow Jr., "Dust, Earth, and Ashes as Symbols of Mourning among the Ancient Hebrews," *JAOS* 20 (1899): 133–50.

17. For instance, 1:21–22 and 2:9–10 are together somewhat redundant, and they separate the scene involving Job's friends from the setting presupposed by this scene. It is possible that one or both of 1:21–22 and 2:9–10 belong to the editorial layer rather than to the earlier narrative. Job's wife is nowhere else mentioned in the story, and her conversation

argument, that the Satan material was added to an earlier Job narrative that contained no such figure, seems secure.

Without entering into the debate over the relationship between Job's prose framework and its poetic dialogue, one may further posit that the Satan material in the current form of the prologue is later than the dialogues. Although the dialogues occasionally use the imagery of bodily deterioration or of physical suffering to describe Job's situation (7:5; 19:20; 30:30), there is no unambiguous reference to Job's sores.[18] More significantly, neither Job nor his friends express any awareness in their dialogues that the Satan or any such figure was responsible for Job's predicament.

That one should expect Job and/or his friends to refer to the Satan if this figure were present in the story from the beginning has been contested by scholars on the grounds that the meetings that took place between God and the Satan were unknown to the human participants in the drama. This objection, however, cannot be upheld. Although Job and his dialogue partners were not aware of the specifics of Job's situation, in which the Satan had challenged God's high estimation of Job, there is no reason to suppose that the theology that serves as the basis for the scenario in this story—the belief that God brings misfortune upon humans through the agency of a superhuman satan—would have been unknown to them. A fundamental presupposition of the Satan material in the prologue is that God brings disaster upon humans via the Satan. This is not to say that the theology of the prologue and that of the dialogues are entirely inconsistent.[19] It is peculiar, however, that in all of the discussion between Job and his friends about Job's trouble and God's hand in it, not once do they allude to the

---

with Job in 2:9–10 echoes some of the second conversation between God and the Satan. These observations may point toward 2:9–10 being part of the supplemental material. Similarly, 1:21–22 contains the divine name, which occurs nowhere else in the narrative prologue outside the Satan material. This may indicate that 1:21–22 entered the text with the later material. Since the divine name occurs several times in the narrative epilogue, however, this criterion is only of limited value in distinguishing the literary strata of the prologue.

18. See also 18:13 and 33:2, 25, which describe the suffering of the wicked in terms of bodily affliction. Carol A. Newsom, "The Book of Job: Introduction, Commentary, and Reflections," *NIB* 4:421, suggests the possibility that 11:15 alludes to Job's disfigurement: "Surely then you will lift up your face without blemish." It is possible, however, that "blemish" should be taken in a moral rather than physical sense in this verse.

19. For recent attempts to account for the absence of the Satan in the dialogues from the perspective of the present form of the book of Job, see Robert Moses, "'The *satan*' in Light of the Creation Theology of Job," *HBT* 34.1 (2012): 19–34; Braden P. Anderson, "The Story of Job and the Credibility of God," *HBT* 34.2 (2012): 103–17.

Satan or any such figure, especially given how integral this figure is to the plot of Job in its present form.[20] This significant silence is likely a clue to the process that produced the book.

To speak of the book of Job's depiction of the Satan is to speak primarily of how the editor who supplied 1:6–12 and 2:1–8 depicts the Satan. This observation raises some interesting questions. Is it possible to distinguish between this particular individual's conception of the Satan and the Satan as this figure is presented by the book as a whole? It could be, for instance, that the addition of the Satan material had interpretive implications for later readers unforeseen even by the editor who added the material. Also, if the Satan material in Job comes from a later era than the rest of the work, then might one reconsider how Job's portrayal of the Satan relates chronologically and conceptually to other depictions of satanic figures in the Hebrew scriptures? These questions will figure into the discussion of Job's Satan below.

The Satan as Attacker/Executioner

The nature of Job's story presents the reader with a special challenge in determining the ideas that underlie it. The story of Job is supposed to be at the same time typical and atypical. Both Job's extreme righteousness and his extreme suffering despite his righteousness are unusual. On the other hand, Job's story is no doubt supposed to be in some way analogous to the experiences of others. Similarly, the Satan's activity in this story is probably to be regarded as typical in some respects and atypical in others. One must very carefully read between the lines of the story in order to distinguish, if possible, what is presumed to be the Satan's business as usual in Job from what is supposed to be unusual. One must also try to distinguish between those aspects of the Satan's activity in Job that are essential to his character and those that are nonessential or accidental.

Presumably, the Satan is one of the "heavenly beings" or "sons of God" (*bənê hāʾĕlōhîm*) who serve God and with whom the Satan comes before God on both occasions in this story (1:6; 2:1). Although some

20. So also König, *Einleitung in das Alte Testament*, 415. Although Lindblom, *Composition du livre de Job*, 24–25, concludes that the Satan material did not belong to the earliest narrative, he argues that it was added to the prose tale before the dialogue was added to the story.

scholars have suggested that the Satan is not a member of this group but is an intruder, this is not the most straightforward reading of the passage.[21] If the Satan is not one of these beings, then the setting of the conversation between God and the Satan on a day when all of the sons of God have gathered to present themselves before Yahweh is superfluous. Although later literature will portray the Satan more as a rebel among heavenly beings than as one who is among God's functionaries, this sort of parting of the ways between God and the Satan does not seem to have taken place yet.

Along the same lines, that this individual is referred to throughout the narrative as *haśśāṭān*, "the Satan," indicates that this designation here, as in Zech 3, refers to a particular officer in the heavenly court, "the Executioner" or "the Attacker" in God's service.[22] The notion of the Satan as God's "Executioner" accounts for much of what this figure says and does in Job. When Yahweh inquires into whence the Satan has come, the Satan replies that he has been "going to and fro on the earth [*šwṭ bāʾāreṣ*] . . . and walking up and down on it" (1:7; 2:2). God then asks whether the Satan has taken note of Job's exceptional piety (1:8; 2:3). From this exchange, one may conclude that the Satan's activity entails surveilling the earth and observing the moral quality of human beings. In light of the fact that satans elsewhere in the Hebrew scriptures typically act as physical assailants, one is probably to understand the business of Job's Satan similarly. When this Satan came across evildoers, he was authorized to dispense corporal or capital punishment on behalf of God.[23] That the Satan, once he has obtained God's permission, proceeds to strike Job with physical illness also comports well with the notion of an attacking satan.

The belief that a satan, whether human or superhuman, would surveil humankind, however, is an idea that we have not encountered up

21. Scholars who take the Satan to be an intruder include Francis I. Andersen, *Job: An Introduction and Commentary,* TOTC (Leicester: InterVarsity Press, 1976), 82; Samuel Terrien, *Job,* 2nd ed., CAT 13 (Geneva: Labor et Fides, 2005), 10.

22. On Peggy Day's proposal (*An Adversary in Heaven: śāṭān in the Hebrew Bible,* HSM 43 [Atlanta: Scholars Press, 1988], 43) that the definite article be translated not as "the" but as "a certain," see the discussion in ch. 1, n22.

23. For examples of texts in which satans function as physical assailants of various sorts, see Num 22:22, 32; 1 Sam 29:4; 2 Sam 19:23 [Eng. 22], and the other passages discussed in the previous chapter, though English translations often misrender the noun *śāṭān* as "adversary" or "accuser" in these passages.

to this point in the study and may be novel to Job. The Satan's role in this respect resembles that of the "eyes of Yahweh" in 2 Chr 16:9, though the latter is mentioned in a positive context: "For the eyes of the LORD range throughout the entire earth [*məšōṭəṭôt bəkol hā'āreṣ*], to strengthen those whose heart is true to him." N. H. Tur-Sinai suggests that the Satan figure in Job is modeled on the "eyes and ears of the king," the Persian "secret police" who would spy out the land and report any suspicious activity.[24]

The role of the Satan in the book of Job involves more than mere surveillance, however. More important for the story of Job is what the Satan is supposed to do when he encounters a wicked person. As is the case with the superhuman satans mentioned in the passages considered in the previous chapter, the Satan in the book of Job is God's agent of punishment. This underlying assumption can be observed, as well, in God's response to the Satan's request to test Job's piety. When the Satan asks God to stretch out God's hand and strike Job, God says simply, "he is in your power" (1:12; 2:6). For God to bring disaster on a person is for the Satan, God's roving emissary of punishment, to bring disaster on that person.

Job's circumstances, however, are exceptional. Since Job has done nothing wrong, the Satan must obtain special permission from God to attack him. The Satan's attack of Job may also deviate from the norm in that the Satan is not permitted to kill Job. As we observed in the previous chapter, the superhuman satans of Num 22, Zech 3, and 1 Chr 21 are presumed to be divine executioners. In the story of Job, each time that the Satan comes before God to request permission to test Job, God restricts the Satan's authority, instructing him not to stretch out his hand against Job to harm him physically or to kill him (1:12; 2:6). It was within the purview of the Satan's power, the story of Job assumes, to kill wicked individuals. The purposes of this narrative, however, require that Job's life be spared so that his response to adversity could be observed. The story of Job envisions a Satan who can kill humans, but who also, at least in exceptional cases, might attack humans in other ways.

24. N. H. Tur-Sinai, *The Book of Job: A New Commentary* (Jerusalem: Kiryath Sepher, 1957), 38–45. Cf. "the eyes of the Lord" in Zech 4:10 and 2 Chr 16:9. See also A. L. Oppenheim, "The Eyes of the Lord," *JAOS* 88.1 (1968): 173–80. Tur-Sinai finds support for his conclusion in an imaginative, yet improbable etymological analysis, in which he derives the noun שׂטן from the verb שׁוט, meaning "to rove." For a critique of Tur-Sinai's etymology, see Day, *Adversary in Heaven*, 17–23.

The Satan Attacks an Innocent Person

While the idea of the Satan as divine executioner underlies the book of Job's depiction of the Satan, the book of Job marks a development in the Satan tradition, moving conceptually well beyond the simple notion of the Satan as an executioner of the wicked in one very significant respect. For the first time, a superhuman satan attacks an innocent person. That this is fundamentally how one should comprehend the Satan's activity in the story of Job is supported by the fact that this is precisely how Yahweh describes the Satan's activity in Job 2:3. In their second meeting, Yahweh summarizes their previous encounter, telling the Satan, "you incited me [*wattəsîttēnî*] against [Job], to destroy him for no reason." This is the primary function of the Satan in the narrative of Job and is a significant innovation in the superhuman satan tradition. In the earlier literature, superhuman satans are supposed to bring trouble upon those whose actions warrant such treatment.

The idea that God would bring suffering upon a righteous individual, of course, is integral to the book of Job. The notion that the Satan might incite God against an innocent person, however, is the creation of the editor who added the Satan material to the book. This editor probably derived from Zechariah the belief that there was a permanent executioner of humans in God's court called "the Satan," as well as the idea that this officer might at times be at odds with God in his opposition of humanity. In Zechariah, the angel of Yahweh rebukes the Satan for his plan to execute Joshua the high priest. In the book of Job, the Satan and God have differing assessments of Job's behavior, and it is the Satan who proposes to test Job with suffering.

There remains the question, however, of how the editor arrived at the peculiar idea that a heavenly satan would "incite" God to bring disaster upon an innocent person. This notion as well was likely derived from an earlier text, specifically 1 Chr 21:1: "a satan stood up against Israel and incited [*wayyāset*] David" to number the people, bringing a plague upon them. This passage retells 2 Sam 24 and probably shares with its source text the assumption that God is punishing Israel for some unspecified sin. Although the Chronicler likely understood that the satan was acting on behalf of an offended Deity, this is not stated explicitly. This silence allowed for later readers to understand this passage in different ways, as can be seen from the long history of the passage's (mis)interpretation. Since it is not stated explicitly in this story, as it was in 2 Samuel, that God was angry with Israel to begin with, it could have appeared to the editor of Job that the satan in Chronicles incited Israel's benevolent ruler to destroy the people without cause. The ambiguity of the Chronicles passage, then, may have opened the door for the editor of Job to imagine the Satan as one who would incite trouble against the innocent.

Scholars have traditionally posited that the Chronicler's depiction of the satan figure depended on the book of Job, not the reverse. This assessment stems in large part from the assumption that the occurrence of the satan figure in 1 Chr 21:1 is later than the Satan material in the book of Job. The traditional reading of the noun *śāṭān* in Chronicles as the name Satan has also contributed to this understanding of the relationship between the two passages, since the name Satan would have been a later development in the tradition than the title "the Satan." The recognition that the Satan material was added to the story of Job by a later editor reopens the question of the two satan passages' relative dating. The observation that Chronicles does not speak of "Satan," but of merely "a satan," likewise yields new possibilities with regard to the tradition-historical relationship between the ideas found in the two texts. The supposition that the editor of Job depended on the census tradition as found in Chronicles, while it must remain hypothetical, accounts best for the book of Job's innovative teaching.[25] The tradition of a superhuman satan had its origins in the Hebrew scriptures as a divine executioner of the wicked. In the story of Job, one observes the most developed and, possibly, the latest manifestation of the satan tradition in the Hebrew scriptures. In this work, the Satan not only brings suffering justly upon the wicked, but also brings it unjustly upon the innocent.

By supplying a satan figure to the story of Job, the editor relieves God of *some* of the burden of responsibility for Job's suffering and, so the readers of Job are led to conclude, also for the misery of other righteous individuals who suffer undeservedly. To be sure, God is not entirely free from responsibility. The Satan challenges God, "stretch out *your* hand" against Job (1:11; 2:5; italics mine). In a sense, ultimate responsibility still resides with Yahweh. Nevertheless, Yahweh is unquestionably the more positive

25. The analysis of 1 Chr 21:1 in ch. 1 allows for the possibility that a previous redactor, not the Chronicler himself, is responsible for the presence of the "satan" in the census story. Cf. the version of the census story in 4QSam[a], which occupies an intermediate position between MT 2 Sam 24 and 1 Chr 21. In this case, it would also be possible that the editor of Job made use of such a version of Samuel rather than Chronicles.

figure in the story, and the Satan is the culprit. Although Yahweh brings Job to the Satan's attention to begin with, the idea to afflict Job originates not with Yahweh but with the Satan. Yahweh speaks only favorably of Job's integrity, but the Satan questions it. The editorial material also portrays God's part in Job's suffering as more passive than in the earlier narrative. God's role in the earlier narrative is summarized by Job's resignation that "the LORD gave, and the LORD has taken away" (1:21). In the editorial material, while God permits the Satan to have his way with Job, the Satan is the villain and the originator of Job's troubles.

Is the Satan an "Accuser" in Job?

Whether one is to regard the Satan as an accuser in the story of Job depends in part on how one defines "accuser." There is little in the prologue of Job to suggest that the Satan was believed to be an "accuser" of sinners or a heavenly "prosecuting attorney," as many scholars have supposed.[26] As already discussed, the title *śāṭān*, "Satan," indicates not that this figure is an accuser but that he is an attacker or executioner. The story of Job also presupposes that physical "attack" is fundamentally the nature of the Satan's work. Job's satan, however, differs notably from the other satans considered up to this point in that he attacks an innocent person. The way that he secures special permission to do this is by calling into question whether Job would maintain his faithfulness under adverse circumstances.

Nevertheless, one must be clear about the role of the Satan in the narrative. The Satan is not the accuser of a sinner. Job has committed no crime in this story. Nor does the Satan accuse Job of having done so.[27] Neither

26. E.g., Pope, *Job*, 10; Edwin M. Good, "The Problem of Evil in the Book of Job," in *The Voice from the Whirlwind: Interpreting the Book of Job*, ed. Leo G. Perdue and W. Clark Gilpin (Nashville: Abingdon, 1992), 52.

27. F. Rachel Magdalene, *On the Scales of Righteousness: Neo-Babylonian Trial Law and the Book of Job*, BJS 348 (Providence: Brown Judaic Studies, 2007), 106–17, argues that the Satan accuses Job of "blasphemous intent." Job's "intent," however, does not seem to be the issue, but the basis of Job's loyalty to God. This legal interpretation of Job 1–2 also presupposes that the title "the Satan" means "the Accuser." Even less likely is the suggestion of Day, *Adversary in Heaven*, 80–83, that the object of the Satan's accusation is not Job but Yahweh. While it is true that the Satan questions God's assessment of Job, given the way that God has blessed Job, it is hardly plausible that the author of this material regards "the Satan" as the accuser of God. Cf. the similar position of John H. Walton and Tremper Longman III, *How to Read Job* (Downers Grove, IL: InterVarsity Press, 2015), 50–56, that

is it evident that the Satan would under normal circumstances prosecute sinners in the heavenly courtroom. Those aspects of the story that have been interpreted to imply that the Satan regularly functions as a superhuman prosecutor (e.g., that he surveils the earth in search of transgressors) are more than adequately accounted for by the belief that the Satan was believed to serve as attacker of the wicked and do not require one to hypothesize that the Satan must have been an accuser. The Satan in this story calls the integrity of the blameless Job into question. Whether the author of the Satan material in Job believed that the Satan would regularly make such allegations about the innocent before God is not clear. That the Satan does this in Job's case may be among those aspects of the story that are supposed to be exceptional. If one is to call the Satan of Job an "accuser," this designation must be qualified considerably. For the author of Job 1:6–12 and 2:1–8, the Satan, more accurately, is an attacker or executioner of evildoers who may on occasion incite God against the innocent.

The Contributions of Job to the Satan Tradition

The book of Job as it now stands paved the way for many subsequent teachings on the Satan. For instance, the sorts of disaster for which the heavenly satan figure was held responsible seem to have been expanded. In earlier passages, heavenly satans, like the "destroyer" of the exodus narrative, bring only death to those who have offended God. In the book of Job, the Satan afflicts Job with sores. Also novel in the book of Job is the Satan's association with foreign invaders. Both 2 Sam 24 and 1 Chr 21 assume that an event such as an enemy invasion was outside the realm of such a heavenly figure's activity. When given a choice between famine, invasion, and plague, David opts for a plague, reasoning, "Let us fall into the hands of the LORD, for his mercy is great; but do not let me fall into the hands of men" (2 Sam 24:12–14 // 1 Chr 21:10–13). Conversely, as part of Job's first trial in the present form of the prologue, the Satan, it is implied, sends the Sabeans and Chaldeans to kill Job's servants and carry off his oxen, donkeys, and camels (1:14–15, 17). Raising up foreign enemies against God's

---

the Satan is "the challenger" of God. This is not to say that the Satan does not challenge God, but that the opposition implied by the title "Satan" is the opposition directed at Job, not that directed at God. Cf. Zech 3:1, where the object of the verb *śṭn* is Joshua, rather than (the angel of) Yahweh.

people would be an important component of the Satan figure's work in early Jewish and Christian literature, notably Jubilees, the War Rule, and the book of Revelation. The belief that the Satan had this ability stems from the book of Job's complex composition.

Further, although the Satan of the book of Job is not yet the accuser that he would become in later tradition, the book portrays the Satan as one who at least in one instance went before God to make allegations about an innocent person. The idea that the Satan might incite God against the righteous in this way likely played a significant role in the rise of the belief that the Satan is the "accuser of our comrades" (Rev 12:10).

What is most revolutionary, however, about the depiction of the Satan in the story of Job is that the Satan attacks the righteous. In Zechariah, although the Satan intends to harm the high priest Joshua, this portrayal of a heavenly satan is consistent with those of Num 22 and 1 Chr 21, in that Joshua is guilty and deserves such treatment. In the book of Job, momentously, the object of the Satan's opposition is an innocent person. While the Satan of Job is not quite yet the evil, antagonistic figure he would eventually become in Jewish and Christian tradition, in the book of Job this enemy of the righteous begins to emerge.

CHAPTER 3

Demons, Evil Spirits, Fallen Angels, and Human Sin

Satanic executioners are not the only superhuman forces that threaten humankind in the world as depicted in the Hebrew scriptures. The literature of Israel also speaks of "demonic" foreign deities worshiped erroneously by Israel, harmful "spirits" that afflict and mislead humans, as well as certain divine beings called "sons of God," who appear in several biblical passages and are associated with various activities. A number of traditions about superhuman figures, including some that are obscure and relatively insignificant in the Hebrew scriptures, would obtain great importance in early Jewish and Christian discussions of Satan and the problem of evil. As later interpreters reflected on the problem of evil, they would make use of diverse and distinct ideas regarding superhuman figures from earlier literature, adapting them and combining them into new, synthetic explanations of evil. In this chapter we briefly consider the biblical texts that speak of these beings and then examine how diverse traditions are brought together and developed in one influential text from the third century BCE, the Book of the Watchers (1 En. 1–36).

Taxonomies and Terminology for Harmful Superhuman Beings

Before beginning an analysis of early biblical and Jewish demonology, a few words are in order about the terminology that is often employed in discussions of this topic. In modern English vocabulary, the word *demon* is used in a very general fashion to refer to nearly any maleficent superhuman being, and the expression *evil spirit* is simply a synonym for *demon.*[1] In other words, in modern theological discourse, both of these designations are generic labels for just about any harmful superhuman entity.

The semantic range of "demon" and "evil spirit" and these labels' synonymy, however, are not the innovations of modern English speakers. Such uses of these designations have a long and venerable history. With regard to the synonymy of "demon" and "evil spirit," some NT books employ *daimonion* and *pneuma* interchangeably with reference to the very same beings (e.g., Luke 9:39–42).[2] The wide semantic range of "demon" has ancient roots, dating as far back as the Jewish translation of the Hebrew scriptures into Greek. The LXX translators used *daimonion* to translate a variety of Hebrew words. For example, the Greek of Isa 13:21 translates *śəʿîrîm,* which appears in a list of beings that inhabit desolate areas, as *daimonia.*[3] So also Hebrew *šēdîm* and *ʾĕlîlîm,* generic designations for foreign deities, are translated with *daimonia* (Deut 32:17; Ps 96:5 [LXX 95:5]; 106:37 [LXX 105:37]).[4] By translating these different Hebrew terms with a single Greek term, whether wittingly or unwittingly, these translators united what were distinct categories in Hebrew into a single overarching Greek category, *daimonion.*[5]

Despite the comprehensive nature of the category "demon" in modern thought, and even in some texts from antiquity, one should not presume that all ancient Israelite and Jewish authors shared this conception of the

1. The first definition that *OED* gives for "demon" is: "Any evil spirit or malevolent supernatural being; a devil" (*OED Online,* s.v. "demon, n. [and adj.]," Oxford University Press, January 2018, accessed March 1, 2018, http://www.oed.com/view/Entry/49788?p=emailAkI6dPyGZAG8g&d=49788). See also the entry for "demon" in *Merriam-Webster,* the first definition of which is "an evil spirit" (*Merriam-Webster,* s.v. "demon," accessed March 1, 2018, https://www.merriam-webster.com/dictionary/demon).

2. On the terminology of the NT, see the discussion in ch. 9.

3. See similarly *daimonia* in LXX Isa 34:14, where the Hebrew seems to refer to animals that have as their habitat regions unfit for humans.

4. In addition, cf. the use of *daimonion* in Isa 65:11 for *gad,* "Fortune."

5. The Gk. *daimonion,* of course, also had a life of its own prior to its appropriation by Jews and Christians with reference to Semitic concepts. For a discussion of why Greek translators chose *daimonion* to translate particular Hebrew words, see Dale Basil Martin, "When Did Angels Become Demons?," *JBL* 129.4 (2010): 658–66. On the association of *śəʿîrîm* and *šēdîm* in Jewish tradition, see the literature cited by Henrike Frey-Anthes, *Unheilsmächte und Schutzgenien, Antiwesen und Grensgänger: Vorstellungen von "Dämonen" im alten Israel,* OBO 227 (Fribourg: Academic Press; Göttingen: Vandenhoeck & Ruprecht, 2007), 201.

superhuman realm. As I will demonstrate, it will not suffice simply to speak of "demons" in the Hebrew scriptures or in the Book of the Watchers. The invisible world was far more rich and varied according to the theology of these texts than a single overarching category such as "demon" suggests. It would also be incorrect, despite the popular usage of the designations, to assume that "demons" are the same as "evil spirits" in all ancient texts. Interestingly, the translators who rendered the Hebrew and Aramaic Scriptures into Greek never translate *rûaḥ*, "spirit," as *daimonion*. This is probably not coincidental. Finally, with regard to terminology, one must be mindful of different and evolving taxonomies of superhuman beings in ancient literature. Not all ancient authors thought of superhuman beings in precisely the same way.

Demons, Evil Spirits, and the Sons of God in the Hebrew Scriptures

Let us consider three distinct traditions from the Hebrew scriptures that would become especially important in early Jewish discussions of evil, its divine agents, and the Satan. One is that of the *šēdîm*, or "demons," as the word is traditionally translated. Among the words in the Hebrew scriptures that ancient and modern translators have rendered as *daimonia*/"demons," the notion of the *šēdîm* has exerted the greatest influence on the developing demonologies of early Judaism. Although *šēdîm* are mentioned only twice in the Hebrew scriptures (Deut 32:17; Ps 106:37), they would figure prominently in early Jewish discussions of evil and its superhuman proponents. The second tradition, one that is distinct from that of the *šēdîm*, pertains to certain maleficent "spirits" that would bring various manners of harm on humans. These "evil spirit" (*rûaḥ rāʿâ*) traditions would also play a significant role in early Jewish discussions of the Satan, sin, and suffering. A third tradition is that of the "sons of God." These divine beings, not to be confused either with "demons" or with "evil spirits," appear in a handful of biblical passages, perhaps most notably in the laconic and enigmatic Gen 6:1–4. This text reports strangely that certain "sons of God" (*bənê hāʾĕlōhîm*) took human wives and had children with them. This peculiar story would intrigue and inspire later interpreters who would reflect on its implications for comprehending the superhuman realm and the human predicament.

Šēdîm, *"Demons"*

The word *šēdîm* occurs twice in the Hebrew scriptures, both times in passages that criticize Israel's worship of foreign deities. Deuteronomy 32:16–17 describes Israel's rebellion against Yahweh:

> They made him jealous with strange gods,
> with abhorrent things they provoked him.
> They sacrificed to demons, not God [*šēdîm lōʾ ʾĕlōah*],
> to deities they had never known,
> to new ones recently arrived,
> whom your ancestors had not feared.

In a similar fashion, Ps 106:34–38 says of Israel's unfaithfulness,

> They did not destroy the peoples,
> as the LORD commanded them,
> but they mingled with the nations
> and learned to do as they did.
> They served their idols,
> which became a snare to them.
> They sacrificed their sons
> and their daughters to the demons [*šēdîm*];
> they poured out innocent blood,
> the blood of their sons and daughters,
> whom they sacrificed to the idols of Canaan.

Since the two passages that mention them say very little about them, precisely what sort of entities (or nonentities) *šēdîm* are presumed to be is not entirely clear. Etymologically, the word has been related to Akkadian *šēdu(m)*, which could refer to either a protective or a malevolent spirit.[6] In both of its biblical occurrences, *šēdîm* designates gods or putative gods other than the God of Israel. The label stands in apposition with "not God" (*lōʾ ʾĕlōah*) in Deut 32. In Ps 106, the objects of Israel's illicit worship are also referred to as "idols" (*ʿăṣabîm*). Despite the traditional translation of *šēdîm* as "demons," one should not assume that the *šēdîm* correspond to "demons" in the modern sense. All that one can conclude with confidence

6. *HALOT* 4:1417–18.

is that the biblical authors considered *šēdîm* to be lesser beings than the God of Israel and inappropriate for Israel to worship. That the Greek translators of these texts chose *daimonia* to translate the word is consistent with their use of *daimonion* elsewhere for words associated with foreign deities (e.g., *'ĕlîlîm* in Ps 96:5 [LXX 95:5]).[7] Jewish interpreters such as the LXX translators and the authors of the Book of the Watchers would bring these texts into conversation with others in an effort to explain just who these *šēdîm* were, how they relate to other superhuman figures, and why it would be a serious error to worship them.

Evil Spirits

The literature of the ancient Near East depicts a world teeming with invisible forces that are out to harm humanity, beings who would arbitrarily attack the righteous and the wicked alike. These beings would cause various sorts of illnesses, and special procedures were prescribed to relieve a person of their afflictions.[8] Although similar notions of the superhuman realm were likely vibrant in ancient Israelite religious thought, the Hebrew Scriptures themselves pay little attention to such ideas, emphasizing rather the sovereignty of Israel's one God in meting out punishment to those who deserve it.[9]

7. This tendency also explains the use of *daimonia* to translate *śāʿîr*. Though the noun *śāʿîr* generally denotes "he-goats," in a couple of passages the plural of the word refers to objects of illicit worship (Lev 17:7; 2 Chr 11:15). This use of the word would have facilitated the identification of the *śəʿîrîm* of Isa 13:21 with such deities and with the *šēdîm* of Deut 32:17 and Ps 96:5. For a discussion of *śəʿîrîm* in the Hebrew scriptures, see Frey-Anthes, *Unheilsmächte und Schutzgenien,* 201–18.

8. See the collection of Mesopotamian texts that pertain to the treatment of individuals who are afflicted by "demons" in Markham J. Geller, *Evil Demons: Canonical Utukkū Lemnūtu Incantations,* SAACT 5 (Helsinki: Neo-Assyrian Text Corpus Project, 2007).

9. Scholars have suggested that a number of "demonic" beings appear in the Hebrew scriptures. Figures identified as "demons" include Azazel, Resheph, Deber, Qeteb, and Lilith. The classic treatment of "demons" in the biblical literature is that of Edward Langton, *Essentials of Demonology: A Study of Jewish and Christian Doctrine, Its Origin and Development* (London: Epworth, 1949). See more recently Karel van der Toorn, "The Theology of Demons in Mesopotamia and Israel: Popular Belief and Scholarly Speculation," in *Die Dämonen: Die Dämonologie der israelitisch-jüdischen und frühchristlichen Literatur im Kontext ihrer Umwelt = Demons: The Demonology of Israelite-Jewish and Early Christian Literature in Context of Their Environment,* ed. Armin Lange, Hermann Lichtenberger, and K. F. Diethard Römheld (Tübingen: Mohr Siebeck, 2003), 61–83; Frey-Anthes, *Unheils-*

Several biblical texts speak of certain "spirits" that carry out God's work of bringing trouble upon human beings. Two episodes involve a *rûaḥ rāʿâ*, "evil spirit," from God (Judg 9; 1 Sam 16–19). First Kings 22 tells a story of a *rûaḥ šeqer*, "deceptive spirit," who misleads Ahab king of Israel into a disastrous battle. A *rûaḥ*, "spirit," is also the agent or means by which God leads the Assyrian king Sennacherib to abandon his military campaign in Judah (2 Kgs 19:7 [// Isa 37:7]). God pours out another sort of spirit, a *rûaḥ tardēmâ*, "spirit of deep sleep," upon the people of Jerusalem, preventing them from comprehending God's message for them (Isa 29:10). While it is probably not correct to speak of a single kind of spirit or even of a single tradition about such spirits to which all these texts point, that each of these passages mentions a *rûaḥ* , "spirit," as a means or agent of God's judgment warrants their consideration together as a very loosely associated group.[10]

First Samuel 16 reports that Yahweh has rejected Saul as king. As a result, the spirit of Yahweh leaves Saul, and another spirit, referred to as a *rûaḥ rāʿâ mēʾēt yhwh*, "evil spirit from the LORD," begins to trouble the king (16:14).[11] Saul's servants notice that an evil spirit from Yahweh is tor-

---

mächte und Schutzgenien. The identification of certain figures in the biblical literature as "demons," however, is disputed. See especially Judit M. Blair, *De-Demonising the Old Testament*, FAT 2/37 (Tübingen: Mohr Siebeck, 2009), who argues that the beings normally labeled "demons" by scholars are not properly considered as such. According to her analysis of the passages in which the relevant terms occur, Azazel is a personification of the forces of chaos; Resheph, Deber, and Qeteb are angels in the service of Yahweh; and a "lilith" is a type of nocturnal bird.

10. Esther J. Hamori, "The Spirit of Falsehood," *CBQ* 72.1 (2010): 15–30, argues that the spirits of Judg 9:23–24; 1 Sam 16:14–23; 18:10–12; 19:9–10; 1 Kgs 22:19–23; 2 Kgs 19:7; and Isa 19:13–14 all reflect a common tradition of a "spirit of falsehood." Although some of the texts considered by Hamori credit these "spirits" with a deluding influence, she overestimates the presence of the theme of delusion in other passages.

11. Some scholars have suggested that the departure of the spirit of Yahweh from Saul created a spiritual "vacuum" into which the evil spirit entered. See, e.g., P. Kyle McCarter Jr., *I Samuel*, AB 8 (Garden City, NY: Doubleday, 1980), 280; Fredrik Lindström, *God and the Origin of Evil: A Contextual Analysis of Alleged Monistic Evidence in the Old Testament*, trans. Frederick H. Cryer, ConBOT 21 (Lund: Gleerup, 1983), 81; Daniel I. Block, "Empowered by the Spirit of God: The Holy Spirit in the Histographic Writings of the Old Testament," *Souhern Baptist Journal of Theology* 1.1 (1997): 51; David T. Tsumura, *The First Book of Samuel*, NICOT (Grand Rapids: Eerdmans, 2007), 428 (citing McCarter). While the evidence for the idea of a "spiritual vacuum" is not as strong as is often assumed, some texts describe a person's illness in terms of the absence of a deity and the presence of a harmful entity. In one ancient Mesopotamian incantation text, a god/goddess is said to

menting him and suggest to Saul that he should find someone to play the lyre before him to provide temporary relief from the symptoms of his spiritual affliction.[12] One of the men in Saul's service suggests David the son of Jesse as one whose musical ability, among his other positive attributes, qualified him for the position. Saul then brings David into his palace. This story offers an explanation of how David, a shepherd from Bethlehem, came to be a member of Saul's royal court. It also provides the setting for two attempts on David's life by the king, who perceives David's success and popularity as a threat to his kingship. "The next day an evil spirit from God [*rûaḥ ʾĕlōhîm rāʿâ*] rushed upon Saul, and he raved [*wayyitnabbēʾ*] within his house, while David was playing the lyre, as he did day by day. Saul had his spear in his hand; and Saul threw the spear, for he thought, 'I will pin David to the wall.' But David eluded him twice" (1 Sam 18:10–11).[13]

The cause of Saul's trouble in these passages is designated alternately *rûaḥ rāʿâ mēʾēt yhwh*, "an evil spirit from the LORD," *rûaḥ yhwh rāʿâ*, "an evil spirit of the LORD," *rûaḥ ʾĕlōhîm rāʿâ*, "an evil spirit of God," *rûaḥ hārāʿâ*, "the evil spirit," and simply *rûaḥ ʾĕlōhîm*, "the spirit of God."[14] That

---

have stepped aside from an afflicted person's body, and an evil curse "like a *gallû*-demon" is said to have come upon him. See Erica Reiner, *Šurpu: A Collection of Sumerian and Akkadian Incantations*, AfOB 11 (Graz: Biblio, 1958), 30 (Tablet V–VI, lines 11–12) and the interpretation of Thorkild Jacobsen, *The Treasures of Darkness: A History of Mesopotamian Religion* (New Haven: Yale University Press, 1976), 158. Conversely, other incantation texts call upon a "demon" to step aside and the deity or a "kindly spirit" to be present or stand beside him. See, e.g., R. Campbell Thompson, *The Devils and Evil Spirits of Babylonia, Being Babylonian and Assyrian Incanations against the Demons, Ghouls, Vampires, Hobgoblins, Ghosts, and Kindred Evil Spirits, Which Attack Mankind: Translated from the Original Cuneiform Texts, with Transliterations, Vocabulary, Notes, Etc.*, 2 vols. (London: Luzac, 1903), 1:80–81, 198–99.

12. Cf. some of the canonical Neo-Assyrian Utukkū Lemnūtu incantations, in which the sound of a copper drum is supposed to drive away the harmful being that afflicts a person. See Geller, *Evil Demons*, Tablet 7, lines 15–22, 47–48; Tablet 9, line 48; Tablet 12, line 87.

13. Several scholars consider 18:10–11 to be an interpolation or the work of a redactor, e.g., Henry Preserved Smith, *A Critical and Exegetical Commentary on the Books of Samuel*, ICC (New York: Scribner's Sons, 1899), 169; McCarter, *I Samuel*, 305–6; Ralph W. Klein, *1 Samuel*, WBC 10 (Waco, TX: Word, 1983), 188. Whether these verses are original to the text or were added at some point by an editor is of little consequence for the present study.

14. My translations. The NRSV and several other modern English translations render *rûaḥ yhwh rāʿâ* as "an evil spirit *from* the LORD" (italics mine). Likewise, the preposition "from" is used to translate the construct relationship in *rûaḥ ʾĕlōhîm rāʿâ*. *Rûaḥ ʾĕlōhîm* without the modifier *rāʿâ* occurs in MT 16:23, though other ancient witnesses attest the adjective specifying that the spirit is "evil."

this spirit is called *rāʿâ* does not constitute a moral assessment of the spirit, but specifies that the spirit is one that inflicts harm.[15] The precise nature of the harm the spirit was supposed to bring upon Saul is unclear.[16] Several scholars attribute Saul's attempts to take David's life in these passages to the evil spirit's influence.[17] But it is probably better to regard Saul's affliction as simply supplying the narrative context for, rather than the cause of, his aggression toward David.

Among the clearer descriptions of Saul's symptoms, 1 Sam 18:10 says that the evil spirit of God caused Saul to "rave" (*yitnabbēʾ*). While Saul's condition would likely be diagnosed by modern readers as a psychological or brain disorder, the biblical narrative portrays Saul's "raving" as a symptom of a spiritual condition. Curiously, in other contexts this same sort of ecstatic activity is regarded more positively. Indeed, the very same activity characterizes Israelite prophets under the influence of the spirit of God in 1 Samuel (10:5; 19:20). In two episodes, Saul encounters a group of prophets engaging in this ecstatic activity. In each of these stories, the spirit of God/Yahweh comes upon Saul so that he himself takes part in the ecstatic behavior, giving rise to the saying, "Is Saul also among the prophets?" (10:6, 10; 19:19–24). Though Saul's evil spirit is clearly distinguished from the spirit of Yahweh mentioned elsewhere in the narrative, these spirits affect Saul similarly. Saul's evil spirit is apparently a negative counterpart to the prophetic spirit of Yahweh.

15. Tsumura, *First Book of Samuel*, 427, suggests that *rûaḥ rāʿâ* should be taken as a construct chain and translated as "a spirit of evilness." With *rāʿâ* functioning as an object genitive, argues Tsumura, one might translate the expression more specifically as "the spirit [of Yahweh] who brings forth disaster." However one analyzes the expression, the work of this spirit is clearly supposed to be that of bringing harm to its victim.

16. In 16:14, the evil spirit "torments" (*bʿt*) Saul. Jacob Hoftijzer, "Some Remarks on the Semantics of the Root *bʿt* in Classical Hebrew," in *Pomegranates and Golden Bells: Studies in Biblical, Jewish, and Near Eastern Ritual, Law, and Literature in Honor of Jacob Milgrom*, ed. David. P. Wright, David Noel Freedman, and Avi Hurvitz (Winona Lake, IN: Eisenbrauns, 1995), 782, argues, "the two main semantic components of the root *bʿt* in Classical Hebrew are fear (most probably a heavy fear) *and* the presence of a bad (incapacitating) state as a result of this fear." The description of the relief brought about by David's lyre playing in 16:23 is also described with a difficult expression: *rûaḥ ləšāʾûl wəṭôb lô*. According to Marten Stol, "Psychosomatic Suffering in Ancient Mesopotamia," in *Mesopotamian Magic: Textual, Historical, and Interpretative Perspectives*, ed. Tzvi Abusch and Karel van der Toorn, Ancient Magic and Divination 1 (Groningen: Styx, 1999), 61–67, in ancient Mesopotamia, fear was considered a common symptom of divine rejection, a rejection often thought to be witchcraft induced.

17. E.g., Klein, *1 Samuel*, 188, 196; P. Kyle McCarter Jr., "Evil Spirit of God," *DDD* 319–20; Tsumura, *First Book of Samuel*, 492.

A harmful spirit of a different sort is mentioned in 1 Kgs 22. This spirit, however, resembles the spirit who troubled Saul in that this spirit also appears in the context of prophetic activity and functions in the narrative as a negative counterpart to the spirit of Yahweh. Ahab king of Israel and Jehoshaphat king of Judah are considering a joint military venture with the objective of retaking Israelite territory that Aram has captured.[18] Before deploying his forces, however, Jehoshaphat wants to ascertain the likelihood that their mission will succeed. In order to do this, Ahab assembles four hundred prophets, who unanimously assure the kings that the mission would be an unqualified victory. When Jehoshaphat requires further assurance of success, Ahab reluctantly summons one final prophet, Micaiah son of Imlah, whose prophecies are said to be frequently at odds with the interests of Ahab. Micaiah initially echoes the optimistic forecast of the other four hundred prophets. When Ahab forces Micaiah to tell the truth, however, the prophet admits that the Israelite king will lose not only the battle but also his life if he attacks Aram. That Micaiah's prophecy contradicts that of the other prophets of Yahweh raises an important question. If Micaiah is correct about Ahab's prospects for success, how is it that the other four hundred prophets have predicted the opposite outcome?

Although Micaiah might merely have alleged that the four hundred prophets of Ahab had conspired to mislead the king, calling into question the authenticity of their prophetic experience, he instead offers a different explanation for the prophetic disagreement.

> I saw the LORD sitting on his throne, with all the host of heaven standing beside him to the right and to the left of him. And the LORD said, "Who will entice Ahab, so that he may go up and fall at Ramoth-gilead?" Then one said one thing, and another said another, until a spirit [*hārûaḥ*] came forward and stood before the LORD, saying, "I will entice him."

18. Certain tensions in 1 Kgs 22 as it now stands have led a number of commentators to posit multiple levels of composition and to suggest that the story at one time applied not to Ahab but to a later Israelite king. See, e.g., the discussions in Simon J. De Vries, *Prophet against Prophet: The Role of the Micaiah Narrative (I Kings 22) in the Development of Early Prophetic Tradition* (Grand Rapids: Eerdmans, 1978), 25–51, 93–111; Simon J. De Vries, *1 Kings,* WBC 12 (Nashville: Nelson, 2003), 259–72; Lindström, *God and the Origin of Evil,* 84–88. Cf., in contrast, Mordechai Cogan, *1 Kings: A New Translation with Introduction and Commentary,* AB 10 (New York: Doubleday, 2001), 496–97, who reads the story as a unified narrative that has been correctly associated with Ahab. For the purposes of this investigation, one need not resolve these issues.

"How?" the LORD asked him. He replied, "I will go out and be a lying spirit [*rûaḥ šeqer*] in the mouth of all his prophets." Then the LORD said, "You are to entice him, and you shall succeed; go out and do it." So you see, Yahweh has put a lying spirit [*rûaḥ šeqer*] in the mouth of all these your prophets; the LORD has decreed disaster [*rāʿâ*] for you. (1 Kgs 22:19–23)[19]

In a society that depends on prophecy, it is necessary for one to discern between those prophets and prophecies that can be trusted and those that are not dependable.[20] Several passages in the Hebrew scriptures indicate that prophets competed to legitimize their prophecies against rival claims to prophetic authority. Jeremiah, based on precedent, contends that the benefit of the doubt should be afforded to a prophet who prophesies disaster, whereas the burden of proof should be borne by a prophet who prophesies peace (Jer 28:8–9). Micah of Moresheth claims that he alone among the prophets of his day has the spirit of Yahweh (Micah 3:5–8). The 1 Kings narrative explains Micaiah's prophecy similarly, claiming that Micaiah alone prophesies by the spirit of Yahweh. The narrative goes beyond this explanation, however, alleging not simply that the other prophets lack Yahweh's spirit, but that they have been misled by a lying spirit from Yahweh.[21]

As for the nature of the spirit in the story, unless one interprets Micaiah's vision figuratively, this spirit is supposed to be a personal being. Further, the *rûaḥ šeqer*, "spirit of falsehood," does not appear to be by nature a deceptive entity. The spirit is identified initially simply as a spirit, with no adjective qualifying it as evil or deceptive in any way. This member of the heavenly court volunteers to act deceptively on this particular occasion, however, in order to bring divine judgment upon Ahab. The spirit's

19. Micaiah's vision and its interpretation are also recounted in 2 Chr 18:18–22.

20. On the distinction of true and false prophecy in ancient Israel, see Richard J. Coggins, "Prophecy—True and False," in *Of Prophets' Visions and the Wisdom of the Sages: Essays in Honour of R. Norman Whybray on His Seventieth Birthday,* ed. Heather A. McKay and David J. A. Clines, JSOTSup 162 (Sheffield: Sheffield Academic Press, 1993), 80–94.

21. Cf. Zech 13:2, in which God says he "will remove from the land the [false] prophets and the unclean spirit." Micaiah also implicitly allows for the theoretical possibility that a prophet might make claims that do not come from Yahweh when he tells the king of Israel, "If you return in peace, the LORD has not spoken by me" (1 Kgs 22:28). On possession by the spirit of Yahweh in ancient Israelite prophecy, see Robert R. Wilson, *Prophecy and Society in Ancient Israel* (Philadelphia: Fortress, 1980), 144–46, 261.

mission is to mislead the king of Israel into battle and to his death. These characteristics distinguish this spirit from Saul's spirit. The presence of Saul's spirit is manifested by physical symptoms, not deception. Nor is it clear, though it is not impossible, that Saul's harmful spirit is supposed to be a personal being. The two spirits, nonetheless, are similar in that they are associated with prophecy and are presented as a negative counterpart to the spirit of Yahweh. Both spirits also bring harm (*rāʿâ*) to their victims.

Other spirits of various sorts appear in the Hebrew scriptures. The designation *rûaḥ rāʿâ*, "evil spirit," occurs in the story of Abimelech and Shechem in Judg 9, though likely with reference to a different sort of "evil spirit" from the one that troubled Saul. In the Judges account, after his father Gideon's death, Abimelech convinces the leaders of Shechem that he should be the one to succeed his father as their ruler. The Shechemites then support Abimelech's massacre of his brothers and make him their king.[22] God, however, disapproves of the violence against Gideon's sons and sends a *rûaḥ rāʿâ* between Abimelech and the leaders of Shechem to punish them (Judg 9:23–24).

As with the story of Saul's affliction in 1 Samuel, the evil spirit here functions as an agent or means of God's judgment, to punish Abimelech and Shechem. The effects of the spirit's work, however, are much different in the case of Abimelech and the Shechemites from what they are in Saul's case. There is no raving in Judg 9, nor any association with the prophetic spirit of God. Instead, the spirit creates discord and hostility between Abimelech and the people of Shechem. The "evil spirit" of Judg 9, then, appears to be no more than a malevolent disposition.[23] As such, the "evil spirit" between Abimelech and Shechem would more closely resemble

22. Several scholars have distinguished between an earlier form of this story in which Abimelech is king of the city-state Shechem only and a later pan-Israelite layer in which he is king of all Israel. See, e.g., C. F. Burney, *The Book of Judges with Introduction and Notes* (London: Rivingtons, 1918), 267; J. Alberto Soggin, *Judges: A Commentary*, trans. John Bowden, OTL (Philadelphia: Westminster, 1981), 180; Volkmar Fritz, "Abimelech und Sichem in JDC. IX," *VT* 32.2 (1982): 129; Lindström, *God and the Origin of Evil*, 74.

23. So Lindström, *God and the Origin of Evil*, 77–78. See S. Tengström and H.-J. Fabry, "רוּחַ *rûaḥ*," *TDOT* 13:388–90) on the use of *rûaḥ* in construct chains to express temperament, emotions, and moral dispositions (e.g., Job 7:11; Ps 51:12, 19 [Eng. 10, 17]; Prov 14:29; 17:27; Isa 65:14). Lindström, *God and the Origin of Evil*, 78–84, also tries to account for the evil spirit of 1 Samuel as something other than a superhuman being. He speculates that in an earlier version of the story Saul merely suffered from a bad mood. The author of the account as we now have it, Lindström argues, transformed the psychological "spirit" of this tradition into God's "negative charisma" (81).

the *rûaḥ qin'â*, "spirit of jealousy," mentioned in Num 5:14, 30, than it would the harmful spirit that afflicted Saul and functioned as the negative counterpart to God's prophetic spirit.

Other passages also speak of God sending a "spirit," in the sense of a (harmful) moral or psychological disposition. For instance, 2 Kgs 19:7 and the parallel account of Isa 37:7 say that God will place a *rûaḥ*, "spirit," in Sennacherib that will cause the Assyrian ruler to return to his own land, where he will be killed. In Isa 29:10, Isaiah informs his people that God has poured out on them a *rûaḥ tardēmâ*, "spirit of deep sleep," which has left them incapable of comprehending God's message to them. While the spirits in these passages and in Judg 9 do not appear to be personal beings or to be of the same sort that afflicted Saul or misled Ahab's prophets, Jewish interpreters of the final centuries before the turn of the era could make creative use of these passages, incorporating them into their understanding of personal evil spirits.[24]

Sons of God

The expression "sons of God" (*bĕnê [hā]'ĕlōhîm*) and related expressions occur in several passages in the Hebrew scriptures with reference to a class of divine beings.[25] In Deut 32:8, the *bĕnê 'ēlîm*, "sons of God," are the gods to whom the Most High allotted all of the nations except for Israel, which belongs to Yahweh.[26] Similarly, Ps 82 speaks of the *bĕnê 'elyôn*, "sons of the Most High," who have been charged with governance of the nations. Psalm 29:1 exhorts the *bĕnê 'ēlîm*, "sons of God," to ascribe glory and strength to Yahweh, and Ps 89:7 (Eng. 6) asks who among these beings might be compared with Yahweh. Job 38 says that the sons of God shouted when God created the earth. Job 1–2 mentions two occasions on which all the sons of God, a group that includes the Satan, assembled before Yahweh.

24. Perhaps, as will be discussed in subsequent chapters, such a reading of Judg 9 is the source of the ideas underlying Jub. 11:5 and 1QapGen[ar] 20:16.

25. For a summary and analysis of the expressions "sons of God" in the Hebrew scriptures, as well as cognate expressions among Phoenician texts, see S. B. Parker, "Sons of (the) God(s)," *DDD* 794–800.

26. The reading *bĕnê 'ēlîm*, "sons of God," supported by 4QDeut[j] and various Greek MSS, represents the earliest version of the text. The expression has been changed to *bĕnê yiśrā'ēl*, "sons of Israel," in the MT, apparently in order to resolve the potentially problematic theology of the passage.

That these divine beings might function individually in the service of God is also presumed in Dan 3, where the fourth individual in the furnace is said to have the appearance of a *bar 'ĕlāhîn*, "son of God," an angel sent by God to protect Shadrach, Meshach, and Abednego (Dan 3:25, 28). The synonymy between "son of God" and "angel" in Dan 3 is characteristic of early Jewish literature, which regarded the "sons of God" as angelic beings (e.g., 1 En. 19:1).[27]

The most perplexing episode involving the sons of God in the biblical literature is also the one that attracted the most interest from early Jewish interpreters. Situated literarily just prior to the flood narrative, it is the brief and allusive story in Gen 6 of those divine beings who married human women and had children with them.

> When people began to multiply on the face of the ground, and daughters were born to them, the sons of God saw that they were fair; and they took wives for themselves of all that they chose. Then the LORD said, "My spirit shall not abide in mortals forever, for they are flesh; their days shall be one hundred twenty years." The Nephilim were on the earth in those days—and also afterward—when the sons of God went in to the daughters of humans, who bore children to them. These were the heroes that were of old, warriors of renown. (Gen 6:1–4)

This passage presents interpreters with several challenges. How is one to understand the mythological events that it reports? Are the Nephilim to be identified with the offspring of the sons of God, and if so, then how did they remain on the earth after the flood? What is the nature of the 120-year limitation placed on human life? How is one to relate these events to the genealogy of Noah that precedes it and to the flood story that follows it? The story's laconic nature, which leaves so many questions unanswered, suggests that this short account alludes to a fuller story with which its earliest readers would have been familiar, but which is no longer available to us.

One should note that the Gen 6 version of these events does not explicitly condemn the actions of the sons of God. Are the marriages between these divine beings and humans regarded as morally neutral, or are they implicitly criticized? Some Jews living in the third century BCE would understand the events reported in this passage as an act of rebellion per-

27. On the reception of the expression "sons of God" in early Judaism, see Ryan E. Stokes, "Sons of God," *EDEJ* 1251–52.

petrated by angelic beings against God. This story, as well as those biblical texts pertaining to demons and evil spirits, would inspire interpreters who sought to understand the superhuman realm more fully and wished to explain how that realm impinges for ill upon the human experience. These three traditions—demons, evil spirits, and the antediluvian sons of God—would be brought together in a synthetic explanation of sin and suffering.

Demons, Evil Spirits, and the Sons of Heaven in the Book of the Watchers

Likely composed sometime in the third century BCE, the Book of the Watchers (1 En. 1–36) contains what is perhaps the earliest known interpretation of the sons of God story in Gen 6:1–4.[28] Some scholars have suggested that 1 En. 6–11 even predates the Genesis version story and that what one reads in the first four verses of Gen 6 is based on this portion of the Book of the Watchers.[29] Whatever their relationship, the third-century

28. The third-century BCE date of the Book of the Watchers is derived primarily from the date of the earliest Aramaic copy of the book discovered among the Dead Sea Scrolls (4QEn^{a}), which J. T. Milik, *The Books of Enoch: Aramaic Fragments of Qumrân Cave 4* (Oxford: Oxford University Press, 1976), 24–25, 140–41, 164, dated paleographically to the first part of the second century BCE, suggesting a slightly earlier date for the original. This date is further supported by the apparent citation of the Book of the Watchers in the second-century BCE book of Jubilees (Milik, *Books of Enoch*, 24–25; James C. VanderKam, "Enoch Traditions in Jubilees and Other Second-Century Sources," in *Society of Biblical Literature 1978 Seminar Papers*, 2 vols., SBLSP 13 [Missoula, MT: Scholars Press, 1978], 1:229–51). Cf., however, Divorah Dimant, "The Biography of Enoch and the Books of Enoch," *VT* 33.1 (1983): 14–29, who argues that certain data common to the Book of the Watchers and Jubilees are the result of their authors' independent use of an ancient haggadic tradition and not evidence of the dependence of Jubilees on the Book of the Watchers. The degree to which Milik's dating of the fragments and of the book's composition has been received by scholars is reflected in an aptly titled article by James H. Charlesworth, "A Rare Consensus among Enoch Specialists: The Date of the Earliest Enoch Books," *Hen* 24 (2002): 225–34.

29. Scholars have generally assumed that it is the Book of the Watchers that makes use of Gen 6:1–4 rather than the reverse. This understanding of the relationship between the two texts was first challenged by Milik, *Books of Enoch*, 30–31. Milik's contention went largely unheeded for decades, but has recently received support from some notable scholars, e.g., Philip R. Davies, "And Enoch Was Not, for Genesis Took Him," in *Biblical Traditions in Transmission: Essays in Honour of Michael A. Knibb*, ed. Charlotte Hempel and Judith M. Lieu (Leiden: Brill, 2006), 97–107; Helge S. Kvanvig, *Primeval History: Babylonian, Biblical, and Enochic: An Intertextual Reading*, JSJSup 149 (Leiden: Brill, 2011), 373–95.

Book of the Watchers contains a version of the sons of God story that goes considerably beyond what one reads in Genesis. In the Book of the Watchers, the sons of God are identified as angelic beings called "watchers," who take human wives and beget monstrous children with them. These hybrid offspring commit various atrocities on the earth. The watchers also reveal forbidden knowledge to humans, such as the art of divination, magico-medicinal practices, and other illicit crafts by which humankind becomes guilty of great sin. The Book of the Watchers further tells of God's response to the problems created by the watchers and of the revelations received by the antediluvian patriarch Enoch.

For a variety of reasons, the Book of the Watchers has figured prominently in recent discussions of early Jewish religious thought. One reason is the intriguing manner in which it addresses the problem of evil. For the authors of the Book of the Watchers, much of humankind's sin and suffering can be traced back to the ancient past when the watchers came to earth to marry human women. This event serves as the origin of many of the world's present problems, including the existence of demons and evil spirits. In its attempt to explain the world's evil, the Book of the Watchers made an enduring contribution to Jewish and Christian thinking on the nature of sin and its superhuman agents.

The Watchers and Forbidden Knowledge

Not only does the Book of the Watchers belong to the collection of works known as 1 Enoch, but it is itself a composite document that comprises the work of several authors who wrote at different times. It is widely held by scholars that 1 En. 6–11, which tells the story of the watchers, is a distinct compositional unit within the book and likely contains the earliest material in the Book of the Watchers.

Within this unit of text, scholars have further distinguished two strands of material.[30] One of these tells how two hundred watchers, led by

30. See Devorah Dimant, "'The Fallen Angels' in the Dead Sea Scrolls and in the Apocryphal and Pseudepigraphic Books Related to Them" [in Hebrew] (PhD diss., Hebrew University, 1974), 23–71; Paul D. Hanson, "Rebellion in Heaven, Azazel, and Euhemeristic Heroes in 1 Enoch 6–11," *JBL* 96.2 (1977): 197; George W. E. Nickelsburg, "Apocalyptic and Myth in 1 Enoch 6–11," *JBL* 96.3 (1977): 383–86; George W. E. Nickelsburg, "Reflections upon Reflections: A Response to John Collins' 'Methodological Issues in the Study of 1 Enoch,'" in *Society of Biblical Literature 1978 Seminar Papers*, 1:311–12; Devorah Dimant,

a watcher named Shemihazah, descend to the earth, marry human women, and have children by them (7:1–2). As a result of their hybrid nature, the watchers' children have superhuman appetites that drive them to kill and devour humans (7:3–5). Another crime that watchers commit in this layer of the story is that they reveal to humans forbidden magico-medical practices (7:1).

This motif of illicit instruction is the focus of the second stratum of the story. In this material, which was added to the narrative by an early editor, the watcher Asael is the primary culprit. Asael teaches humans how to manufacture cosmetics, jewelry, and weapons. With the knowledge of these crafts, humankind becomes not merely the victims of superhuman sexual immorality and violence, but themselves perpetrators of those very sins (8:1–2). By means of these etiologies, 1 En. 6–11 explains the origin of certain of the world's sins. Divination, magico-medical practices, and the knowledge of how to manufacture those items that give rise to violence and sexual immorality, according to the Book of the Watchers, were revealed to humans by rebellious divine beings.

The Origin and Activity of Evil Spirits

The Book of the Watchers contains two passages that address the activity of evil spirits. The first, 1 En. 15–16, elaborates on the inappropriateness of the watchers' relationships with human women. These chapters teach that the sexual intermingling of immortal, spiritual beings with mortal flesh violated the order of creation. The product of these forbidden unions, as

"1 Enoch 6–11: A Methodological Perspective," in *Society of Biblical Literature 1978 Seminar Papers*, 1:323–24; Carol A. Newsom, "The Development of 1 Enoch 6–19: Cosmology and Judgment," *CBQ* 42.3 (1980): 313–14; George W. E. Nickelsburg, *1 Enoch 1*, Hermeneia (Minneapolis: Fortress, 2001), 165, 171–72; Siam Bhayro, *The Shemihazah and Asael Narrative of 1 Enoch 6–11: Introduction, Text, Translation, and Commentary with Reference to Ancient Near Eastern and Biblical Antecedents*, AOAT 322 (Münster: Ugarit-Verlag, 2005), 11–20. Cf. the misgivings of John J. Collins, "Methodological Issues in the Study of 1 Enoch: Reflections on the Articles of P. D. Hanson and G. W. Nickelsburg," in *Society of Biblical Literature 1978 Seminar Papers*, 1:315–16, about such a division, though he has since affirmed that 1 En. 6–11 interweaves distinct traditions (*The Apocalyptic Imagination: An Introduction to Jewish Apocalyptic Literature*, 3rd ed. [Grand Rapids: Eerdmans, 2016], 61). Eibert J. C. Tigchelaar, *Prophets of Old and the Day of the End: Zechariah, the Book of Watchers and Apocalyptic*, OTS 35 (Leiden: Brill, 1996), 165–76, argues that chs. 6–11 are the result of an author joining various traditions into a literary text.

a result of their hybrid origin, would have both a fleshly and a spiritual component. Thus the Book of the Watchers accounts for the origin of evil spirits.

> But now the giants who were begotten by the spirits and flesh—
> they will call them evil spirits on the earth,
> for their dwelling will be on the earth.
> The spirits that have gone forth from the body of their flesh are evil spirits,
> for from humans they came into being, and from the holy watchers was the origin of their creation.
> Evil spirits they will be on the earth, and evil spirits they will be called.
> The spirits of heaven, in heaven is their dwelling;
> but the spirits begotten on the earth, on the earth is their dwelling. (1 En. 15:8–10)[31]

Although the halves of these creatures that are mortal and fleshly perished long ago, the passage explains, the creatures' immortal, spiritual halves have survived in the form of evil spirits that will continue to afflict humans until the final judgment.[32]

31. Unless otherwise noted, English translations of 1 Enoch are from George W. E. Nickelsburg and James C. VanderKam, *1 Enoch: The Hermeneia Translation* (Minneapolis: Fortress, 2012).

32. In addition to this etiology, in which evil spirits are the spirits of the formerly embodied offspring of the watchers, some scholars further detect in this passage a second etiological tradition, according to which the children of the watchers were never embodied but existed as evil spirits from the time of their birth. If one removes those statements from the passage that speak of the spirits proceeding from the bodies of the giants (15:9a and 16:1), these scholars argue, one is left with the teaching that evil spirits were never embodied at all but were born as spirits. See Dimant, "Fallen Angels," 49, 61–62, 76–77; Ronald Anthony Pascale, "The Demonic Powers of Destruction in 1 Enoch 15:3–16:1 and Jubilees 10:5, and the Demonizing of the Avenging Angels" (PhD diss., Harvard University, 1980), 56–58, 61, 63–64; Esther Eshel, "Demonology in Palestine during the Second Temple Period" [in Hebrew] (PhD diss., Hebrew University, 1999), 35–44; Michael Segal, *The Book of Jubilees: Rewritten Bible, Redaction, Ideology and Theology*, JSJSup 117 (Leiden: Brill, 2007), 150–54.

There are several problems with positing the existence of such a hypothetical tradition, according to which the offspring of the watchers were from the very beginning of their existence evil spirits. First, in order to find this idea in 15:7b–16:1, one must remove 15:9a and 16:1 from the passage for no other reason than to arrive at this hypothesized teaching. There is no indication in the text itself that this passage is composite. Second, even with the passage reconstructed accordingly, arguments for such a belief amount to no more than an

So as to distinguish these "spirits" from their fathers, the disembodied spirits of the giants are designated "*evil* spirits." The designation "evil spirits" (*pneumata ponēra*) recalls the *rûaḥ rāʿâ* from God that torments King Saul (1 Sam 16:14–23; 18:10; 19:9) and perhaps also the *rûaḥ rāʿâ* that God sends between Abimelech and Shechem (Judg 9:23). The author of this passage interprets the Hebrew tradition of the *rûaḥ rāʿâ* in light of the sons of God story of 1 En. 6–11 and Gen 6:1–4. Similarities between the etiology in 1 En. 15:8–10 and Greek and Mesopotamian accounts of the origin of superhuman figures may also suggest that the author made use of these or similar extrabiblical traditions in his telling of the sons of God story to address the origin of evil spirits.[33] Although the terminology of

---

argument from silence. The reconstructed passage does not require one to interpret it in a way that blatantly contradicts its context in the Book of the Watchers, taking it to mean that the children of the watchers were never giants but were disembodied spirits from birth. Third, they are "*giants* who were begotten by the spirits and flesh" (15:8, italics mine). It is difficult to imagine "giants" (*gigantes*) who do not have bodies. Positing that an Aram. *npylyn* or *gbryn* lay behind the Gk. *gigantes* does little to resolve this difficulty. Fourth, 1 En. 10:15 ("Destroy all the spirits of the half-breeds and the sons of the watchers, because they have wronged men"), which is adduced as evidence of the hypothesized etiology, if this text indeed refers to evil spirits, is incompatible with an etiology of evil spirits. What would be the purpose of the teaching that the children of the watchers were evil spirits if those spirits no longer existed? More likely, this command is simply to kill the watchers' gigantic offspring. Finally, the etiology of this passage must take into account the emphasis on the hybrid origins of the evil spirits, who are "begotten by the spirits *and flesh*" (15:8, italics mine). It is to be expected, given the logic of the passage, that the fruit of such a union would possess, at least initially, both spirit and flesh.

While it is possible that the tradition of the watchers' gigantic offspring circulated independently of the evil spirit etiology (e.g., as in 1 En. 6–11), there is no compelling evidence that the reverse is also true, that the etiology of evil spirits ever circulated in Jewish literature of this period apart from the belief that these beings were at one time embodied in the form of giants. And, as Archie T. Wright points out in *The Origin of Evil Spirits: The Reception of Genesis 6.1–4 in Early Jewish Literature*, WUNT 198 (Tübingen: Mohr Siebeck, 2005), 152–53; and in "Evil Spirits in Second Temple Judaism: The Watcher Tradition as a Background to the Demonic Pericopes in the Gospels," *Hen* 28.1 (2006): 148–49, whether these traditions were ever independent or not, they constituted a whole in the form of the Book of the Watchers in the third-second centuries BCE and influenced Second Temple Judaism as such.

33. T. Francis Glasson, *Greek Influence in Jewish Eschatology: With Special Reference to the Apocalypses and Pseudepigraphs* (London: SPCK, 1961), 57–59, observes that the identification of the "evil spirits" in this passage with the children of divine beings resembles the etiology of *daimones* in Plato, *Apology* 15 (27B-E), and that their identification with deceased individuals from the primeval past resembles that found in Hesiod, *Works and Days* 110–27. Nickelsburg, however, says that these parallels are not substantial, since the two etiologies

"evil spirits" associates the spirits of the watchers' children with some of the spirits one encounters in the Hebrew scriptures, this passage clearly expands upon the ideas of the earlier texts, bringing the notion of evil spirits into conversation with various other traditions.

One way in which the Book of the Watchers supplements the biblical data pertaining to evil spirits is by supplying additional information concerning these spirits' activity.

> And the spirits of the giants consume, do violence, make desolate, and attack and wrestle and hurl upon the earth and make races. They eat nothing, but abstain from food and are thirsty and smite. These spirits (will) rise up against the sons of men and against the women, for they have come forth from them.
>
> From the day of the slaughter and destruction and death of the giants, from the soul of whose flesh the spirits are proceeding, they are making desolate without (incurring) judgment. Thus they will make desolate until the day of the consummation of the great judgments, when the great age will be consummated. It will be consummated all at once. (15:11–16:1)[34]

Unfortunately, textual uncertainties obscure our understanding of some of the items listed.[35] The general nature of these activities, nonetheless, is

---

are not combined in Greek literature as they are in the early Jewish literature and since the Greek *daimones* are thought to be good beings (*1 Enoch 1*, 273). The similarities between these traditions, nonetheless, are difficult to dismiss as pure coincidence, and it seems reasonable to infer that a common tradition lies behind both the Greek and Jewish versions of the etiologies. The Jewish version diverges from its Greek counterparts in that it construes these superhuman entities and the events that led to their existence in unequivocally negative terms. Parallels also exist between these etiologies and Near Eastern traditions, namely the Neo-Assyrian Utukkū Lemnūtu incantations. On the points of contact between the Book of the Watchers' teaching and the Utukkū Lemnūtu texts, see below.

34. Verse 11 poses multiple textual difficulties. The translation above follows Nickelsburg except in the two instances in which he emends the text (*1 Enoch 1*, 267–68, 274). Nickelsburg emends "consumes" (Gk. *nemomena*, which he supposed to be from Aram. *rʿyn*) to read "lead astray" (Aram. *tʿyn*). He also posits that Aram. *mrwʾ*, "illness," is behind "races" (Gk. *dromous*). Syncellus's version of this list also includes "produce hallucinations."

35. For example, what does it mean that the spirits "make races" (δρόμους ποιοῦντα)? Perhaps Nickelsburg and Charles are correct to emend the text at this point. Based on the Ethiopic, R. H. Charles, *The Book of Enoch* (Oxford: Oxford University Press, 1912), 37, suggests that *dromous* is more likely to have been *tromous*, "tremblings." But, as Michael A. Knibb, *The Ethiopic Book of Enoch: A New Edition in the Light of the Aramaic*

clear: evil spirits attack humans by causing illnesses and physical afflictions of various sorts.[36]

Despite their association with the "evil spirit" that bothered Saul, the evil spirits in this passage have much more in common with the malevolent entities that are spoken of in Neo-Assyrian incantation texts than they have in common with Saul's spirit. The incantation texts speak of invisible beings who trouble humans and livestock with a variety of physical afflictions.[37] These entities are unable to eat and drink (cf. Mark

---

Dead Sea Fragments, 2 vols. (Oxford: Oxford University Press, 1978), 2:102, points out, *tromous* hardly explains the Ethiopic *ḥazan,* "sorrow." On Nickelsburg's emendations, see further n36 below.

36. Nickelsburg, *1 Enoch 1,* 267–68, 273, emends v. 11 so as to expand the activity of these spirits to include leading humans astray. He understands the first word in the list, *nemomena,* according to Syncellus, to denote "pasturing," which does not make sense with reference to evil spirits. He does not find helpful the reading of Codex Panopolitanus, *nephelas,* "clouds." Rather, he supposes that *nemomena* is a translation of Aram. *r'yn,* "pasturing," which could be a corruption of either *t'yn* , "leading astray," or *r''yn* , "shattering." Given that these spirits are said to lead humans astray in 1 En. 19 and in several passages in Jubilees (e.g., 7:27; 10:2), Nickelsburg concludes that "an omission of the idea here would be strange." There does not, however, appear to be sufficient grounds for emending the text in this way. Since this is perhaps the earliest extant reference to evil spirits outside the Hebrew scriptures, one should not presume that it would necessarily be strange for the concept of leading astray to be absent. Evil spirits in the Hebrew scriptures are not said to be responsible for human sin. How widespread the belief was that "evil spirits" would lead a person astray at the time of this text's composition is not clear. In a passage of the Book of the Watchers dating to a slightly later period than 1 En. 12–16, "spirits" are said to lead humans to worship demons (19:1). (Dating the various segments of the Book of the Watchers with precision is difficult. Nickelsburg, *1 Enoch 1,* 230, 279, dates 1 En. 12–16 between 300 and 250 BCE. He argues that 1 En. 17–19 presupposes 12–16 and probably derives from the second half of the third century BCE.) The book of Tobit, which may be roughly contemporaneous with the Book of the Watchers, does speak of evil spirits afflicting humans with sickness and death, but not as deceiving anyone (Tob 6:7). Furthermore, the concept of leading astray does not fit well in this lengthy list that consists otherwise entirely of physical afflictions. Perhaps also Nickelsburg is too quick to dismiss Panopolitanus's *nephelas* as a clue to the original text. This reading, which is followed by the Ethiopic, could be related to *nplyn.* Furthermore, it is possible to make sense of Syncellus's Greek text as it stands. The middle voice of *nemō* can refer to the "grazing" of cattle, but it can also refer to "eating" more generally. It can also carry the metaphorical meaning of "devouring" or "consuming" as a fire would do, or to the "spread" of disease (e.g., ulcers, gangrene) in a human (LSJ 1167). It can also mean "to dwell in," "to inhabit," or "to possess" in terms of property. Either the notion of inhabiting or of consuming the human body as a disease would fit the context of the passage well.

37. See, e.g., Geller, *Evil Demons,* Tablet 6, lines 55–90, and Tablets 13–15, lines 220–30, of the canonical Utukkū Lemnūtu incantations.

3:20–22).[38] Their origin is also portrayed in terms similar to the evil spirits in the Book of the Watchers. Like the spirits of the giants, some of the troublesome entities in the incantation texts are believed to be the ghosts of individuals who have died before their time, often as the result of some tragedy or an act of violence.[39] Also relevant to our discussion is that some of the harmful beings mentioned in the incantation texts are described as "the offspring of earth spawned by the seed of Anu [i.e., heaven]."[40]

One important way that the evil spirits of the Book of the Watchers resemble the evil beings of incantation texts more closely than they do Saul's spirit is that the spirits of the Book of the Watchers are not said to be affiliated with God. In 1 Samuel, the evil spirit that comes against Saul is from God, and the spirit's presence marks God's rejection of Saul as king over Israel. In the present passage, conversely, nothing explicitly associates evil spirits with the creator and God of Israel. This is not to say that this passage would not allow for a scenario in which Israel's God might send an evil spirit to torment a sinner.[41] To attribute the existence of evil spirits to the rebellious watchers' violation of proper boundaries, nevertheless, does more to distance God from these spirits than to associate the Creator with them. They were not a part of God's creative work, but came into existence as a result of angelic rebellion and an unauthorized mixing of the heavenly with the earthly. This passage also implies no distinction between the righteous and the wicked in these spirits' dealings. As in the incantation texts, the evil spirits of this passage are simply in the world troubling humans indiscriminately.

38. E.g, Utukkū Lemnūtu Tablet 4, lines 158–75. The idea that demons would hunger and thirst without being able to eat and drink would continue to be mentioned in Jewish incantation texts several centuries into the Common Era. See Amulet 7, lines 16–22, in Joseph Naveh and Shaul Shaked, *Amulets and Magic Bowls: Aramaic Incantations of Late Antiquity,* 3rd ed. (Jerusalem: Magnes, 1998), 70–71. In Mark 3:20–22, when Jesus and his followers are unable to eat, Jesus's opponents allege that he has Beelzebul.

39. E.g, Utukkū Lemnūtu Tablet 4, lines 130–49.

40. Utukkū Lemnūtu Tablet 5, line 10; translated by Geller, *Evil Demons,* 209. Cf. this idea in 11Q11 v 6. Pascale, "Demonic Powers of Destruction," 121–73, also notes this similarity between the Book of the Watchers and the Utukkū Lemnūtu texts.

41. This is what one finds in Jubilees, which adopts the Book of the Watchers' etiology of evil spirits, but also regards these spirits as beings through whose agency God punishes the wicked (e.g., Jub. 10:1–14).

Demons, Evil Spirits, Fallen Angels, and the Worship of False Gods

First Enoch 17–19 offers a brief account of Enoch's tour of the mythical world. In ch. 19, he arrives at the edge of the earth, where he observes pillars of fire standing in a great chasm. Uriel, Enoch's angelic tour guide, comments, "There stand the angels who mingled with the women. And their spirits—having assumed many forms—bring destruction on men and lead them astray to sacrifice to demons as to gods until the day of the great judgment, in which they will be judged with finality" (19:1). Here, as in the previous etiology, harmful spirits are associated with the watchers who sinned prior to the flood. In the present passage, however, the evil spirits are referred to as "their spirits," that is, the sinful angels' spirits. It is possible that a different etiology from that of 1 En. 15 is implied here. This passage does not say that the spirits are the disembodied spirits of the watchers' half-breed children. Instead, some scholars have suggested that the spirits here are supposed to be the spirits of the watchers themselves.[42] Since this understanding of the passage requires the transgressing angels to be simultaneously imprisoned and causing trouble on the earth, it is unlikely that the spirits are the same persons as the angels. The spirits in this passage are likely, as in 15:7b–16:1, thought to be the watchers' offspring. However the author of this text conceived of these spirits' origin, the concern of this text is not to provide an etiology of these spirits. By referring to the spirits as the angels' spirits, this text emphasizes rather the present relationship of the spirits to the sinful angels.[43]

As in 15:8–16:1, the spirits in this passage receive blame for harming humans. But, unlike the previous passage, which lists a number of physical afflictions for which evil spirits were supposed to be responsible, physical assault on humans is merely one of two items for which the spirits are given credit in 19:1. The second is the worship of "demons" (Gk. *daimonia*; Eth. *'agānənt*). To characterize the worship of deities other than the God of Israel as the worship of "demons" is rooted in the biblical polemic of

42. Matthew Black, *The Book of Enoch or 1 Enoch: A New English Translation,* SVTP 7 (Leiden: Brill, 1985), 161, argues that according to this passage the watchers' bodies are imprisoned while their disembodied spirits roam the earth. So also Kelley Coblentz Bautch, "What Becomes of the Angels' 'Wives'? A Text-Critical Study of 1 Enoch 19:2," *JBL* 125.4 (2006): 769.

43. So Nickelsburg, *1 Enoch 1*, 287. In Panopolitanus's account, this etiology of evil spirits is followed by an etiology of the mythological sirens. See Bautch, "What Becomes of the Angels' 'Wives'?," 766–80, on the text-critical challenge of this second etiology.

Deut 32:17 and Ps 106:37. This polemic appears in several early Jewish and Christian texts (e.g., LXX Ps 95:5; 1 En. 99:7; Bar 4:7; 1 Cor 10:20).

It should be noted that the spirits of the angels do *not* appear to be identical with demons in 1 En. 19.[44] Based on the texts considered thus far, we would expect that these two categories of superhuman beings would be distinguished. As noted above, the notions of "evil spirit" (*rûaḥ rāʿâ*) and "demons" (*šēdîm*) are distinct in the Hebrew scriptures. In later literature, "demons" and "evil spirits" come to be more or less synonymous. This terminological overlap, however, does not appear to be present in the Book of the Watchers. But this may be the earliest passage in which the concepts of (evil) spirits and demons are associated with each other, an association that would later lead to their equation.[45] In this passage, nevertheless, spirits harm humans and lead them to worship false gods; demons, on the other hand, are the false gods themselves.

As for the identity of the demons, it is likely that the imprisoned angels with whom the spirits are connected are believed to be the "demons" worshiped by idolaters. Connecting demons with the sinful angels would have made sense to an early Jewish interpreter of Gen 6, who would have had no problem interpreting the Genesis passage in light of other "sons of God" texts in the Hebrew scriptures. Deuteronomy 32, which in v. 17 criticizes the worship of foreign gods as the worship of "demons" (*šēdîm*), just a few verses prior to this speaks of the gods of the nations as "sons of God" (*bənê ʾĕlōhîm*).[46] Psalm 82 uses the related designation "sons of the Most High" (*bənê ʿelyôn*) to refer to the gods of the nations. In 1 En. 19:1, an interpreter has brought together a number of distinct biblical traditions. The sons of God of Gen 6:1–4 are regarded as sinful angels and are identified with the demons worshiped by the nations.[47] If this understanding of the text is correct, then this passage

44. So Nickelsburg, *1 Enoch 1*, 287.

45. The book of Tobit, which was written near this time, also associates evil spirits with demons. In this work, the angel Raphael instructs Tobias as to how he might use the heart and liver of a fish to help a person "afflicted by a demon or evil spirit" (6:7). It is unclear whether an evil spirit and a demon are the same thing in this passage, but both designations are used with reference to beings that physically afflict humans.

46. On the text of Deut 32:8, I agree with the majority of interpreters who follow the reading of 4QDeut^{j}, *bny ʾlhym*, "sons of God," instead of the MT *bənê yiśrāʾēl*, "sons of Israel." See the explanation of this text in Emanuel Tov, *Textual Criticism of the Hebrew Bible*, 2nd ed. (Minneapolis: Fortress; Assen: Van Gorcum, 1992), 269.

47. Isa 24:21–22 may be another biblical text of which the author of this passage made use: "On that day the LORD will punish the host of heaven in heaven and on earth the kings

is the earliest example of "demons" being identified as rebel or "fallen" angels.[48] The sinful angels who are imprisoned at the end of the earth are the demons worshiped erroneously by the nations. The spirits, on the other hand, are not demons, but are probably thought to be the illegitimate children of those demons, who mislead humans to worship the imprisoned angels.

That the spirits would mislead humans to worship demons is an innovation. The evil spirit who troubled Saul caused physical distress, as do the evil spirits of 1 En. 15:8–16:1. In 1 En. 19:1, in contrast, spirits have been transformed from beings who merely afflict humans with illness into instigators of sin. Their work as deceivers, however, should not be overestimated. It is not yet the case that these spirits' activity in the moral realm is comprehensive. This verse gives no indication that spirits lead humans to commit all sorts of moral wrongdoings. Even less do they appear to be assigned in deterministic fashion the ultimate responsibility for all human sin. They do, however, play a role in the propagation of evil, promoting the worship of false gods, which is no small error by early Jewish standards.

Although the connection with the worship of false gods is a new take on the "(evil) spirit" tradition, this concept has roots in earlier literature. A number of passages in the Hebrew scriptures allow that a prophet's revelatory experiences might on occasion be misleading, especially when they encouraged the worship of a deity other than Yahweh. In Deuteronomy, Moses warns, "If prophets or those who divine by dreams appear among you and promise you omens or portents, and the omens or the portents declared by them take place, and they say, 'Let us follow other gods' (whom you have not known) 'and let us serve them,' you must not heed the words of those prophets or those who divine by dreams" (13:1–3). Such a prophet would be trying "to turn you from the way in which the LORD your God commanded you to walk" (13:5).

---

of the earth. They will be gathered together like prisoners in a pit; they will be shut up in a prison, and after many days they will be punished."

48. Contra Martin, "When Did Angels Become Demons?," 657–77, who argues that demons were first identified as fallen angels in the second century CE by Christians. Cf. also Kevin Sullivan, "The Watchers Traditions in *1 Enoch* 6–16: The Fall of the Angels and the Rise of Demons," in *The Watchers in Jewish and Christian Traditions,* ed. Angela Kim Harkins, Kelley Coblentz Bautch, and John C. Endres (Minneapolis: Fortress, 2014), 96–99, 102, who does not appear to distinguish "demons" and "evil spirits" in the Book of the Watchers, but does distinguish the "watchers" from demons/spirits.

Zechariah 13:2 draws a connection between idolatry, prophecy, and an "unclean spirit": "On that day, says the LORD of hosts, I will cut off the names of the idols from the land, so that they shall be remembered no more; and also I will remove from the land the prophets and the unclean spirit [*rûaḥ haṭṭūm'â*]."[49] Recall that an "evil spirit" inspires Saul to prophesy (*hitnabbē'*) just as the spirit of Yahweh had done earlier in the king's reign (1 Sam 10:6, 10; 18:10). Another "lying spirit" in 1 Kgs 22 deceived Ahab's prophets so that they would encourage the Israelite king to go to war and to his death.[50]

A century or so after the Book of the Watchers was composed, the Epistle of Enoch also speaks of evil spirits and demons in the context of idolatry. In this passage, Enoch warns idolaters, "the visions of (your) dreams will lead you astray" (1 En. 99:8).[51] The author of 1 En. 19:1 recognizes that even idols have the allure of prophetic revelations. According to this passage, these revelations are nothing more than the deceptive tactics of spirits bent on harming humans. These spirits are the spirits of sinful angels who are imprisoned at the end of the earth.

Possibly related to this work of deception is the statement that these spirits have "assumed many forms" (*polymorpha genomena*). It is not clear exactly what kind of multiformity the author of this passage has in mind. Aramaic magic bowls and amulets from the first millennium CE speak of spirits appearing to persons in dreams or visions in the form of animals or of other frightening creatures.[52] In the present context, the polymorphic nature of the spirits probably has to do with their work of destruction or

49. Whether the "unclean spirit" of this passage is an attitude or a "superhuman" being is not clear. Armin Lange, "Considerations Concerning the 'Spirit of Impurity' in Zech 13:2," in *Dämonen,* ed. Lange, Lichtenberger, and Römheld, 254–68, argues that it is a living, "demonic" being that manifests itself in human beings in their attitude and behavior.

50. Cf. Jer 23:9–40, which criticizes prophets who have lying dreams and lead people astray.

51. Cf. also 1 John 4:1, "Beloved, do not believe every spirit, but test the spirits to see whether they are from God; for many false prophets have gone out into the world." That evil beings might appear to a person in a dream or vision is a common theme in Aramaic incantations from the first millennium CE. See Charles D. Isbell, *Corpus of the Aramaic Incantation Bowls,* SBLDS 17 (Missoula, MT: Society of Biblical Literature, 1975), texts 11.10; 19.8; Naveh and Shaked, *Amulets and Magic Bowls,* Bowl 13, lines 11–13.

52. See A. Ya. Borisov, "Epigraphical Notes: Four Hermitage Aramaic Magic Bowls" [in Russian], *Epigrafika Vostoka* 19 (1969): 7; Naveh and Shaked, *Amulets and Magic Bowls,* Bowl 13, lines 11–13; Joseph Naveh and Shaul Shaked, *Magic Spells and Formulae: Aramaic Incantations of Late Antiquity* (Jerusalem: Magnes, 1993), Amulet 12, lines 12–13; Bowl 18, lines 1–2; 25, lines 9–10.

deception. Nickelsburg cites as potential parallels the transformation of the watchers into human form in T. Reu. 5:6 and, more pertinently, the appearance of the devil to Eve as an angel in Apoc. Mos. 17:1.[53] In 2 Cor 11:14, Paul says that the Satan disguises himself as an angel of light. The idea that a spirit might change its appearance in order to mislead someone would fit the context in 1 En. 19:1.

It is perhaps more likely, however, that the mention of the spirits' various forms refers simply to the belief that spirits may afflict humans in various ways. "Having assumed many forms" immediately precedes not the statement that the spirits "lead astray," but that they "bring destruction on men." First Enoch 15:11 lists several ways in which these spirits attack humans. In an effort to leave no stone unturned, ancient Near Eastern incantations would regularly list various types of evil beings that might attack an individual and the different ways they might do this.[54] Saying that the spirits of the angels have assumed many forms may be an attempt to account for the variety of harmful spirits that trouble humans with a single etiology. That the spirits would also employ a variety of deceptive tactics and assume different appearances in order to lead unsuspecting victims astray is not out of the question.[55]

Superhuman Beings and Human Sin

The Book of the Watchers offered its readers an explanation of many of the world's problems. More precisely stated, the Book of the Watchers provided various explanations to account for a variety of humankind's troubles. The third-century pseudepigraphon's etiologies of evil trace certain kinds of sin and suffering to the period before the flood when a group of rebellious angels descended to the earth, married human women, and revealed forbidden secrets to humans.[56] Angelic revelation of heavenly secrets is to blame for some of humankind's problems. Other forms of sin and suffering stem from these angels' sexual immorality and the terrible offspring that this immorality produced.

53. Nickelsburg, *1 Enoch 1*, 287.

54. E.g., Utukkū Lemnūtu Tablet 6, lines 40–90.

55. Cf. Jub. 10:12, where Noah writes down the spirits' "deceptions."

56. Other passages in the book make use of the Eden tradition of Gen 2–3 rather than the sons of God story to explain certain of the world's problems (1 En. 24:2–25:7; 32:3–6).

Although the story of the sinful angels would enjoy widespread popularity in early Judaism, it is the Book of the Watchers' teaching on demons and evil spirits that appears to have had the most significant and enduring influence on Jewish and Christian theology. The Book of the Watchers made use of traditions from the Hebrew scriptures pertaining to demons, evil spirits, and sons of God, bringing these distinct concepts into conversation with one another in order to address the problems of sin and suffering. According to the Book of the Watchers, evil spirits are the disembodied children of the sons of God, who inflict human beings with various manners of bodily harm (15:8–16:1; 19:1). Especially innovative is the work's use of these traditions to account for the worship of false gods. First Enoch 19:1 credits evil spirits explicitly with leading humans into sin, seducing unsuspecting humans so that they worship demons as though these lesser beings are actually gods. In fact, these demons are none other than the imprisoned angels who sinned prior to the flood. In the next century, the book of Jubilees would develop the Book of the Watchers' teachings about spirits, demons, and the threats they pose to humankind. Jubilees would further elaborate that these menacing beings serve the Satan.

CHAPTER 4

The Prince of Mastema and His Deceptive Spirits

The book of Jubilees devotes a great deal of attention to maleficent superhuman beings. This work also marks a number of significant shifts in Jewish thinking about evil spiritual forces and their involvement in human sin and suffering. In Jubilees, the Satan and evil spirits join forces to rule over the nations of the earth, deceiving and afflicting humankind in various ways. The Satan, called "(the) Prince (of) Mastema" in Jubilees, also appears in a number of tales as the superhuman adversary of Israel. As the author of Jubilees reflected on the stories of Israel's ancestors, posing questions to these stories about Israel's status among the nations of the world, the figure of the Satan and ideas about other harmful superhuman forces supplied answers. In the present chapter I introduce the Prince of Mastema and other maleficent superhuman characters who appear in Jubilees. I address how these figures function within the created order and within God's plan for Israel as described in Jubilees. In the next chapter I will consider how Jubilees also, in contrast, depicts the Prince of Mastema as one who opposes God's plan for Israel.

Interpreting Jubilees

Often referred to as a "rewriting" or "retelling" of the Hebrew scriptures, the book of Jubilees recounts many of the stories told in Genesis and the first nineteen chapters of Exodus.[1] Jubilees also uses other lit-

1. Much has been written on the generic classification of Jubilees; it is typically identified as a "rewritten Bible" or a like designation. For a recent discussion of Jubi-

erature pertaining to Israel's ancestors, such as the Enochic Book of the Watchers. Jubilees does not merely recite the stories as told in Genesis, Exodus, and other sources, but offers its readers interpretive adaptations of these stories. Jubilees, however, presents itself as more than an interpretation and expansion of Israel's sacred traditions; it casts itself as an authoritative revelation given by God through the agency of the angel of the presence to Moses on Sinai.[2] One of its major concerns is to demonstrate that God from the very moment of creation has purposed to set Israel apart as a special people. Accordingly, Jubilees claims that many of the divinely revealed laws that distinguish Israel from the other nations of the world were in effect long before the time of Moses and were faithfully observed by Noah, Abraham, and other noteworthy patriarchs.

In order to comprehend fully what Jubilees has to say about the Satan, evil spirits, and related figures, as well as where Jubilees fits into the history of these traditions, one must have some sense of how the book was composed. The compositional process that produced Jubilees has become in recent years a matter of scholarly debate. The point of contention concerns the way that Jubilees' "author" incorporated earlier narratives into his work. Did Jubilees' author rework his sources so thoroughly that Jubilees is a relatively seamless unity, the details of which, for the most part, reflect the thinking of its author? Or did Jubilees' author incorporate much of his source material largely without modification, leaving observable tensions in his final product that allow one to distinguish the portions of the work that were produced by the author of Jubilees himself from those portions that derived from earlier sources? These questions bear directly on the present discussion, since one must consider to what extent Jubilees' depictions of the Satan reflect either a single notion or diverse notions of this figure.

The prevailing scholarly opinion until recently was that Jubilees is largely the work of a single author writing sometime in the second century BCE and that the ideas expressed in the work represent the opinions of

---

lees' genre and how the work defies a simple generic classification, see John J. Collins, "The Genre of the Book of *Jubilees*," in *A Teacher for All Generations: Essays in Honor of James C. VanderKam*, ed. Eric F. Mason et al., 2 vols., JSJSup 153 (Leiden: Brill, 2012), 2:737–55.

2. On these aspects of Jubilees' self-presentation and other authority-conferring strategies employed by the work, see Hindy Najman, "Interpretation as Primordial Writing: Jubilees and Its Authority Conferring Strategies," *JSJ* 30.4 (1999): 379–410.

Jubilees' author.[3] Michael Segal has challenged this assumption, arguing that the person who produced Jubilees was not really an "author" in the sense that most people today think of authorship. This person, rather, is more appropriately considered a "redactor" or "composer" who incorporated various written sources into one book, supplying commentary along the way.[4] Segal points out a number of contradictions in the book

3. Dating Jubilees with precision is difficult. James C. VanderKam (*Textual and Historical Studies in the Book of Jubilees*, HSM 14 [Missoula, MT: Scholars Press, 1977], 207–85; and "Jubilees, Book of," *EDSS* 1:434–45) dates the work to the period between 160 and 150 BCE on the following basis. The earliest copy of Jubilees among the Dead Sea Scrolls (4Q216) dates paleographically to the Hasmonean period. Since this copy may be dated between 125 and 100 BCE, the work must have been composed by this time. The author of Jubilees also appears to have made use of the Book of Dreams (1 En. 83–90; ca. 164 BCE), so the work could have been composed no earlier than this. Since Jubilees shares many concerns with the Qumran sect but does not reveal any evidence of a schism such as that between the Qumran community and the rest of society, the work was probably composed before the Qumran group split off from Jewish society. Jonathan A. Goldstein, "The Date of the Book of Jubilees," *PAAJR* 50 (1983): 63–86, has argued that Jubilees should be dated between 169 and 167 BCE. He observes that the author seems to have been aware of the sack of Jerusalem in 169 but is silent on Antiochus IV's banning of certain Jewish customs later in his reign. Conversely, Doron Mendels, *The Land of Israel as a Political Concept in Hasmonean Literature: Recourse to History in Second Century B.C. Claims to the Holy Land*, TSAJ 15 (Tübingen: Mohr Seibeck, 1987), 57–88, situates Jubilees within the religio-political climate between 130 and 109 BCE. Martha Himmelfarb, *A Kingdom of Priests: Ancestry and Merit in Ancient Judaism* (Philadelphia: University of Pennsylvania Press, 2006), 72–77, reads Jubilees' passages pertaining to Edom and those pertaining to intermarriage against the backdrop of the conversion of Idumeans to Judaism under Hasmonean rule. She places the composition of Jubilees in the last third of the second century BCE. Michael Segal, *The Book of Jubilees: Rewritten Bible, Redaction, Ideology and Theology*, JSJSup 117 (Leiden: Brill, 2007), 319–22, has made the case that Jubilees' redactional framework (on which see below) is characterized by inner-Jewish polemic that reflects the beginning of a rift in the nation that "reached its full expression in the sectarian literature preserved at Qumran" (322). For this reason, Segal claims that the work of the redactor should be dated to the period following the formation of the Essene stream of Judaism. More recently, Eibert J. C. Tigchelaar, "The Qumran *Jubilees* Manuscripts as Evidence for the Literary Growth of the Book," *RevQ* 26.4 (2014): 579–94, and Matthew Phillip Monger, "4Q216 and the State of *Jubilees* at Qumran," *RevQ* 26.4 (2014): 595–612, have argued based on the Qumran manuscript evidence that Jubilees as attested in the Ethiopic translation was the product not of a single author writing at one time, but of a process of *Fortschreibung*, some of which took place subsequent to the second century BCE.

4. Segal summarizes his arguments in *Book of Jubilees*, 21–35. See also his more recent article, "The Dynamics of Composition and Rewriting in Jubilees and Pseudo-Jubilees," *RevQ* 26.4 (2014): 555–77.

that can be explained if one grants that a redactor has compiled earlier rewritten narratives. Not all of the ideas expressed in Jubilees, according to Segal, represent the thinking of its redactor, who in numerous instances did not bother to reconcile his sources with one another or with his own viewpoint.

Based on some of Segal's observations, James Kugel suggests a different process of composition for the book. He argues that Jubilees is a unified work, written by a single author, to which an "interpolator" added his own interpretations here and there.[5] Kugel claims that he can identify these interpolations, twenty-nine in total, based on the interpolator's distinctive terminology. If one simply removes these passages, then Jubilees reads as a consistent, coherent work.[6] Other scholars, however, while they allow that Jubilees makes use of a variety of sources, are not persuaded that one can distinguish the work's literary strata.[7] These scholars draw attention instead to the book's overall unity.

The matter of precisely how Jubilees was written is yet to be completely resolved, and it need not be entirely resolved for our purposes. My approach is to take seriously the complex nature of the work under consideration. Reading Jubilees simply as a unity runs the risk of glossing over the variety of perspectives that the book contains. While one may contest the specifics of Segal's hypothesis, his contention that the person who composed Jubilees combined a number of earlier texts and traditions without reconciling all the tensions created in the process seems indisputable. The work no doubt exhibits a large degree of unity that one can attribute to its "author," but numerous and important tensions remain in

5. Kugel makes a case for his understanding of Jubilees' composition in several publications. His arguments appeared initially in "On the Interpolations in the *Book of Jubilees*," *RevQ* 24.2 (2009): 215–72; and most recently in *A Walk through Jubilees: Studies in the Book of Jubilees and the World of Its Creation*, JSJSup 156 (Leiden: Brill, 2012), 227–96.

6. Kugel, "On the Interpolations," 266.

7. See James C. VanderKam's critical assessment of Segal's and Kugel's arguments in "Jubilees as the Composition of One Author?," *RevQ* 26.4 (2014): 501–16. See also Todd R. Hanneken, "The Watchers in Rewritten Scripture: The Use of the Book of the Watchers in Jubilees," in *The Fallen Angels Traditions: Second Temple Developments and Reception History*, ed. Angela Kim Harkins, Kelley Coblentz Bautch, and John C. Endres; CBQMS 53 (Washington, DC: Catholic Biblical Association of America, 2014), 25–68. Though she apparently does not reject a redaction-critical approach to the work, Betsy Halpern-Amaru, *The Perspective from Mt. Sinai: The Book of Jubilees and Exodus*, JAJSup 21 (Göttingen: Vandenhoeck & Ruprecht, 2015), 21, reads Jubilees "as a unitary text that may reflect the work of a single author or the hand of a final editor."

the text. This assessment holds true even after one removes those passages that Kugel attributes to an "interpolator."[8]

Given Jubilees' compositional complexity, one must remain alert to the possibility that the book contains not one systematic presentation of the Satan and evil spirits but multiple presentations that stand in some degree of tension with one another. Perhaps these reflect differences in thought among the sources of Jubilees, or perhaps they reflect differences between the thinking of Jubilees' author and the sources he appropriated.[9] With regard to the Satan, Jubilees portrays the Prince of Mastema in two different ways. In some passages, he appears as the divinely appointed chief of the evil spirits who mislead and afflict the nations of the earth. In other passages, he is the antagonist of Israel who attempts to harm God's elect unprovoked, presumably simply because of his character. While these two conceptions of the Prince of Mastema are not necessarily contradictory, they nonetheless differ and should be distinguished. Additionally, other incongruities remain in the text of Jubilees that seem to point to the work's inclusion of earlier material pertaining to the Satan and/or evil spirits, the teaching of which material may have differed somewhat from that of Jubilees' author. The way that Jubilees' author has incorporated earlier material, allowing incongruities to remain in the final product, obscures to some extent the book's teaching. One challenge for interpreters of Jubilees is to assess such tensions in an effort to discern precisely what Jubilees as a whole was supposed to communicate.

Taxonomy, Terminology, and Titles for Harmful Superhuman Beings

Jubilees' vocabulary and categories for describing the superhuman realm, while indebted to earlier literature, also differ from those of the texts considered up to this point. As in the writings of the Hebrew scriptures, one encounters in Jubilees various kinds of satanic beings, some human and some superhuman. Different from Job and Zechariah, however, the pri-

8. An example of such a tension created by Jubilees' incorporation of earlier material is that the "testament" of Noah in Jub. 7:20–39 is separated from the account of Noah's death (10:14–17) by three chapters. According to the chronology of Jubilees, Noah delivers his testamentary address to his children about three hundred years before he dies.

9. Hanneken, "Watchers in Rewritten Scripture," argues that the tensions in the present form of Jubilees reflect not differences between the work of the redactor and his sources, but tensions that already existed in Jubilees' sources.

mary superhuman satan figure in Jubilees goes by the title "the Prince of Mastema," rather than "the Satan," though Jubilees likely makes use of this latter designation in one instance (10:11). With regard to evil spirits and demons, Jubilees employs familiar vocabulary but conceives of these categories of harmful beings somewhat differently from earlier literature.

Unfortunately, the analysis of Jubilees' terminology for the superhuman realm is complicated by the fact that, aside from the small portion of the work preserved on Dead Sea Scroll fragments, we do not have access to the work in the language of its composition, but only via translation.[10] Jubilees was composed in Hebrew, from which it was translated into Greek. From Greek, it was then translated into Latin and Ethiopic. Although bits of the Greek remain and a portion of the Latin has survived, the work is available in its entirety only in Ethiopic.[11] This means that for the large majority of the book, one has access only to a translation of a translation of the original, which can be problematic when it comes to discerning the ideas that were initially expressed and read in Hebrew. Fortunately, however, the translators of Jubilees have done modern interpreters a service in that they have transliterated those words they perceived as names or titles for the Satan rather than translating them. Since these Hebrew words could have been common nouns as well as names or titles, however, the task remains of determining whether the ancient translators have correctly understood these designations.

We should also keep in mind that Jubilees' author typically avoids calling superhuman beings by their names. The highest class of angelic beings who assist the righteous are not referred to by their names as in some early Jewish works, but are called simply "angels of the presence" (2:2). The angel who speaks to Moses on Sinai and who serves as the protector of God's

10. James C. VanderKam, "The Jubilees Fragments from Qumran Cave 4," in *The Madrid Qumran Congress: Proceedings of the International Congress on the Dead Sea Scrolls, Madrid, 18–21 March 1991*, ed. Julio Trebolle Barrera and Luis Vegas Montaner, STDJ 11, 2 vols. (Leiden: Brill, 1992), 2:642. VanderKam identifies at least fourteen MSS of Jubilees among the fragmentary remains of the Dead Sea Scrolls: 1Q17, 1Q18, 2Q19, 2Q20, 3Q5 (frags. 3, 1), 4Q176[a] (frags. 19–21), 4Q216, 4Q218, 4Q219, 4Q220, 4Q221, 4Q222, 4Q223–224, 11Q12. Recently, Monger, "4Q216," 599–600, and Tigchelaar, "Qumran *Jubilees* Manuscripts," 582–84, have called into question whether each of these MSS indeed represents a complete copy of Jubilees rather than simply a copy of a portion of the work.

11. The Greek survives only in the form of quotations and allusions by ancient Christian authors, and one third of the Latin is extant in the form of a fifth/sixth-century palimpsest. On the textual witnesses of Jubilees, see James C. VanderKam, *The Book of Jubilees*, 2 vols., CSCO 510–511 (Leuven: Peeters, 1989), 1:8–16.

people (2:1; 18:9; 48:4) corresponds to the angel named Michael in other texts (1 En. 10:11; Dan 10:21; 12:1). In Jubilees he is merely "the angel of the presence." The angel who gives Noah the book of healing to counter the work of harmful spirits is simply "one of us," that is, one of the angels of the presence (10:10). This unnamed figure corresponds to the angel Raphael in other literature (e.g., 1 En. 10:4–8; Tob 3:16–17). This aversion to referring to heavenly beings by their names also applies to sinful angels. In Jubilees' version of the watcher story, the names Shemihazah, Asael, and others that appear in the Book of the Watchers are nowhere to be found (Jub. 5:1–11). With respect to designations for the Satan, in those passages where there is some question as to whether a particular term is functioning as a name for this figure, a title, or simply a common noun, Jubilees' tendency to avoid names for such figures should lead one to suspect that it is more probably a title or a common noun than a proper name. Certainty in these cases, however, may not be possible.

Satanic Titles and Terminology

The usual title for the Satan figure in Jubilees is "the Prince of Mastema" (18:9, 12; 48:2, 9, 12, 15) or "Prince Mastema" (11:5, 11; 17:16). In one passage, the Ethiopic speaks of "Mastema, the leader of the spirits" (10:8).[12] That the Prince of Mastema is to be identified with the Satan is clear from Jub. 10:11, where the designation "Satan" or "the Satan" refers to this figure. Jubilees also draws from earlier traditions about the Satan in its portrayal of the Prince of Mastema. For instance, Jubilees' account of the binding of Isaac in Jub. 17 reworks the story of Abraham's trial into a tale that very much resembles that of Job.[13] It portrays God's seemingly unreasonable

12. It may be that in the original Hebrew of Jubilees *mśṭmh* appeared exclusively as a common noun, as in the titles "Prince of Mastema" (i.e., "Prince of Hostility"). Cf. Jubilees' account of the Passover, which speaks of the "forces of Mastema/hostility," who are sent by God to kill the Egyptian firstborn (Jub. 49:2). The noun *mśṭmh* also occurs in designations for harmful angelic beings in several of the Dead Sea Scrolls: *ml'ky hmśṭmwt*, "Angels of Hostility" (4Q390 1:11; 2 i 7; 4Q387 2 iii 4), and, with reference to Belial, *ml'k hmśṭmh*, "a hostile angel" (1QM 13:11; CD 16:5 [or "Angel of Obstruction"]). On the vocabulary of *mastema* in the Dead Sea Scrolls, see J. W. van Henten, "Mastemah," *DDD* 553–54; Armin Lange, "מַשְׂטֵמָה *maśṭēmāh*," *ThWQ* 2:796–802. Though it is possible that the author of the Hebrew book of Jubilees was consistent in his use of *mśṭmh* simply as a common noun, the Ethiopic translator of the work nonetheless understood the word in some instances as a name.

13. J. T. A. G. M. van Ruiten, "Abraham, Job and the Book of *Jubilees*: The Intertextual

demand that Abraham sacrifice his son as a test of Abraham's character instigated in heaven by the Prince of Mastema.

As for the significance of the title "Prince of Mastema," the noun *mśṭmh* and the cognate verb *śṭm* occur in a small number of passages in the Hebrew scriptures and denote hostile activity of various sorts.[14] The verb *śṭm* is used, for instance, in Gen 27:41 with reference to Esau's plan to kill Jacob for stealing the blessing intended for Esau. In some passages, humans are the objects of God's hostility. Job complains to God, "with the might of your hand, you persecute me [*tiśṭəmēnî*]" (Job 30:21).[15] The idea of divine hostility is probably at the root of the title in Jubilees, according to which the Prince of Mastema is tasked by God with punishing wicked humans (Jub. 10:8). The title may be doubly significant in Jubilees, since some of its stories speak as well of God's people as the objects of the Prince of Mastema's undeserved hostility.

With regard to the noun "satan" (*śāṭān*), Jubilees reflects the diverse usage that one observes in the Hebrew scriptures, which use *śāṭān* as a common noun that means "attacker." It can refer to human attackers, at times in a military context (e.g., 1 Sam 29:4; 1 Kgs 5:18 [Eng. 5:4]). In other passages, the attacker is superhuman (e.g., Num 22:22, 32). With the definite article, *haśśāṭān*, "the Satan," in two passages it is the title for a particular heavenly individual who serves God as the heavenly attacker or executioner of humans (Zech 3:1–2; Job 1–2). A similar range or referents for this word is found in Jubilees. Ethiopic *sayṭān*, a transliteration of Heb. *śāṭān* (presumably via Gk. *satanas* or *satan*), occurs five times in Jubilees. In one instance, it refers to *the* Satan, the Prince of Mastema (Jub. 10:11). In the other four occurrences (23:29; 40:9; 46:2; 50:5), the designation

---

Relationship of Genesis 22:1–19, Job 1–2:13 and *Jubilees* 17:15–18:19," in *The Sacrifice of Isaac: The Aqedah (Genesis 22) and Its Interpretations,* ed. Ed Noort and Eibert Tigchelaar, TBN 4 (Leiden: Brill, 2002), 83–85, disagrees with the scholarly consensus that Jub. 17 was influenced by Job. See also Jacques van Ruiten, *Abraham in the Book of Jubilees: The Rewriting of Genesis 11:26–25:10 in the Book of Jubilees 11:14–23:8,* JSJSup 161 (Leiden: Brill, 2012), 212–14. On Jubilees' version of the sacrifice/binding of Isaac, see the discussion below. For now, it will suffice to observe that, whether Jub. 17 was influenced directly by Job or is merely coincidentally similar to it, the similarities between Job 1–2 and Jub. 17 suggest that the Prince of Mastema in Jubilees corresponds to the Satan of earlier literature.

14. The noun occurs twice in Hos 9:7–8. The verb occurs in Gen 27:41; 49:23; 50:15; Job 16:9; 30:21; Ps 55:4 (Eng. 3).

15. See also Job 16:9. The two instances of the noun *maśṭēmâ* in Hos 9:7–8 may refer to God's hostility to sinful humans, but the meaning of these verses is unclear.

appears to denote a generic "attacker" rather than a particular individual.[16] Some of these attackers appear to be of the human variety, whereas others are more likely superhuman.

All four passages that use "satan" generically borrow from the language of 1 Kgs 5, which describes the peaceful conditions of the early period of Solomon's reign. During this time, the historian reports, *ʾên śāṭān wəʾên pegaʿ rāʿ*, "there is neither adversary nor misfortune" (1 Kgs 5:18 [Eng. 4]). Since Jewish literature could appropriate the terminology of 1 Kgs 5, which speaks of a human attacker, in order to speak of a superhuman attacker, determining with certainty what sort of satan is intended in these texts is not always simple. In three of these texts in Jubilees, the notion of a human, military attacker makes very good sense. Jubilees 40:9 describes the time during which Joseph ruled Egypt as a time when "there was no satan or any evil one."[17] Likewise, Jub. 46:2 relates that, because the Egyptians honored the Israelites as long as Joseph was alive, "there was no satan or evil one throughout all of Joseph's lifetime." Jubilees 50:5 speaks of a future era in which Israel will live securely in its land and during which "they will no longer have any satan or any evil person."

Jubilees 23 employs the language of 1 Kgs 5 to describe the eschatological period as well, but does so likely with reference to a superhuman rather than a human satan: "There will be no old man, nor anyone who has lived out his lifetime, because all of them will be infants and children. They will complete and live their entire lifetimes peacefully and joyfully. There will be neither a satan nor any evil one who will destroy. For their entire lifetimes will be times of blessing and healing" (23:28–29).[18] The

16. R. H. Charles, *The Book of Jubilees or The Little Genesis* (London: Black, 1902), 150, 227, 245, 258, renders *sayṭān* as the proper name Satan in these texts (Jub. 23:29, 40:9; 46:2; 50:5) and refers the reader to As. Mos. (= T. Mos.) 10:1, which predicts the eschatological end of the devil. O. S. Wintermute, "Jubilees: A New Translation and Introduction," *OTP* 2:102, 130, 137, 142, likewise translates the word in each of these passages as "Satan." Ronald Anthony Pascale, "The Demonic Powers of Destruction in 1 Enoch 15:3–16:1 and Jubilees 10:5, and the Demonizing of the Avenging Angels" (PhD diss., Harvard University, 1980), 194–95, interprets the "satan" and "evil one" of these verses as "Satan and the evil powers of destruction" (195). Gene L. Davenport, *The Eschatology of the Book of Jubilees*, StPB 20 (Leiden: Brill, 1971), 39n1, argues that these statements pertain to gentile opponents of Israel.

17. Unless otherwise indicated, all English quotations of Jubilees are from VanderKam, *Book of Jubilees*, vol. 2.

18. In addition to Jub. 23:28–29 and 50:5, see 4Q504 17:13–14 for an example of a text that adopts the phraseology of 1 Kgs 5:18 (Eng. 4) to describe the eschatological era.

context of this statement, which concerns human health and longevity in the final age, suggests that the sort of satan who will not be present during this period is not a human threat, but the sort of superhuman satan who would bring sickness and a shortening of the human lifespan.[19] It is not impossible, however, that even this text refers to a human satan. If a superhuman satan is in mind, this satan does not seem to be a chief satanic figure, such as the "Prince of Mastema," but simply a member of a class of satanic beings.[20] In the context of the entire book of Jubilees, this satan would probably be identified with those beings who are elsewhere called "(evil) spirits."

In the remaining occurrence of *sayṭān*, Jub. 10:11, ninety percent of evil spirits are bound, but ten percent of the harmful spirits are left to serve "the satan." There is some ambiguity in the Ethiopic as to whether *sayṭān* reflects the title, "the Satan," or the name Satan. Since there is no definite article in Ethiopic, either *śāṭān* or *haśśāṭān* could have appeared in the Hebrew original.[21] In literature prior to Jubilees, "satan" does not appear to be used as a name, only as a common noun or in the title *haśśāṭān*, "the Satan."[22] Although Jub. 10:11 could in theory contain the earliest occurrence of the word as a name, nothing in this verse indicates that the word has come to be a name. Furthermore, given that Jubilees typically does not call superhuman beings by name, it is likely that neither is "satan" supposed to be a name. Despite the ambiguity with regard to the particular usage of the word "satan" in this passage, the identity of the person to whom this designation refers is not in doubt. This individual is supposed to be identical with the figure referred to elsewhere as "the Prince of Mastema," the chief of the evil spirits.[23]

19. For another example of the use of 1 Kgs 5:18 (Eng. 4) with reference to a superhuman satan, see Bowl 22 in Joseph Naveh and Shaul Shaked, *Magic Spells and Formulae: Aramaic Incantations of Late Antiquity* (Jerusalem: Magnes, 1993), 130–31.

20. Cf. the reference to such a satan in the Aramaic Levi Document: *ʾl tšlṭ by kl śṭn*, "let not any satan have power over me" (4Q213[a] 1 i 17). The word *kl*, "any," makes clear that a class of beings is in mind. The statement in Jubilees that no satan will exist in the eschaton similarly seems to presume the existence of a class of satanic beings.

21. VanderKam, *Book of Jubilees*, 2:60, translates *sayṭān* in 10:11 as "the satan." Those who interpret the word as the proper name Satan include Charles, *Book of Jubilees*, 81; Davenport, *Eschatology*, 39n1; George H. Schodde, *The Book of Jubilees Translated from the Ethiopic* (Oberlin, OH: Goodrich, 1888), 36; and Wintermute, "Jubilees," *OTP* 2:76.

22. 1 Chr 21:1 is traditionally taken to be the earliest example of Satan as a name, but as I argued in ch. 1, *śāṭān* in this verse should be translated as "a satan."

23. Davenport, *Eschatology*, 39n1, offers no explanation for his claim that this passage

Another designation that some scholars have claimed that Jubilees uses for the Satan is "belial" (*blyʿl*). Belial is a name for the Satan figure that occurs with frequency in the Dead Sea Scrolls.[24] As is the case with "mastema" and "satan," the word *blyʿl* is not the name of a superhuman being in the Hebrew scriptures. It is a common noun, the precise meaning of which is somewhat ambiguous. It is used to describe "wicked" or "worthless" persons, often as part of the expression "son/daughter/man of belial" (e.g., Deut 13:14; 1 Sam 1:16; Job 34:18; Prov 19:28). In poetry, *blyʿl* appears in parallelism with "death" and "Sheol" (2 Sam 22:5; Pss 18:5 [Eng. 4]; 41:9 [Eng. 8]). The Ethiopic transliteration of this word occurs twice in Jubilees (1:20; 15:33).[25] In 15:33, the angel of the presence tells Moses that some Israelites will disobediently leave their children uncircumcised. These disobedient descendants of Jacob are referred to as "sons of belial"

---

implies a distinction between the Satan and Mastema. Verses 8–9 say that a tenth of the spirits are to be left under Mastema's supervision, and v. 11 says that they are left under the control of the Satan. The simplest explanation for this is that the Satan and Mastema are thought to be the same individual. Neil Forsyth, *The Old Enemy: Satan and the Combat Myth* (Princeton: Princeton University Press, 1987), 188–90, also holds that Jubilees distinguishes between Mastema and the Satan. Forsyth, however, bases this supposed distinction on false premises. First, he regards the satans mentioned in those texts that speak of a time when there is no "satan" as "Satan," the proper name of an angelic figure distinct from Mastema. These statements are found in Jub. 23:29, 40:9, 46:2, and 50:5. I concluded above, however, that "satan" in these verses is used generically, not to refer to a particular individual. Second, and more strangely, Forsyth regards "Mastema" as Jubilees' name for either the angel Shemihaza or the angel Asael of the Book of the Watchers. There is no evidence that Jubilees intends one of these angels by the name Mastema. In Forsyth's tradition history, the Mastema and Satan traditions begin to converge in 10:8–11, which links the two figures. A simpler explanation is that the designation "(the Prince of) Mastema" is Jubilees' preferred appellative for the Satan figure. There is no evidence that the title was ever employed otherwise.

On the basis of a parallel account in the *Book of Asaph the Physician*, Todd R. Hanneken, *The Subversion of the Apocalypses in the Book of Jubilees*, EJL 34 (Atlanta: Society of Biblical Literature, 2012), 74–75, argues that the original text of Jub. 10:11 read "the Prince of Mastema" rather than "the Satan." Cf., however, the counterargument of Thomas J. Farrar, "New Testament Satanology and Leading Suprahuman Opponents in Second Temple Jewish Literature: A Religion-Historical Analysis," *JTS* (forthcoming). Even were one to remove this explicit identification of the Prince of Mastema as the Satan, it remains clear from other passages in Jubilees (e.g., 17:15–18:16) that the Prince of Mastema is to be identified with this figure.

24. E.g., CD 4:12–19; 5:17–19; 1QM 13:10–12. Belial may also appear as a name in some of the fragments of so-called Pseudo-Jubilees (4Q225–226), on which see ch. 7.

25. The transliteration is *beləḥor* in 1:20 and *belə'ar* or *belə'or* (depending on the MS) in 15:33. Cf. βελιάρ in 2 Cor 6:15.

(*wəluda belə'ar*). Although most translators take "belial" in this statement as a name, as the Greek and Ethiopic translators seem to have understood it, in the Hebrew it may simply have been a common noun, as in the identical expression (*bny blyʿl*) in earlier literature.[26] To describe Israelites as "sons of Belial" would also be atypical in Jubilees, which emphasizes that the entire nation of Israel belongs to God and has been granted immunity to evil superhuman forces (e.g., 19:28). "Wicked people" is a more likely translation.

Those scholars who understand belial in 15:33 as a name probably do so based on the assumption that this name also occurs in 1:20. "May your mercy, Lord, be lifted over your people. Create for them a just spirit. May the spirit of Belial not rule them so as to bring charges against them before you and to trap them away from every proper path so that they may be destroyed from your presence. . . . Create for them a pure mind and a holy spirit" (1:20–21).[27]

Although Belial is a common name for the satan figure in the Dead Sea Scrolls, it is not obvious that the word is used this way in Jubilees.[28] *Rwḥ blyʿl*, from which the Eth. *manfasa beləḥor* of 1:20 probably derives, could be translated simply as "a wicked spirit." That the antitheses of the "spirit of belial" are a "just spirit" and a "holy spirit" points toward taking it as a common noun, meaning "wickedness." That the only other use of "belial" in the book (15:33) should likely be understood in this way also supports this interpretation. Furthermore, again, given Jubilees' tendency to avoid calling angelic figures by name, it is doubtful that Jubilees employs "belial" as a name in this passage. Nonetheless, in light of Jubilees' teaching concerning "evil spirits" and "demons," there is little question about the nature of the spirit of whom Moses speaks in this passage. It is a spirit such

26. Those who translate it as a proper name in this instance and in 1:20 include Charles, *Book of Jubilees*, 113; Wintermute, "Jubilees," *OTP* 2:87; Pascale, "Demonic Powers of Destruction," 196; VanderKam, *Book of Jubilees*, 2:94. VanderKam, *The Book of Jubilees*, Guides to the Apocrypha and Pseudepigrapha (Sheffield: Sheffield Academic Press, 2001), 127–28, however, allows that this word may be a common noun. For examples of *bny blyʿl* and related expressions in the Hebrew scriptures, see Deut 13:14; Judg 19:22; 20:13; 1 Sam 1:16; 2:12; 10:27; 25:17; 1 Kgs 21:10, 13; 2 Chr 13:7.

27. The expression "bring charges against" in VanderKam's translation is an acceptable rendering of Eth. *'astawādaya* and has thus been retained. For reasons that will be given in the next chapter, however, it is unlikely that "bring charges against" accurately reflects the meaning of the original Hebrew.

28. Those who translate *manfasa beləḥor* in 1:20 as "the spirit of Belial" include Charles, *Book of Jubilees*, 6; Wintermute, "Jubilees," *OTP* 2:53; VanderKam, *Book of Jubilees*, 2:5.

as those who rule the nations and lead them astray. Moses prays that one of these wicked spirits will not be permitted to rule Israel.

Designations for Demons and Evil Spirits

Jubilees employs a wide range of vocabulary to refer to harmful spirits. In addition to the designations "spirit of belial" (1:20) and "satan" (23:29), one finds "spirit(s)" (10:5, 8; 11:5; 15:31–32), "evil spirits" (10:3, 13; 12:20), "savage spirits" (11:4), "spirits of Mastema [or 'hostility']" (19:28), "forces of Mastema [or 'hostility']" (49:2), "evil ones" (10:11), and even "the Lord's forces" (49:4). One also encounters "demons" (1:11; 7:27; 10:2; 22:17) and "impure demons" (10:1).

Jubilees generally follows the terminological distinctions we observed in earlier literature, but is not entirely consistent in this respect. As do the Book of the Watchers and earlier biblical texts, Jubilees refers to those beings who afflict and mislead humans as "spirits" (Eth. *manāfəst*) and employs the term "demons" (*'agānənt*) for those beings who are the objects of the nations' (and occasionally Israel's) misguided worship (e.g., 1:11, 20; 11:4–5; 22:17). Indeed, passages in Jubilees that describe the religion of the gentiles use exclusively "demons" to refer to their objects of worship, never "spirits."

Nevertheless, Jubilees does not in every instance maintain the distinction between "spirits" and "demons." While the beings who mislead and cause illness are typically referred to as "spirits," they are in two instances referred to as "demons" (7:27; 10:2–3). In other words, Jubilees consistently refers to those beings that are worshiped by nations as "demons"; but, with reference to those beings who mislead and harm humans, Jubilees will occasionally use "spirits" and "demons" interchangeably. Although Jubilees typically preserves the terminological distinctions found in the Book of the Watchers and earlier biblical texts, those instances in which Jubilees does not maintain these distinctions indicate a taxonomy of the superhuman realm that differs from that found in earlier literature. In Jubilees, the categories of evil spirits and demons, which were distinct in earlier writings, have been collapsed into a single category. These demons/spirits afflict, mislead, and receive worship from humankind.[29]

29. Jubilees may not have been the first composition to combine these categories. See Tob. 6:7, which attributes the activity of physically afflicting humans to "a demon or an evil

The Prince of Mastema, Deceptive Spirits, and the Nations

Numerous passages in Jubilees speak of the Prince of Mastema and evil spirits/demons, and different passages present these figures in different ways. In some passages, one can observe a systematizing tendency. These pericopes incorporate the Prince of Mastema and evil spirits into an overarching understanding of harmful superhuman beings and situate them within Jubilees' teaching concerning Israel's unique status among the nations of the earth. According to these passages, the Prince of Mastema is the chief of the evil spirits, who mislead and afflict the nations. Israel, however, is protected from these spirits' deceptive and harmful influence.

Although the Prince of Mastema is leader of these spirits, the evil spirits themselves seem to be the main concern of these passages rather than their leader. Numerous passages in Jubilees address the threat that evil spirits pose to humankind and, potentially, to Israel. The Prince of Mastema appears only in a small number of these passages, where his significance derives primarily from his association with the evil spirits. Indeed, the Prince of Mastema is not mentioned at all in Jubilees until ch. 10, where he figures into the book's explanation for the existence of evil spirits. While the Prince of Mastema outranks evil spirits in the divine hierarchy, from a literary standpoint the Prince of Mastema plays more of a supporting role to the evil spirits.

The Danger of Deceptive Spirits

In many respects, the problems created by evil spirits in Jubilees resemble those attributed to spirits in the earlier Book of the Watchers. In other important ways, Jubilees expands the activity and importance of evil spirits from what they possess in earlier literature. As in the Book of the Watchers, evil spirits in Jubilees are responsible for physical maladies. In 10:3, for instance, Noah's children complain to him that the spirits/demons are blinding and killing his grandchildren. Also, like the Book of the Watchers, Jubilees credits evil spirits with misleading humans. Jubilees differs from the Book of the Watchers, however, in the prominence that Jubi-

spirit" (*daimonion ē pneuma ponēron*). It is not certain whether "demon or evil spirit" is a hendiadys in Tobit, referring to a single kind of harmful being, or indicates two different types of being, both of which may harm humans.

lees accords the spirits' deceptive activity. Just one verse in the Book of the Watchers mentions that the spirits bring destruction on humans and mislead them to worship demons (1 En. 19:1). Neither does this verse give any indication that the spirits' deceptive work constitutes a more significant problem for humans than the physical harm they cause. In Jubilees, conversely, it is the spirits' ability to mislead nations into error that poses their greatest threat to humankind. Jubilees addresses this activity of the spirits repeatedly and, as will be demonstrated below, at critical junctures in the narrative.

Jubilees also expands the scope of the spirits' delusion. In 1 En. 19:1, the spirits mislead humans only to worship false gods. In Jubilees, by contrast, spirits lead humans to worship false gods *and* to commit all sorts of other wrongdoing, especially to shed human blood (Jub. 7:27; 11:5). The attribution of human bloodshed to the influence of spirits makes sense, if one presumes an etiology of the spirits such as one finds in the Book of the Watchers, which claims that harmful spirits are the spiritual remnants of the violent giants (1 En. 15:8–16:1).[30] Early interpreters may have also found an exegetical basis for evil spirits' involvement in human bloodshed in Judg 9, where God sends an "evil spirit" between Abimelech and the people of Shechem that pits the two parties against each other in deadly conflict.[31]

Jubilees raises the issue of spiritual delusion in its very first chapter, where Moses implores God, "May a spirit of belial not rule [Israel] so as . . . to trap them away from every proper path so that they may be destroyed from your presence" (1:20).[32] Should Israel be led astray by a spirit of belial, they would run the risk of being destroyed. One next encounters these spirits/demons in the days just after the flood, when they are misleading Noah's descendants. Noah tells his children, "For I myself see that the demons have begun to lead you and your children astray; and now I fear regarding you that after I have died you will shed human blood on the earth and (that) you yourselves will be obliterated from the surface of the earth"

30. Jub. 10:5 identifies the spirits as the children of the watchers, but does not state specifically that the spirits are what remains of the slain giants.

31. Additional texts that could have contributed to an association of seductive spirits with violence include 1 Kgs 22, where a lying spirit leads Ahab and Israel to war with Aram, and Ps 106:37–38, where the worship of "demons" (who are identified with spirits in Jubilees) entails human sacrifice. Perhaps, also, interpreters blamed the "evil spirit" that tormented Saul for the king's violent aggression toward David (1 Sam 18:10–11; 19:9–10).

32. VanderKam has "the spirit of Belial" rather than "a spirit of belial."

(7:26–27). Noah worries, as does Moses, that spiritual delusion could have disastrous consequences.

The Prince of Mastema, Chief of the Deceptive Spirits

Jubilees 10 introduces the character of the Prince of Mastema and brings him to bear on Jubilees' doctrine of harmful spirits and their deceptive activity. In this passage, Noah learns that evil spirits are misleading, blinding, and killing his grandchildren. As in Jub. 7:27, the patriarch voices his fear that evil spirits will bring about the total obliteration of humanity. In his prayer for divine assistance, Noah compares the spiritual/demonic threat with the flood that nearly put an end to humankind. Noah asks God to intervene a second time in order to save his family.

> God of the spirits which are in all animate beings—you who have shown kindness to me, saved me and my sons from the flood waters, and did not make me perish as you did to the people (meant for) destruction—because your mercy for me has been large and your kindness to me has been great: may your mercy be lifted over the children of your children; and may the wicked spirits not rule them in order to destroy them from the earth. Now you bless me and my children so that we may increase, become numerous, and fill the earth. You know how your watchers, the fathers of these spirits, have acted during my lifetime. As for these spirits who have remained alive, imprison them and hold them captive in the place of judgment. May they not cause destruction among your servant's sons, my God, for they are savage and were created for the purpose of destroying. May they not rule the spirits of the living for you alone know their punishment; and may they not have power over the sons of the righteous from now and forevermore. (10:3–6)

If the evil spirits are able to continue their work of deception and death unchecked, Noah predicts, they will completely destroy his descendants from the earth. Therefore, Noah asks God to have the spirits incarcerated and to save his descendants and humanity once again from total annihilation.

There are several ambiguities and tensions in Noah's prayer for protection from the spirits. What is the relationship between the physical harm caused by the spirits and their deceptions? Is Noah worried that the spirits will kill his grandchildren, or that they will lead his grandchildren into sin for which God will then destroy them? It is possible that Noah is concerned that the spirits will lead his family into sin, which would render humankind vulnerable to other sorts of attacks by these punishing spirits, but this is not stated explicitly. Also, does Noah seek protection for all of humankind or for the righteous only? The prayer seems to concern all humankind, though the final part of v. 6 specifically mentions the "sons of the righteous."[33] Perhaps we have in this pericope what was originally a story about Noah procuring protection for humankind from the physical maladies caused by evil spirits, which story has been reworked into one about Noah securing protection specifically for the elect against spiritual deception, befitting the theological message of Jubilees.

Initially, in response to Noah's request to have the spirits bound, God orders the angels of the presence to imprison all the evil spirits. Mastema, however, objects to their incarceration.

> When Mastema, the leader of the spirits, came, he said: "Lord creator, leave some of them before me; let them listen to me and do everything that I tell them, because if none of them is left for me I shall not be able to exercise the authority of my will among mankind. For they are meant for (the purpose of) destroying and misleading before my punishment because the evil of mankind is great." (10:8)

The spirits who are about to be imprisoned, Mastema argues, are necessary for his work of punishing human wickedness. God must leave a sufficient number of spirits in Mastema's service so that they may inflict harm that is commensurate with humankind's sin. In the end, so that humankind will not be altogether destroyed, God has ninety percent of the spirits bound. God leaves ten percent of the spirits in the service of Mastema, however, for the purpose of punishing human wickedness (10:9, 11).

Mastema's request for God to leave some spirits free to serve him presumes, as do Job 1–2 and Zech 3, that the Satan, here identified as "Mastema,

33. The tension between a concern for all humankind and a concern for the righteous in particular may also be reflected in the textual tradition. In v. 3, VanderKam's text and translation (quoted above) follow those MSS that read "children of your children" (*Book of Jubilees*, 1:60; 2:58). Some copies, however, read "(children of) my children" (MSS 12, 35, and 58) or "children of your servant" (MSS 21, 39, and 48). VanderKam suggests that the "my/your" confusion may have taken place in the Greek interchange of μου and σου. The tension between concern for humanity in general and for the righteous in particular may have contributed to the confusion regarding whose children are in jeopardy in this verse.

the leader of the spirits," has been tasked by God with punishing wicked humans.[34] In other respects, this passage contains many new ideas that we have not yet encountered regarding the Satan figure. One new feature of the tradition is the association of the Satan and harmful spirits. Not only are spirits and the Satan for the first time in extant literature incorporated into a single system of thought, but a hierarchy of the superhuman realm is articulated, in which the spirits/demons are subordinate to the Prince of Mastema.

Another of Jubilees' departures from earlier traditions about the Satan figure, and one that relates to this figure's association with evil spirits, is its depiction of the Prince of Mastema as the deceiver of the nations. The role of evil spirits as deceivers of humankind is mentioned in the Book of the Watchers and is, as discussed above, expanded in Jubilees. By virtue of his association with evil spirits, the Prince of Mastema becomes the leader of these deceptive forces. The prince appears in this capacity most clearly in Jub. 11, which describes the time between Noah and Abraham as one in which people were led astray by evil spirits to worship idols and commit acts of violence. Jubilees explains, "Prince Mastema was exerting his power in effecting all these actions and, by means of the spirits, he was sending to those who were placed under his control (the ability) to commit every (kind of) error and sin and every (kind of) transgression; to corrupt, to destroy, and to shed blood on the earth" (11:5).[35]

While the notion of the Prince of Mastema as the chief deceiver of the nations is new, it is not altogether without precedent. According to 1 Chr

34. On the nature of the Satan in Zech 3 and Job 1-2, see the discussion in chs. 1-2. In the case of Zech 3, the Satan stands ready to punish the high priest Joshua for his iniquity. With regard to Job, although Job himself is innocent, the story presumes that the Satan's usual business was to punish evildoers.

35. VanderKam's translation of Jub. 11:5, quoted here, and that of Wintermute follow the majority of the Ethiopic MSS, which say that Prince Mastema sent the spirits "to those" (*la'əlla*) under his control (VanderKam, *Book of Jubilees*, 2:65; Wintermute, "Jubilees," *OTP* 2:78). Segal, *Book of Jubilees*, 181, however, follows MSS 21 and 58, which say that Prince Mastema sent the spirits "who" (*'əlla*) were under his control. According to the majority reading, those under the prince's authority are the humans to whom he sends the spirits. MSS 21 and 58, on the other hand, identify those under his authority as the evil spirits whom he sends to the humans. Support for the majority text is found in 10:8–14 and 15:31–32, where Mastema and/or his spirits are given authority over all the peoples of the world, except for the elect. As discussed above, Jub. 10:8–14 also speaks of Mastema having authority over the spirits, so the minority reading is not inconsistent with Jubilees' teaching elsewhere. Whatever version of 11:5 is the earlier, the Prince of Mastema in this passage is exercising his God-given authority in leading humanity astray by agency of the spirits who serve him.

21, a satan incites David to number the people, bringing guilt upon Israel, and strikes the nation with a plague as a consequence. The satan figure in Chronicles does not appear to be *the* Satan, but merely *a* satan. Nor does deception appear to be a regular part of this figure's work, but is only an activity in which he happens to engage on this particular occasion in order to bring divine judgment on Israel. In Jubilees, deception of the nations through the agency of evil spirits appears to be a regular and integral component of the Prince of Mastema's business. As chief of the evil spirits, this Satan figure leads the nations to worship idols and to shed blood.

Although the Prince of Mastema is identified as the leader of the evil spirits, there is a question as to whether he himself is one of them. Does the Prince of Mastema, according to Jubilees, belong to those spiritual beings created by God on the first day of creation (2:2), or is he among the illegitimate offspring of the watchers? What is potentially at stake in this question is whether Jubilees teaches that God designed evil into creation or, rather, that evil arose subsequent to creation and is not part of God's original design.

Jubilees does not address the origin of the Prince of Mastema explicitly, and the implicit evidence is ambiguous. The story of the binding of the spirits itself seems to assume that Mastema is not himself one of the evil spirits. Mastema's plea that some of these spirits be left before him so that he may do his work of punishing humanity implies that the prince himself is not among those who are in jeopardy of being imprisoned. Mastema is not worried that he will be bound with the spirits. This punisher is a functionary of God and has an assignment to carry out whether the spirits are imprisoned or not. His concern is only that he will be understaffed. On the other hand, Jubilees does not mention the Prince of Mastema among the angelic beings created by God on the first day (2:2). His absence from the creation account is conspicuous, given the important place he and his spirits occupy in Jubilees.[36] The first acknowledgment of the Prince of Mastema in Jubilees' history is in ch. 10, where he is associated with the watchers' children.

Some of the challenge in ascertaining the precise nature of the Prince of Mastema in Jubilees relates to the book's terminology for superhuman

36. Segal, *Book of Jubilees*, 178, says that it is reasonable to assume that the Prince of Mastema is implicitly included in the different types of angels created by God in Jub. 2:2. On the other hand, John J. Collins, "The Origin of Evil in Apocalyptic Literature," in *Seers, Sibyls and Sages in Hellenistic-Roman Judaism*, JSJSup 54 (Leiden: Brill, 1997), 290, says, "Mastema first appears in *Jub* 10, and is presumably one of the spirits of the giants."

beings, which is not consistent. The categories "angel" and "spirit" in Jubilees are not absolutely distinct.[37] The designation "satan" is used with reference to the Prince of Mastema (10:11) as well as, perhaps, to a class of harmful spirits (23:29). Jubilees is also inconsistent in its interpretation of the expression "sons of God" in earlier literature. According to Job 1–2, which Jubilees uses, the Satan is a member of this class of divine beings. The author of Jubilees may regard these "sons of God" as angels (cf. LXX Job 1:6; 2:1). Jubilees follows its Enochic sources in identifying the "sons of God" of Gen 6:1–4 as angelic watchers (Jub. 5:1; 7:21).[38] Jubilees 15:31–32, however, interprets the "sons of God" of Deut 32 in terms of the evil spirits, the offspring of angelic beings who lead the nations astray. If the Prince of Mastema is supposed to be one of the "sons of God" in Jubilees, even this would allow for different accounts of his origin.

Although the story of the binding of the spirits, a tradition that likely predates the composition of Jubilees, assumes that the satan figure is not himself one of the spirits, it is possible that the author of Jubilees believes that the Prince of Mastema is one of these evil spirits. The larger question of evil's origin in Jubilees I take up in the next chapter.

Evil Spirits and the Election of Israel

Evil spirits who mislead and harm humanity under the guidance of the Prince of Mastema are no trivial matter in Jubilees, but figure fundamentally into the theology and message of the book. According to Jubilees, on the seventh day of creation when God instituted the Sabbath, God at that time declared the divine intent to set Israel apart among the nations as a holy people (2:19–20). They were to be God's people, and God would be their God. Were Israel to fall prey to the seductive and deadly influence of evil spirits, however, the divine plan for Jacob's descendants would be jeopardized. For this reason, at several important points in the narrative Jubilees addresses the potential danger of evil spirits for Israel.

The network of relationships among Israel, God, the nations, and evil spirits is most clearly articulated in Jub. 15. This chapter of Jubilees corresponds to Gen 17, where God makes a covenant with Abram (changing

37. For the use of "spirit" and "angel" side by side, see Jub. 2:2; 15:32.

38. See also Dan 3:25–28, which uses "a son of the gods" (NRSV mg.) and "angel" interchangeably.

his name to Abraham) and Abraham circumcises all of the males in his household. Amid Jubilees' discussion of circumcision as a mandatory sign of Israel's special status before God, Jub. 15:31–32 provides further information regarding the difference between God's relationship with Israel and the Deity's relationship with other nations.

> For there are many nations and many peoples and all belong to [God]. He made spirits rule over all in order to lead them astray from following him. But over Israel he made no angel or spirit rule because he alone is their ruler. He will guard them and require them for himself from his angels, his spirits, and everyone, and all his powers so that he may guard them and bless them and so that they may be his and he theirs from now and forever.

According to these verses, God has subjected all of the nations of the world, except for Israel, to the deluding influence of evil spirits.

This passage merges Jubilees' teaching on "evil spirits" with the theology of Deut 32:8–9: "When the Most High apportioned the nations, when he divided humankind, he fixed the boundaries of the peoples according to the number of the sons of God; the Lord's own portion was his people, Jacob his allotted share."[39] According to Deuteronomy, the nations of the world have been allotted to certain divine beings called "sons of God." The notion of divine rulers of nations is found elsewhere in the Hebrew scriptures. In Ps 82, the "sons of the Most High," also referred to in this psalm as "gods" (*'ĕlōhîm*), govern the nations of the earth. In the later, apocalyptic book of Daniel, the nations of Persia, Greece, and Israel have superhuman princes who fight on behalf of their respective nations (Dan 10:13, 20, 21; 12:1). In Deut 32:8–9, the Most High assigns each nation to one of the sons of God, except for Israel, whom Yahweh governs directly.[40] It is not clear how the author of Jubilees would have assessed

39. This reading of Deut 32 follows the LXX and 4QDeut[j] rather than the MT. Depending on the version of Deut 32:8 one is reading, the boundaries of the peoples correspond to the number of the "sons of Israel" (MT, Samaritan Pentateuch, Targum, Vulgate, Peshitta), the number of the "sons of God" (LXX, 4QDeut[j]), or the number of the "sons of the angels of God" ($\text{LXX}^{\text{Alexandrinus, Vaticanus, Hexapla}}$). The reading of the LXX and 4QDeut[j], "the sons of God," explains the other variants, and scholarly consensus correctly regards it as the earliest reading.

40. See also Sir 17:17, which follows Deut 32 in teaching that God has assigned every nation a ruler except Israel.

the claims of Daniel, though the two works seem to be at odds in at least one respect. Both Jubilees and Daniel place representative superhuman beings over nations, but Daniel does not exempt Israel from this policy. Daniel says that Michael is Israel's prince (10:21; 12:1). Conversely, Jub. 15:31–32 states that, whereas the other nations fall under the dominion of lesser divine beings, God did not entrust Israel to any such angelic or spiritual delegate.[41]

Jubilees 15 interprets the "sons of God" of Deut 32 as "spirits," "angels," or "powers." It would be difficult to delineate Jubilees' taxonomy of the superhuman realm based on this text. Nevertheless, there can be little doubt that superhuman rulers of the nations to whom these verses refer are supposed to be (or at least to include) the same beings that Jubilees elsewhere calls "evil spirits" and "demons."[42] Their work of delusion and their jurisdiction, which is restricted to the gentile nations, confirm their identification with the spirits mentioned in other passages in Jubilees.

That Jub. 15:31–32 identifies the biblical "sons of God" with "angels" is consistent with other Jewish writings from the period. As we saw in the previous chapter, the Book of the Watchers understands the "sons of God" of Gen 6 as angelic beings called watchers.[43] In the present passage, which is indebted to Deut 32, the "sons of God" seem also to be identified with the spirits who are the offspring of the angelic watchers. The Hebrew *bənê 'ĕlōhîm* could have been interpreted by the author of this passage as "sons of angels." A reading preserved in some Greek manuscripts of Deut 32:8 makes this understanding of the verse explicit: "When the Most High apportioned the nations, as he divided the sons of Adam, he established the boundaries of the nations according to the number of the *sons of the angels*

41. Cf. also the allegorical Animal Apocalypse (1 En. 85–90), in which God entrusts Israel, represented by a flock of sheep, for a limited time to seventy superhuman beings, represented by shepherds (1 En. 89:59–90:19). Similarly, 4Q387 2 iii 4 and 4Q390 2 i 7 speak of God handing Israel over to "angels of hostilities" (*ml'ky hmśṭmwt*). See below, as well, on Jubilees' teaching concerning the angel of the presence, whose role in protecting God's people against the Prince of Mastema resembles that of Michael, who fights on behalf of Israel in Daniel (Jub. 17:17–18; 48:2–4).

42. Pascale, "Demonic Cosmic Powers of Destruction," 196, incorrectly infers, "Since no mention is made of Satan, Mastema, or Belial in Jub 15:31–32, it is doubtful that these spirits are to be regarded as evil spirits under the rule of the archdemon. Certainly there is no connection between the demonic offspring of the watchers in Jub 10:1–14 and these spirits or angels."

43. Similarly, see Jub. 5:1 and 7:21. See also Dan 3:25–28, which interchanges the designations "a son of the gods" (NRSV mg.) and "angel."

of God."[44] Both Jubilees and this Greek tradition hold that the nations are distributed among the children of angels. In Jubilees, the children of the angels are evil spirits/demons.[45]

The work of these spirits among the nations is that of leading people astray. Presumably they lead the nations under their control to commit idolatry, but bloodshed and other sorts of sin that Jubilees elsewhere attributes to spiritual delusion may be in mind here as well. Israel, conversely, is not to fall prey to these spirits. The children of Jacob are to worship God exclusively. All the nations of the earth belong to God, but the Creator has a unique, direct relationship with Israel. Thus Israel is not to be subject to the deceptions of evil spirits as are the other nations.

One consequence of Jubilees' incorporating Deut 32:8 into its discussion of evil spirits is that the God of Jubilees is given full responsibility for the deception that these spirits work among the nations. It was for this purpose that God appointed spirits over the nations. This passage says unequivocally, "[God] made spirits rule over all in order to lead them astray from following him" (Jub. 15:31).[46] While Jub. 15:31–32 very much aligns with other passages in Jubilees that teach that God has spared only Israel among the nations of the world from the spirits' deceptive control, the claim of this passage is more explicitly deterministic. God takes an active part in leading the nations astray. Elsewhere in the work, God is only to keep the spirits from deceiving Israel. The claim that God plays an active part in human sin bothered some early Jewish readers. As we will see in ch. 6, this view drew criticism from some who were more inclined to defend God against charges of complicity in wrongdoing and to attribute sin, instead, to the human will. To be fair, Jubilees is less interested in blaming God for the sins of the nations than in giving God credit for the preservation of a special people. In Jub. 15:31–32, however, these are presented as two sides of the same coin.

44. Emphasis mine. On the text of Deut 32:8, see n39 above.

45. We have already encountered the notion that the "demons" were the "gods" worshiped by the nations. See the discussions of *šēdîm* in Deut 32 and Ps 109 and of demons in 1 En. 19:1 in ch. 3.

46. According to Segal, *Book of Jubilees*, 229–45, Jub. 15:25–34 is one of those legal passages penned by Jubilees' redactor/composer. In Kugel's assessment, Jub. 15:31–32 belongs to one of those twenty-nine passages added by an interpolator ("On the Interpolations," 248–50). He argues that Jub. 15:25–34 was added to address certain issues pertaining to circumcision. On the whole, this text is quite consistent with others in Jubilees that speak of the deceptive influence of spirits.

The way that God accomplishes the divine plan of setting Israel apart from the other nations of the world in Jubilees is by providing the chosen people with divinely revealed literature that protects them from evil spirits. At three crucial moments in Jubilees' history (and prehistory) of God's people, an important figure asks God for assistance against harmful spirits on behalf of the chosen line. In each of these instances, God responds to the request by granting the elect access to divinely revealed literature. The first installment of this literature occurs just after the flood in response to Noah's request that God would protect his children and the children of the righteous from the harmful spirits. After God has ninety percent of the spirits bound, saving humanity from annihilation, God takes further steps to ensure the spiritual safety of the chosen line. God instructs the angel of the presence to reveal to Noah how one may further defend oneself against evil spirits. Noah records this information in a book, which he entrusts to his son Shem (10:10–14).[47] Similarly, upon his conversion from idolatry, Abram prays that God will not allow evil spirits to rule over him or his descendants. God responds by having the angel of the presence teach Abram the Hebrew language, which, Jubilees explains, had been lost since the tower of Babel incident. In this way, Abram acquires the ability to read the books of his ancestors (12:19–27). The final installment of this protective literature mentioned in Jubilees is the book of Jubilees itself. In the introduction to the work, Moses asks God not to allow a spirit of belial to rule over Israel. God responds by having the angel of the presence dictate the heavenly tablets to Moses, who records this revelation, producing the book of Jubilees (1:19–28).

The Satan and the Deception of the Nations

Deceptive spirits play important theological roles in the teaching of Jubilees. Harmful spirits serve to distinguish the chosen people of God from

47. That this protection is intended for the righteous elect and not for humankind in general is indicated in a number of ways. The reason for the revelation is that the spirits will not "fight fairly," i.e., they will not merely harm the wicked (10:10). That the revelation to Noah also included information about the spirits' "deceptions" (10:12) associates this revelation with Jubilees' teaching that God intends the nations to be deceived by spirits, but not Israel (e.g., 15:31–32), and with the other passages in Jubilees that present revelatory literature as the means by which the chosen people defends itself spiritually (1:19–28; 12:19–27). Finally, that Noah bequeaths the book he writes to Shem narrows the recipients of the revelation to the chosen line. Contra Segal, *Book of Jubilees*, 172–73.

the rest of humankind. They do this by leading all of the nations, except for the descendants of Jacob, into sin. In contrast, Israel has received divinely revealed written instruction that affords them protection from spiritual delusion.

The Prince of Mastema fits into this theological scheme as the chief of the evil spirits who deceive the nations. Although the Prince of Mastema outranks the spirits in the superhuman hierarchy, he is less important to the theology of Jubilees than are the spirits themselves. That Jubilees associates the Prince of Mastema with the harmful and deceptive spirits in this way, however, marks several important developments in the Satan tradition. From this point forward in the history of the tradition, it becomes commonplace for early Jewish texts to speak of the Satan as the leader of evil spiritual forces. Also, as a result of his association with deceptive spirits, the Prince of Mastema/the Satan himself becomes a deceiver of humankind, not merely a punisher or attacker. Additionally, Jubilees' depiction of the whole world except for the elect as under the deceptive control of the Satan and his spirits would find a home in the theology and literature of early Judaism and Christianity.

CHAPTER 5

The Prince of Mastema, Enemy of God's People

In the theology of Jubilees, evil spirits have an important function, demarcating Israel from the nations. These spirits rule over the nations, leading them into sin and destroying them. Israel is protected from these spirits by the Torah that God revealed to Moses. The Prince of Mastema's significance in this scheme is as the chief of those evil spirits who lead the world into sin and threaten to do the same with Israel. The Prince of Mastema is not especially important as an independent actor. He impinges on human existence only through the work of deceptive spirits over whom God has given him command.

A different understanding of the Prince of Mastema is found in other passages in Jubilees. In these passages, the prince acts alone, apart from the agency of evil spirits. His intentions, moreover, do not accord with God's plans for Israel, but are contrary to them. He creates problems for humans not as a deceiver and punisher, but simply attacks them in an effort to do them harm. These stories serve to account for the evils that befall individuals and, more importantly, those evils that threaten the nation of Israel, but in a way that maintains God's benevolence toward the chosen people. The Prince of Mastema, rather than God, is the one who threatens the well-being of God's people.

The Prince of Mastema Attempts to Harm God's People

Three stories in Jubilees depict the Prince of Mastema not as a deceiver or punisher, as did the passages discussed in the previous chapter, but as an unprovoked troubler of humankind. Two of these stories, Jubilees' version of the sacrifice of Isaac and Jubilees' retelling of Israel's exodus from Egypt, portray the Prince of Mastema as the enemy of Abraham's descendants in particular and even, in one instance, as the protector of Israel's enemies. In all three of these stories, the Prince of Mastema opposes or is opposed by God's people.

The Prince of Mastema Causes a Famine

In Jub. 11:11–24, the Prince of Mastema appears as a troubler of humans who is thwarted by a teenage Abram. According to this story (which is not found in Genesis), in the days of Terah, the Prince of Mastema induced a famine that impoverished humankind. When farmers would sow seed, the Prince of Mastema would send birds to devour the seed before it could be plowed into the earth, rendering the earth barren (11:11–13). The young Abram was gifted with a unique ability to keep the birds from eating the seed, a talent that kept him very busy during sowing season as farmers would frequently call upon him to assist them. Eventually, Abram invented a tool that allowed people to sow seed in such a way that it could not be eaten by birds (11:18–24). Thus Abram blocked the Prince of Mastema's attempt to deprive humans of agricultural produce.

This story involving the Prince of Mastema is unique in Jubilees. The prince does not lead the nations astray through the agency of evil spirits, as he does in the passages discussed in the previous chapter. Nor does the Prince of Mastema attack God's people in this story, as he does in the passages to be discussed below. The Prince of Mastema's hostility in this pericope appears to be directed at humankind in general, not specifically at Abram's family. Nevertheless, that it is Abram who frustrates the prince's hostile plan anticipates the coming conflicts between the Prince of Mastema and Abram's descendants.

The Prince of Mastema Tests Abraham

In Jubilees' account of the binding of Isaac, the Prince of Mastema appears specifically as the enemy of God's people.[1] Jubilees' version of Abraham's

1. Michael Segal, *The Book of Jubilees: Rewritten Bible, Redaction, Ideology and Theology*, JSJSup 117 (Leiden: Brill, 2007), 189–202, distinguishes between the rewritten source for the

ordeal, which draws from the story of Job, opens as Abraham's faithfulness is lauded in heaven (Jub. 17:15; cf. Job 1:8; 2:3).[2] The Prince of Mastema, however, devises a test to ascertain the extent of Abraham's devotion: "Abraham does indeed love his son Isaac and finds him more pleasing than anyone else. Tell him to offer him as a sacrifice on an altar. Then you will see whether he performs this order and will know whether he is faithful in everything through which you test him" (Jub. 17:16; cf. Job 1:9–11; 2:4–5).[3]

Even though God does not doubt Abraham's devotion, God assents to the satanic antagonist's request and orders Abraham to offer Isaac as a sacrifice. As in the Genesis story, Abraham obediently goes about preparing to offer his son. He travels to the site of the sacrifice, builds an altar, binds Isaac, and places him on the altar. At this point in the story, which an angel of the presence narrates to Moses, the angel speaks autobiographically, "Then I stood in front of [Abraham] and in front of the prince of Mastema" (Jub. 18:9). The image of the angel of the presence standing before

---

Akedah in Jub. 17:15–18:17 and the work of the redactor in 18:18–19. James Kugel, "On the Interpolations in the *Book of Jubilees*," *RevQ* 24.2 (2009): 233–36, identifies 18:18–19 as the work of the interpolator, but attributes 17:15–18:17 to Jubilees' author. On the composition of Jubilees, see the discussion in the previous chapter.

2. Jacques van Ruiten ("Abraham, Job and the Book of *Jubilees*: The Intertextual Relationship of Genesis 22:1–19, Job 1–2:13 and *Jubilees* 17:15–18:19," in *The Sacrifice of Isaac: The Aqedah (Genesis 22) and Its Interpretations*, ed. Ed Noort and Eibert Tigchelaar, TBN 4 [Leiden: Brill, 2002], 83–85; *Abraham in the Book of Jubilees: The Rewriting of Genesis 11:26–25:10 in the Book of* Jubilees *11:14–23:8*, JSJSup 161 [Leiden: Brill, 2012], 212–14) contests the scholarly consensus that Jub. 17 borrows from the book of Job in its retelling of the story of Abraham's test. According to van Ruiten, though Jub. 17 shares many elements with Job's prologue, there are also several differences between the two stories. For example, Jubilees uses the language of "testing" to describe the event, as does Gen 22, whereas the language of "testing" does not appear in Job's prologue. Similarly, in Jubilees, as in the Genesis story, God conducts the test of Abraham, whereas in Job, God delegates this work to the Satan. That Jubilees retains certain elements of Gen 22, however, is what one should expect in a retelling of Gen 22; this does not mean that the author cannot have also made use of the story of Job. The same may be said of other differences between Jub. 17 and Job 1–2. One should expect the author of a rewritten tale to incorporate into his rewriting elements from the base story (e.g., Gen 22) and from other texts or traditions (e.g., Job 1–2 and Zech 3), as well as other elements reflecting the author's purpose for the retelling (e.g., information concerning the date of the event).

3. A similar interpretation of the Akedah along the lines of Job 1–2 and Zech 3 that also mentions "the Prince of the Mastema" appears in the work from Qumran known as 4QPseudo-Jubilees (4Q225 2 i–ii). For the text and a translation of this fragmentary document, see J. C. VanderKam and J. T. Milik, "Jubilees," in *Qumran Cave 4, VIII: Parabiblical Texts, Part 1*, by Harold Attridge et al., DJD 13 (Oxford: Clarendon, 1994), 141–75.

Abraham and the Prince of Mastema draws on Zech 3:1, where Joshua, with the Satan at his right, stands before the angel of Yahweh. Just as the angel of Yahweh intervenes on behalf of Joshua in Zech 3, so the angel of the presence intervenes in Jubilees and prevents Abraham from sacrificing his son (Jub. 18:9–11). Perhaps the shaming of the Prince of Mastema in 18:12 corresponds to the rebuke of the Satan in Zech 3:2.

In Jubilees' version of the Akedah, the Prince of Mastema is a participant in God's heavenly court. He does not, however, merely take orders from God. He is capable of independent thought and action, and his contrariness is integral to the story. The Prince of Mastema convinces God to test Abraham, even though God had already done so more than adequately to be confident of the quality of Abraham's piety.[4]

> Now the Lord was aware that Abraham was faithful in every difficulty which he had told him. For he had tested him through his land and the famine; he had tested him through the wealth of kings; he had tested him again through his wife when she was taken forcibly, and through circumcision; and he had tested him through Ishmael and his servant girl Hagar when he sent them away. In everything in which he tested him he was found faithful. He himself did not grow impatient, nor was he slow to act; for he was faithful and one who loved the Lord. (Jub. 17:17–18)

The test that the Prince of Mastema devises for Abraham is entirely unnecessary. He convinces God to examine Abraham even though, as Jubilees makes very clear, the patriarch had already proven his faithfulness repeatedly. The idea that the Prince of Mastema might launch an attack on someone that is completely without cause is borrowed from Job's prologue, where the Satan incites God against Job for no reason (Job 2:3). This passage differs from Job, however, in that the Satan's proposal in Job at least has the merit of being based on the fact that Job's integrity was as of yet untested by adversity. Abraham, according to Jubilees, has already proven his steadfast loyalty by being obedient in a number of difficult circumstances.

An editor has supplemented the story of Abraham's test, much as the editor supplemented the story of Job's test, adding the Satan to it as

4. Cf. b. Sanh. 89b, where Satan incites God to test Abraham, and LAB 32:1–2, where it is the angelic hosts' jealousy that provokes God's command for Abraham to sacrifice his son.

the ultimate source of the difficulty that befalls the faithful. While God ordered Abraham to sacrifice Isaac, according to Jubilees' retelling of the events, it was actually the Prince of Mastema who was behind the command for Abraham to kill his son. One purpose of this version of Isaac's near sacrifice is to remove any suspicion that God might harm the elect without provocation and to present the Prince of Mastema instead as the superhuman individual behind the chosen people's undeserved troubles.[5] According to Jubilees, it is the Prince of Mastema, not God, who would have Isaac killed. Indeed, Jubilees gives no indication that the Prince of Mastema intends to stop Abraham from sacrificing his son. If the malevolent prince has his way, we are left to assume, the test will run its full course, Abraham will once again prove faithful, and Isaac will be dead. Fortunately for Abraham, Isaac, and their descendants, the angel of the presence intervenes just in time to save Isaac from the Prince of Mastema's malicious plot.

Some interpreters of Jubilees have suggested that another aim of this passage is to assert God's omniscience.[6] The doctrine of God's comprehensive knowledge or omniscience, at least as classically defined, however, does not seem to be at stake. The reason that the test is unnecessary is not that God knows all things by virtue of divine omniscience, but that Abraham had already been tested sufficiently to demonstrate his unswerving loyalty. Jubilees' version of the story makes clear, nonetheless, that there is no deficiency in God's ability to assess Abraham's character and no malevolence on God's part that brings Isaac so near to death. Rather, it is the Prince of Mastema who puts the fate of God's people at risk.

5. Jubilees even goes beyond Job in an effort to exculpate God. Unlike the story of Job, where it is God who broaches the topic of Job with the Satan (Job 1:8; 2:3), Jubilees says that unspecified voices in heaven praised Abraham's faithfulness. It is in response to these voices, rather than to an inquiry by God, that the Prince of Mastema proposes to test Abraham. This alteration to the tradition may stem in part from an interpretation of Gen 22:1, which says, "After these things/words [*wayyəhî 'aḥar haddəbārîm hā'ēllê*] God tested Abraham." The effect of this change, however, is to diminish the Deity's involvement in the events that led to Abraham's test.

6. Segal, *Book of Jubilees*, 189–91. After Abraham has proven himself faithful in the Gen 22 account, the (angel of the) Lord says, "now I know that you fear God" (22:12). According to Segal, the God of Jubilees is not one who must test humans in order to ascertain their faithfulness, but knows all things by virtue of the Deity's omniscience. See also van Ruiten, "Abraham, Job," 71.

The Prince of Mastema Assists the Egyptians

The Prince of Mastema is portrayed very similarly as the leading antagonist in Jubilees' exodus account.[7] The Prince of Mastema makes his first appearance in this narrative in the retelling of Exod 4:24. In Exod 4, Moses begins his journey from Midian to Egypt, where God has instructed him to demand the Israelites' release from Pharaoh. On his way to Egypt, an event transpires, the details of which are obscure. It appears that Moses encounters Yahweh, who inexplicably seeks to take Moses's life (4:24). God stops short of killing Moses, however, when Moses's wife Zipporah circumcises their son and touches the circumcised foreskin to Moses's feet (4:25–26). Interpreters, ancient and modern alike, have found it perplexing that God would seek to take the life of Moses, whom God had just commissioned to deliver the Israelites from bondage.[8] Among ancient attempts to deal with this enigmatic text, the LXX clarifies the identity of the one who seeks Moses's life. It is not God who tries to kill Moses, but an "angel of the Lord."

In Jubilees, such an attack on the life of God's servant was the work not of the Deity or of one of the angels of the presence, but of the Prince of Mastema. The angel of the presence who speaks with Moses on Sinai reminds him,

> You know who spoke to you at Mt. Sinai and what the prince of Mastema wanted to do to you while you were returning to Egypt—on the way at the shady fir tree. Did he not wish with all his strength to kill you and to save the Egyptians from your power because he saw that you were sent to carry out punishment and revenge on the Egyptians? I rescued you from his power. (Jub. 48:2–4)

Once again the Prince of Mastema tries to harm God's people, but the angel of the presence steps in on behalf of Moses and Israel. Although the

7. Segal, *Book of Jubilees*, 203–28, attributes the exodus story of Jub. 48 to a rewritten source, but its legal interpretation in Jub. 49 to Jubilees' redactor. Kugel, "On the Interpolations," 254–57, credits 49:2–17, 22–23 to the interpolator, but the rest of the exodus material to Jubilees' author.

8. On the interpretation of Exod 4:24–26, see the discussions and bibliographies of Brevard S. Childs, *Exodus: A Commentary*, OTL (London: SCM, 1974), 95–101; John I. Durham, *Exodus*, WBC 3 (Waco, TX: Word, 1987), 56–59; William H. C. Propp, *Exodus 1–18: A New Translation with Introduction and Commentary*, AB 2 (New York: Doubleday, 1999), 218–20, 233–38.

text is silent on the point of whether God authorizes the attack, it is clear that it is not God who intends to kill Moses; the Prince of Mastema does. This attempt on Moses's life is part of an effort on the prince's part to protect the Egyptians, Israel's enemy. As with Abraham's test, the angel of the presence steps in to defend the chosen people from the hostile prince's attacks. The irony of this pericope within the context of the book of Jubilees is that, according to Jub. 10:1–13, the Prince of Mastema is supposed to be God's agent of punishment, as is the Satan of earlier tradition. In Jub. 48, by contrast, the Prince of Mastema tries to kill Moses in order to prevent him from bringing divine punishment upon the Egyptians.

The Prince of Mastema comes to the aid of Egypt a second time when Moses arrives there. Moses performs miraculous signs in order to convince Pharaoh to release the Israelites. In response, the Prince of Mastema enables the Egyptian magicians to match Moses sign for sign (48:9). As we have come to expect, however, the angels of the presence come to Israel's aid. In this case, the angels limit the Egyptian magicians' ability to compete with Moses (48:9–10). When, after a number of disastrous plagues, Pharaoh finally permits the Israelites to leave Egypt, the Prince of Mastema rouses the Egyptians so that the Egyptian army pursues the Israelites. As before, the angel of the presence comes to Israel's rescue and stands between the Israelites and the Egyptian army (48:13).[9] God then makes a way for the Israelites to cross the sea as on dry ground and throws the Egyptians into the sea.

The book of Exodus answers the question of why the Egyptians would be so emboldened as to pursue Israel, even after suffering powerful plagues at the hand of Moses and Israel's God. According to Exodus, God hardens the Egyptians' hearts so that they will pursue the Israelites (Exod 14:4, 8, 17). In Jubilees, however, it is the Prince of Mastema who hardens the hearts of Pharaoh and the Egyptians (Jub. 48:12, 17),[10] though this does not appear to be an attempt to defend God against charges of causing someone to sin.[11] In the book of Exodus, God hardens the Egyptians and then

9. The role of the angel(s) of the presence in the exodus story is probably based in part on Isa 63:9. Isa 63 speaks of the gracious acts of God toward Israel and their deliverance from Egypt in particular. The *qere* of v. 9 says that an angel of the presence saved the people (*ûmal'ak pānāyw hôšî'ām*). The *ketiv* of this verse, which is followed by the LXX, says just the opposite, that no angel saved Israel, but that God's very presence accomplished this.

10. Cf. T. Jos. 20:2, which says that "Belial" was with the Egyptians at the time of the exodus.

11. Segal, *Book of Jubilees*, 218, assumes that both Mastema's attack on Moses and Mas-

punishes them for the actions to which this hardening gives rise. Nothing in the account of Jubilees, however, suggests that this seeming injustice troubled the author of this retelling. Jubilees 48:17 even says that it was also God who hardened the Egyptians' hearts so that they would be thrown into the sea.[12] Jubilees reveals little concern to dissociate God from human sin, but Jubilees retells the story in a way that avoids the implication that God is responsible for Israel's troubles. The Prince of Mastema's activity in this story is similar to his testing of Abraham, his attempt on Moses's life, and his empowering of the Egyptian magicians. The Prince of Mastema is the enemy of God's people. He, not God, is behind the threats to Israel's well-being. Accordingly, Egyptian hostility toward Israel is the work of this prince.

Jubilees 48:15–19 explains more fully the Prince of Mastema's activity, and inactivity, in the events surrounding Israel's exodus from Egypt.

> On the fourteenth day, the fifteenth, the sixteenth, the seventeenth, and the eighteenth the Prince of Mastema was bound and locked up behind the Israelites so that he could not accuse them. On the nineteenth day we released them so that they could help the Egyptians and pursue the Israelites. He stiffened their resolve and made them stubborn. They were made stubborn by the Lord our God so that he could strike the Egyptians and throw them into the sea. (48:15–17)[13]

The reason that the Israelites enjoyed the Egyptians' favor just long enough to pack their belongings and get out of Egypt is that for five days the Prince of Mastema was bound and unable to cause trouble for the Israelites. During these days, the wicked prince could not harden the hearts of the Egyptians. According to 48:18–19, with the Prince of Mastema incapacitated, the Israelites were able to plunder the Egyptians. When the Israelites asked the Egyptians for clothing and for utensils of silver, gold, and bronze,

---

tema's hardening of the Egyptians' hearts "defend the notion that God is completely good." The problem addressed in these stories is not God's absolute goodness, however, but God's goodness toward Israel. For this reason, Jub. 48:17 can say that God hardened the Egyptians' hearts so that they would be thrown into the sea.

12. Jub. 48:14 may also attribute this act to God. See, however, n15 below.

13. As in the case of Jub. 1:20, Eth. *'astawādaya,* "accuse," in this passage probably does not accurately convey the sense of the original Hebrew. On the translation of this verse and the nature of the Prince of Mastema's activity, see the discussion below concerning whether the Prince of Mastema is an "accuser" in Jubilees.

the Egyptians gladly handed these goods over to them. Exodus 12:35–36 says that the Egyptians' generosity was a result of the Lord making them favorably disposed toward the people of Israel. In Jubilees, God brings about this change of attitude on the part of the Egyptians by binding the Prince of Mastema, who up to this point had been hardening the Egyptians' hearts. The Egyptians' good favor, however, is short-lived. After five days, the angels release the Prince of Mastema, who again hardens the Egyptians' hearts and incites them to attack Israel.[14]

Jubilees' exodus account depicts an interesting dynamic in the relationship between God and the Prince of Mastema. As elsewhere in Jubilees, God is clearly the superior of the two. The Prince of Mastema in this story, however, is no mere functionary of the Deity, obediently executing a duty that God has assigned him. He has an agenda of his own that is contrary to God's: to harm God's people by assisting Egypt against them. God, in contrast, has Israel's interest in mind and intends to punish the Egyptians. Despite this independence on the part of the Prince of Mastema, ultimately he unwittingly serves God's purpose and accomplishes the will of the Deity. God has the prince bound so that he will not oppose the Israelites and has him released so that the Egyptian army will pursue them and be thrown into the sea. For this reason, 48:17 can say both that "[the Prince of Mastema] stiffened their resolve and made them stubborn" and that "they were made stubborn by the Lord our God so that he could strike

14. According to most of the Ethiopic MSS, in 48:16, after the Prince of Mastema has been bound for five days, the angels "released *them* so that *they* could help the Egyptians pursue the Israelites" (italics mine). Although the passage speaks of the Prince of Mastema alone being bound and hardening the Egyptians (48:15, 17), the Ethiopic witnesses overwhelmingly support the reading that has more than one individual being released. Two different explanations have been suggested for this incongruity. The first, given by Klaus Berger and James VanderKam, is that the plural refers to the spirits under Mastema's control (Klaus Berger, *Das Buch der Jubiläen*, in vol. 3 of *Unterweisung in erzählender Form*, JSHRZ 2 [Gütersloh: Gütersloher Verlagshaus Gerd Mohn, 1981], 545; James C. VanderKam, *The Book of Jubilees*, 2 vols., CSCO 510–511 [Leuven: Peeters, 1989], 2:314). Cf. the association of these spirits with "Mastema" in 10:8–11 and 11:5. The second, offered by Moshe Goldmann, Michael Segal, and Betsy Halpern-Amaru, is that the passage originally spoke of the Prince of Mastema alone being released, but that it was either mistakenly altered or modified intentionally in order to bring this passage into line with those that associate the spirits with Mastema (Moshe Goldmann, "The Book of Jubilees," in *The Apocryphal Books* [in Hebrew], ed. Abraham Kahana, 2 vols. [Tel Aviv: Masada, 1956], 1:310; Segal, *Book of Jubilees*, 219; Halpern-Amaru, *The Perspective from Mt. Sinai: The Book of Jubilees and Exodus*, JAJSup 21 [Göttingen: Vandenhoeck & Ruprecht, 2015], 77).

the Egyptians and throw them into the sea."[15] The relationship between God and the Prince of Mastema is such that the actions of the Egyptians can be attributed both to the work of God and to the work of the Prince of Mastema. The intentions of the Prince of Mastema and those of God are at odds, but ultimately God manipulates the prince in order to bring about good for Israel. Jubilees simultaneously teaches that it is the Prince of Mastema who is behind attacks on the elect and that God manipulates this prince for the good of the elect. At the end of the story, the Prince of Mastema is shamed, as he was when he attempted to have Abraham sacrifice Isaac (48:12; cf. 18:12).

Two Perspectives on the Prince of Mastema

Jubilees depicts the Prince of Mastema in two different ways. First, in some passages the prince leads the nations of the world astray through the agency of evil spirits (Jub. 10:1–14; 11:5). Second, in other stories the Prince of Mastema is simply out to harm God's people (17:15–18:16; 48). Most importantly, these two groups of texts portray the relationship between the activity of the Prince of Mastema and the purposes of God very differently. In one set of texts, the Prince of Mastema through the agency of harmful spirits serves God's purpose of leading all of the nations except Israel astray. In the other, the Prince of Mastema opposes God's plan for Israel.

This is not to say that the two portrayals of the Prince of Mastema are completely different or are incompatible. Indeed, they have some im-

15. Segal, *Book of Jubilees*, 218–22, regards the statements in 48:17 that the Prince of Mastema hardened the Egyptians' hearts, on the one hand, and that God hardened them, on the other, to be a "clear contradiction." He suggests that the explanation of the Egyptians' hardening as the work of the Deity is a later interpolation. That the angels release the Prince of Mastema (*or* his spirits) for this very purpose (48:16), however, demonstrates the Deity's involvement in the Egyptians' hardening. Jub. 48:14 may also credit God with bringing the Egyptians out after the Israelites: "All of the people whom he brought out to pursue the Israelites the Lord our God threw into the sea." The subject of the verb "brought out" in the first half of this sentence is not explicit. It would be natural to infer that God is the implied subject of the verb, since the Deity appears most immediately in the context of this statement. On the basis of the broader context of the narrative, however, Segal identifies the subject as the Prince of Mastema. It is possible that the statement in 48:17 that God hardened the Egyptians is an interpolation, but the tension between this statement and others in the passage is not so great as to require this conclusion.

portant commonalities that probably account for the inclusion of both traditions in the book of Jubilees. In both groups of texts, the Prince of Mastema is associated with the nations. In both groups of texts, the Prince of Mastema also threatens to harm the elect, who are protected by God. In these general respects, one can speak of unity and coherence in Jubilees' depiction of the Prince of Mastema.

Nevertheless, the Mastema material in Jubilees exhibits significant diversity as well. Although the Prince of Mastema is associated with the nations in both sets of passages, his relationship to the nations is portrayed differently in them. In one case, the Prince of Mastema is the deceiver and punisher of the nations. In the other, he is Egypt's protector. Although the Prince of Mastema threatens to harm the elect in both groups of texts, he goes about this in very different ways. In one case, he threatens to mislead Israel from following God. In the other, he is simply out to harm Israel and to protect Israel's enemies. And, while God protects the elect from the Prince of Mastema's attacks in both groups of texts, this protection takes quite different forms. In one case, Israel's defense comes in the form of divinely revealed literature that the people must observe. In the other, angels of the presence directly hinder the Prince of Mastema.

Also, harmful spirits figure very differently into these two portrayals of the Prince of Mastema. In one group of texts, the Prince of Mastema deceives humankind through the agency of these spirits. In the other, the Prince of Mastema acts independently. Interestingly, in Jubilees' account of the Passover, "all the forces of Mastema [or 'hostility'] were sent to kill every first-born in the land of Egypt" (49:2).[16] Recall that, according to Jub. 10, harmful spiritual beings are to serve the Prince of Mastema, afflicting and killing wicked humans. In Jubilees' exodus story, in contrast, the Prince of Mastema is trying to protect Egypt from God's judgment and to harm Israel. The forces of Mastema/hostility are sent, presumably by God, to kill the Egyptians, frustrating the efforts of the Prince of Mastema. It is possible that the "forces of Mastema/hostility" who punish the Egyptians in Jub. 49:2 are not to be identified with the "spirits/demons"

16. One should understand this passage in the context of various traditions with regard to exactly who killed the firstborn of Egypt. While some statements in the book of Exodus say simply that Yahweh killed them (e.g., Exod 12:23a), Exod 12:23b attributes this activity to "the destroyer" (*hammašḥît*), who is sent by Yahweh. Ps 78:49 says that God let loose on the Egyptians "a company of harmful angels" (*mišlaḥat mal'ăkê rā'îm*). With regard to the composition of Jub. 49:2, Segal, *Book of Jubilees*, 223–28, attributes this verse to Jubilees' redactor. Kugel, "On the Interpolations," 217–18, argues that this verse is an interpolation.

who are supposed to serve as agents of divine punishment and are said to be under the leadership of the Prince of Mastema in other passages in Jubilees. Whether these passages speak of the same harmful beings or not, it is apparent that diverse traditions regarding the Prince of Mastema, agents of divine punishment, the relationships of these beings to one another, and their relationship to God's purposes are present in Jubilees.

Primarily, these two groups of texts portray the relationship between the Prince of Mastema's activity and God's purposes differently. In the stories in Jubilees where the Prince of Mastema misleads the nations through the agency of evil spirits, his activity is in accordance with the purposes of God. In these texts, he punishes the wicked and misleads those nations whom God has destined for religious delusion (see Jub. 15:31–32). In Jubilees' version of the exodus and of Isaac's binding, on the other hand, the Prince of Mastema's actions are at odds with God's plan for Israel. At best, the prince in these texts is manipulated by God so that he unwittingly accomplishes God's purpose.

Both of these perspectives on the Prince of Mastema have their basis in the earlier biblical literature, in which the Satan is supposed to be a functionary of God who is in some instances at odds with God's benevolent purposes (Zech 3; Job 1–2). Some of the early narrative traditions regarding this figure, those to which Jubilees was the heir, apparently dealt with this complexity in different ways. Some likely portrayed the Prince of Mastema primarily in terms of his role as God's agent of punishment, dealing with the wicked in ways that befit their wickedness. Others, however, elaborated on the contrast between the Satan's malevolence and the Deity's benevolence toward the righteous, depicting the Prince of Mastema as a more nefarious character who is out to harm God's people. Jubilees incorporates both of these perspectives into its story.

The Prince of Mastema as "Accuser"

The belief that the Satan was an "accuser" is one that developed over time, not one that was part of the Satan tradition from its inception. Zechariah 3 portrays the Satan as an executioner, rather than a prosecutor. The book of Job also regards the Satan as an executioner or attacker, though as one who may also incite God to harm the righteous. Three passages in Jubilees are pertinent to the questions of when and how the Satan came to be regarded as an accuser. Two of these passages, at least in the Ethiopic text, refer to the Prince of Mastema or a related figure accusing Israel. The third passage speaks of the Prince of Mastema persuading God to test Abraham as God tested Job.

Jubilees 48:15–19 relates that the angels of the presence bound the Prince of Mastema for five days so that Israel could plunder the Egyptians and depart from Egypt. According to the Ethiopic translation of this passage, the angels' purpose for binding the Prince of Mastema was to prevent him from "accusing" (Eth. *'astawādaya*) Israel during those particular days. This statement seems to presuppose the belief that one responsibility of the Prince of Mastema among the heavenly host was to serve as an accuser or a prosecuting attorney of sorts in the heavenly courtroom. Moses's prayer in Jub. 1:20 that "the spirit of Belial" would not be allowed to "bring charges against" (*'astawādaya*) Israel seems to assume that a spirit of belial could serve in a similar capacity.

Since the Ethiopic text of Jubilees is a translation of a translation, however, one cannot take for granted that such an understanding of the Prince of Mastema and his spirits was found in the original Hebrew of Jubilees. Indeed, upon closer examination, certain aspects of the text lead one to suspect that the second-century BCE Hebrew work did not depict the Prince of Mastema or his spirits as figures whose responsibilities included the accusation of sinners.

First, behind Eth. *'astawādaya*, "accuse," is very probably the Hebrew verb *śāṭan*. According to Wolf Leslau, *'astawādaya* has a more literal meaning of "to throw something against someone."[17] This meaning resembles that of Gk. *endiaballō*, which in the LXX translates Heb. *śāṭan*. Indeed, a survey of the Ethiopic OT reveals that in five of the six instances of *endiaballō* in the LXX, this word is translated into Ethiopic by the verb *'astawādaya*. These also correspond to the five instances in which *endiaballō* translates the verb *śāṭan*.[18] The use of this particular Ethiopic word indicates that the Hebrew of Jubilees probably contained the verb *śāṭan*.

17. Wolf Leslau, *Comparative Dictionary of Ge'ez* (Wiesbaden: Harrassowitz, 1991), 605, defines *'astawādaya* as follows: "accuse (from 'throw something against someone'), make accusations, make false charges, slander, abuse, calumniate." The G stem of the word is *wadaya*, which Leslau defines as "put, put in, add, put on (adornments), put under, lay, place, set, throw, cast."

18. The Gk. *endiaballō* appears in the place of the MT's *śāṭān* in Num 22:22. It translates the verb *śāṭan* in Ps 37:21 (MT 38:21); 70:13 (MT 71:13); Ps 108:4, 20, 29 (MT 109:4, 20, 29). For the Ethiopic text of the OT, I consulted Hiob Ludolf, ed., *Psalterium Davidis Aethiopice et Latine* (Frankfurt: Zunner, 1701).

When one considers that the two passages in which these words occur speak either of the Satan or of a related figure, it is quite likely that it was the verb *śāṭan* that appeared in the Hebrew. As argued in earlier chapters, this Hebrew verb typically, if not exclusively, denotes physical attack and never clearly refers to accusation.

Furthermore, the contexts of these statements in Jubilees portray the Prince of Mastema and the spirit of belial as attackers rather than as accusers. This is most obvious in Jub. 48. In this retelling of the exodus story, the Prince of Mastema tries to kill Moses on his way to Egypt. The Prince of Mastema is bound for five days while Israel departs from Egypt. Once he is released, he does not rush immediately into God's heavenly courtroom to bring charges against them, but stirs up the Egyptians to attack Israel militarily. The reason that the Prince of Mastema is bound is so that he will not attack Israel as they begin their departure from Egypt. As soon as he is released, he resumes his hostile activity, leading the Egyptians to launch a military attack on Israel.[19]

Similarly, although Moses's request for protection from a "spirit of belial" in Jub. 1:20 appears within the context of a prayer rather than a narrative, this prayer also contains a clue as to the nature of this spirit's activity. Moses's request may be broken into parallel lines as follows:

> May the spirit of Belial not rule them
> so as to bring charges against [or 'attack'] them before you
> and to trap them away from every proper path
> so that they may be destroyed from your presence.

19. Assuming that the Ethiopic of Jub. 48:18 accurately conveys the sense of the Hebrew, Miryam T. Brand, *Evil Within and Without: The Source of Sin and Its Nature as Portrayed in Second Temple Literature*, JAJSup 9 (Göttingen: Vandenhoeck & Ruprecht, 2013), 185n60, attempts to account for the peculiar reference to accusation in the context of Jubilees' exodus story. She speculates that, according to Jubilees, the Israelites duplicitously acquired goods from the Egyptians, pretending only to borrow them. Therefore, it would have been necessary for the Prince of Mastema to be bound so that he would not accuse the Israelites of this crime before God. There is nothing in Jubilees' exodus account, however, that suggests that the Israelites' request was duplicitous or sinful. On the contrary, Jubilees portrays the plundering of the Egyptians as justifiable recompense for Israel's treatment by the Egyptians (Jub. 48:18–19). It was not an act of injustice that the angels of the presence arranged for God to overlook. In addition, once the Prince of Mastema is released, he does not seize the opportunity to accuse the Israelites of any crime before God, but leads the Egyptians to attack them. It was in order to postpone this sort of attack that the angels of the presence temporarily confined the Prince of Mastema.

Arranged in this manner, the spirit's ruling Israel in the first line corresponds to the spirit's leading them astray in the third line. The activity of the spirit in question, which is referred to in the second line, corresponds to the people being destroyed from before God in the fourth line. Moses prays that such a spirit would not be allowed to wield its deceptive influence over Israel and, as a result, to attack and destroy them. That Moses would be concerned with spiritual deception that leads to destruction fits well Jubilees' understanding of evil spirits and the threat they pose. Recall Noah's prayer for his children: "may the wicked spirits not rule them in order to destroy them from the earth" (10:3). Were a spirit to mislead Israel, they would become vulnerable to attack and destruction by the spirit. It is the threat of attack, not accusation, by a spirit of belial that prompts Moses's prayer in Jub. 1:20.[20]

Although Jubilees does not portray the Prince of Mastema or any of his associates as superhuman prosecutors of sinners, it may offer one insight into how the Satan came to be regarded as a heavenly accuser. As discussed above, Jubilees' rewritten account of the binding of Isaac incorporates elements from the Job story (Jub. 17:15–18:6). In this version of the story, the Prince of Mastema suggests that God should command Abraham to kill his son as a test of Abraham's allegiance. Using Job's situation as a paradigm, Jubilees tells of an instance in which the Prince of Mastema calls the resolve of a faithful individual into question, resulting in hostility from God.

Retelling the story in this fashion, Jubilees does not presume that the Prince of Mastema is a prosecutor of sinners. The Prince of Mastema does not accuse Abraham of having committed any sin. Nor does the prince necessarily even allege that Abraham would sin if tested, as the Satan alleges of Job (Job 1:11; 2:5). The prince simply contends that Abraham loves no one more than he loves his son and that only by commanding Abraham to sacrifice Isaac will God truly ascertain whether Abraham is faithful to God in everything (Jub. 17:16). Accordingly, God's command to Abraham is not a punishment for any alleged crime on Abraham's part, but is a test of Abraham's faithfulness. The Prince of Mastema does not function as

20. In theory, it is possible that the author of Jubilees envisions a scenario in which a spirit leads Israel into sin, then accuses or prosecutes Israel before God, securing permission to attack and destroy them. While such an understanding of spiritual activity is not impossible, Jubilees contains no evidence of a process involving prosecution by spirits. Jubilees says only that spirits mislead and destroy. Apart from the questionable Ethiopic translation of 1:20, they are never said to accuse.

a prosecutor in this story, nor does the story assume that the Prince of Mastema ever serves in such a capacity.

The purpose of Jubilees' version of the story is to diminish God's role in endangering Isaac by presenting the Prince of Mastema as the real source of divine hostility. Borrowing the idea of a test inspired by the Satan from the story of Job, Jubilees blames the Prince of Mastema for Abraham's ordeal. Jubilees' retelling of the exodus account, which involves attacks by the Prince of Mastema against Moses and Israel, accomplishes a similar purpose. A related account of the sacrifice of Isaac also appears in a fragment of Pseudo-Jubilees (4Q225 2 i 9–10), which says that the Prince of Mastema approached God "and caused Abraham to be hostile against Isaac" (*wyśṭym 't 'brhm byśḥq*).[21] The Prince of Mastema's purpose in this story is not to accuse, but to create hostility toward God's people, diminishing the Deity's responsibility for their trials.

In Jubilees' retelling of Gen 22, the Prince of Mastema is the enemy of the righteous, not the accuser of sinners. While the story of Abraham's test in Jubilees neither portrays the Prince of Mastema as a heavenly prosecutor of sinners nor assumes that the prince holds such an official prosecutorial post, the story resembles Job in that the Prince of Mastema creates trouble for a righteous person by calling his commitment to God into question. In this sense, the Prince of Mastema functions as an accuser of sorts in Jubilees. Eventually, Jewish theologians would formalize this activity on the Satan's part, depicting him as the official accuser of the righteous before God, as well as the prosecutor of sinners, but the Prince of Mastema does not yet hold such an office in Jubilees.

Jubilees on the Origin of Evil

The book of Jubilees says much about the relationship between the superhuman realm and human sin and suffering. Jubilees addresses this matter more systematically than previous literature, creating a hierarchy in which

21. The translation of *wyśṭym* in this fragment as "accused" is without basis apart from the assumption that the Prince of Mastema must function in this capacity in the text. See, e.g., VanderKam and Milik, "Jubilees," 147; Armin Lange, "מַשְׂטֵמָה *maśṭemāh*," *ThWQ* 2:798. The verb *śṭm* appears elsewhere in the qal stem (Gen 27:41; 49:23; 50:15; Ps 55:4 [Eng. 3]; Job 16:9; 30:21; 4Q174 4 4) with the meaning "to be at enmity with, be hostile toward" (*HALOT* 3:1316). 4Q225 contains the sole occurrence of the verb in the hiphil, with an expected meaning along the lines of "to cause to be hostile toward."

the Prince of Mastema as the superhuman punisher of wicked humans commands a host of spirits/demons, who mislead, harm, and kill the nations of the earth. Jubilees also expands the scope of the spirits'/demons' activity, crediting them with misleading humankind into various sins, not merely idolatry as in the Book of the Watchers.

Jubilees, however, does not appear to be concerned about the problem of evil for its own sake and nowhere attempts to offer an explanation for sin's ultimate existence.[22] Jubilees takes on the issue of sin's origin in the context of addressing Israel's special status among the nations of the world. It is the matter of election rather than theodicy that drives Jubilees' theology. The sins of the nations are attributed to the deceptive work of the Prince of Mastema and his host of spirits, whom God has placed in authority over the nations. Israel, however, is protected from this deception. God has provided Israel alone with immunity to the spirits' deception in the form of Jubilees' Torah. Nevertheless, there seems to remain some danger that Israel will allow itself to be ruled by the spirits, should Israel fail to heed the teachings of Jubilees.

Like the Book of the Watchers before it, Jubilees traces the genesis of evil spirits back to the union of the heavenly watchers with human women. Gabriele Boccaccini finds in Jubilees the same idea that he claims is fundamental to Enochic Judaism, "that evil is superhuman and is caused by the sin of the Watchers."[23] Other scholars argue that the watcher story is less important as an explanation for the existence of evil in Jubilees than it is in the Book of the Watchers.[24] In Michael Segal's assessment, Jubilees (as

22. This conclusion is consistent with that of Loren T. Stuckenbruck, "The Book of Jubilees and the Origin of Evil," in *Enoch and the Mosaic Torah: The Evidence of Jubilees,* ed. Gabriele Boccaccini and Giovanni Ibba (Grand Rapids: Eerdmans, 2009), 294–308. Stuckenbruck identifies five "beginnings" of sin in the book of Jubilees: (1) the misdeed of Adam and Eve in the garden (3:8–31), (2) Cain's murder of his brother Abel (4:1–6, 9, 31–32), (3) the watcher story (5:1–19; 7:20–39; 8:1–4; 10:1–14), (4) Ham's looking upon Noah's nakedness (7:7–15), and (5) the tower of Babel incident (10:18–11:6). In Stuckenbruck's assessment, "None of the five episodes . . . has anything to do with the question of 'where evil originally came from' or 'how the activity of sinning got to be'" (307).

23. Gabriele Boccaccini, *Beyond the Essene Hypothesis: The Parting of the Ways between Qumran and Enochic Judaism* (Grand Rapids: Eerdmans, 1998), 87. Similarly, Helge S. Kvanvig, "Jubilees—Read as a Narrative," in *Enoch and Qumran Origins: New Light on a Forgotten Connection,* ed. Gabriele Boccaccini (Grand Rapids: Eerdmans, 2005), 78, says, "The Watcher story is not only a paradigm for sin and evil, it also constitutes the root cause for the evil that haunts men."

24. E.g., James C. VanderKam "The Angel Story in the Book of Jubilees," in *Pseud-*

shaped by its redactor) does not teach that sin had its origin in the activity of the watchers, but that God ordered the universe in a dualistic fashion and that evil has existed from the very moment of creation.[25] Segal is certainly correct that Israel's election, according to Jubilees, was declared from the moment of creation (2:19–33). To say that God also created evil itself at this point in time, however, seems to go beyond what Jubilees claims. Jubilees does not mention the Prince of Mastema or his harmful spirits among those beings that God created. Evil spirits, and very possibly the Prince of Mastema himself, come into existence as the result of the watchers' transgression. This is the only explanation that Jubilees offers for the existence of evil. Although Jubilees is aware of sin before the descent of the watchers (3:17–25; 4:1–6), it is not the sin of Adam and Eve or of Cain that endangers Israel's existence, but those spirits fathered by the watchers.

The issue of evil in Jubilees, to be sure, is connected with God's plan from creation to preserve a special people. Although evil cannot be traced all the way back to Israel's election at the moment of creation, Israel's unique status is much more important to Jubilees' understanding of evil than is the watcher myth. That certain evil beings have existence as a result of the watchers' transgression is less significant than how God implements the creation plan to preserve a special people in a world where these menacing beings exist. Appropriately, Jubilees does not even mention these spirits or their leader in its account of the watcher episode. These evil beings enter the story only after the flood as humankind is poised to separate into the nations of the world and steps must be taken to preserve the chosen line.

Although Jubilees surpasses the Book of the Watchers in the extent of the sins attributed to spirits/demons and in the important role that these beings occupy in Jubilees' understanding of God's plan for Israel and humankind, the importance of the watcher story itself is diminished in the theology of Jubilees. While the watcher myth serves as the etiology for

---

epigraphic Perspectives: The Apocrypha and Pseudepigrapha in Light of the Dead Sea Scrolls, ed. Esther G. Chazon and Michael Stone, STDJ 31 (Leiden: Brill, 1999), 154; Todd Russell Hanneken, "Angels and Demons in the Book of Jubilees and Contemporary Apocalypses," *Hen* 28.1 (2006): 14–16. Annette Yoshiko Reed, "Enochic and Mosaic Traditions in Jubilees: The Evidence of Angelology and Demonology," in *Enoch and the Mosaic Torah*, ed. Boccaccini and Ibba, 353–68, argues that the watcher myth is not an explanation for the existence of sin in Jubilees, but serves as a warning for those Jews who would sin by adopting the customs of the nations.

25. Segal, *Book of Jubilees*, 97–269.

those sins that distinguish Israel from the nations, this particular etiology is not really the point of Jubilees. What is truly significant is that God from the moment of creation has purposed to set Israel apart from the rest of humankind. Accordingly, from the very instant that the world's peoples began to emerge as distinct entities, God has maintained the chosen people's unique status by affording them alone protection from misleading and harmful spirits.

A second set of narratives in Jubilees, those that depict the Prince of Mastema attempting to harm God's people, also relates to the problem of evil. These stories, including Jubilees' version of the near sacrifice of Isaac and of Israel's exodus from Egypt, address not the cause of sin but the cause of Israel's suffering. Opposition to Israel's well-being, these narratives teach, comes not from Israel's benevolent God but from the Prince of Mastema, who intends to harm God's people. These texts borrow Job's notion of the Satan who would harm an innocent person, but applies this teaching at the national level. The Prince of Mastema is the enemy not simply of innocent individuals but of the entire nation of Israel.

Unity and Diversity in the Portrayal of the Satan in Jubilees

In this chapter we have discussed those passages in Jubilees in which the Prince of Mastema appears as the enemy of God's people. Jubilees retells the stories of Isaac's near sacrifice and of Israel's exodus from Egypt in a way that places the blame for divine hostility toward the elect on the Prince of Mastema rather than on God. These passages contrast with those discussed in the previous chapter, in which the Prince of Mastema leads the nations of the world astray through the agency of evil spirits. Most importantly, these two depictions of the Prince of Mastema differ with respect to how they conceive of the Prince of Mastema's relationship to God and God's plan for Israel. According to those texts discussed in the previous chapter, the Prince of Mastema is the chief of those spirits who carry out God's command of misleading and destroying the nations of the earth. In Jubilees' retelling of the exodus and sacrifice of Isaac, the Prince of Mastema opposes God's plan for Israel and fights on behalf of Israel's national enemies.

If we read Jubilees as a unity, it is difficult to know exactly what to make of passages that stand in tension with one another. It is easier to determine how individual passages portray the Prince of Mastema than to ascertain how the book of Jubilees as a whole conceives of him. The idea of evil spirits who lead the nations astray seems integral to Jubilees' theology. Some passages in Jubilees incorporate the figure of the Prince of Mastema into this systematic understanding of evil spirits and Israel's election. Other passages do not obviously relate to this system (e.g., Jub. 17:15–18:16) or are in tension with it, such as Jubilees' exodus account, in which the Prince of Mastema assists the Egyptians while the angels of the presence and the forces of Mastema/hostility assist Israel. These are more difficult to comprehend in the context of Jubilees. The various depictions of the Prince of Mastema in Jubilees share the understanding that God and the angels of the presence protect the descendants of Jacob from the superhuman forces who would destroy them. This understanding is perhaps where the unity of Jubilees' material pertaining to the Satan resides. Whatever Jubilees' author intended by incorporating these diverse traditions, Jubilees presents the Prince of Mastema both as one who serves God in leading the nations astray and as one who supports the nations in an effort to destroy God's people. This Satan figure, who is responsible both for the sins of the world and for the troubles of the righteous, would be the Satan received by Jewish and Christian tradition.

CHAPTER 6

Demons, Evil Spirits, the Satan, and Human Responsibility for Sin

Up to this point, we have followed the development of beliefs about evil spirits and the Satan from their roots in the Hebrew scriptures through the Enochic Book of the Watchers and Jubilees' account of Israel's origin. We have observed a trajectory in the later literature increasingly to credit these superhuman beings with responsibility for human wickedness. Other writings, however, reveal that not all theologians of the Second Temple period were comfortable with the teaching that forces external to humanity were ultimately behind human sin. Blaming humanity's moral downfall on the work of superhuman beings ran into conflict with some theologians' conception of human volition. Especially troubling to these thinkers was the implication that God was somehow responsible, even indirectly, for human sin. How, they asked, could God hold humans accountable for what was entirely out of their control? What is more, how could God punish humans for actions that God ultimately caused?

Several works composed in the late Second Temple period came to the defense of God's character and offered an alternative explanation for humanity's moral failings. Those who are looking for someone to blame for sin need only to look to the sinners themselves. In the first quarter of the second century BCE, Ben Sira produced an anthology of wisdom teachings. Ben Sira's book of wisdom addresses a number of issues, one of which is the relationship between the Creator and human sin. The sage admonishes his pupils, "Do not say, 'It was the Lord's doing that I fell away'" (Sir 15:11). Another work that objected to the idea that forces external to human beings determined human morality is the Epistle of Enoch (roughly 1 En. 91–108). Composed somewhat later than Sirach, the Epistle contends, "lawlessness was not sent upon the earth; but men created it by themselves" (1 En. 98:4b).[1] The NT Epistle of James also enters into the discussion of human responsibility for sin, as well as, perhaps, the thanksgiving hymn Barkhi Nafshi (4Q434) from the Dead Sea Scrolls.

Human Responsibility for Sin according to the Wisdom of Ben Sira

The book of Sirach is among those early Jewish writings that were not included in the Hebrew scriptures but that seem to have enjoyed a fairly wide circulation and even obtained canonical status in some Christian circles. Sirach was composed by a teacher named Jesus son of Eleazar son of Sirach, probably in the first quarter of the second century BCE (50:27).[2] Ben Sira's work is appropriately considered among those ancient writings to which the label "Wisdom" has been assigned. As such, it joins the earlier books of Proverbs, Job, and Qoheleth (Ecclesiastes), the later Wisdom of Solomon, and the various fragmentary sapiential texts that were discovered among the Dead Sea Scrolls. Of these works, Sirach most closely resembles the book of Proverbs, both formally and theologically.[3] Sirach

1. Unless otherwise noted, all English quotations of 1 Enoch are from George W. E. Nickelsburg and James C. VanderKam, *1 Enoch: The Hermeneia Translation* (Minneapolis: Fortress, 2012).

2. The prologue to the Greek translation supplies us with our most substantial clue to Ben Sira's date. Although the translator does not give us his own name, he identifies himself as the author's grandson, who immigrated to Egypt during the thirty-eighth year of the reign of Euergetes II. Since there is no real reason to doubt the translator's claim, this places the arrival of Ben Sira's grandson in Egypt in 132 BCE. Allowing a couple of generations from the career of Ben Sira to that of his grandson, scholars date the Hebrew composition to sometime in the first quarter of the second century BCE. Other factors in the dating of this work are Ben Sira's panegyric on Simeon II, who was high priest from 219 to 196 (50:1–21), and the fact that Ben Sira reveals no awareness of the turbulence in Judah under the Seleucid ruler Antiochus IV Epiphanes in the mid-second century BCE. On the authorship and dating of Ben Sira, see Patrick W. Skehan and Alexander A. Di Lella, *The Wisdom of Ben Sira*, AB 39 (New York: Doubleday, 1987), 8–16.

3. As Ben Sira seeks to impress upon his readers the value of his wisdom, one of his objectives seems to have been to reassert the validity of a this-worldly act-consequence relationship (*Tun-Ergehen-Zusammenhang*) as taught in the more ancient book of Proverbs. Ben Sira repudiates, on the one hand, the teaching found in Qoheleth that there is no such relationship between one's deeds and one's outcome, that the end of the sinner is the same as the end of the righteous (e.g., Qoh 9:1–3). He also rejects, on the other hand, the apocalyptic eschatology found in works such as the Book of the Watchers, in which recompense for one's deeds is postponed until the eschaton or afterlife (e.g., 1 En. 10:14; 25:3–7).

comprises a variety of material. The work contains a number of pithy sayings as well as some more lengthy treatments of various moral, theological, and practical matters. It offers advice on a wide range of topics, including money (e.g., 10:30–31), health (e.g., 30:14–17), relationships between men and women (e.g., 7:19, 24–26; 25:13–26:18), sin (e.g., 15:11–20), and death (e.g., 38:16–23). Prudence with respect to all of these facets of human life, for Ben Sira, falls under the umbrella of "wisdom."[4] The nature and value of wisdom occupy the sage's attention in a number of passages (e.g., 6:18–37; 24:1–31). An extended praise of Israel's national heroes spans several chapters near the end of the book (44:1–50:21).

The problem of theodicy is one that Ben Sira visits in multiple passages. Sin and humankind's accountability before its Maker are matters of particular importance to the sage. He addresses the problem of sin most directly and extensively in 15:11–20.

> Do not say, 'It was the Lord's doing that I fell away';
> for he does not do what he hates.
> 12Do not say, 'It was he who led me astray';
> for he has no need of the sinful.
> 13The Lord hates all abominations;
> such things are not loved by those who fear him.
> 14It was he who created humankind in the beginning,

According to Ben Sira, there is no postmortem existence (e.g., Sir 38:21). Those who obtain wisdom will receive the reward of an eternal name (e.g., 37:26). And the wicked, despite appearances to the contrary, will also receive their just deserts. Though a wicked individual may prosper throughout his life, a moment of suffering on the day of his death can set justice aright (e.g., 11:26–27). On Ben Sira's teaching concerning the relationship between act and consequence, see Gabriele Boccaccini, *Middle Judaism: Jewish Thought, 300 B.C.E. to 200 C.E.* (Minneapolis: Fortress, 1991), 78–80; and Samuel L. Adams, *Wisdom in Transition: Act and Consequence in Second Temple Instructions*, JSJSup 125 (Leiden: Brill, 2008), 153–213.

4. Ben Sira also departs from his forebears by subsuming into his wisdom the Mosaic Torah, which does not occupy a place of prominence in the earlier wisdom literature. (Cf. Deut 4:5–6, which also associates the Mosaic law with "wisdom.") On the relationship between wisdom and the law in Ben Sira, see Johannes Marböck, "Gesetz und Weisheit: Zum Verständnis des Gesetzes bei Jesus Ben Sira," *BZ* 20.1 (1976): 1–21; Eckhard J. Schnabel, *Law and Wisdom from Ben Sira to Paul: A Tradition Historical Enquiry into the Relations of Law, Wisdom, Ethics*, WUNT 16 (Tübingen: Mohr Siebeck, 1985), 8–92; John J. Collins, *Jewish Wisdom in the Hellenistic Age*, OTL (Louisville: Westminster John Knox, 1997), 54–61; Johannes Marböck, *Weisheit im Wandel: Untersuchungen zur Weisheitstheologie bei Ben Sira*, BZAW 272 (Berlin: de Gruyter, 1999), 81–96; Adams, *Wisdom in Transition*, 198–204.

and he left them in the power of their own free choice [*yēṣer*].
15If you choose, you can keep the commandments,
and to act faithfully is a matter of your own choice.
16He has placed before you fire and water;
stretch out your hand for whichever you choose.
17Before each person are life and death,
and whichever one chooses will be given.
18For great is the wisdom of the Lord;
he is mighty in power and sees everything;
19his eyes are on those who fear him,
and he knows every human action.
20He has not commanded anyone to be wicked,
and he has not given anyone permission to sin.

The way that Ben Sira begins this discourse ("Do not say, 'It was the Lord's doing that I fell away'") gives one the impression that he is countering a belief that some of his contemporaries held. His warning implies that a rival explanation of human sin, one that attributed it to the Lord, was available to his readers. Ben Sira advocates instead a doctrine of free will. He warns his students that they should not blame God for their misdeeds. God does not lead people to sin. God hates sin, indeed, but has given individuals the ability to choose whether they will engage in it.

Ben Sira argues that humans are responsible for sin, stating that God has left each person in the power of his or her own *yēṣer*. The NRSV translates *yēṣer* as "free will," though elsewhere this term means something like "inclination" (e.g., Gen 6:5; 8:21).[5] According to Ben Sira, it is not God, but a person's own *yēṣer* that leads a person to sin. Granted, Ben Sira's argument is not airtight. Since it was God who created the human *yēṣer* by which moral decisions are made, is not God still ultimately responsible for sin?[6] Blaming God even indirectly for sin, however, is not the intent of Ben Sira, whose goal rather is to exculpate God of any blame for sin.

Ben Sira does not seem to have in mind the Book of the Watchers' teaching on evil spirits as the object of his rebuttal. Nothing in Ben Sira's

5. On the meaning of *yēṣer* in Ben Sira, see Miryam T. Brand, *Evil Within and Without: The Source of Sin and Its Nature as Portrayed in Second Temple Literature*, JAJSup 9 (Göttingen: Vandenhoeck & Ruprecht, 2013), 100–103, who argues that *yēṣer* in Sirach is not a negative concept as it is in some texts, but is a neutral term, denoting the human ability to choose.

6. John J. Collins, *Apocalypticism in the Dead Sea Scrolls* (London: Routledge, 1997), 35.

teaching in 15:11–20 suggests that he is refuting a doctrine of "evil spirits"; he is refuting only the claim that God might lead a person into sin.[7] Also, if one may take Ben Sira's rhetoric at face value, then he is warning his pupils that it would be inappropriate for *them* to blame *their* transgressions on God. The Book of the Watchers does not appear to have its own community in mind in its teaching on deceptive spirits. The claim is made only that evil spirits mislead those who worship idols.[8] Similarly, in Jubilees the domain of evil spirits is the nations; Israel has been granted immunity from those spirits who would lead them astray. There is no indication that the authors of the Book of the Watchers or of Jubilees would have said, "God (through the agency of evil spirits) led *me* to sin."[9]

To what teaching Ben Sira is responding is not entirely clear. He would have likely been uncomfortable with texts such as 2 Sam 24, where God incites David to number Israel's fighting men and then punishes David and the people for this sin. He may have also felt uneasy about the parallel account in 1 Chr 21, where God accomplishes this through the agency of a satanic emissary. Even though Ben Sira does not seem directly to dispute teachings on evil spirits, he almost certainly would have taken issue with explanations of idolatry that are found in 1 En. 19 and Jub. 15. According to Sir 15, God has endowed humankind with free will, "has not commanded anyone to be wicked," and "has no need of the sinful."[10]

7. Several scholars have observed that Ben Sira addresses many of the same themes as do the writings that make up 1 Enoch, but that Ben Sira does so from a perspective that is at variance with the Enochic corpus. See Randal A. Argall, *1 Enoch and Sirach: A Comparative Literary and Conceptual Analysis of the Themes of Revelation, Creation, and Judgment*, EJL 8 (Atlanta: Scholars Press, 1995); Benjamin G. Wright III, "Putting the Puzzle Together: Some Suggestions concerning the Social Location of the Wisdom of Ben Sira," in *Conflicted Boundaries in Wisdom and Apocalypticism*, ed. Benjamin G. Wright III and Lawrence M. Wills, SymS 35 (Leiden: Brill, 2006), 89–112; Adams, *Wisdom in Transition*, 191–98. Nevertheless, Ben Sira does not appear to respond directly to the Book of the Watchers' teaching on evil spirits.

8. The Book of the Watchers does not address the issue of whether Jews are susceptible to the deceptive influence of evil spirits.

9. Menahem Kister, "The Yetzer of Man's Heart, the Body and Purification from Evil: Between Prayer Terminologies and Worldviews," in *Meghillot: Studies in the Dead Sea Scrolls VIII*, ed. M. Bar-Asher and D. Dimant (Jerusalem: Bialik Institute and Haifa University Press, 2010), 241-82 (Hebrew) argues that Sir 22:27-23:6 appropriates the language of an apotropaic prayer, but asks for deliverance from one's own evil inclination rather than from any evil superhuman being. This passage perhaps constitutes evidence that Ben Sira was aware of and rejected the belief that evil superhuman beings instigated human sin.

10. Brand, *Evil Within and Without*, 95–97, suggests that Ben Sira in this passage re-

Despite what appears to be an unequivocal declaration of human free will in Sir 15, Ben Sira's wisdom anthology elsewhere emphasizes God's sovereignty over humankind. Following a passage in which Ben Sira compares the relationship between human beings and their Maker with "clay in the hand of the potter, to be molded as he pleases" (33:13), the sage describes creation as consisting of pairs of opposites.

> Good is the opposite of evil,
> and life the opposite of death;
> so the sinner is the opposite of the godly.
> Look at all the works of the Most High;
> they come in pairs, one the opposite of the other. (33:14–15)

This passage teaches that God has built good and evil into creation and implies that God creates human beings as either godly or sinful. This viewpoint stands in considerable tension with the statements on free will in 15:11–20. It appears that Ben Sira included different perspectives on the problem of sin in his collection of wisdom, a fact that complicates attempts to determine precisely where Ben Sira himself came down on the matter.[11]

Another text that may give one insight into Ben Sira's understanding of sin is a comment that the sage makes in 25:24. In the midst of a series of warnings to his male readers about the dangers of women, Ben Sira offers the following perspective on womankind's role in humanity's downfall: "From a woman sin had its beginning, and because of her we all die" (25:24). This statement alludes to the story of the first human couple in Gen 3, which would come to figure prominently in Jewish and Christian accounts of the origin of sin. Nevertheless, one cannot assume that this interpretation of Gen 3 figured as prominently in Ben Sira's understanding of sin. This passing

---

sponds to a Jewish view that derived from Hellenistic thought, in which a sort of determinism was fairly widespread.

11. For discussions of theodicy in Sirach, see, e.g., James L. Crenshaw, "The Problem of Theodicy in Sirach: On Human Bondage," *JBL* 94.1 (1975): 47–64; Gian Luigi Prato, *Il Problema della Teodicea in Ben Sira*, AnBib 65 (Rome: Pontifical Biblical Institute, 1975); David Winston, "Theodicy in Ben Sira and Stoic Philosophy," in *Of Scholars, Savants, and Their Texts: Studies in Philosophy and Religious Thought*, ed. R. Link-Salinger (New York: Lang, 1989), 239–49; Collins, *Jewish Wisdom*, 79–96; Pancratius C. Beentjes, "Theodicy in Wisdom of Ben Sira," in *Theodicy in the World of the Bible*, ed. Antti Laato and Johannes C. de Moor (Leiden: Brill, 2003), 509–24; James L. Crenshaw, *Defending God: Biblical Responses to the Problem of Evil* (Oxford: Oxford University Press, 2005), 136–37.

remark probably reflects Ben Sira's negative view of women or of troublesome wives more so than it reflects his understanding of the nature of sin or of the events that transpired in the garden of Eden.[12] The negative portrayal of a woman in this verse is not unique in Ben Sira's wisdom anthology (see, e.g., Sir 42:14). The belief that the woman of Gen 3 introduced death into the world also runs counter to Ben Sira's teaching in 17:1–7, which says that God created humankind mortal and gave them the knowledge of good and evil.

Ben Sira's collection of wisdom preserves for his readers more than one perspective on the origin of the world's problems. One of these perspectives insists that humans, not God, are responsible for sin.

Demons, Evil Spirits, and Human Responsibility for Sin in the Epistle of Enoch

The Epistle of Enoch is one of the several works that make up the collection known as 1 Enoch.[13] The Epistle, which itself may be divided into a

12. John J. Collins, "Before the Fall: The Earliest Interpretations of Adam and Eve," in *The Idea of Biblical Interpretation: Essays in Honor of James L. Kugel*, ed. H. Najman and J. H. Newman (Leiden: Brill, 2004), 298.

13. Although the title "Epistle of Enoch" can designate any of the material collected in chs. 91–108 of 1 Enoch, scholars generally regard the final few chapters of the work as a separate appendix. George W. E. Nickelsburg, *1 Enoch 1,* Hermeneia (Minneapolis: Fortress, 2001), 416, limits the title "Epistle" to 1 En. 92–105 (including 91:11–17 between 93:10 and 11). One can further distinguish between the Epistle itself (92:1–5; 93:11–105:2) and the Apocalypse of Weeks (93:1–10; 91:11–17), though scholars disagree about the relationship between these two literary units. For the argument that the Apocalypse of Weeks once existed independently of the Epistle, see Loren T. Stuckenbruck, *1 Enoch 91–108*, CEJL (Berlin: de Gruyter, 2007), 62–64. For arguments in favor of regarding the Epistle and the Apocalypse of Weeks as a unity, see James C. VanderKam, *Enoch and the Growth of an Apocalyptic Tradition,* CBQMS 16 (Washington, DC: Catholic Biblical Association of America, 1984), 144–45. In recent years, based in part on manuscript evidence and in part on internal considerations, some scholars have also come to hold that the material that now introduces and concludes the Epistle once circulated independently from the body of the work. Gabriele Boccaccini, *Beyond the Essene Hypothesis: The Parting of the Ways between Qumran and Enochic Judaism* (Grand Rapids: Eerdmans, 1998), 104–13, 134–35, distinguishes between what he calls the "Proto-Epistle of Enoch," which did not contain 1 En. 94:6–104:6, and the Epistle as we now have it, which includes those chapters. Nickelsburg, *1 Enoch 1*, 23–24, 336–37, holds that the Epistle at one time formed part of an Enochic testament without 94:6–104:8. Stuckenbruck, *1 Enoch 91–108*, 191–92, distinguishes between Epistle A (the fragments that lie behind the framework of the book) and Epistle B (the main body of the Epistle itself, 94:6–104:8).

number of smaller literary units of various genres and of diverse origins, promises that a final judgment is coming in which God will reward the righteous and the wicked as their respective deeds merit.[14] Among those sins deserving of God's wrath, this Enochic pseudepigraphon singles out the oppression of the righteous by the wealthy (e.g., 96:4–8; 97:8–10). The Epistle also castigates its opponents for mishandling the "words of truth" (e.g., 98:15–16; 99:2; 104:9–11).

It is difficult to date the Epistle of Enoch with precision. Since this work makes extensive use of the Book of the Watchers, which was likely completed by the end of the third century BCE, this date may serve as a definite *terminus post quem* for the Epistle.[15] And since sections of the work appear in two Qumran manuscripts dating to the first century BCE, a *terminus ante quem* for at least these sections of the book is firmly established.[16] More controversial, however, is how one might go about narrowing the period during which the Epistle must have been written.

Much of the debate over precisely when the Epistle of Enoch was written revolves around whether the author of Jubilees was aware of the Epistle. Jubilees 4:16–26, which gives an account of Enoch's life and work, includes a synopsis of the patriarch's putative literary activity. It refers to some of the early Enochic writings that are known to us, including the Book of the Watchers, the Astronomical Book, and the Book of Dreams.[17] Scholars disagree, however, as to whether this passage at any point refers to the Epistle. If Jubilees does mention the Epistle, this allows one to date the Epistle prior to Jubilees. But if Jubilees does not mention the Epistle, then this significant silence could indicate that the Epistle was composed after Jubilees. Complicating matters further, there is no consensus as to when Jubilees itself was composed. Jubilees has

14. On the various literary forms appearing in the Epistle, see Nickelsburg, *1 Enoch 1*, 416–20; and Stuckenbruck, *1 Enoch 91–108*, 192–204.

15. The third-century date of the Book of the Watchers is based on J. T. Milik, *The Books of Enoch: Aramaic Fragments from Qumrân Cave 4* (London: Oxford University Press, 1976), 25, 140, 164, who, based on paleography, dates two Qumran MSS of this work (4QEn^{a,b}) to the first half of the second century BCE. One of these MSS (4QEn^{a}), according to Milik (141), was copied from a MS dating no later than the third century BCE.

16. Milik, *Books of Enoch*, 178–79, dates 4QEn^{c}, which contains 1 En. 104–107, to the last third of the first century BCE. Milik (246) dates 4QEn^{g}, which contains 91:1–94:2, to the middle of the first century BCE.

17. James C. VanderKam, "Enoch Traditions in Jubilees and Other Second-Century Sources," in *Society of Biblical Literature 1978 Seminar Papers*, 2 vols., SBLSP 13 (Missoula, MT: Scholars Press, 1978), 1:231–41.

been dated as early as 169 BCE and as late as 109 BCE.[18] Were one to determine with certainty whether Jubilees' author knew of the Epistle, one would still be in a position to date the Epistle with only a limited degree of exactness.

While it is not impossible that the author of Jubilees knew of and even mentioned the Epistle of Enoch, evidence for such knowledge is meager. In arguing that Jubilees does refer to the Epistle, Stuckenbruck cites Jubilees' claim that Enoch wrote a "testimony" (Jub. 4:18, 19). The noun "testimony" (Eth. *samā't*), says Stuckenbruck, occurs in the Enochic corpus only in the Epistle.[19] Others, however, find no reference to the Epistle of Enoch in Jubilees.[20] Although one cannot dismiss the possibility that the author of Jubilees was familiar with some of the traditions now contained in the Epistle (e.g., the Apocalypse of Weeks), evidence that he was aware of the Epistle of Enoch as we have it is ambiguous at best. And Jubilees never refers to the primary contents of the Epistle, which pertain to tensions between the rich and poor and between the wise and those who are in religious error. What is more, as will be demonstrated below, the evidence of the Epistle itself suggests that its author may have been aware of Jubilees' teaching on evil spirits.[21]

Lawlessness Was Not Sent upon the Earth

The Epistle of Enoch does not typically figure into discussions of early Jewish beliefs about evil spirits. Its neglect in this regard is understand-

18. On the date of Jubilees, see ch. 4, 77n3.

19. Stuckenbruck, *1 Enoch 91–108*, 215. There is some question as to whether the latter half of Jub. 4:18 describes this "testimony" or begins a new literary unit describing another work. If the literature referred to in 4:18 is taken as a single writing, then the testimony described cannot be the Epistle. VanderKam, "Enoch Traditions in Jubilees,"231-41, also suggests, "with some hesitation," that Jubilees presupposes some of the Epistle's contents. He finds possible references to the Epistle's contents in Jub. 4:18, 19, and 7:29 (and somewhat less likely in 4:17 and 10:17).

20. R. H. Charles, *The Book of Jubilees or the Little Genesis* (London: Black, 1902), lxviii–lxxi; Nickelsburg, *1 Enoch 1*, 427; and Milik, *Books of Enoch*, 48. Charles also lists a number of passages in the Epistle that, he claims, rely on Jubilees.

21. For the sake of simplicity, I will refer to the "author" of the Epistle in the singular, though the Epistle is a composite work with multiple authors. Properly speaking, the author in mind for the present chapter's purposes is the author of the "body" of the Epistle or Epistle B (see n13).

able. The Epistle mentions evil spirits only once and speaks of them as merely one item in a list of objects of illicit worship (1 En. 99:7). Given the more exciting teachings on malevolent spirits in the Book of the Watchers and Jubilees, the Epistle's passing reference to these beings seems hardly worthy of mention. Nevertheless, there is much more to this work's teaching on evil spirits than is obvious at first glance. Indeed, a closer look at the Epistle reveals a polemic directed against the teachings on evil spirits found in the Book of the Watchers and Jubilees.

The passage in which the Epistle of Enoch most clearly addresses the origin of human sin, though not explicitly evil spirits, is 98:4–5.

> I swear to you, sinners,
> that it was not ordained <for a man> to be a slave,
> nor was <a decree> given for a woman to be a handmaid;
> but it happened because of oppression.
> Thus lawlessness was not sent upon the earth;
> but men created it by themselves,
> and those who do it will come to a great curse.
> Likewise, neither is a woman created barren,
> but because of the works of her hands she is disgraced with childlessness.[22]

These lines state unequivocally that the blame for human sin is not to be placed on any force outside humanity. Humans themselves created it, and (therefore) those who do it will justifiably be cursed. Commentators have rightly compared this passage with Sir 15:11–20, in which Ben Sira similarly addresses the question of sin's source with statements like, "Do not say, 'It was the Lord's doing that I fell away'"; "Do not say, 'It was he who led me astray'"; and, "[the Lord] has not commanded anyone to be wicked." According to Ben Sira, humans are responsible for their own sin. The NT book of James also echoes this sentiment: "No one, when tempted, should say, 'I am being tempted by God'" (Jas 1:13). Each of these passages expresses the concern that humans bear the responsibility for their actions. The guilty cannot escape judgment

22. The first few lines of this passage present the interpreter with a text-critical challenge, but the meaning of the passage as a whole is sufficiently clear. On the text-critical problem, see George W. E. Nickelsburg, "Enoch 97–104: A Study of the Greek and Ethiopic Texts," in *Armenian and Biblical Studies*, ed. Michael E. Stone (Jerusalem: St. James, 1976), 113–17.

by shifting responsibility for their wrongdoing to God or to one of God's superhuman agents.[23]

Although it is not impossible that the Epistle was influenced by Ben Sira's teaching in this regard, one also perceives a difference between the Epistle's remark, on the one hand, and those of Ben Sira and the later James, on the other. Ben Sira and James warn individuals not to think that God leads them to commit acts of sin. "Do not say, 'It was the Lord's doing that *I fell away*'" (Sir 15:11). "*No one, when tempted*, should say, '*I am being tempted* by God'" (Jas 1:13). According to these two authors, God does not instigate acts of sin. The Epistle of Enoch, on the other hand, appears to be addressing the origin of human sin more generally. "Lawlessness was not *sent upon the earth*; but *men created it* by themselves" (1 En. 98:4b).[24] Hence, the Epistle implies, sin is not beyond human control; humans are justly condemned for it.

The Epistle's comments may be governed by the same ideology and rationale as those that govern Ben Sira and James. All three authors likely found it difficult to believe that a righteous God would punish humans for actions that were beyond their control. The question to which the Epistle's rhetoric directly responds, however, differs from that of Ben Sira and James. Admittedly, it is not clear that 1 En. 98:4–5 offers an explanation of why moral evil *ultimately* came into being in the first place. The Epistle, nevertheless, is a step closer to offering this sort of explanation than are Ben Sira and James.

Presumably, the Epistle of Enoch did not invent the idea that lawlessness was "sent upon the earth" solely for the sake of refuting it. The Epistle's author, like Ben Sira, was almost certainly responding to a belief held by some of his contemporaries. Most scholars contrast the Epistle's perspective with the perspective of the Book of the Watchers.[25] Many of

23. In addition, see Pss. Sol. 9:4–5:

Our works (are) in the choosing and power of our souls,
to do right and wrong in the works of our hands,
and in your righteousness you oversee human beings.
The one who does what is right saves up life for himself with the Lord,
and the one who does what is wrong causes his own life to be destroyed;
for the Lord's righteous judgments are according to the individual and the household.

Translation is that of R. B. Wright, "Psalms of Solomon," *OTP* 2:660. Cf. also Philo of Alexandria, *Fug.* 79.

24. Italics in the three preceding quotations are mine.

25. E.g., Maxwell Davidson, *Angels at Qumran: A Comparative Study of 1 Enoch 1–36, 72–108 and Sectarian Writings from Qumran*, JSPSup 11 (Sheffield: Sheffield Academic Press,

these scholars identify the Book of the Watchers' supposed version of evil's origin as the very teaching that the Epistle seeks to refute.[26] Florentino García Martínez avers, "It is impossible not to conclude that the author of the Epistle is completely turning around the conclusion of the Book of the Watchers in order to arrive at the opposite conclusion."[27] According to the scholars who find in these verses a critique of the earlier watcher tradition, the Book of the Watchers views the descent of the watchers as the introduction of moral evil into the world. Angels who rebelled before the flood, not humans, brought about the existence of sin on the earth. The Epistle of Enoch counters this idea, contending that humans themselves did this. So the common interpretation of 1 En. 98:4–5 goes.

The issue of evil's origin in the Book of the Watchers, however, is much more complex than these scholars acknowledge. The Book of the Watchers is a composite document, with its different literary components approaching the issue of evil in different ways. As a result, one cannot claim simply that the Epistle of Enoch disagrees with *the* conclusion of the Book of the Watchers regarding the origin of sin.[28] What one can and should ask instead is whether 1 En. 98:4–5 is reacting to one or more of the traditions regarding the origin of sin that are preserved in the Book of the Watchers.[29] And one should not limit one's consideration to the Book

---

1992), 46, 123, 294, 296; James C. VanderKam, *Enoch: A Man for All Generations* (Columbia, SC: University of South Carolina Press, 1995), 91; Nickelsburg, *1 Enoch 1*, 477; John J. Collins, *The Apocalyptic Imagination: An Introduction to Jewish Apocalyptic Literature*, 3rd ed. (Grand Rapids: Eerdmans, 2016), 84–85.

26. E.g., Milik, *Books of Enoch*, 53–54, 55; Paolo Sacchi, *Jewish Apocalyptic and Its History*, trans. William J. Short, JSPSup 20 (Sheffield: Sheffield Academic Press, 1990), 103, 146, 165; Florentino García Martínez, *Qumran and Apocalyptic: Studies on the Aramaic Texts from Qumran*, STDJ 9 (Leiden: Brill, 1992), 88; Florentino García Martínez, "Apocalypticism in the Dead Sea Scrolls," in *The Origins of Apocalypticism in Judaism and Christianity*, ed. John J. Collins; vol. 1 of *The Encyclopedia of Apocalypticism*, ed. John J. Collins, Bernard McGinn, and Stephen J. Stein (New York: Continuum, 1998), 166; Collins, *Apocalypticism*, 23; Annette Yoshiko Reed, *Fallen Angels and the History of Judaism and Christianity: The Reception of Enochic Literature* (Cambridge: Cambridge University Press, 2005), 78, 95. While Stuckenbruck, *1 Enoch 91–108*, 345–46, seems to be in general agreement with those scholars who set the Epistle in opposition to the Book of the Watchers, he prefers to focus on "how it is that the [watcher] tradition is being reappropriated" by the Epistle.

27. García Martínez, "Apocalypticism in the Dead Sea Scrolls," 166.

28. For a helpful discussion of the Book of the Watchers' take on the origin of sin, see Brand, *Evil Within and Without*, 158–67.

29. Stuckenbruck, *1 Enoch 91–108*, 346, proposes that the Epistle may be addressing

of the Watchers. It is also possible that the Epistle addresses a teaching found in another work.[30]

Fortunately, 1 En. 98:4–5 offers the reader a helpful clue as to what particular teaching it is refuting. Specifically, the Epistle's contention that lawlessness was not sent upon the earth seems a strange way of summarizing the watcher story. The sinful practices mentioned in the Book of the Watchers were not sent to the earth, but were taught or revealed to humans by rebellious angels. The notion that sin was sent upon the earth, and humans were compelled to commit it, however, does appear in the book of Jubilees.

In Jubilees' retelling of Genesis, the years between Noah's death and Abraham's birth were those during which Noah's descendants settled their allotted territories and became nations. Also during this period, the fledgling nations of the earth established those patterns of behavior that would characterize them throughout history. From the perspective of Jubilees, these patterns were not commendable ones, but were characterized by idolatry and bloodshed (Jub. 11:1–6). This moral degeneration among the

what was perceived to be "a potential misperception to which the myth of the watchers could have given rise."

30. Another teaching that has been suggested as that against which the Epistle is reacting is the deterministic doctrine of the Dead Sea Scrolls sect. According to Boccaccini, *Beyond the Essene Hypothesis*, 104–13, 134–35; and Gabriele Boccaccini, "Enoch, Qumran, and the Essenes: The Rediscovery of a Forgotten Connection: A Response to 'The Epistle of Enoch and the Qumran Literature,'" in *George W. E. Nickelsburg in Perspective*, ed. Jacob Neusner and Alan J. Avery-Peck, JSJSup 80 (Leiden: Brill, 2003), 128, 1 En. 98:4 belongs to a lengthy section (94:6–104:6) interpolated into the Epistle by an anti-Qumranic segment of the Essenes. In Boccaccini's estimation, this passage distinguishes between evil, which the author believes was caused by angels, and individual acts of sin, which the author blames on humans. In this way, Boccaccini reconciles the Epistle's teaching with that of the Book of the Watchers, as he interprets it. The Book of the Watchers, in Boccaccini's mind, deals with the origin of evil, while the Epistle addresses the matter of sinful acts themselves. As noted above, such a simplistic reading of the Book of the Watchers is problematic. It is the Epistle of Enoch, moreover, that seems to address the issue of evil's origin more generally and not merely the individual acts themselves. Boccaccini is correct, nonetheless, that the Epistle, inasmuch as it is concerned with whether humans have it within their power to reject lawlessness, does not necessarily contradict the overall thrust of the Book of the Watchers, as far as such a thrust can be determined. With respect to Boccaccini's proposal that the deterministic doctrine of the Qumran community is the target of the Epistle's teaching, this theory is not impossible. The author of the Epistle of Enoch would without a doubt have disagreed with the teachings of some of the Dead Sea Scrolls in the debate over how divine determinacy relates to human responsibility, but it is not clear that the particular teachings of the Dead Sea Scrolls group were those that the Epistle's author had in mind.

nations, according to Jubilees, took place with some goading from the superhuman realm. Evil spirits under the direction of their leader, the Prince of Mastema, were responsible for the nations' sins.

Jubilees 11:5	**1 Enoch 98:4b**
Prince Mastema was exerting his power in effecting all these actions and, by means of the spirits, he was **sending [*fannawa*]** to those who were placed under his control (the ability) to commit [*gabra*] every (kind of) error and sin [*ḫāṭi'at*] and every (kind of) transgression; to corrupt, to destroy, and to shed blood ***on the earth [diba mədər].***	Thus lawlessness [*ḫāṭi'at*] was not **sent [*fannawa*] upon the earth [*diba mədər*]**; but men created it by themselves, and those who do it [*gabra*] will come to a great curse.

The terminological correspondence between these two passages, albeit in Ethiopic translation, suggests that these texts are taking part in the same discussion. Perhaps one even responds directly to the other. The idea of "sin" or "lawlessnesss" being "sent" is a concept that we have encountered only in Jubilees up to this point.[31] Jubilees also specifies that humans "commit" these misdeeds "upon the earth." These are precisely the ideas that the Epistle is addressing in 98:4.[32] In Jubilees, it is the Prince of Mastema and his spirits who lead the nations to sin. The Epistle of Enoch does not mention the Prince of Mastema or evil spirits in this passage, since the author of the Epistle is primarily concerned here with defending God's righteousness. Such a defense of the Deity against the charge of involvement in human sin is an understandable response to Jubilees' teaching on the Prince of Mastema and evil spirits. Since Jubilees presents the deceptive work of these beings as part of their God-given commission (10:1–13;

31. This idea will be adopted by the Damascus Document as well, a writing that clearly knows and makes use of Jubilees.

32. This is not to claim that Jubilees' teaching about the cause of sin is the only teaching that the Epistle of Enoch contradicts, but that, at the very least, the teaching of Jubilees that evil is sent among humans by the agency of deceptive spirits is prominent among those beliefs contradicted by the Epistle in this passage. If Nickelsburg's reconstruction of the first part of 98:4 is correct, then the Epistle may also be addressing human responsibility for oppression, not just those sins said to be caused by evil spirits in Jubilees.

15:31–32), an objection to implicating God in human sin makes sense as a response to Jubilees' teaching. For the author of the Epistle, God is not to blame for human sin. It is humankind who created sin, and those humans who do it will justly come to a great curse.

Demons and Evil Spirits as Mere Objects of Worship

That the Epistle objects specifically to the teaching that humans are led into idolatry through the agency of evil spirits can be inferred from another passage in the Epistle. In 1 En. 99:6–9, one can discern a polemic against the teaching that superhuman forces are behind human transgression. These verses contain the Epistle's sole explicit reference to evil spirits.

> Those who worship stones—
> and who carve images of silver and gold and wood and stone and clay
> and worship phantoms and demons and abominations and evil spirits
> and all errors, not according to knowledge;
> no help will you find from them.
> They will be led astray by the folly of their hearts,
> and their eyes will be blinded by the fear of their hearts,
> and the visions of (your) dreams will lead you astray—
> You and the false works which you have made and constructed of stone,
> you will be destroyed together. (99:7–9)

These lines, which promise the eschatological judgment of idolaters, resemble 1 En. 19:1.

> There stand the angels who mingled with the women. And their spirits—having assumed many forms—bring destruction on men and lead them astray to sacrifice to demons as to gods until the day of the great judgment, in which they will be judged with finality.

In both 1 En. 99:7–9 and 19:1, evil spirits are associated with "demons" (Gk. *daimonia*; Eth. *ʾagānənt*), which idolaters worship.[33] These passages differ significantly, however, in that whereas evil spirits lead people to worship demons in the Book of the Watchers, evil spirits in the Epistle

33. The Ethiopic of 99:7 has "unclean spirits."

appear side by side with demons in a list of objects of idolatrous worship, a list that also includes carved images, phantoms, abominations, and "all errors."

The significance of the Epistle's listing evil spirits along with demons in this manner should not be overlooked, though many scholars have missed the innovation of this passage. In the Hebrew scriptures, "demons" (*šēdîm*) are those beings that stand behind the idols worshiped by the nations. An "evil spirit" (*rûaḥ rāʿâ*) was a being sent by God to punish an evildoer for sin (Judg 9:23; 1 Sam 16:14–23; 18:10–11). First Enoch 19:1 is one of the earliest texts to bring these two traditions into conversation. Keeping with the biblical tradition, however, only "demons" in the Book of the Watchers receive worship. The evil spirits are another kind of being. They themselves do not receive worship; their work, as described in 1 En. 19:1, is to mislead people to worship the demons. Although some passages in Jubilees treat "demons" as synonymous with evil spirits, the designation "evil spirits" is reserved for those passages in which these beings are deceiving or otherwise troubling humanity.

What is novel in Jubilees is also to employ on occasion the designation "demons" for those beings that engage in this troublesome activity (e.g., 10:1).[34] Jubilees nowhere says that idolaters worship "evil spirits." Although Jubilees may assume that the evil spirits who govern the nations are those beings erroneously worshiped by them, Jubilees preserves some of the earlier terminological distinction, according to which only "demons" are worshiped. The Epistle differs from Jubilees and other earlier works in that it identifies the objects of idolatrous worship as "evil spirits."

Furthermore, the Epistle says nothing more of the evil spirits' nature or activity. No mention is made of their misleading humanity. It is possible that these spirits' deceptive activity is assumed in this passage. Given the claim that humans are responsible for the existence of sin in 1 En. 98:4, however, it is very probably more than coincidental that the Epistle depicts evil spirits only as passive objects of worship and does not give them credit for leading the people astray into this erroneous worship. The innovation of the Epistle of Enoch is to claim that "evil spirits" receive worship and to relegate their role in idolatrous worship to mere passivity.

Consistent with the Book of the Watchers, Jubilees, and earlier biblical literature (e.g., Isa 44:20), those who worship idols are said to be "led

34. See also Tobit, which assumes that a person can be troubled by an "evil spirit" or a "demon" (Tob 6:7).

astray."[35] One of the ways they are misled is by dreams. As noted in ch. 3, 1 En. 19:1 may have false prophecy in mind when it speaks of the spirits' deceptive activity. In the Epistle, however, the evil spirits are not said to be responsible for seductive visions, but the folly of the idolaters' own hearts gives rise to their delusion. The Epistle describes idolaters with the traditional language, claiming that they have been "led astray" and "blinded."[36] Isaiah 44:18–20 says of idolaters, "their eyes are shut," and "a deluded heart has led [them] astray."[37]

The three concepts of demons, going astray, and blindness all converge in the book of Jubilees. For instance, Jub. 22:17–18 claims that those who worship demons have no eyes to see and that they wander astray. Likewise, Noah's children report to their father in Jub. 10:1–2 that the demons are "misleading, blinding, and killing" his grandchildren. Although Jub. 10:1–2 and the Epistle share the language of "blinding" and "leading astray," the later Enochic work does not give evil spirits or demons credit for this delusion. Rather, humans are "led astray by the folly of their hearts" and "blinded by the fear of their hearts" (1 En. 99:8a, b). While the author of the Epistle is happy to adopt the terminology of Jubilees with reference to demons, evil spirits, and idolatry, he parts ways with the earlier work when it comes to understanding the activity of these beings. Jubilees teaches that evil spirits mislead idolaters, but the Epistle of Enoch contends that idolaters are deceived only by themselves.

Admittedly, one would probably be going beyond what the evidence allows were one to conclude that these spirits are merely inanimate, according to the Epistle, and have no real existence. There may be an intended contrast between the lifeless images of silver, gold, wood, and stone mentioned in 99:7a and the (living?) beings listed in 99:7b, implying that the latter are the very real objects of worship behind the idols.[38] The implication, nevertheless, is that these phantoms, spirits, and demons have no power or influence over humankind. God certainly did not give them charge over the nations in order to lead the nations astray, as Jub. 15:31–32 maintains. Evil spirits cannot be blamed for idolatry on the part of morally responsible human beings.

35. Ethiopic has "they will fall into error."

36. The line claiming that the eyes of idolaters are blinded is omitted from the Chester Beatty–Michigan Greek papyrus.

37. NRSV has "mind" instead of "heart" for *lēb*.

38. Nickelsburg, *1 Enoch 1*, 492.

The Epistle contradicts the teaching that evil spirits are at work in the world leading humans to worship false gods. It is not clear that the Epistle's author has any problem with the watcher myth as it is presented in chs. 6–11 of the Book of the Watchers. Indeed, the Epistle's author, on the whole, seems to find the Book of the Watchers congenial to his own teaching, making extensive use of it.[39] By presenting itself as the teaching of Enoch, the Epistle also positions itself squarely and unabashedly within the Enochic literary tradition. The Epistle, nevertheless, does not agree entirely with the earlier Enochic work. It does not hold evil spirits responsible for the sin of idolatry as does 1 En. 19:1. The terminology of the Epistle is especially at variance with Jubilees on this matter. According to the Epistle, sin was not "sent upon the earth" as Jubilees claims. Rather, a person's blindness and delusion originate within a person's own heart.

The reason that the Epistle's author was averse to the teaching of Jubilees and 1 En. 19 on the origin of evil is not known. One may presume that, like many theologians through the ages, the Epistle's author was unable to reconcile such divine determinism with human accountability without compromising his belief in God's justice. For God justly to hold humankind morally responsible for their deeds, the author of the Epistle may have reasoned, humans must be the ones who ultimately determine their actions.

Pertinent to this issue are the differing notions of election in Jubilees and the Epistle. Jubilees draws a clear line of distinction between God's people and the rest of humankind. The line between Israel and the other nations was established by God from the moment of creation (Jub. 2:17–24). God enforces this distinction throughout history (beginning in Noah's day) by allowing deceptive spirits dominion over the nations, but keeping the chosen line directly under the Deity's own governance (Jub. 1:20; 15:25–32). Conversely, outside the Apocalypse of Weeks, there is no mention of "the elect" in the Epistle of Enoch.[40] Indeed, in Nickelsburg's assessment, an openness to outsiders characterizes the Epistle.[41] For instance, the Epistle tells of a time in the future when "the wise among men will see the truth, and the sons of the earth will contemplate these words of this epistle, and they will recognize that their wealth cannot save them

39. Stuckenbruck, *1 Enoch 91–108*, 206–9, compiles an impressive list of allusions to the Book of the Watchers in the Epistle.

40. George W. E. Nickelsburg, "The Epistle of Enoch and the Qumran Literature," *JJS* 33.1–2 (182): 346.

41. Nickelsburg, "Epistle of Enoch," 343–45.

when iniquity collapses" (100:6). In light of the possibility that the "sons of the earth" might realize their error and reform their ways, the Epistle encourages them, "So contemplate, O human beings, the deeds of the Most High and fear to do evil in his presence" (101:1).[42]

Nickelsburg concludes that, although the Epistle is meant to encourage those inside its group, it nevertheless makes an appeal for those outside the group to repent.[43] Perhaps for the author of the Epistle of Enoch, in order for this appeal to be genuine, there must exist the real possibility that human beings can choose to abandon their error and obey God's commandments. The doctrine of Jubilees, that God determined long ago those groups who would and would not be obedient to him and maintains this distinction by use of deceptive spirits, would not have been easy to reconcile with the universalistic outlook of the Epistle.

"Evil Inclination" instead of the Satan in Barkhi Nafshi?

The thanksgiving hymn Barkhi Nafshi ("Bless, O My Soul") is one of the fragmentary works discovered among the Dead Sea Scrolls.[44] Although chs. 7–8 will deal more fully with what the Dead Sea Scrolls have to say about the Satan and related figures, one passage in Barkhi Nafshi is relevant to our present discussion of superhuman beings and human responsibility for sin:

> [the heart of stone] you have [dri]ven with rebukes far from me, and have set a pure heart in its place. The evil inclination [you] have driven with rebukes [from my inmost parts] *vacat* [and the spirit of ho]liness you have set in my heart. Adulterousness of the eyes you have removed from me, and it gazed upon [all your ways. The s]tiffness of neck you have sent away from me, and you have made it into humility. Wrathful anger you have removed [from me, and have set in me a spirit of lo]ng-suffering. Haughtiness of heart and arrogance of eyes you have

42. Similarly, see 1 En. 105:1–2.

43. Nickelsburg, "Epistle of Enoch," 344–45.

44. M. Weinfeld and D. Seeley, "4QBarkhi Nafshi[a-e]," in *Qumran Cave 4, XX: Poetical and Liturgical Texts, Part 2*, by Esther Chazon et al., DJD 29 (Oxford: Clarendon, 1999), 255–334, describe the five copies of this work paleographically as Herodian (4Q434–437) or late Hasmonean or early Herodian (4Q438), which indicates a date sometime in the latter half of the first century BCE or the first half of the first century CE for these copies of the work.

> for[got]ten to reckon to me. [A spirit of deceit you have destroyed] and a [bro]ken heart you have given to me. (4Q436 1 i 10–ii 4)[45]

Eibert Tigchelaar argues that there is an intertextual relationship between Barkhi Nafshi and Zech 3.[46] If Tigchelaar is correct, then, intriguingly, Barkhi Nafshi differs from Zech 3 in that the hymn has *yṣr rʿ*, "an evil inclination," as the object of God's rebuke (*gʿr*) rather than *hśṭn*, "the Satan."

If Barkhi Nafshi replaces the Satan with an evil inclination, this raises some interesting possibilities with regard to the theology of this text. In our discussion of Sirach we noted Ben Sira's use of *yēṣer* as a neutral concept to refer to the faculty by which a person is able to choose to do either good or evil. The belief also arose in early Judaism, based in part on biblical texts such as Gen 6:5 and 8:21, that a person's *yēṣer* could be predisposed toward sin (e.g., 4QInstruction[c] [4Q417] 1 ii 12). The substitution of an evil inclination for the Satan in Barkhi Nafshi could reflect an emphasis in this text on human responsibility for sin rather than on superhuman responsibility for it.[47] In this case, perhaps the author is among those Jews who would deny that forces external to humans cause humans to do evil, but this conclusion probably goes beyond what the evidence of this fragmentary text allows.

The Satan and Human Responsibility for Sin in the Epistle of James

The NT Epistle of James also emphasizes that humans are responsible for sin. James 1:13–15 was mentioned above in conjunction with Sir 15:11–20

45. Translation is that of Weinfeld and Seeley, "4QBarkhi Nafshi[a-e]," 299.

46. Eibert Tigchelaar, "The Evil Inclination in the Dead Sea Scrolls, with a Re-edition of 4Q468I (4QSectarian Text?)," in *Empsychoi Logoi: Religious Innovations in Antiquity: Studies in Honour of Pieter Willem van der Horst,* ed. Alberdina Houtman, Albert de Jong, and Magda Misset-van de Weg, AJEC 73 (Leiden: Brill, 2008), 351–52, observes the following common vocabulary between Zech 3 and Barkhi Nafshi (4Q436 1 i–ii and 4Q437 4 // 4Q438 4 ii): *gʿr, hsyr, hʿbyr, hlbyš,* and *śym.*

47. Brand, *Evil Within and Without,* 48. Cf. Tigchelaar, "Evil Inclination," 351–52, who interprets the "evil inclination" in Barkhi Nafshi not as an internal, psychological disposition, but as a personified entity that is external to the speaker. Brand, however, correctly notes the parallelism between "evil inclination" and other sinful attributes of the speaker with which God deals in this text (e.g., "adulterousness of the eyes," "wrathful anger," "haughtiness of heart") and interprets the "evil inclination" in this context as an internal disposition of the speaker rather than a personal, superhuman being.

and 1 En. 98:4–5 as an example of a text that stresses that humans rather than God are to blame for sin.

> No one, when tempted, should say, "I am being tempted by God"; for God cannot be tempted by evil and he himself tempts no one. 14But one is tempted by one's own desire, being lured and enticed by it; 15then, when that desire has conceived, it gives birth to sin, and that sin, when it is fully grown, gives birth to death. (Jas 1:13–15)

Interestingly, in spite of this unequivocal endorsement of human responsibility for sin, James goes on to express the belief that his readers are vulnerable to the seductive influence of "the devil" and the "demonic." James 3:14–15 warns, "But if you have bitter envy and selfish ambition in your hearts, do not be boastful and false to the truth. 15Such wisdom does not come down from above, but is earthly, unspiritual, demonic [*daimoniōdēs*]."[48] And again in 4:7–8a, "Submit yourselves therefore to God. Resist the devil [*tō diabolō*], and he will flee from you. 8Draw near to God, and he will draw near to you."

James is able to hold together both the teaching that God is free from blame with regard to human sin and the belief that evil superhuman forces are out to lead his readers astray.[49] For James, these beliefs are not mutually exclusive. According to James, humans have the ability to resist the devil's attempts to lead them into sin. Moreover, the devil's attempts to mislead humanity do not implicate God in any way. For James, the devil does not mislead humans in the service of God. The devil and the demonic are opposed to God. Thus the wisdom about which James warns his readers "does not come down from above, but is . . . demonic" (3:15). In James's understanding, resisting the devil is tantamount to submitting to or drawing near to God (4:7–8). God does not tempt people; the devil does. And humans are capable of resisting the devil.

48. The NRSV has "devilish" for *daimoniōdēs*.

49. For a recent and extensive discussion of James's view of temptation/testing in its early Jewish context, see the study by Nicholas Ellis, *The Hermeneutics of Divine Testing: Cosmic Trials and Biblical Interpretation in the Epistle of James and Other Jewish Literature*, WUNT 2/396 (Tübingen: Mohr Siebeck, 2015).

Superhuman Beings and Human Responsibility for Sin in Early Jewish Literature

In the second century BCE, as theologies attributing human wickedness to unseen, superhuman powers are growing in popularity among Jews, some writers express dissatisfaction with such beliefs. They argue that God is just and that humans alone are to blame for sin. The Epistle of Enoch disagrees in particular with the idea found in the Book of the Watchers and Jubilees that evil spirits are active in the world, leading humans to worship false gods. In the Epistle of Enoch, humans may worship evil spirits and demons, but they do this without any goading from the superhuman realm. Lawlessness has not been sent upon the earth. Humankind has created it and will be punished for it. Barkhi Nafshi may deal with human wickedness similarly, emphasizing the role of a person's character in determining whether a person will sin and de-emphasizing the Satan's role. James, in contrast, is able to assert both humankind's responsibility for sin and the devil's role in leading humans astray. While some Jews rejected explanations of human sin that attributed it to forces external to human beings (as will be discussed in the following two chapters), others had no misgivings about such theologies. Indeed, some writings surpass even the Book of the Watchers and Jubilees in teaching that humans are under the dominion of dark powers bent on wickedness.

CHAPTER 7

Belial, Sin, and Sectarianism

In the Dead Sea Scrolls one encounters a variety of beliefs about the Satan figure, who typically goes by the name Belial. One finds in the scrolls many of the perspectives on the Satan and other maleficent superhuman entities that are attested in earlier literature, as well as some novel ideas about these beings. The Damascus Document, in particular, adopts much of Jubilees' teaching about the Prince of Mastema and his spirits, but adapts this teaching to suit its authors' sectarian interests. One can also observe in the Dead Sea Scrolls a shift in thinking about the Satan in comparison with earlier literature, as this figure is conceived of primarily in terms of wickedness and his role as an instigator of sin becomes more prominent.

The Corpus of the Dead Sea Scrolls

The designation "Dead Sea Scrolls" in our study refers to the remains of approximately nine hundred manuscripts discovered between 1947 and 1956 in eleven caves near Qumran. Although many consider the Dead Sea Scrolls a single corpus of writings, they comprise documents that were composed by a large number of individuals over a span of centuries and represent a wide range of Jewish beliefs and practices. Some of the texts were apparently composed by members of a particular group or sect within Judaism, whereas others reflect the thinking of Judaism more broadly. Among the Dead Sea Scrolls are copies of biblical books (i.e., those works that would eventually be deemed canonical by Judaism and Christianity), several apocryphal and pseudepigraphal writings that were previously known to scholars and appear to have enjoyed fairly wide circulation among Jews around the turn of the era, and other writings of various sorts that were unknown to scholars prior to the discovery of the Dead Sea Scrolls. Some of these previously unknown texts, though not all of them, appear to have been unique to the Jewish group responsible for collecting the Dead Sea Scrolls. With regard to literature that mentions satanic and related figures, one finds among the Dead Sea Scrolls copies of the works discussed in previous chapters of this book: Zechariah, Chronicles, Job, the Book of the Watchers, Jubilees, and the Epistle of Enoch. My focus in the present chapter and the following one, however, will be those texts that are found only (or primarily) among the Dead Sea Scrolls. One should bear in mind, nonetheless, that those Jews who made use of these texts did so in the context of a larger body of literature, including those writings considered in previous chapters.

The diversity of the Dead Sea Scrolls also means that this collection of writings does not present a single coherent, systematic doctrine of the superhuman realm. Different texts depict satanic figures in different ways. On the other hand, some ideas, such as the notion of a "dominion of Belial" and the belief in an opposition between light and darkness, appear in several texts. Those texts that represent the thinking of the sect, though not completely uniform in their description of satanic figures, share a number of characteristics. For the most part, in the present and following chapters I limit discussion to the teachings of individual texts, considering each work in its own right. Occasionally, however, it will be helpful to ask questions about the group that possessed and used these texts and how these texts may have related to one another both diachronically and synchronically. One ought to ask what the diversity of writings attested among the Dead Sea Scrolls reveals about the beliefs of those who read them. For example, what is the significance of the fact that the Book of the Watchers, with its etiology of evil spirits, existed in multiple copies among the scrolls alongside the Treatise on the Two Spirits and its very different etiology of the spirit of darkness?

Taxonomies, Terminology, and Titles for Harmful Superhuman Beings

Satanic and other harmful superhuman entities go by numerous appellatives in the Dead Sea Scrolls. The profusion of terminology for such beings in the scrolls is due in part to the aforementioned diversity of the literature that the scrolls comprise. As one would expect, different texts sometimes prefer different designations for the same figure. The individual referred to as Belial in one document may be called Melchiresha or the Angel of Darkness in another. The variety of terminology in the Dead Sea Scrolls is also a result of expansive taxonomies of the superhuman realm within individual texts that conceive of several different types of harmful beings. For instance, the Songs of the Maskil in one line lists "spirits of the destroying angels, spirits of the bastards, demons, Lilith, howlers and [desert dwellers]" (4Q510 1 5).[1] Another copy of the document also mentions a "destroyer" and "wicked spirits" (4Q511 1 6–7), though whether these two items are to be understood as distinct from the other classes of being mentioned or overlap with the others is not clear. Before we hone in on specific scrolls and what they have to say about the Satan and related figures, it will be helpful to gain a sense of the different types of harmful superhuman beings spoken of in the Dead Sea Scrolls as well as the terminology and titles by which the scrolls refer to them.[2]

Demons

Among the Hebrew and Aramaic scrolls, the word *šd*, "demon," appears several times.[3] In just one text, Pseudo-Daniel, *šd* is used as it is in the

1. Unless otherwise specified, translations of the Dead Sea Scrolls are from *DSSR*. Fragment, column, and line numbers are also cited as they are in this edition of the scrolls.

2. For excellent surveys of the types of "demonic beings" or "evil spirits" in the Dead Sea Scrolls, see Loren T. Stuckenbruck, "The Demonic World of the Dead Sea Scrolls," in *Evil and the Devil*, ed. Ida Fröhlich and Erkki Koskenniemmi, LNTS 481 (London: Bloomsbury T&T Clark, 2013), 51–70, also published as "Demonic Beings and the Dead Sea Scrolls," in *The Myth of Rebellious Angels*, WUNT 335 (Tübingen: Mohr Siebeck, 2014), 78–102; Eibert J. C. Tigchelaar, "Evil Spirits in the Dead Sea Scrolls: A Brief Survey and Some Perspectives," in *Dualismus, Dämonologie und diabolische Figuren: Religionshistorische Beobachtungen und theologische Reflexionen*, ed. Jörg Frey and Enno Edzard Popkes (Tübingen: Mohr Siebeck, forthcoming). On apotropaism in the Dead Sea Scrolls (not addressed here), see Philip Alexander, "The Demonology of the Dead Sea Scrolls," in *The Dead Sea Scrolls after Fifty Years: A Comprehensive Assessment*, ed. P. Flint and J. C. VanderKam, 2 vols. (Leiden: Brill, 1999), 2:331–53; Ida Fröhlich, "'Invoke at Any Time . . .': Apotropaic Texts and Belief in Demons in the Literature of the Qumran Community," *BN* 137 (2008): 41–74; David Lincicum, "Scripture and Apotropaism in the Second Temple Period," *BN* 138 (2008): 63–87.

3. Martin G. Abegg Jr., James E. Bowley, and Edward M. Cook, *The Non-Biblical Texts from Qumran*, vol. 1, part 2, of *The Dead Sea Scrolls Concordance*, 3 vols. in 5 (Leiden: Brill, 2003–2016), has fourteen entries for *šd*. This number includes five occurrences in the Aramaic copies of the book of Tobit (4Q196 14 i 5, 12; 4Q197 4 i 13; 4 ii 9, 13). Four of the remaining nine occurrences are in 11Q11 (i 10; ii 3, 4; v 12). *Šd* is extant in a total of six different

Hebrew scriptures and Enochic literature, to refer to the (false) gods worshiped by the nations (4Q243 13 2 // 4Q244 12 2). In Tobit, the Apocryphal Psalms, and the Songs of the Maskil, *šd* designates a class of harmful beings.[4] In Tob 6:14–18, it refers to a particular demon, Asmodeus, who kills any man who attempts to marry Sarah (4Q196 14 i 5, 12; 4Q197 4 ii 9, 13). *Šd* also appears with reference to a harmful being in Tob 6:7. In this verse, "demon" is mentioned alongside "[evil] spirit." In the Apocryphal Psalms, as well, "demon" appears just after a word that may be reconstructed as *hrw*]*ḥwt*, "[the spi]rits" (11Q11 ii 3). It is not clear precisely how the terms "demons" and "spirits" relate to each other in Tobit and the Apocryphal Psalms. They could refer to distinct types of harmful beings, or they could be more or less synonymous. The Songs of the Maskil lists "demons" among several different types of harmful beings (4Q510 1 5).[5]

Another use of *šd*, one that we have not yet observed in our literature, occurs in Pseudo-Ezekiel. This text draws from Isa 13:21, which prophesies that Babylon will be laid waste and will become a dwelling place for a number of wild creatures, including *śʿrym*. The term *śʿrym* in this verse has been translated variously as "goats" or "goat demons."[6] The LXX renders this term with *daimonia*, "demons."[7] The Hebrew Pseudo-Ezekiel clarifies that they are indeed *šdym*, "demons," who are promised to inhabit Babylon (4Q386 1 iii 4). The presence of these beings emblematizes disaster, though whether they are supposed also to be the cause of disaster in this text is not stated.

Spirits

The Dead Sea Scrolls frequently use *rwḥ*, "spirit," with reference to various types of harmful superhuman beings.[8] *Rwḥ* can also refer to various types

---

documents in the Dead Sea Scrolls. The words *daimōn* and *daimonion* are not preserved in the few Greek fragments found among the scrolls.

4. Perhaps the occurrence of *šd* in 4QAmram (4Q547 3 1) also belongs in this category, though the fragmentary state of this text prevents certainty.

5. Ida Fröhlich, "Evil in Second Temple Texts," in *Evil and the Devil*, ed. Fröhlich and Koskenniemi, 35–49, helpfully distinguishes and describes various demonic figures in the book of Tobit and the Dead Sea Scrolls.

6. On the meaning of *śʿrym*, see Henrike Frey-Anthes, *Unheilsmächte und Schutzgenien, Antiwesen und Grensgänger: Vorstellungen von "Dämonen" im alten Israel*, OBO 227 (Fribourg: Academic Press; Göttingen: Vandenhoeck & Ruprecht, 2007), 201–18.

7. Cf. a similar statement regarding "demons" inhabiting Edom in LXX Isa 34:14.

8. There is one possible occurrence of *pneuma* among the Greek fragments. The char-

of beneficent beings. Often *rwḥ* is qualified by a word or phrase in order to specify just what sort of spirit is being mentioned (e.g., *rwḥ ṭmʾh*, "unclean spirit," in 11Q5 19:15). "Spirit" can refer to an angelic being created by God, but also to a being whose nature and origin are aberrant. Recall, for example, the "spirits of the destroying angels" and the "spirits of the bastards" mentioned in the Songs of the Maskil (4Q510 1 5). "Spirits of the destroying angels" probably refers to punishing angels.[9] "Spirits of the bastards," in contrast, refers to those spirits who came about as a result of the illicit union between the watchers and human women, as told in the Book of the Watchers (1 En. 15:1–16:1). Further, "spirits" can refer both to beings whose work is to punish sinners or otherwise harm humans and to those who mislead humans into sin. In the Genesis Apocryphon, God sends a *rwḥ mkdš*, "baneful spirit" (also referred to as a *rwḥ bʾyšʾ*, "evil spirit," and a *rwḥ šḥlnyʾ*, "spirit causing discharges of pus") to afflict Pharaoh's house with illness (1QapGen[ar] 20:16–17, 26). The Damascus Document mentions spirits who are associated with the Satan figure, *rwḥwt blyʿl*, "spirits of Belial," who inspire apostasy among humans (CD 12:2). Additional designations for harmful spirits include the *rwḥ hṭmʾh*, "spirit of impurity" (4Q444 1–4 i + 5 8), *rwḥwt ʿwlh*, "spirits of iniquity" (1QH[a] 25:8), *rwḥy ršʿ*, "wicked spirits" (4Q511 1 6), and *rwḥy ḥbl*, "spirits of destruction" (4Q511 43 6).[10]

Satans

The noun *śṭn*, "satan," occurs six times in the nonbiblical Dead Sea Scrolls, always without the definite article. With one possible exception, the personal name Satan does not appear in the Dead Sea Scrolls. Rather, in the scrolls *śṭn* refers exclusively, or almost exclusively, to a class of harmful beings.

In some cases, it is not clear whether *śṭn* refers to a human or a superhuman being. The Words of the Luminaries borrows the language of 1 Kgs 5, depicting the eschatological era as one in which there is no *śṭn*, per-

acters *PNEU* are preserved just before the right margin of the very fragmentary 7Q4 1 4. There is no indication that the word in this fragment refers to a harmful superhuman being, though it is not impossible.

9. Cf. 1QM 13:11–12, which refers to "the spirits of his [i.e, Belial's] lot, angels of destruction."

10. For a more comprehensive discussion of the semantic range of "spirit" and its collocations in the Dead Sea Scrolls, see Eibert Tigchelaar, "רוּחַ *rūaḥ*," *ThWQ* 3:618–32.

haps understood as in 1 Kings, in the sense of a human military aggressor (4Q504 17:13–14).[11] Two passages in the Hodayot use *śṭn* to refer to a class of attacker (1QH[a] 22:25; 24:23). Though the context of these references does not permit one to be certain whether this *śṭn* is supposed to be human or superhuman, the collocation of *śṭn* with *mšḥyt* in both Hodayot passages (cf. 1 Chr 21:1, 12, 15) and with *gʿr* in 1QH[a] 22:25 (cf. Zech 3:2) may indicate that *śṭn* in these passages refers to a superhuman attacker.[12]

In other documents, *śṭn* clearly refers to a class of harmful superhuman beings. The Aramaic Levi Document contains the prayer *ʾl tšlṭ by kl śṭn*, "let not any satan have power over me" (4Q213[a] 1 i 17). A similar prayer is found in the "Prayer for Deliverance" in 11QPsalms[a]: *ʾl tšlṭ by śṭn wrwḥ ṭmʾh*, "let not a satan or an unclean spirit have dominion over me" (11Q5 19:15). The word *kl*, "any," in the Aramaic Levi Document makes clear that *śṭn* in this text is a class of beings rather than a particular individual. The absence of *kl* in the "Prayer for Deliverance," in contrast, allows for the possibility that *śṭn* refers to a particular individual, "Satan."[13] Similarities with other prayers for protection from superhuman beings, such as that of the Aramaic Levi Document, that unambiguously refer to classes of beings, however, suggest that *śṭn* is also a class of being rather than a name in the "Prayer for Deliverance."[14] The parallelism between *śṭn* and *rwḥ ṭmʾh* may also indicate that "satan" is a category of harmful being rather than a particular individual.[15] While it is possible that the "Prayer for Deliver-

11. Armin Lange, "Satanic Verses: The Adversary in the Qumran Manuscripts and Elsewhere," *RevQ* 24.1 (2009): 39, regards the *śṭn* of 4Q504 as a "category of demons which will no longer exist in the eschaton." Since the language of 1 Kgs 5:18 (Eng. 4) could be appropriated either to refer to a human or a superhuman *śṭn* (e.g., Jub. 23:28–29; 46:2; 50:5), it can be difficult to ascertain just what sort of satan is intended in texts such as 4Q504 17:13–14. The human interpretation, however, is well suited to the international/political context of this passage, in which it is predicted that the nations will bring their silver, gold, and jewels to glorify Israel, Jerusalem, and the temple. Though a superhuman interpretation of the word is not impossible, nothing in the context suggests that the *śṭn* of 4Q504 is superhuman.

12. Cf. also 1QM 13:10–11, which uses *šḥt* with reference to the activity of Belial. For a later example of the collocation of *śṭn* in a superhuman sense and *mšḥyt*, "destroyer," see, e.g., b. Ber. 16b, where Rabbi Judah asks for protection from *śṭn hmšḥyt*, "Satan, the destroyer."

13. For this argument, see Stuckenbruck, *Myth of Rebellious Angels*, 95. Cf. also *DSSR* 2:453, which in this case reproduces the translation of Michael Wise, Martin Abegg, and Edward Cook, *The Dead Sea Scrolls: A New Translation* (New York: HarperCollins, 1996): "Let Satan have no dominion over me, nor an unclean spirit."

14. See also the prayers for relief from harmful spirits in Jub. 10:3, 6; 12:20.

15. So argues Lange, "Satanic Verses," 40. It is possible, however, as Miryam Brand, *Evil Within and Without: The Source of Sin and Its Nature as Portrayed in Second Temple*

ance" contains the earliest extant occurrence of "Satan" as the name of an individual, it is perhaps more likely that this text simply uses the word in the same manner as other texts up to this point in time, as a common noun denoting a class of attacker.[16]

Although no extant text from the Dead Sea Scrolls clearly refers to a figure by the designation "(the) Satan," this does not mean that a figure corresponding to "the Satan" of the Hebrew scriptures or to "the Prince of Mastema" of Jubilees is absent from the scrolls. It only means that the Dead Sea Scrolls, at least in those portions that have been preserved, do not appear to refer to this figure by the title or name Satan. Numerous texts mention figures that correspond to the Satan of earlier literature. Although they go by appellatives other than "the Satan," these chief superhuman antagonists clearly belong to the reception history of the Satan tradition. These include the Angel of Darkness, the Angel of Hostility, Belial, and Melchiresha. Some of these figures behave similarly to the Satan of Zechariah and Job. Others, at first glance, appear to have little in common with the Satan of the Hebrew scriptures. Only when viewed in the context of developing beliefs about the Satan in early Judaism can one perceive that these figures indeed belong to this tradition.

Other Harmful Superhuman Beings

In addition to demons, spirits, and satans, the scrolls mention several other harmful beings, for example, the *mšḥyt*, "destroyer" (4Q511 1 6; cf. Exod 12:23), *ml'ky ḥbl*, "angels of destruction" (1QM 13:12), and *ml'ky hmśṭmwt*, "angels of animosity" (4Q387 2 iii 4).[17] Juxtaposed with "spirits of the de-

Literature, JAJSup 9 (Göttingen: Vandenhoeck & Ruprecht, 2013), 209, contends, that "unclean spirit" is not a personal being but a sinful disposition. Cf. "spirit of faithfulness and knowledge" in line 14.

16. The final occurrence of *śṭn* in the scrolls does not have sufficient context for a full analysis. In 1QSb 1:8, a *lamed* is preserved before *śṭn*, and the text should very likely be reconstructed *k*]*l śṭn*, "a]ny/every satan" (cf. 1QH[a] 4:6; 45:3; 4Q213[a] 1 i 17). As is the case with the other occurrences of the word in the Dead Sea Scrolls, *śṭn* in 1QSb probably denotes a class of harmful being.

17. *DSSR* 2:809 in this case reproduces the translation of Devorah Dimant, *Qumran Cave 4, XXI: Parabiblical Texts, Part 4: Pseudo-Prophetic Texts*, DJD 30 (Oxford: Clarendon, 2001), 187, rendering *ml'ky hmśṭmwt* as "angels of Mastemot."

stroying angels" and "spirits of the bastards" in the Songs of the Maskil are *lylyt*, "Lilith," *'ḥym*, "howlers," and *hpwg'ym pt' pt'wm lt'wt*, "those which fall upon men without warning to lead them astray" (4Q510 1 5–6).[18] Some of these categories are very likely synonymous or overlap to some degree with types of demons and spirits mentioned elsewhere in the scrolls. For instance, 1QM 13:12 identifies the "angels of destruction" with the "spirits of [Belial's] lot." The beings listed in the Songs of the Maskil, however, are presumably supposed to be distinct. Again, one should expect the Dead Sea Scrolls to attest not a consistent taxonomy of harmful superhuman beings but differing taxonomies reflecting the diversity of the writings that the scrolls comprise.

Melchiresha in the Visions of Amram

Several copies of an Aramaic work called the Visions of Amram were found among the fragments from Cave 4. The earliest of these copies have been dated to the latter half of the second century BCE.[19] In one scene in the work, Moses's father Amram has a vision in which he sees two individuals quarreling over him. When Amran asks them who they are that they exercise authority over him, they inform him that they have rule and authority over all the human race.[20] The text is in such poor condition that precisely what happens next in the vision account is difficult to determine. The two figures ask Amram a question, the content of which is uncertain.[21] Amram observes that one of the figures has a frightening appearance, wears dyed clothing, and is associated with darkness. The name given for this figure

18. A similar list seems to have occurred in 4Q444, but the text is too fragmentary to be certain: "[b]astard [spirits] and the unclean spirit [. . . .]" (4Q444 2 i 4).

19. Émile Puech, "4Q543–4Q549: 4QVisions de 'Amram^{a-g} ar," in *Qumrân Grotte 4, XII: Textes araméens, première partie: 4Q529–549*, DJD 31 (Oxford: Oxford University Press, 2001), 283–87. Puech dates 4Q543, 4Q544, and 4Q547 to the second half of the second century BCE.

20. Amram's conversation with the figures is fragmentarily preserved in 4Q543 frags. 5–9; 4Q544 frag. 1; 4Q547 1–2 iii.

21. 4Q544 offers us the most intact copy of this passage. See the reconstructed text, based also in part on 4Q543 and 4Q547, in Puech, "4Q543–4Q549," 322. The conversation is typically reconstructed to indicate that Amram is offered a choice of which individual will rule him. Andrew Perrin, "Another Look at Dualism in *4QVisions of Amram*," *Hen* 36.1 (2014): 109–12, however, correctly warns that not enough text is preserved to demonstrate that this is the nature of the question posed to Amram.

is Melchiresha (*mlky rš*ʿ), "King of Wickedness."[22] The other figure has a more pleasant appearance and is associated with light. The name of this individual is not preserved in the text, though the name Melchizedek is a reasonable guess as to what it might have been. Melchizedek is the name given for the superhuman representative of good who opposes Belial in 11QMechizedek. The name Melchizedek, which would have been taken to mean "Righteous King" or "King of Righteousness," would also be an apt antithesis to Melchiresha.[23] Further, Melchizedek would be a fitting identity for the superhuman protagonist in the Visions of Amram, the message of which pertains to the priesthood.[24] That Melchizedek was the name for this figure, however, remains a guess.

Though one's ability to analyze the Visions of Amram is hindered by its fragmentary state, what is preserved of Amram's vision exhibits dependence on Zech 3. That two superhuman figures dispute the judgment of a human being, that this judgment has implications for the priesthood, and the matter of clothing all have their basis in Zechariah's vision of the disagreement between the angel of Yahweh and the Satan over the high priest Joshua. That these figures "rule" over all humankind, however, would seem to have more in common with traditions such as those found in Jubilees, where patriarchs, including Amram's son Moses, express their concern about the possibility of a deceptive and harmful spirit ruling the elect (e.g., Jub. 1:20).[25] The association of the Satan figure with wickedness, as the

22. The name Melchiresha also occurs in 4Q280. 4Q544, frag. 3, contains the words "three names," so it may be that Melchiresha and/or his good counterpart had three different names. On the possible names for these two figures, see Maxwell J. Davidson, *Angels at Qumran: A Comparative Study of 1 Enoch 1–36, 72–108 and Sectarian Writings from Qumran*, JSPSup 11 (Sheffield: Sheffield Academic Press, 1992), 267–68.

23. For this meaning of the name Melchizedek in early Jewish literature, see Philo, *Allegorical Interpretation* 3.79; Josephus, *Jewish Antiquities* 1.180; *Jewish War* 6.438; Heb 7:1–2.

24. On the priestly nature of the dispute between Melchiresha and the good figure, see Robert R. Duke, *The Social Location of the Visions of Amram (4Q543–547)*, StBibLit 135 (New York: Lang, 2010), 79–88; Blake Alan Jurgens, "Reassessing the Dream-Vision of the *Vision of Amram* (4Q543–547)," *JSP* 24.1 (2014): 22–39.

25. Shared traditions between Jubilees and the Visions of Amram are not limited to those about evil superhuman beings. Both documents also speak of a Canaanite-Egyptian war that took place during the period that Jacob's descendants sojourned in Egypt. Puech, "4Q543–4Q549," 285–87, says that the author of Jubilees knew the Visions of Amram. However, James C. VanderKam, "Jubilees 46:6–47:1 and 4QVisions of Amram," *DSD* 17.2 (2010): 141–58, argues that these two works independently made use of a common tradition about a Canaanite-Egyptian war.

name Melchiresha suggests, is also a concept that is not found in Zech 3 but that appears in Jubilees and later texts.[26]

In other important regards, this text more closely resembles some of the Dead Sea Scrolls than it does either Zechariah or Jubilees. The name Melchiresha occurs in 4QCurses, and a plausible name for this figure's opponent, Melchizedek, is used to refer to a heavenly being in 11QMechizedek. The name Melchiresha, which draws attention to the figure's association with wickedness, also resembles the emphasis on the Satan's role in human sin in some of the scrolls. Moreover, the language of light and darkness, as we will see, appears very prominently in the Treatise on the Two Spirits and in the War Rule. Finally, the belief that two opposing superhuman beings rule humankind also shows up in both the Treatise on the Two Spirits and the War Rule. The notion of superhuman rulers is absent from Zechariah. In Jubilees, the nations are ruled by their respective spirits who answer to the Prince of Mastema. The patriarchs pray that God will not allow one of these spirits to rule over the elect, but they never ask to be ruled instead by a good angelic figure. Jubilees 15:31–32 goes as far as to declare that there is no such figure, but that God rules Israel. The date for the Visions of Amram is probably too early to be considered one of the works produced by the Dead Sea Scrolls sect, but its view of the opposition between light and darkness and between their respective superhuman representatives is one that would find a home among the writings preserved by this group.[27]

26. Contra Liora Goldman, "Dualism in the *Visions of Amram*," *RevQ* 24.3 (2010): 431, who argues that "*Visions of Amram* contains no traces of moral judgment in its treatment of the forces of darkness, Malchiresha, and those who fall under Malchiresha's rule." Goldman argues instead that Melchiresha's role in these texts parallels that of Death in the Testament of Abraham. The supposed parallels between Melchiresha and Death, however, are based on the vision's serpent imagery and on Amram's choice between the two superhuman figures, both of which Perrin, "Another Look at Dualism," 106–17, has argued persuasively are not present in the fragments of the Visions of Amram but have been invented by scholarly reconstructions of the text. Even if Melchiresha's role in some ways resembles that of Death in other texts, as would not be surprising for a "satan" (i.e., attacker/executioner) figure, this would not necessarily exclude a moral judgment. Cf. Jubilees, where the Prince of Mastema is a punisher of the wicked, but also leads the nations into sin.

27. In addition to its early date, that the Visions of Amram is written in Aramaic rather than Hebrew may also suggest that this work was not a product of the sect. On the place of the Aramaic writings among the Dead Sea Scrolls, see Devorah Dimant, "The Qumran Aramaic Texts and the Qumran Community," in *Flores Florentino: Dead Sea Scrolls and Other*

Belial in the Damascus Document

Although the Damascus Document figures fundamentally into most scholarly discussions of the Dead Sea Scrolls, this work was actually known to scholars about fifty years prior to the discovery of the Dead Sea Scrolls. Two medieval manuscripts of the Damascus Document were published by Solomon Schechter in 1910. He had discovered them more than a decade earlier in a genizah in Cairo.[28] For Schechter and those scholars who wrote during the first half of the twentieth century, there was very little context, relatively speaking, within which to study this work. But that situation changed drastically in the middle of the twentieth century with the discovery of the Dead Sea Scrolls, which included several copies of the Damascus Document.[29] Since that time, it has become standard for scholars to discuss the Damascus Document in the

---

Early Jewish Studies in Honour of Florentino García Martínez, ed. Anthony Hilhorst, Émile Puech, and Eibert Tigchelaar, JSJSup 122 (Leiden: Brill, 2007), 197–205.

28. Solomon Schechter, *Documents of Jewish Sectaries Edited from Hebrew Manuscripts in the Cairo Genizah Collection Now in the Possession of the University Library, Cambridge* (Cambridge: Cambridge University Press, 1910). Schechter had brought the fragments of what is now called the Damascus Document to Cambridge from Cairo in 1896. The common designation for those MSS that Schechter brought from Cairo is CD, an abbreviation for "Cairo Damascus": Cairo being the place where the MSS for the work were first discovered and Damascus being a place of historical importance for the group whose origins are described in the Damascus Document (e.g., 6:5, 19; 7:15, 19; 8:21). More recently, photographs of the Damascus Document were published by the Israel Exploration Society, along with a transcription by Elisha Qimron, in Magen Broshi, ed., *The Damascus Document Reconsidered* (Jerusalem: Israel Exploration Society, 1992).

29. Fragments of the Damascus Document were found in Caves 4, 5, and 6. The eight copies of the work from Cave 4 were published in J. M. Baumgarten, *Qumran Cave 4, XIII: The Damascus Document (4Q266–273)*, DJD 18 (Oxford: Clarendon, 1996). The Caves 5 and 6 fragments were published in M. Baillet, J. T. Milik, and R. de Vaux, *Les "Petites Grottes" de Qumrân: Exploration de la falaise, le grottes 2Q, 3Q, 5Q, 6Q, 7Q, à 10Q, le rouleau de cuivre*, DJD 3 (Oxford: Clarendon, 1962). For a complete list of editions of the Cairo and Qumran MSS, see the bibliography in Charlotte Hempel, *The Damascus Texts*, Companion to the Scrolls 1 (Sheffield: Sheffield Academic Press, 2000), 9–14. According to Joseph M. Baumgarten and Daniel R. Schwartz, "Damascus Document," in *Damascus Document, War Scroll, and Related Documents*, vol. 2 of *The Dead Sea Scrolls: Hebrew, Aramaic, and Greek Texts with English Translations*, ed. James H. Charlesworth, PTSDSSP (Tübingen: Mohr Siebeck; Louisville: Westminster John Knox, 1995), 4, "Initial study of the fragments from Cave IV indicates that the main Genizah text (MS A) appears to be a substantially reliable copy, where we now have ancient parallels. . . . Nevertheless, it is wise to note that comparison with Qumran texts at times indicates that the medieval copies are less than perfect texts."

context of the scrolls.[30] That several copies of the Damascus Document turned up among the scrolls suggests that this work was held in high regard by those to whom the scrolls belonged.

The Damascus Document, like many of the texts considered in this study, is likely a composite work, though there is as of yet no consensus among scholars regarding how exactly the document came to be in its present form.[31] The earliest copy of the Damascus Document has been dated to the first half or the middle of the first century BCE, and this date serves as the *terminus ante quem* for the text as we have it.[32] Since the Damascus Document refers explicitly to the book of Jubilees, "the Book of the Divisions of the Times in Their Jubilees and in Their Weeks" (CD 16:3–4), one can be confident that the Damascus Document was written after that work.[33] That the author(s) of the Damascus Document regarded Jubilees as a reliable source of doctrine and made use of it is an observation

30. Though the relationship between the Damascus Document and the other Qumran writings is a matter of debate, it is common these days for scholars to speak of the Damascus Document as a product of the same stream of Judaism as that which produced the Rule of the Community, but not necessarily of the particular group that many scholars believe resided at Qumran. For a brief overview of the relationship between the Damascus Document and the other sectarian writings from the Dead Sea Scrolls, see Baumgarten and Schwartz, "Damascus Document," 6–7; John J. Collins, *Beyond the Qumran Community: The Sectarian Movement of the Dead Sea Scrolls* (Grand Rapids: Eerdmans, 2010), 12–51.

31. See Hempel, *Damascus Texts*, 44–53, for a survey of source- and redaction-critical work on the Damascus Document. See also the extensive discussion of the work's literary history in Stephen Hultgren, *From the Damascus Covenant to the Covenant of the Community: Literary, Historical, and Theological Studies in the Dead Sea Scrolls*, STDJ 66 (Leiden: Brill, 2007). Interesting in the context of the present study is Hultgren's suggestion that all of the passages in the Damascus Document that mention Belial were not part of the original writing, but are part of a Qumran redaction of the work (392–405). Engaging Hultgren's argument would take us beyond the scope of the present study, which is more concerned with the teachings about Belial in the Damascus Document than the history of the Damascus sect or the literary development of the Damascus Document before the Belial material entered it, whenever and however that happened.

32. Baumgarten, *Damascus Document*, 26–30.

33. The composite nature of the Damascus Document complicates the work's dating somewhat. As noted by Philip R. Davies, *The Damascus Covenant: An Interpretation of the "Damascus Document,"* JSOTSup 25 (Sheffield: JSOT Press, 1982), 203, the Damascus Document's citation of Jubilees only proves that this particular portion of the Damascus text is later than Jubilees. Nevertheless, there are other reasons to suspect that the author(s) of the Damascus Document made use of Jubilees. For example, Davies, *Damascus Covenant*, 82–83, suspects that CD 2:14–4:12b relies on Jub. 6:7–14. As I show in this chapter, other passages in the Damascus Document also seem to build on the theology of Jubilees.

of no little significance as it relates to the Damascus Document's teaching on evil superhuman beings.[34]

With regard to sin, although the Damascus Document appeals to its readers to align themselves with the remnant of Israel that faithfully follows God's precepts, the work articulates a deterministic theology similar to that found in other sectarian writings from the scrolls (CD 2:7–13). This sort of doctrine, which speaks of God choosing or, alternatively, rejecting individuals and causing them to stray, is quite compatible with the firmly predestinarian Treatise on the Two Spirits found in some copies of the Rule of the Community, which we discuss in the next chapter.

Those who stray, the Damascus Document explains, do so on account of a "sinful urge and lecherous eyes" (CD 2:16). The concept of a "sinful urge" (*yṣr 'šmh*) that is at the root of humanity's disobedience derives from

34. The relationship between the Damascus Document and Jubilees is an issue unto itself. Davies, *Damascus Covenant*, 203, proposes that both the Damascus Document and Jubilees come from the same circles, those that were also responsible for some of the Enochic writings. Devorah Dimant, "Qumran Sectarian Literature," in *Jewish Writings of the Second Temple Period: Apocrypha, Pseudepigrapha, Qumran Sectarian Writings, Josephus*, ed. Michael E. Stone, CRINT 2.2 (Assen: Van Gorcum; Philadelphia: Fortress, 1984), 530, compares the halakah of Jubilees with that of other sectarian writings from Qumran (including CD) and concludes, "though *Jubilees* and the Qumran scrolls share the same tradition in respect to many *halakhot*, yet they differ in various details and therefore cannot be simply identified. In consequence the question of the nature and the origin of the sect's *halakhah* remains open." Michael A. Knibb, "*Jubilees* and the Origins of the Qumran Community," in *Essays on the Book of Enoch and Other Early Jewish Texts and Traditions*, ed. Michael A. Knibb, SVTP 22 (Leiden: Brill, 2009), 253, says, "there can be no question that the Palestinian priestly reform movement that lies behind Jubilees belongs in the prehistory of the Qumran sect and of the wider Essene movement." He further claims that it is plausible to link the movement that lies behind Jubilees with the "root of planting" of whom CD 1 speaks. Charlotte Hempel, "Community Origins in the Damascus Document in the Light of Recent Scholarship," in *The Provo International Conference on the Dead Sea Scrolls: Technological Innovations, New Texts, and Reformulated Issues*, ed. Donald W. Parry and Eugene Ulrich, STDJ 30 (Leiden: Brill, 1999), 328–30, identifies the pious group whose postexilic origin is described in certain passages of the Damascus Document with those groups whose emergence is described in 1 Enoch and Jubilees. According to Hempel, these passages in the Damascus Document were composed by this group. On the basis of his developmental hypothesis pertaining to the dualism of the Dead Sea Scrolls sect, Peter von der Osten-Sacken, *Gott und Belial: Traditionsgeschichtliche Untersuchungen zum Dualismus in den Texten aus Qumran*, SUNT 6 (Göttingen: Vandenhoeck & Ruprecht, 1969), 197–200, argues that the teaching of Jubilees is later than that of the Damascus Document. Scholars have been correct to reject Osten-Sacken's understanding of the relationship between the two works. As we will see below, it is more likely that the Damascus Document adapts Jubilees' teaching.

the assessment of Gen 8:21 that "the inclination [*yṣr*] of the human heart is evil from youth" (cf. Gen 6:5). As prime examples of individuals who succumbed to their sinful urge, the Damascus Document adduces the sexually immoral watchers and their gigantic offspring, whose actions warranted the flood (CD 2:17–21).

The Damascus Document's teaching on humankind's "urge" or "inclination" differs somewhat from that of Ben Sira, who, as we saw in the previous chapter, mentions a person's *yṣr* in the context of his teaching on free will: "Do not say, 'It was the Lord's doing that I fell away.' . . . It was he who created humankind in the beginning, and he left them in the power of their own free choice [*yṣr*]. If you choose, you can keep the commandments" (Sir 15:11–15). While one might contest the NRSV's translation of *yṣr* as "free choice," the *yṣr* for Ben Sira is certainly more neutral than it is for the author(s) of the Damascus Document. In the Damascus Document the "inclination" seems to be something akin to a proclivity for wickedness that the large majority of humankind gratifies, but that the righteous few successfully resist. Near the end of the first century CE, 4 Ezra speaks similarly of an "evil heart" that humans must overcome if they are to be righteous (4 Ezra 3:20–26; 4:30; 7:92). Later, the Mishnah speaks of two "inclinations" within the heart of a person, a *yṣr ṭwb*, "good inclination," and a *yṣr rʿ*, "bad inclination" (e.g., m. Ber. 9:5).[35] The Damascus Document, like Genesis and 4 Ezra, speaks only of a proclivity for wickedness, which humans are expected to resist, though only a small number actually do.

Although humanity's innate propensity for wickedness alone might seem to account sufficiently for the ubiquity of sin in the world, another passage in the Damascus Document makes clear that God does not simply leave humans to their own depraved devices. Instead, God plays an active part in humankind's error. Regarding those whom God rejects, this passage explains, "God had not chosen them from ancient eternity"; instead "He caused [them] to stray" (CD 2:7, 13). Nothing is said in this passage about any personal agent through whom God leads the nonelect astray, but other passages in the Damascus Document further elucidate the superhuman workings behind human transgression.

The primary designation for the superhuman proponent of wickedness in the Damascus Document is *blyʿl*, "Belial" (CD 4:13, 15; 5:18; 8:2; 12:2;

35. Ishay Rosen-Zvi, *Demonic Desires: "Yetzer Hara" and the Problem of Evil in Late Antiquity* (Philadelphia: University of Pennsylvania Press, 2011), helpfully analyzes notions of the human *yṣr* in rabbinic and prerabbinic Jewish literature.

19:14). As noted in ch. 4, *bly'l* is not the name of a superhuman individual in the Hebrew scriptures, but is a common noun. It is often translated as "worthlessness" or "wickedness" and can carry connotations of "death" (e.g., Deut 13:14; 2 Sam 22:5; Ps 18:5 [Eng. 4]). "Wickedness" appears to be the sense in which the word is used in Jubilees (1:20; 15:33). It is frequently used this way in the Dead Sea Scrolls as well (e.g., 1QH^a 11:30, 33).

Belial comes to be used as a name for the Satan in the centuries prior to the turn of the era and is the preferred name for this figure in several of the Dead Sea Scrolls, such as 11QMelchizedek, the Rule of the Community, and the War Rule.[36] The Greek form of the name, *Beliar*, appears in later texts, such as the Testaments of the Twelve Patriarchs and the Sibylline Oracles.[37] The Greek form also occurs once in the NT (2 Cor 6:15). The preference for the name Belial (i.e., "worthlessness" or "wickedness") in certain Dead Sea Scrolls likely reflects these texts' emphasis on the figure's role as an instigator of sin, as opposed to simply a punisher or attacker of humans, though Belial continues to play these other roles in these documents as well.

In addition to the name Belial, the Damascus Document in one passage uses *ml'k hmśṭmh*, "the Angel of Obstruction [or 'Hostility']" (16:5).[38] This title, which designates an angel who troubles those Israelites who do not keep the law of Moses, is probably an alternate title for Belial (cf. CD 8:1–2). Similarly, 1QM 13:10–11 refers to Belial as *ml'k mśṭmh*, "a hostile angel."[39] The application of such terminology to the Satan figure recalls Jubilees' "Prince of Mastema/Hostility."

The activity of Belial very much resembles that of the Satan of earlier literature and of the Prince of Mastema of Jubilees in particular. Given

36. For a discussion of how one may distinguish between those occurrences of *bly'l* in the scrolls as a common noun and those as a personal name, see Devorah Dimant, "Between Qumran Sectarian and Non-Sectarian Texts: Belial and Mastema," in *The Dead Sea Scrolls and Contemporary Culture*, ed. Adolfo Roitman, STDJ 93 (Leiden: Brill, 2010), 237–41. On the use of "Belial" in the scrolls, see also Corrado Martone, "Evil or Devil? Belial from the Bible to Qumran," *Hen* 26.2 (2004): 115–27; Annette Steudel, "Der Teufel in den Texten aus Qumran," in *Apokalyptik und Qumran*, ed. Jörg Frey and Michael Becker (Paderborn: Bonifatius, 2007), 192–94; Samuel Thomas, "בְלִיַּעַל I *b^{e}lijja'al*," *ThWQ* 1:452–57.

37. T. Reu. 4:11; 6:3; T. Levi 3:3; 19:1; T. Jud. 25:3; T. Iss. 6:1; T. Dan 5:1; SibOr 3:63–74.

38. Alternatively, it is possible to translate *ml'k hmśṭmh* as "angel from Mastema," with Mastema serving as a name. As Dimant, "Belial and Mastema," 247, and Stuckenbruck, *Myth of Rebellious Angels*, 97, have observed, this translation is unlikely due to the definite article attached to *mśṭmh*. The *DSSR* renders this expression "Angel of Obstruction" (1:109).

39. *DSSR* 1:265 has "an angel of malevolence."

the Damascus Document's indebtedness to the book of Jubilees, such correspondence with respect to their understanding of the Satan is to be expected. For instance, CD 5:17–19 claims that Belial assisted the Egyptians who opposed Moses and Aaron: "For in times past Moses and Aaron stood in the power of the Prince of Lights and Belial raised up Yannes and his brother in his cunning <when seeking to do evil> to Israel the first time." In early Jewish tradition, Yannes (or Jannes) and his brother Jambres were the Egyptian magicians who opposed Moses in Pharaoh's court (e.g., 2 Tim 3:8). The belief that these opponents were helped by Belial recalls Jub. 48:9, which says that Prince Mastema assisted the Egyptian magicians against Moses. Further, as Moses is helped by the angel(s) of the presence in Jub. 48:2–4, so Moses and his brother are empowered by the "Prince of Lights" in the Damascus Document.[40]

The Damascus Document also resembles Jubilees in its depiction of Belial as an agent of divine punishment against the wicked: "And such is the verdict on all members of the covenant who do not hold firm to these laws: they are condemned to destruction by Belial" (CD 8:1–2).[41] In contrast, another passage in the Damascus Document speaks of divine judgment being executed by a group of angelic beings: "But Strength, Might, and great Wrath in the flames of fire <with> all the angels of destruction shall come against all who rebel against the proper way and who despise the law" (CD 2:5–6). The angels of destruction in this passage resemble the "forces of Mastema" who are sent to kill the firstborn of Egypt in Jub. 49:2, or the envoy of "destroying angels" (*ml'ky r'ym*) that is given this task in Ps 78:49. It could be that the traditions brought together in the Damascus Document are not uniform with regard to exactly what superhuman being(s) will

40. Early studies of the Damascus Document expressed uncertainty over how 5:17c–19 relates to the surrounding material (e.g., Solomon Schechter, *Documents of Jewish Sectaries*, Library of Biblical Studies [1910; repr., New York: Ktav, 1970], 69n32; R. H. Charles, *APOT* 2:811). Building on this uncertainty, several scholars have suggested that these lines were added to the text by an editor: e.g., Jerome Murphy-O'Connor, "An Essene Missionary Document? CD II, 14–VI, 1," *RB* 77.2 (1970): 224–25; Jean Duhaime, "Dualistic Reworking in the Scrolls from Qumran," *CBQ* 49.1 (1987): 53–54; Michael A. Knibb, *The Qumran Community*, CCWJCW 2 (Cambridge: Cambridge University Press, 1987), 46; Hultgren, *From the Damascus Covenant*, 397–401. Whether this passage was part of the earliest compositional layer of the Damascus Document or belongs to a subsequent layer, it fits its current context well. The opposition to Moses and Aaron at the time of the exodus provides a pertinent example from Israel's history of individuals who opposed Moses and God's anointed, which is the subject of CD 5:20–6:1.

41. See also the similar statement in the alternate version of this passage in CD 19:13–14.

carry out God's judgment against sinners, with one tradition holding that Belial is God's heavenly punisher, and another that this responsibility falls to certain "angels of destruction." That the Damascus Document makes use of Jubilees, which itself comprises diverse traditions, may account for some of the variation in the Damascus Document. Nevertheless, a harmonistic reading of these two passages in the Damascus Document, according to which Belial leads a group of punishing angels, is equally possible. See, for instance, the War Rule, in which Belial commands a host of "angels of destruction" (1QM 13:11–12).

The Damascus Document indeed presupposes a hierarchy in the superhuman realm. CD 12:2–3 indicates that Belial has a host of deceptive spirits at his disposal: "Everyone who is controlled by the spirits of Belial and advises apostasy will receive the same verdict as the necromancer and the medium." This theology resembles Jubilees' teaching concerning the Prince of Mastema and the spirits that he employs to lead humankind astray (Jub. 10:1–14; 11:4–5). Furthermore, the Damascus Document shares with Jubilees the belief that keeping the law is Israel's means for protecting itself from the Angel/Prince of Mastema's attacks: "Therefore let a man <take upon> himself the oath to return to the law of Moses, for in it everything is laid out in detail in the 'Book of Time Divisions by Jubilees and Weeks.' On the day a man promises to return to the law of Moses the Angel of Obstruction will leave him, if he keeps His words" (CD 16:1–5). This passage, which refers the reader to the book of Jubilees, follows the earlier work in prescribing the Mosaic Torah as the means for warding off the Angel of Obstruction/Hostility/Mastema.[42]

Nevertheless, there are some very significant differences between the portrayals of the Satan figure in the Damascus Document and Jubilees. These pertain to Belial's role as the chief superhuman instigator of sin. I have already mentioned the Damascus Document's preference for the name Belial (i.e., "wickedness"), rather than Mastema (i.e., "hostility"). Another difference pertains to the scope of Belial's deceptive work. Jubilees distinguishes only between the nations, which are controlled by spirits under the Prince of Mastema's authority, and Israel, which is governed by God. The Damascus Document, in contrast, speaks explicitly of a period of time when even some among Israel are ruled by Belial. This is the assumption of CD 12:2–3, quoted in the previous paragraph, which stipulates

42. A similar statement is found in the NT epistle of James: "Submit yourselves therefore to God. Resist the devil, and he will flee from you" (Jas 4:7).

severe punishment for any Israelite who, falling under the influence of Belial's spirits, speaks apostasy.[43]

What is more, that Belial would gain power over an Israelite, according to the Damascus text, is no mere isolated incident, but is a pandemic that characterizes the present evil age. The Damascus Document declares that the whole people of Israel—except for the group represented by the Damascus text—is for the time being under Belial's deception.

> But in the present age Belial is unrestrained in Israel, just as God said by Isaiah the prophet, the son of Amoz, saying, "*Fear and pit and snare are upon thee, dweller in the land*" (Isa 24:17). The true meaning of this verse concerns the three traps of Belial about which Levi son of Jacob said that Belial would catch Israel in, so he directed them towards three kinds of righteousness. The first is fornication; the second is wealth; the third is defiling the sanctuary. Who escapes from one is caught in the next, and whoever escapes from that is caught in the other. (CD 4:12–19)

These lines contain an interpretation of Isa 24:17. The reference to "three nets of Belial" appears to derive from an otherwise unknown tradition associated with the patriarch Levi. The present passage claims that Belial has been allowed to work his delusion among the people of Israel, causing them to engage in certain wicked deeds, mistaking them for works of righteousness. What is perhaps a hypothetical possibility in Jubilees has become a terrible reality in the Damascus Document. Belial has gained dominion over Israel.

It is possible that this passage also relates to the conversation between Jubilees and the Epistle of Enoch that we observed in the previous chapter, regarding whether sin has been "sent" upon the earth. Though English translations of the Damascus Document typically obscure the possible connection, the Hebrew of the Damascus Document may reflect Jubilees' teaching about the Prince of Mastema's part in leading the nations astray. The Hebrew of CD 4:12–13 says that in the present age, *bly'l mšwlḥ byśr'l*. This verb *mšwlḥ* has been translated variously as "is unrestrained," "will run unbridled," "is let loose," and "shall be unleashed."[44] While these and

43. Lev 20:27 required death by stoning for any Israelite who functioned as a medium. CD 12:2–3 instructs that this sentence is to apply as well in the case of apostasy, which is attributed to deception by the spirits of Belial.

44. In addition to *DSSR* 1:89, see Davies, *Damascus Covenant*, 243; Geza Vermes, *The*

similar words denoting permission of various sorts are possible translations of this word, it is also possible to render it "sent." In Jubilees, various sins are said to have been "sent" upon the earth by the Prince of Mastema via his host of evil spirits (Jub. 11:5). The Epistle of Enoch, taking issue with this explanation of evil, argues that lawlessness was not "sent" upon the earth (1 En. 98:4). Perhaps, given the Damascus Document's reliance on Jubilees, this statement should be understood in the context of this discussion. According to the Damascus Document, not only has "Belial" (or "Wickedness") been sent upon the earth, but he has been sent even among the people of Israel. The one sending Belial is, presumably, God.[45]

Another difference between the Damascus Document and Jubilees has to do with the sins for which Belial and the Prince of Mastema are supposed to be responsible. In Jubilees, the Prince of Mastema leads the nations into various sins, idolatry and violence in particular. These are the sins of the nations, not of Israel. According to the Damascus Document, Belial is credited with using three nets to trap Israel: fornication, wealth, and defilement of the sanctuary. These sins, however, are defined according to sectarian standards. Those who did not belong to the Damascus group and did not interpret the Mosaic law as that group did, this text claims, were deceived by Belial. These Israelites, however, were not aware of their sin. According to the Damascus Document, the failure of other Israelites to recognize their error resulted from their being deceived by Belial.

Are Belial and the Prince/Angel of Mastema the Same Person?

Until recently, the scholarly consensus has held that the Dead Sea Scrolls speak of a single leader of the forces of evil. According to this view, Belial is

Complete Dead Sea Scrolls in English (New York: Allen Lane/Penguin, 1997), 130; Baumgarten and Schwartz, "*Damascus Document*," 19.

45. In arguing for this particular translation of the passage, I see two points that are at stake. The first is the connection of the Damascus Document's teaching with the doctrine that is debated by Jubilees and the Epistle of Enoch regarding the source of human sin. The second is the degree to which God is believed to play an active part in causing human sin. Although the distinction between "releasing" Belial for the purpose of misleading Israel and "sending" Belial for this purpose may be largely semantic, the latter carries a more active nuance, a nuance that seems appropriate for the deterministic outlook of the Damascus Document.

the name of the Satan in the Dead Sea Scrolls, and the figure of Belial corresponds to the Prince of Mastema in the book of Jubilees.[46] This is also the position I espouse in the present study. In a 2011 essay, however, Devorah Dimant challenged the consensus view.[47] She contended that there are two leaders of the forces of evil in the Dead Sea Scrolls; Belial and the Prince/Angel of Mastema are to be distinguished. Belial should be understood as one of the harmful superhuman beings who is subordinate to the Prince/Angel of Mastema.

While Dimant is to be commended for her willingness to scrutinize the scholarly consensus, her hypothesis in this case is not supported by the textual evidence. Belial is called "a hostile angel" (or "angel of Hostility/Mastema") in 1QM 13:11. Indeed, several passages in the scrolls connect Belial with *mśṭmh*, "hostility," and related vocabulary: *śṭm*, "to be hostile toward," and *śṭmh*, "hostility, hatred" (1QM 13:4; 14:9; 4Q174 4 4; 4Q286 7 ii 2). Not only are there terminological points of contact, but there are significant conceptual parallels as well. Similar to the Prince of Mastema in Jubilees, Belial punishes wicked humans (CD 8:1–2), commands a host of spirits (e.g., CD 12:2), leads humans to sin (e.g., CD 4:13–18), and sides with Israel's national enemies against God's people in battle (e.g., 1QM 1:1). Belial is also credited with empowering the Egyptian magicians' opposition to Moses in CD 5:17–19, as is the Prince of Mastema in Jub. 48:9.

One piece of evidence that Dimant adduces for her hypothesis is the very fragmentary text Pseudo-Jubilees, which contains both the designations "Belial" and "Prince of Mastema" within a relatively brief text. Unfortunately, too little of this text remains to determine whether Belial and the Prince of Mastema are supposed to be one and the same or two distinct persons in this document. In support of regarding them as one and the same, other passages refer to the Satan by more than one designation ("Mastema" and "the Satan" in Jub. 10:8–12; "Belial" and "a hostile angel" or "Angel of Mastema/Hostility" in 1QM 13:11). In support of regarding

46. See, e.g., Theodore J. Lewis, "Belial," *ABD* 1:655–56; Ryan E. Stokes, "Belial," *EDEJ* 435–36; Chad T. Pierce, "Satan and Related Figures," *EDEJ* 1198–99.

47. Dimant, "Belial and Mastema," 235–56. Dimant was not the first scholar to express an awareness of the possibility that the different appellatives might refer to distinct beings. See, e.g., Annette Steudel, "God and Belial," in *The Dead Sea Scrolls Fifty Years after Their Discovery*, ed. Lawrence H. Schiffman, Emanuel Tov, and James C. VanderKam (Jerusalem: Israel Exploration Society, 2000), 333, who says with respect to Belial, Mastema, Melchiresha, etc., "every single text has to be examined closely to see whether in fact exactly the same entity is meant."

them as distinct persons, on the other hand, is the tentative reconstruction of one passage in Pseudo-Jubilees by James VanderKam and J. T. Milik, which reads, "Belial listened to [the Prince of the Mastema . . .]."[48] This reconstruction is based on a combination of 4QPseudo-Jubilees[a], which preserves the words "Belial listened to [ ]" (4Q225 frag. 2, col. ii), with what appears to be the corresponding line of 4QPseudo-Jubilees[b], which preserves "to (the) prince" (4Q226 frag. 7).

While this reconstruction of Pseudo-Jubilees is possible, it is far from certain. No copy of the work preserves the complete statement. This is important, because 4Q225 and 4Q226 are not identical. Differences between them lead some scholars to regard them as distinct (albeit related) works.[49] In light of such differences, one must be cautious regarding any conclusions about the theology of the document, if it is indeed a single document, that are drawn from a simple combination of the two texts. Even if the two texts were identical in the passage under consideration, it is not clear that "the prince" of 4QPseudo-Jubilees[b] is the Prince of Mastema. The combined text would only read, "Belial listened to the prince." While the prince in this line might in theory be the Prince of Mastema, it is also possible that he should be identified as the Prince of Lights. If the Prince of Mastema and Belial are regarded as distinct beings in this document, it would be the only place in the literature we have considered where there appears to be any such distinction, a fact that renders this reconstruction all the more unlikely.

Although numerous titles are given for the superhuman representative of wickedness in the Dead Sea Scrolls, there is no indication that these point to different figures. The scholarly consensus that these are simply multiple titles for one satanic individual appears to be correct. Given the great similarity between Jubilees' depiction of the Prince of Mastema and what the Damascus Document and other Dead Sea texts claim about Belial, there can be little doubt that Belial is a designation that the Dead Sea Scrolls use for the superhuman individual whom Jubilees calls (the Prince of) Mastema, the individual known as "the Satan" in the Hebrew scriptures. The different designations for this figure, however, are not in-

48. J. C. VanderKam and J. T. Milik, "Jubilees," in *Qumran Cave 4, VIII: Parabiblical Texts, Part 1*, by Harold Attridge et al., DJD 13 (Oxford: Clarendon, 1994), 149–51.

49. See the discussion and bibliography in Michael Segal, "Dynamics of Composition and Rewriting in Jubilees," *RevQ* 26.4 (2014): 566, who regards 4Q225 and 4Q226 as different versions of the same work.

significant, since they point to different emphases pertaining to the activity of this individual. Whereas "the Satan" and "the Prince of Mastema" emphasize the harm that this figure inflicts on humans, the name Belial draws attention to this figure's association with sin.

Belial in the Rule of the Community

The work known as the Rule of the Community was very important to the Jews of the Dead Sea Scrolls sect, as is evident from the dozen or so copies of the work found among the scrolls. In this rule book are the teachings and regulations according to which a sectarian community organized itself. Its rules include stipulations for membership in the group, policies for disciplining its members, and instructions for maintaining the group's purity and its covenant with God. Differences among the various copies of this work, as well as indicators within the document itself, reveal that the Rule of the Community underwent several stages of composition and editing.[50] On the basis of the manuscript evidence, this work appears to have taken the form(s) known to us by around 75 BCE.[51]

Interestingly, although the Rule of the Community mentions Belial four times, the work does not have much to say about the nature or activity

50. See Jerome Murphy-O'Connor, "La genèse littéraire de la *Règle de la Communauté*," *RB* 76.4 (1969): 528–49; J. Pouilly, *La règle de la communauté de Qumran: Son évolution littéraire*, CahRB 17 (Paris: Gabalda, 1976); Robert A. J. Gagnon, "How Did the Rule of the Community Obtain Its Final Shape: A Review of Scholarly Research," *JSP* 10 (1992): 61–79; Philip S. Alexander, "The Redaction-History of *Serekh ha-Yahad*: A Proposal," *RevQ* 17.65–68 (1996): 437–56; Sarianna Metso, *The Textual Development of the Qumran Community Rule*, STDJ 21 (Leiden: Brill, 1997); Hartmut Stegemann, *The Library of Qumran: On the Essenes, Qumran, John the Baptist, and Jesus* (Leiden: Brill; Grand Rapids: Eerdmans, 1998), 107–12; Michael A. Knibb, "Rule of the Community," *EDSS* 2:793–97.

51. The copy of the Rule of the Community found in Cave 1 (1QS), which serves as the basis for most studies of this document, was made sometime between 100 and 75 BCE (James H. Charlesworth in Elisha Qimron and James H. Charlesworth, "Rule of the Community," in *Rule of the Community and Related Documents*, vol. 1 of *The Dead Sea Scrolls: Hebrew, Aramaic, and Greek Texts with English Translations*, ed. James H. Charlesworth, PTSDSSP [Tübingen: Mohr Siebeck; Louisville: Westminster John Knox, 1994], 2). Scholars believe that the work had its origin in the mid-second century BCE, since some of the Cave 4 MSS of it have been dated to the end of that century (J. T. Milik, "Le travail d'édition des fragments manuscrits de Qumrân," *RB* 63.1 [1956]: 61; Philip S. Alexander and Geza Vermes, *Qumran Cave 4, XIX: Serekh ha-Yaḥad and Two Related Texts*, DJD 26 [Oxford: Clarendon, 1998], 20–21).

of Belial. It is much more concerned with how humans conduct themselves in relation to Belial than with Belial himself.[52] Three of the four references to Belial in the work occur in the expression *mmšlt blyʿl*, "dominion/reign of Belial" (1QS 1:18, 23–24; 2:19). The remaining occurrence appears in the expression *gwrl blyʿl*, literally "lot of Belial" (1QS 2:5). While it is possible that *blyʿl* in these expressions simply means "wickedness," parallel statements in other Dead Sea texts, in which Belial is clearly a person, suggest that the Rule of the Community also refers to the person Belial (e.g., 1QM 1:5; 14:9).[53]

The "dominion of Belial" is described in 1QS as one of trial, during which the covenanters' faithfulness to God is tested by adversity. The Rule of the Community warns its readers that those who enter the covenant "must not turn back from following after [God] because of any terror, dread, affliction, or agony during the time of Belial's dominion" (1QS 1:17–18). The dominion of Belial was also a time during which Israel transgressed God's commands: "the Levites . . . shall rehearse the wicked acts of the children of Israel, all their guilty transgressions and sins committed during the dominion of Belial" (1QS 1:22–24). If one can harmonize the Rule of the Community and the Damascus Document on this point, the era of Belial's dominion probably corresponds to that period of time mentioned in the Damascus Document during which Belial was sent amid Israel to lead them into sin (CD 4:12–21; cf. 1QM 14:9–10).[54] The wicked are referred to in this work as the "lot of Belial" (1QS 2:5). The expression "lot of Belial" also occurs in the War Rule with reference to the enemies of Israel who are ruled by Belial (1QM 1:5; 4:2). The Community Rule contains a lengthy passage that prescribes a number of curses that the Levites are to utter against these guilty individuals (1QS 2:4–18). This ceremony was to be performed "annually, all the days of Belial's dominion" (1QS 2:19).[55]

52. Brand, *Evil Within and Without*, 243–48.

53. The word *blyʿl* occurs one further time in 1QS: "I shall give no refuge in my heart to *blyʿl*" (10:21). The context of this statement, in which *blyʿl* appears in parallel with "foolishness," "sinful deceit," "fraud," and "lies," indicates that *blyʿl* in this passage should be understood as "wickedness."

54. Brand, *Evil Within and Without*, 242, states that 1QS conceives of two periods of Belial's dominion, one that corresponds to the history of Israel's rebellion against God and another that corresponds to the present time of persecution.

55. See also the prescription for cursing Belial and the spirits of his lot in 4QBerakhot (4Q286, frag. 7a; 4Q287, frag. 6).

Although the Rule of the Community does not speak directly about Belial's nature and activity, it clearly associates Belial with wickedness and human sin. The Rule of the Community refers to evil humans as the "lot of Belial." Belial's dominion is characterized by sin in Israel. The Rule of the Community also describes Belial's dominion as one in which otherwise faithful individuals experience considerable pressure to turn away from following after God. Since it is Belial who holds dominion during this era, he is, presumably, supposed to be the instigator of the sin and persecution.[56] The Rule of the Community, however, stops short of saying this explicitly. Whatever his particular role may be, Belial in this work, as in the Damascus Document, is a wicked figure.

The Dead Sea Scrolls, the Satan, and Sin

In the Dead Sea Scrolls considered in this chapter, Belial (or Melchiresha) resembles in many respects the Satan figures of earlier literature. These beings are particularly close conceptually to the Prince of Mastema in Jubilees. These documents, however, also mark some significant developments in the Satan tradition. The main difference between these scrolls and earlier literature is the degree to which the scrolls view Belial as a wicked figure. The association of the Satan figure with sin is not new but can be observed in Jubilees as part of a complex depiction of the Prince of Mastema. In the Visions of Amram, the Damascus Document, and the Rule of the Community, however, the association with wickedness is primary. The names Belial and Melchiresha are indicators of this shift in thinking about the figure's relationship to sin. Belial's sphere of influence has also been extended to include members of Israel who are deceived and led into sin by him. This idea is particularly prominent in the Damascus Document, which states that Belial has trapped in nets those members of Israel outside the Damascus group, making them believe that they are righteous when they are in serious error. Also, the sins for which Belial is supposed to be responsible now include violations of the Mosaic Torah. Furthermore, language of "light" and "darkness," which appears in these texts in connection

56. Contra Brand, *Evil Within and Without*, 243–48, who argues that the Rule of the Community denies Belial any agency in human sin. While Brand may be correct that the work emphasizes human responsibility, it is probably going too far to conclude that the work denies Belial any sort of role whatsoever in human wickedness.

with Belial/Melchiresha, points to yet another significant development in the relationship between the Satan and evil. (I discuss this development in the next chapter.) While there can be little doubt that the superhuman antagonist of these Dead Sea Scrolls belongs to the tradition of satanic figures that extends back into the Hebrew scriptures, he is beginning to look quite different from those figures.

CHAPTER 8

Belial and the Powers of Darkness

Two texts from the Dead Sea Scrolls depict reality primarily in terms of a cosmic conflict between light and darkness. One of these texts, the Treatise on the Two Spirits, describes the activity of the Angel of Darkness, a superhuman figure who is associated with the spirit of falsehood and leads all of humankind to practice the deeds of falsehood. The other text, the War Rule, offers instructions pertaining to the eschatological conflict between the Sons of Light and the Sons of Darkness. In this text, Belial leads the Sons of Darkness against the Sons of Light, who are aided by Michael. This text portrays Belial as one who is at odds with God. This Satan in this work appears less like one of God's superhuman functionaries and more like God's enemy.

The Angel of Darkness in the Treatise on the Two Spirits

The Treatise on the Two Spirits is a unit of text found in some copies of the Rule of the Community.[1] This intriguing passage has attracted perhaps more scholarly attention than any other in the Dead Sea Scrolls. Since the Treatise appears in the copy of the Rule of the Community from Cave 1, it was among the initial texts from the vicinity of Qumran to be discov-

1. The Treatise appears in 1QS and 4QS[c]. Eibert J. C. Tigchelaar, "'These Are the Names of the Spirits of . . .': *4QCatalogue of Spirits* (*4Q230*) and New Manuscript Evidence for the *Two Spirits Treatise*," *RevQ* 84.4 (2004): 543–45, argues that 1Q29a (=1Q29 frags. 13–17) may have belonged to an additional copy of the Treatise. The Treatise on the Two Spirits appears in its entirety only in 1QS (3:13–4:26).

ered and made available to scholars. Owing to its availability early on, its perspective on the nature of the struggle between good and evil was for a time believed to represent the quintessential theology of the Dead Sea Scrolls group.[2] More recently, since the publication of the complete corpus of the Dead Sea Scrolls, scholars have come to acknowledge that this teaching may not have been as important for the group(s) who possessed the Dead Sea Scrolls as was previously assumed.[3] Many scholars now also suspect that the Two Spirits Treatise existed at one time independently of its present context in the Rule of the Community and that it may not be "sectarian" at all.[4] Nevertheless, the Treatise on the Two Spirits bears witness to at least one strand of thinking in the scrolls regarding good, evil, and their superhuman proponents.

The Two Spirits

The Treatise on the Two Spirits derives its name from 1QS 3:17–19.

2. The opinion that the Treatise's teaching characterized the Dead Sea Scrolls group was bolstered by the identification of this group with the Essenes, whose theology Josephus summarizes as follows: "The sect of the Essenes . . . declares that Fate is the mistress of all things, and that nothing befalls men unless it be in accordance with his decree" (*Antiquities* 13.172–73 [Marcus, LCL]). Cf. the opening of the Treatise: "All that is now and ever shall be originates with the God of knowledge. Before things come to be, He has ordered all their designs, so that when they do come to exist—at their appointed times as ordained by His glorious plan—they fulfill their destiny, a destiny impossible to change" (1QS 3:15–16).

3. Charlotte Hempel, "The Teaching on the Two Spirits and the Literary History of the Community Rule," in *Dualism in Qumran,* ed. Géza G. Xeravits, LSTS 76 (London: T&T Clark, 2010), 102–4.

4. Sarianna Metso, *The Textual Development of the Qumran Community Rule,* STDJ 21 (Leiden: Brill, 1997), 145, says that it is likely that the Two Spirits passage existed independently of the Rule of the Community and was later made to address the *maskil* in order to fit into its present context. Hempel, "Teaching on the Two Spirits," 102–20, acknowledges this likely explanation for the presence of the Treatise in some copies of the Rule of the Community, but further observes that the Treatise seems to share some of the redactional history of the Rule. An alternative explanation for the presence of the Treatise in certain copies of the Rule of the Community has been suggested by Philip Alexander, "The Redaction-History of *Serekh ha-Yaḥad*: A Proposal," *RevQ* 17 (1996): 437–56, who argues, based on the paleographical dating of the pertinent MSS, that 1QS and 4QS[c] (which contain the Two Spirits Treatise) represent the earlier form of the Rule of the Community, which later editions abbreviated.

> [God] created humankind to rule over the world, appointing for them two spirits in which to walk until the time ordained for His visitation. These are the spirits of truth and falsehood.

These two spirits are referred to additionally in 1QS 3:25 as the "spirits of light and darkness." The Treatise teaches that the spirits of truth/light, on the one hand, and of falsehood/darkness, on the other, are the basis for all human activity, good and evil.

It is difficult to define precisely what sort of "spirits" the two spirits are supposed to be, whether they are superhuman beings or simply psychological dispositions within humans.[5] That the brief treatise uses the word *rwḥ*, "spirit," in differing ways does not help to clarify the matter. In 1QS 4:3, for example, *rwḥ* seems to be used much as it is elsewhere in the Rule of the Community to refer to the moral dispositions of human beings.[6] In 1QS 3:24, on the other hand, one reads of the *rwḥy gwrlw*, "spirits allied with him [lit. 'of his lot']," of the Angel of Darkness, likely referring to maleficent superhuman spirits who serve the Angel of Darkness.[7]

Adding further complexity to the discussion is the controversial question of whether the Two Spirits teaching bears the mark of Zoroastrian influence. From the early days of Dead Sea Scrolls studies, scholars have noted the resemblance between the Two Spirits discourse and the teaching of the Iranian Gathas.[8] This text, which is supposed to contain the

5. For a brief summary of the two major views on the nature of the two spirits, see John R. Levison, "The Two Spirits in Qumran Theology," in *The Dead Sea Scrolls and the Qumran Community,* vol. 2 of *The Bible and the Dead Sea Scrolls*, ed. James H. Charlesworth (Waco, TX: Baylor University Press, 2006), 169–85. See also the helpful discussion of Mladen Popović, "Anthropology, Pneumatology and Demonology in Early Judaism: The *Two Spirits* Treatise (1QS 3:13–4:26) and Other Texts from the Dead Sea Scrolls," in *Sibyls, Scriptures, and Scrolls: John Collins at Seventy*, ed. Joel Baden, Hindy Najman, and Eibert Tigchelaar, JSJSup 175, 2 vols. (Leiden: Brill, 2017), 2:1029–67.

6. *Rwḥ* may also be used in this psychological sense in 3:14 and 4:10.

7. For a discussion of the use of *rwḥ* in the Dead Sea Scrolls and in the Two Spirits passage, see A. A. Anderson, "The Use of 'Ruaḥ' in 1QS, 1QH and 1QM," *JSS* 7 (1962): 293–303; Arthur Everett Sekki, *The Meaning of Ruaḥ at Qumran*, SBLDS 110 (Atlanta: Scholars Press, 1989), 193–219; Maxwell J. Davidson, *Angels and Qumran: A Comparative Study of 1 Enoch 1–36, 72–108 and Sectarian Writings from Qumran*, JSPSup 11 (Sheffield: Sheffield Academic Press, 1992), 152–56. Davidson correctly identifies the "spirits" of the lot of the Angel of Darkness as "supernatural" beings, but he incorrectly assumes that they must be "angels," in particular. They are more likely to be connected with the "evil spirit" (*rwḥ rʿh*) tradition of earlier literature, which is not necessarily the same category of being as an "angel" (*mlʾk*).

8. A. Dupont-Sommer, "L'instruction sur les deux Esprits dans le 'Manuel de Disci-

teaching of Zoroaster himself, likewise claims that the existence of good and evil stems from the activity of two superhuman spirits, one good and the other evil (*Yasna* 30:3–5). If the Two Spirits Treatise is indeed indebted to this Zoroastrian belief, as scholars have hypothesized, the likelihood that the two spirits of the Treatise are likewise superhuman beings is increased. Other scholars, however, prefer to emphasize the continuity of the Two Spirits Treatise's teaching with earlier biblical traditions, and do not find Iranian parallels to be determinative for interpretation of the Treatise.[9] In this case, there is less reason to take the two spirits as superhuman, personal beings.

Within the Treatise itself, one can find support for both a superhuman and psychological interpretation. In favor of the superhuman interpretation is that the Treatise refers unambiguously to two important angelic figures in the struggle between truth and falsehood, the "Prince of Lights" and the "Angel of Darkness." Some scholars believe that the "spirits of truth and falsehood" are alternative designations for these angelic beings.[10] This identification is not impossible, though it seems preferable to distinguish the two spirits from the Angel of Darkness and the Prince of Lights. Another passage in the Two Spirits Treatise speaks of the spirits of truth and falsehood struggling within the heart of a person (1QS 4:23–25), which suggests that the spirits are different from the angels themselves. The statement that the spirits contend within a person leads some scholars to conclude that the "spirits" are no more than psychological dispositions like the good and bad inclination of later rabbinic tradition (e.g., m. Ber. 9:5).[11]

---

pline,'" *RHR* 142.1 (1952): 16–17, 21, 25, 28–30, 34; Karl Georg Kuhn, "The Sektenschrift und die iranische Religion," *ZTK* 49.3 (1952): 296–316.

9. E.g., P. Wernberg-Møller, "A Reconsideration of the Two Spirits in the Rule of the Community (1 Q Serek III,13–IV,26)," *RevQ* 3.3 (1961): 413–41; Marco Treves, "The Two Spirits of the Rule of the Community," *RevQ* 3.3 (1961): 449–52.

10. E.g., Davidson, *Angels and Qumran*, 146. So also James H. Charlesworth, "A Critical Comparison of the Dualism in 1QS 3:13–4:26 and the 'Dualism' Contained in the Gospel of John," in *John and the Dead Sea Scrolls*, ed. James H. Charlesworth (New York: Crossroad, 1990), 78, who provides a list of earlier scholars who identify the two spirits likewise.

11. Wernberg-Møller, "Reconsideration of the Two Spirits," 413–41; Treves, "Two Spirits," 449–52. In his earlier commentary on the Rule of the Community, P. Wernberg-Møller, *The Manual of Discipline: Translated and Annotated with an Introduction*, STDJ 1 (Leiden: Brill; Grand Rapids: Eerdmans, 1957), 67, 70, allowed that the Two Spirits teaching made use of Zoroastrian traditions and that the two spirits of 1QS 3:18 had a "metaphysical" dimension. He refers to this position as "erroneous" in his later article.

The majority of scholars, however, have been correct to reject a purely psychological interpretation of the passage.[12]

Some of the apparent contradiction between the superhuman and psychological interpretations of the two spirits may be alleviated if one recognizes that the distinction between the psychological forces within a person and the invisible forces that act upon a person from without is much clearer to modern thinkers than it was to some ancient theologians. Recall the "spirit of deep sleep" that Isaiah says God has poured out upon Israel (Isa 29:10), or the "evil spirit" that God sends between Abimelech and Shechem, creating hostility between them (Judg 9:23). The two spirits of the Treatise are not to be equated with the Prince of Lights and the Angel of Darkness, but to say that they are simply dispositions internal to individual humans probably does not do justice to their full substance as described in the Treatise. More likely, the spirits of truth and deceit are to be regarded as impersonal "forces," which, by God's design, are at work in the world and within human beings.

Whatever the spirits' precise nature, the Two Spirits discourse teaches that God created the spirit of truth and the spirit of falsehood and that humankind is caught in a superhuman conflict between the two. The spirits of truth and falsehood, according to the Treatise, did not enter the world subsequent to the creation of humanity. Unlike other Jewish literature from this era that claims either that sin was created by humans (Epistle of Enoch) or that certain evils came about as a result of angelic rebellion (Book of the Watchers, Jubilees), the Two Spirits discourse says that God created the spirit of falsehood at the time of humanity's creation. Accordingly, rather than looking to Gen 3 or 6 for the biblical account of evil's origin, the Two Spirits teaching looks to Gen 1.

Although the Treatise nowhere explicitly cites the text of Genesis, it draws liberally from the Gen 1 creation story, among other biblical passages, in formulating its teaching.[13] The opposition between good and evil, the Treatise states, was established by God at creation and is rooted in an even more fundamental polarity between light and darkness: "[God] created humankind to rule over the world, appointing for them two spirits in which to walk until the time ordained for His visitation. These are the

12. E.g., John J. Collins, *Apocalypticism in the Dead Sea Scrolls* (London: Routledge, 1997), 40–41.

13. More accurately stated, the Treatise makes use of Gen 1:1–2:4a, the creation material attributed to P by source critics.

spirits of truth and falsehood. Upright character and fate originate [*twldwt*] with the Spring of Light; perverse, with the Fountain of Darkness" (1QS 3:17–19).[14]

The polarity between light and darkness can be found in a number of passages in the Hebrew scriptures.[15] In Isa 45:7, God says, "I form light and create darkness, I make weal and create woe; I the LORD do all these things." Light and darkness appear prominently in the Genesis creation account, where they are the object of God's creative activity on the first day of ordering the heavens and the earth (Gen 1:3–5). This day, according to Jub. 2:2, is also that on which God created the various "spirits" through whom God would govern the world. That 1QS 3:19 uses the word *twldwt* in describing the origins of truth and falsehood likewise recalls the Genesis narrative, which recounts "the generations [*twldwt*] of the heavens and the earth when they were created" (Gen 2:4).[16]

The notion of two opposite spirits from God can also be found in the Hebrew scriptures. First Samuel 16:14 says that "the spirit of the LORD departed from Saul and an evil spirit from the LORD tormented him."[17] It is possible, however, that the Treatise derives even this idea along with the imagery of watery origins for truth and falsehood from the opening verses of Genesis. Genesis 1:2 says that when God created the heavens and the earth, "darkness was over the face of the deep, and the spirit of God was moving over the face of the waters." An early Jewish interpreter could have seen in this verse a reference to two water sources, one associated

14. Here I follow those scholars who translate *mʿyn* as "spring" in line 19 instead of *mʿwn*, "habitation, dwelling." See, e.g., James H. Charlesworth in Elisha Qimron and James H. Charlesworth, "Rule of the Community," in *Rule of the Community and Related Documents*, vol. 1 of *The Dead Sea Scrolls: Hebrew, Aramaic, and Greek Texts with English Translations*, ed. James H. Charlesworth, PTSDSSP (Tübingen: Mohr Siebeck; Louisville: Westminster John Knox, 1994), 13; *DSSSE* 1:75. Given that (1) the context of this statement pertains to the origins (not the abode) of truth; (2) this word is parallel with *mqwr*, "well"; and (3) the expression *mʿyn ʾwr*, "spring of light," occurs with *mqwr* (along with other language related to creation) in 1QH[a] 14:20, the reading *mʿyn*, "spring," is preferable.

15. In many of these, "light" and "darkness" connote good and evil, respectively (e.g., Job 30:26; Qoh 2:13; Isa 5:20; 45:7; 59:9; Jer 13:16; Amos 5:18, 20).

16. The Treatise also uses *twldwt* with reference to the origin of the humankind in 1QS 3:13; 4:15.

17. Oscar J. F. Seitz, "Two Spirits in Man: An Essay in Biblical Exegesis," *NTS* 6.1 (1959): 82–95, argues that the idea of two spirits in the Treatise (and also in the Testaments of the Twelve Patriarchs and the Shepherd of Hermas, *Mandate*) comes from an exegesis of 1 Sam 16:14.

with "darkness" and another connected with the "spirit of God." It would have been easy for such an interpreter to infer that the reverse was true as well, that the waters connected with the spirit of God were also associated with light and that those associated with darkness were also related to a negative counterpart of the spirit of God.[18] While a number of biblical texts, including 1 Sam 16:14, likely contributed to the formation of the "two spirits" teaching, the Treatise conceives of the origins of truth and falsehood primarily in the terms of the Gen 1 creation story.[19]

The Angel of Darkness

The belief that God has placed before humankind two modes of conduct, one good and the other evil, would not have been controversial among Jews of the second and first centuries BCE. The teaching of this passage may be compared to the "two ways" teaching found in wisdom writings (e.g., Prov 4:11–19). As discussed in ch. 6, Ben Sira teaches that God has presented human beings with a choice between fire and water, life and death (Sir 15:11–20).[20] Where the theology of the Treatise departs from that of Sir 15 and works such as the Epistle of Enoch is in how it explains why some humans opt to walk in the "spirit of truth" while others elect to

18. Cf. Jub. 2:2, which also expands upon the opening verses of Genesis and addresses the origin of waters and spirits, though differently from the Treatise on the Two Spirits: "For on the first day he created the heavens that are above, the earth, the waters, and all the spirits who serve before him" (James C. VanderKam, *The Book of Jubilees*, 2 vols., CSCO 510–511 [Leuven: Peeters, 1989], 2:7).

19. Wernberg-Møller, *Manual of Discipline*, 67, states that the phraseology of the Treatise "suggests that the whole of the essay is based on Gen. I ff." Other references to the creation account in the Two Spirits discourse include the reference to various "kinds" of spirits in 1QS 3:14 (cf. Gen 1:11, 12, 21, 24, 25) and to "Adam" in 1QS 4:23 (Gen 1:26, 27). The idea that God created humankind for the dominion of the world in 1QS 3:17–18 may also reflect Gen 1:27–30. In addition, some scholars reconstruct 1QS 4:26 so that it mentions "the knowledge of good [and evil]." If this is correct, this passage would allude to the tree of the knowledge of good and evil, which figures prominently in Gen 2–3. On the likelihood of this reconstruction of 1QS 4:26 and the use of the Genesis creation account in the Treatise more generally, see Shane Alan Berg, "Religious Epistemologies in the Dead Sea Scrolls: The Heritage and Transformation of the Wisdom Tradition" (PhD diss., Yale University, 2008), 127–39.

20. Michael A. Knibb, *The Qumran Community*, CCWJCW 2 (Cambridge: Cambridge University Press, 1987), 95, notes the affinity of the "Two Spirits" passage with the "two ways" tradition in Barn. 18–21 and Did. 1–6.

walk in the "spirit of falsehood." While Sir 15 says that sin originates with humans, the Treatise on the Two Spirits explains things differently: "The authority of the Prince of Light extends to the governance of all righteous people; therefore, they walk in the paths of light. Correspondingly, the authority of the Angel of Darkness embraces the governance of all wicked people, so they walk in the paths of darkness" (1QS 3:20–21). This teaching divides humankind into two camps, the righteous and the wicked. Individuals in each group behave as they are governed by the group's respective angelic leader. The person who possesses authority over the wicked is the Angel of Darkness.

That the Angel of Darkness belongs properly to the Satan tradition is perhaps less than obvious. The Treatise does not refer to the Angel of Darkness as "the Satan." Nor does the Treatise apply one of the other satanic appellatives we have encountered in other literature (e.g., Belial, Prince of Mastema) to the Angel of Darkness. The Angel of Darkness also has very little in common with the punishing Satan of the Hebrew scriptures. Perhaps it is for this reason, in addition to a desire to emphasize the polarity between light and darkness, that the author of the Treatise chose not to use the designation "Satan" for this figure. The Treatise does not depict the Angel of Darkness as an attacker of sinners.

Nevertheless, there is more than sufficient justification for associating the Angel of Darkness with the Satan tradition. While this figure does not have much in common with the Satan of Zechariah or Job, his activities overlap considerably with those of Belial and the Prince of Mastema in other literature. 1QS 3:20–21 says that the Angel of Darkness has authority over the wicked, whom he leads astray (cf. Jub. 11:5, CD 4:12-18). He opposes the angel of light (cf. CD 5:17-18). One also reads in the Treatise that the Angel of Darkness has a host of harmful spirits aligned with him (1QS 3:24; cf. Jub. 10:7-9, CD 12:2-3), that he afflicts the righteous (1QS 3:23; cf. Jub. 17:15–18:12), and that his authority is characterized by *mśṭmh*, "hostility" ("his diabolic rule," 1QS 3:23; cf. Jub. 11:11; 48:2, CD 16:4-5). Further, if one is to read the Treatise on the Two Spirits in the context of the Community Rule, one is probably to identify the Angel of Darkness with Belial, whose association with the earlier biblical Satan tradition is less ambiguous.

More specifically, the Treatise on the Two Spirits' teachings about good and evil and about their superhuman representatives may derive from a theological tradition similar to that of the Visions of Amram. Both of these texts speak of two superhuman authorities over humankind.

In both the Treatise on the Two Spirits and the Visions of Amram, one of these figures is associated with light and the other is associated with darkness.[21] Presumably, the Visions of Amram divides humankind between the two authorities, as does the Treatise, though the fragmentary state of the Visions of Amram limits one's ability to ascertain many of its details.[22]

Although the Treatise divides humankind into two camps, the righteous and the wicked, each with its respective angelic leader, this division is not as neat and tidy as it at first appears. "The authority of the Angel of Darkness further extends to the corruption of all the righteous. All their sins, iniquities, shameful and rebellious deeds are at his prompting, a situation God in His mysteries allows to continue until His era dawns" (1QS 3:21–23). Even though the righteous are under the dominion of the Prince of Lights, they may on occasion succumb to the influence of the Angel of Darkness and be led into sin.

Column 4 further elaborates on the human condition: "Until now the spirits of truth and perversity have contended within the human heart. All people walk in both wisdom and foolishness. As is a person's endowment of truth and righteousness, so shall he hate perversity; conversely, in proportion to bequest in the lot of evil, one will act wickedly and abominate truth" (1QS 4:23–25). Each human, this passage seems to say, has been allotted a share of truth and a share of evil. The degree to which a person is righteous or wicked depends on his or her respective share of the truth and of evil. Since this sort of anthropology stands in tension with the simple bifurcation of humanity into two distinct groups, some scholars have

21. The portions of Visions of Amram relevant to this discussion are found on 4Q543 frags. 5-9; 4Q544 frag. 1; 4Q547 1-2 iii.

22. It is also possible that the Treatise, like the Visions of Amram, is presectarian in origin. Hartmut Stegemann (*The Library of Qumran: On the Essenes, Qumran, John the Baptist, and Jesus* [Leiden: Brill; Grand Rapids: Eerdmans, 1998], 110) and Armin Lange (*Weisheit und Prädestination: Weisheitliche Urordnung und Prädestination in den Textfunden von Qumran*, STDJ 18 [Leiden: Brill, 1995], 168–69; "Wisdom and Predestination in the Dead Sea Scrolls," *DSD* 2.3 [1995]: 348) have hypothesized a presectarian origin for the Treatise. There is nothing inherently sectarian about the division of humankind into the Sons of Righteousness and the Sons of Deceit. Nothing in this Treatise itself suggests that the Sons of Righteousness are to be identified exclusively with a select remnant within Israel. God is referred to in 1QS 3:24 as the "God of Israel," which indicates that the Sons of Light and Darkness were conceived of in national categories. Despite its possible presectarian origins, the Treatise would no doubt have been read from a sectarian perspective as part of the Rule of the Community.

suggested that this text has undergone editorial revision.[23] Whether this combination of ideas took place at the literary level or happened at the preliterary stage, the Treatise on the Two Spirits adapts a tradition that divided humanity simply into two groups in order to accommodate a more complex understanding of human morality.

This complex approach to humankind's struggle lends a psychological dimension to the opposition between good and evil. But this opposition is not one that is merely internal to individual members of humanity, as are the good and bad inclinations of the Mishnah (e.g., m. Ber. 9:5). It is part of a greater superhuman struggle between the forces of truth and falsehood that involves the Prince of Lights and the Angel of Darkness.

To classify humans on the basis of such a graded scale as is implied by the Treatise on the Two Spirits nevertheless diminishes the absolute distinction between the righteous and the wicked. That the Treatise distinguishes humans in such a nuanced fashion may support the hypothesis that this teaching is not strictly sectarian in outlook. The world does not consist simply of those within the sect and of those outside it, but of a spectrum of righteous and wicked persons. On the other hand, this understanding of morality would have been very compatible with the practice prescribed by the Rule of the Community of ranking community members annually according to the degree to which each had attained moral perfection (1QS 5:20–24).[24]

In addition to causing sin, according to the Treatise, the Angel of Darkness and all the spirits of his lot afflict the Sons of Light. "Moreover, all the afflictions of the righteous, and every trial in its season, occur because of this Angel's diabolic rule. All the spirits allied with him share but a single resolve: to cause the Sons of Light to stumble. Yet the God of Israel (and the Angel of His Truth) assist all the Sons of Light" (1QS 3:23–25). The Sons of Light (= the righteous) are not left defenseless against the Angel of Darkness and his spirits, for the God of Israel and the Angel of His Truth come to their help. "Angel of His Truth" is likely another designation for the Prince of Lights. This teaching resembles that of Jubilees' exodus narrative and

23. Peter von der Osten-Sacken, *Gott und Belial: Traditionsgeschichtliche Untersuchungen zum Dualismus in den Texten aus Qumran*, SUNT 6 (Göttingen: Vandenhoeck & Ruprecht, 1969), 17–27; Jean Duhaime, "L'instruction sur les deux esprits et les interpolations dualistes à Qumrân," *RB* 84.4 (1977): 566–94; Jean Duhaime, "Dualistic Reworking in the Scrolls from Qumran," *CBQ* 49.1 (1987): 40–43.

24. Compare the language of 1QS 5:20–24 with that of the introduction to the Two Spirits teaching in 1QS 3:13–14.

of CD 5:17–19, which teach that the Prince of Mastema or Belial opposes the people of God, who receive support from a beneficent angelic figure.[25]

Its similarities to other Jewish literature notwithstanding, the Two Spirits text differs in several notable regards from Jubilees and the Damascus Document. For instance, although Jubilees addresses the problem of evil within the context of its teaching on Israel's elect status, it is only Israel's election, not the existence of evil itself, that God establishes at the moment of creation. Jubilees is not concerned with the ultimate origin of evil. The Two Spirits discourse, on the other hand, claims that God created the very spirits of truth and falsehood. Another divergence from earlier literature is that the Satan figure in the Two Spirits Treatise, the Angel of Darkness, is said to mislead even the elect, the Sons of Truth. In Jubilees, the realm of the Prince of Mastema's activity is limited to the nations. The Damascus Document extends Belial's sphere of influence to include those Jews who are outside the sect. The Two Spirits teaching is unique among the works we have considered up to this point in that the Angel of Darkness plays a significant role in misleading even the "righteous" (1QS 3:21–23). Finally, the Two Spirits Treatise's graded understanding of humankind's spiritual condition, according to which individuals are righteous and evil to differing degrees depending on their differing shares in truth and falsehood, is unique in this literature.[26]

Perhaps what is most distinctive about the Two Spirits discourse is how it conceives of truth and falsehood. The Two Spirits Treatise considers moral evil in a far more comprehensive way than do the other writings we have considered up to this point; and in doing so, it must deal with

25. "Prince of Lights" is the designation that CD 5:18–19 uses for the angelic being who assisted Moses and Aaron against the Egyptian magicians, who were raised up by Belial. Jub. 48:9–12 says that the angel(s) of the presence helped Moses against the Egyptians, who were supported by the Prince of Mastema. A similar sort of opposition can be observed in the War Rule.

26. At one time, it was common for scholars to compare the two spirits teaching in this respect with another Dead Sea text, 4QZodiacal Physiognomy (4Q186). More recent studies suggest, however, that the similarities between the Treatise and this text are superficial and that the texts do not have comparable views of humankind's spiritual makeup. See Matthias Albani, "Horoscopes in the Qumran Scrolls," in *The Dead Sea Scrolls after Fifty Years: A Comprehensive Assessment*, ed. Peter W. Flint and James C. VanderKam, 2 vols. (Leiden: Brill, 1999), 2:279–330; Mladen Popović, *Reading the Human Body: Physiognomics and Astrology in the Dead Sea Scrolls and Hellenistic–Early Roman Period Judaism*, STDJ 67 (Leiden: Brill, 2007), 172–208; Mladen Popović, "Light and Darkness in the Treatise on the Two Spirits (1QS III 13 –IV 26) and in 4Q186," in *Dualism in Qumran*, ed. Xeravits, 148–65.

the origin of sin more absolutely than do the other texts. The Book of the Watchers does not explain the ultimate origin of evil but offers etiologies of particular evils: sorcery, divination, sexual immorality, and the worship of demons. Jubilees' teaching on the Prince of Mastema and his spirits accounts for the existence of those sins that distinguish the nations of the world from God's people Israel, particularly idolatry and military aggression. The Damascus Document proffers that Belial has entrapped those Jews outside their sect's covenant with specific practices that are contrary to the Damascus group's understanding of the Mosaic Torah. The sins with which the Two Spirits teaching deals, however, are not simply those sins that characterize outsiders, but also those vices of which the insiders, the Sons of Light, are themselves guilty.

> The operations of the spirit of falsehood result in greed, neglect of righteous deeds, wickedness, lying, pride and haughtiness, cruel deceit and fraud, massive hypocrisy, a want of self-control and abundant foolishness, a zeal for arrogance, abominable deeds fashioned by whorish desire, lechery in its filthy manifestation, a reviling tongue, blind eyes, deaf ears, stiff neck and hard heart—to the end of walking in all the ways of darkness and evil cunning. (1QS 4:9–11)

Similarly, the virtues that characterize the spirit of truth are not purely nationalistic or sectarian in nature, but more comprehensive.

> This spirit engenders humility, patience, abundant compassion, perpetual goodness, insight, understanding, and powerful wisdom resonating to each of God's deeds, sustained by His constant faithfulness. It engenders a spirit knowledgeable in every plan of action, zealous for the laws of righteousness, holy in its thoughts and steadfast in purpose. This spirit encourages plenteous compassion upon all who hold fast to truth, and glorious purity combined with visceral hatred of impurity in its every guise. It results in humble deportment allied with a general discernment, concealing the truth, that is, the mysteries of knowledge. (1QS 4:3–6)

Such lists of virtues and vices appear frequently in early Jewish and Christian literature (e.g., Gal 5:19–23; 2 Tim 2:22–23).[27] Although the

27. David E. Aune, "Lists, Ethical," *NIDB* 3:671, says that catalogs of virtues and vices,

Treatise's lists contain some concerns that could be regarded as particularly Jewish, such as "hatred of impurity," other virtues (e.g., "humility, patience, abundant compassion, perpetual goodness") do not appear to be exclusively Jewish or sectarian.[28] Neither could the "righteous" claim that they had absolutely perfected the virtues of truth and utterly shunned the vices of falsehood. At the root of the Treatise's teaching is a view of good and evil that encompasses much more than an obedience to a narrowly defined set of boundary-marking rules. "Truth" and "falsehood," according to the Treatise, have to do with moral attributes that are not so easily quantifiable, the full spectrum of what constitutes "right" and "wrong," moral "good" and "evil," for human beings.

In order to account for this more comprehensive and inclusive understanding of sin and righteousness, the previous explanation(s) of the human moral condition required some modification. First, the origin of evil could not be explained primarily on the basis of an event that took place long after the world was created. Human beings, according to Gen 1–5, had learned how to sin well before the sons of God descended. Since the Book of the Watchers and Jubilees were not concerned to explain the ultimate origin of evil, there was no tension between their explanations of the world's problems and instances of human wickedness prior to the watchers' descent (e.g., Adam and Eve's disobedience in the garden and Cain's murder of Abel, which are mentioned or alluded to in both the Book of the Watchers and Jubilees). The Two Spirits Treatise, defining sin as it does, must account for all unrighteousness, and must therefore trace the origins of good and evil all the way back to the very beginning of creation.

Similarly, the Treatise's view of sin required that the Satan's sphere of influence be expanded in comparison with the other texts. Since the concern of Jubilees was the boundary between Israel and the nations, that the Prince of Mastema's authority would be restricted to the nations is appropriate. In the Damascus Document, it is also fitting that Belial's realm of influence would include those members of Israel outside the covenant group in order to explain why some Jews were not obedient to the Torah as

---

which occur only rarely in the Hebrew scriptures, were more common in Greek ethical discourse and were adopted by various cultures during the Hellenistic period.

28. This is not to say, however, that the list of virtues in the Treatise is not particularly apt for a sectarian community such as the one represented by the Rule of the Community. On the appropriateness of these virtues and vices for the Dead Sea Scrolls sect, see Carol A. Newsom, *The Self as Symbolic Space: Constructing Identity and Community at Qumran*, STDJ 52 (Atlanta: Society of Biblical Literature, 2004), 128–32.

interpreted by the sect. When sin includes those vices of which even members of the Sons of Light are guilty, however, it makes sense to place the righteous as well to some degree under the Angel of Darkness's dominion (1QS 3:21–23). By implication, the sins for which the Angel of Darkness is supposed to be responsible in the Treatise are more comprehensive than is the case with Satan figures in other texts. Although the Sons of Light and the Sons of Darkness alike are subject to the devices of the Angel of Darkness and are guilty of various vices, the Sons of Light are ruled primarily by the Prince of Lights and are thus predominantly characterized by those virtues associated with light.

Truth and falsehood in the Treatise on the Two Spirits are not simply a matter of belonging either to Israel or to another nation. Nor is it a matter solely of either keeping a narrowly defined Mosaic Torah or failing to do so. Truth and deceit included virtues and vices that are practiced to varying degrees by all people. While the Two Spirits teaching inherited the division of humankind into two groups from earlier works, its view of sin and righteousness required a more nuanced approach to the human condition than a simple bipartite classification system. Although persons fall into one of two camps, belonging either to the righteous or the wicked, they are also arranged along a graduated spectrum depending on the extent to which they are characterized by truth and falsehood.

The Two Spirits discourse is not the first Jewish text to tackle the question of why even the supposedly faithful fail to live up to the standards of righteousness.[29] Ben Sira, as we saw in ch. 6, instructs his readers, "Do not say, 'It was the Lord's doing that I fell away'" (Sir 15:11). But the Two Spirits teaching is the first we have encountered that answers the question, at least in part, by claiming that an evil angel has a hold on every single human being, leading them to follow the ways of falsehood.

This state of affairs, in which truth and falsehood, light and darkness, are locked in conflict, is not expected to last. God, according to the Treatise, will not remain a neutral observer, but will eventually intervene once and for all on the side of truth. In the end, God would destroy perversity and

29. As Jörg Frey, "Different Patterns of Dualistic Thought in the Qumran Library: Reflections on Their Background and History," in *Legal Texts and Legal Issues: Proceedings of the Second Meeting of the International Organization for Qumran Studies, Cambridge 1995*, ed. Moshe Bernstein, Florentino García Martínez, and John Kampen; STDJ 23 (Leiden: Brill, 1997), 293, puts it, the problem addressed by this teaching was that it seemed "that even the Sons of Light commit sin and thus share in the spirit of wickedness (4:24) as well, at least to a certain extent."

purify humankind (1QS 4:18–21). In an effort to make sense of all the evil in the world, the author of the Two Spirits passage is willing to posit that God created it. The Angel of Darkness is the superhuman being who leads humans to commit evil deeds. Nevertheless, this passage maintains that God is ultimately on the side of truth and will eventually eliminate falsehood.

Belial, the Enemy, in the War Rule

Another fascinating document, multiple copies of which were found among the Dead Sea Scrolls, is the Rule of the War of the Sons of Light against the Sons of Darkness, or simply the War Rule.[30] This document, which has been compared with Greco-Roman military manuals, contains instructions for the anticipated eschatological battle between the Sons of Light and the Sons of Darkness.[31] The War Rule was probably composed in the period between the mid-second century and mid-first century BCE.[32] Most scholars agree that the War Rule was not written de novo by a single author.[33] Rather, like nearly all of the works we have considered up to this point, it is a composite work that took its present shape through a multistage process of composition and editing. A number of inconsistencies between the work's different sections evince the work's composite nature. The war described in column 1, for instance, is one that is divided into seven phases, with the upper hand alternating between the Sons of Light and the Sons of Darkness.[34] Column 2, in contrast, speaks of a war lasting forty years, during the course of which Israel does not appear to suffer any setbacks.

30. Maurice Baillet, *Qumrân Grotte 4, III*, DJD 7 (Oxford: Clarendon, 1982), identified six copies of the War Rule among the scrolls discovered in Cave 4.

31. Jean Duhaime, "The *War Scroll* from Qumran and the Greco-Roman Tactical Treatises," *RevQ* 13 (1988): 133–51.

32. Most copies of the document have been dated paleographically to sometime in the first century BCE, with only 4Q494 and 11Q14 dated to the early first century CE. See the discussion and bibliography in Brian Schultz, *Conquering the World: The War Scroll (1QM) Reconsidered*, STDJ 76 (Leiden: Brill, 2009), 32–33.

33. Yigael Yadin, *The Scroll of the War of the Sons of Light against the Sons of Darkness*, trans. Batya and Chaim Rabin (Oxford: Oxford University Press, 1962), is in the minority in that he treats the War Rule as though it is the product of a single hand.

34. The division of the war into seven phases in 1QM has been compared to the Zoroastrian belief recorded by Plutarch (*On Isis and Osiris*, 47) that the forces of light and darkness are evenly matched in a war and that dominance alternates between the two. See Collins, *Apocalypticism*, 101–3.

Scholars commonly identify four blocks of material in the book, corresponding roughly to columns 1, 2–9, 10–14, and 15–19. Nevertheless, there is currently no consensus as to how the book's various pieces came together.[35] Pertinent to the present study is that some of the literary hypotheses for the War Rule have been tied to theories about a shift in the theology of the Dead Sea Scrolls sect. According to these theories, the sect's understanding of the origin of evil evolved over time. The earlier portions of the War Rule represent the group's earlier theology, and the later parts of it reflect a development in that theology.[36] Such hypotheses, however, have not proven persuasive. The particular order in which the various pieces of the War Rule came together is not apparent. Nor is it evident that the composition history of the work corresponds to a shift in thinking on the nature of good and evil. What is clear is that the person(s) responsible for the War Rule in its present form incorporated a variety of earlier traditions about the forces of evil to create the work as we have it.

One can further observe that the War Rule exhibits a great deal of unity despite its undeniably composite character. With regard to the conflict between good and evil, all four major sections of the War Rule share certain very basic elements. They all speak of the eschatological war between Israel (or certain tribes of Israel) and the wicked nations of the world. They conceive of this battle as a conflict between the forces of "light" and the

35. For example, Philip Davies, *1QM, the War Scroll from Qumran: Its Structure and History*, BibOr 32 (Rome: Biblical Institute Press, 1977), identifies three documents in the War Rule, consisting of cols. 2–9, 15–19, and 10–12. These documents, says Davies, all circulated independently, as did two fragments (cols. 13 and 14). Eventually, these texts were joined together, with col. 1 being added to the book as an introduction. Schultz, *Conquering the World*, 382–85, has suggested that the War Rule initially consisted of cols. 1–9 and was later expanded by the addition of cols. 10–19. For a summary of the scholarship on the composition and date of the War Rule see Jean Duhaime, "War Scroll," in *Damascus Document, War Scroll, and Related Documents*, vol. 2 of *The Dead Sea Scrolls: Hebrew, Aramaic, and Greek Texts with English Translations*, ed. James H. Charlesworth, PTSDSSP (Tübingen: Mohr Siebeck; Louisville: Westminster John Knox, 1995), 83–84.

36. Osten-Sacken, *Gott und Belial*, 28–196, holds that the "eschatological war dualism" found in 1QM 1 is early and that the ethical dimension to the conflict between the forces of good and evil in the Dead Sea Scrolls is a later development. Duhaime argues that the War Rule, along with other Dead Sea writings, underwent a "dualistic" reworking, in which material about opposition between heavenly beings was inserted into earlier writings. See, e.g., Jean L.-Duhaime, "La rédaction de *1 QM* XIII et l'évolution du dualisme à Qumrân," *RB* 84.2 (1977): 210–38. Philip R. Davies, "Dualism and Eschatology in the Qumran War Scroll," *VT* 28.1 (1978): 28–36, also argues that the "dualistic" material in the War Rule is later than the "nationalist-ethical" material.

forces of "darkness."[37] The nations of the world are said to be under the authority of Belial, who is responsible for these nations' hostility toward God's people.[38] Each section of the War Rule also portrays the eschatological battle as one in which God and the angels fight on behalf of Israel.[39]

Belial, Sin, and Punishment

In other ways, the War Rule exhibits a great deal of diversity. It contains an assortment of the traditions that are found in earlier writings, sometimes combining them harmonistically. Some passages in the work credit Belial with leading the nations, the Sons of Darkness, into wickedness. These passages are found in the third section of the work, columns 10–14. Column 13 records a curse that the people are to pronounce against Belial and the spirits of his lot: "Cursed be Belial for the hostile plan and may he be denounced for his guilty authority! Cursed be all the spirits of his lot, for their wicked plan and may they be denounced for all their service of impure uncleanness! For they are the lot of darkness, but the lot of God is for [everlast]ing light!" (1QM 13:4–6).[40] This curse holds Belial and his spirits responsible for wickedness and uncleanness, though it does not specify exactly what sorts of wrongdoing his work includes.

Similarly, just a few lines later, War Rule directs the following remarks to God:

> You have cast us in the lot of light according to your truth. The commander of light, long ago, you entrusted to our rescue . . . all the spirits of truth are under his dominion. You have made Belial to destroy, a hostile angel. In the darkne[ss] . . . his counsel is aimed towards wickedness and guiltiness. All the spirits of his lot, angels of destruction, are behaving according to the statutes of darkness. (1QM 13:9–12)

37. The designation "Sons of Darkness" occurs frequently and in all four sections of the work (e.g., 1QM 1:10; 3:6, 9; 13:16; 14:17; 16:11). "Sons of Light" appears less frequently, but is implicit as the counterpart to the "Sons of Darkness." "Sons of Light" occurs several times in col. 1. Otherwise, it may appear in 14:17, but this is not certain. The related designation "lot of light," however, appears in 13:9.

38. E.g., 1QM 1:5, 13; 4:1–2; 11:8; 13:2; 14:9; 18:1, 3.

39. E.g., 1QM 1:10–11; 7:5–6; 9:14–15; 12:7–13; 17:6–8.

40. Unless otherwise specified, translations of the War Rule are taken from Duhaime, "War Scroll," 96–141.

Parallels between this text and others we have considered abound. The belief that God has created Belial in order to destroy (*lšḥt*) is consistent with earlier depictions of the Satan as a functionary of God who attacks the wicked.[41] "Hostile angel" (*ml'k mśṭmh*) recalls CD 16:5 and the "Mastema" terminology of Jubilees. That Belial and his spirits, the angels of destruction, lead humans into wickedness and punish them for it also recalls these two works. The language of light and darkness echoes the Treatise on the Two Spirits' teaching and the Visions of Amram. The Prince of Lights appears in the Treatise (1QS 3:20) and in the Damascus Document (CD 5:18).

Despite the statement that Belial was created for the purpose of destruction, Israel is instructed to curse Belial (13:4–5). This indicates that the War Rule's author(s) did not regard all of Belial's activity as condoned by God. This view differs from those texts where the Satan and his spirits function largely within parameters established by God (e.g., Jub. 10) and has more in common with those in which the Satan opposes God's plan (Jub. 48). 1QM 13:4–12 speaks of Belial both as a functionary of God and as wicked and accursed. Perhaps the War Rule deems Belial's role as "destroyer" to be acceptable, since Belial is supposed to have been created by God for this purpose. Belial's promotion of wickedness and impurity, on the other hand, is probably the activity for which he is condemned. Unfortunately, the War Rule does not explicitly sort this out.

The belief that Belial is responsible for sin also surfaces in column 14. This text's sectarian outlook most closely resembles that of the Damascus Document: "You have shown through wonders your mercy for the remna[nt . . .] during the dominion of Belial. With all the mysteries of his hatred, he has not drawn [us] away from your covenant; you have driven his spirits of [des]truction far from u[s]" (1QM 14:9–10). Although the War Rule typically distinguishes between Israel and the nations, 1QM 14:9–10 corresponds to the Damascus Document, claiming that it is only a select

41. Duhaime, "War Scroll," 123, translates *šḥt* in 13:11 as "corrupt" instead of "destroy." Given Belial's association with the "angels of destruction" (*ml'ky ḥbl*) in this passage and the use of *šḥt* in the sense of "destroy" in connection with the activity of satan figures in other texts (e.g., 1 Chr 21:1, 12, 15; 1QH[a] 22:25; 24:23), it is probably physical destruction rather than moral corruption that is intended here. Cf. also Jub. 10:5, which says that harmful spirits "were created for the purpose of destroying." The notion of Belial as a destroyer would also contrast nicely with the depiction of the Prince of Lights as the rescuer in these lines. A third possibility is to take the word as the noun *šaḥat*, "pit, grave." Since the passage goes on to speak of the defeat of the Sons of Darkness, this translation is not out of the question. The verb "destroy," however, better suits the more immediate context.

group or "remnant" within Israel that has remained faithful to the covenant and is protected from Belial's harmful spirits (cf. CD 4:12–19; 16:1–5). The sectarian character of this passage is further suggested by the fact that "dominion of Belial" is an expression that occurs several times in the Rule of the Community (1QS 1:18, 23–24; 2:19).

Belial and the Sons of Darkness versus Israel

Other passages in the War Rule have more in common with the rewritten exodus story of Jub. 48, in which the Prince of Mastema does not lead people astray and punish them, but simply attacks God's elect. In Jubilees, the Prince of Mastema rouses the Egyptians' hostility so that they attack Israel. The precedent for the belief that the Satan might attack God's people in this way may be found in Job 1:15, 17, where the Satan (it is implied) sends the Sabeans and Chaldeans against the righteous Job's servants and herds. The War Rule combines this idea of the Satan figure as the enemy of the righteous with the biblical tradition of an eschatological battle (e.g., Ezek 38–39).

Even the passages in the War Rule that describe Belial as the leader of Israel's enemies in the eschatological battle are not completely uniform in how they envision the final conflict. The diversity of the War Rule in this regard stems in part from the variety of earlier traditions of which the work makes use. John Collins has shown, for example, that the War Rule is heir to an ancient Near Eastern conception of war, in which divine beings battle on behalf of their human subjects.[42] The Hebrew scriptures contain more than one depiction of such divine combat. According to some texts, Yahweh and the host of heaven do battle against Israel's human foes. For example, Judg 5 says that Yahweh marches down from Seir and that the stars fight against the enemies of Israel from heaven.[43] Another portrayal of divine combat pits the divine representatives of nations not against humans but against one another in battle. The clearest example of this is found in Dan 10:13, 20–21, where Michael, the prince of Israel, and another

42. John J. Collins, "The Mythology of Holy War in Daniel and the Qumran War Scroll: A Point of Transition in Jewish Apocalyptic," *VT* 25.3 (1975): 596–604.

43. This view of God's role in war is also found in Deut 23:14: "Because the LORD your God travels along with your camp, to save you and to hand over your enemies to you, therefore your camp must be holy, so that he may not see anything indecent among you and turn away from you."

superhuman figure fight the corresponding superhuman princes of Persia and Greece. In the War Rule, one finds both of these traditions.

The War Rule says that God and the angels join in the fight against Israel's human enemies: "the congregation of [God's] holy ones (is) in our midst for an everlasti[ng] help. . . . For the Lord is holy, and the glorious king (is) with us, together with the holy ones . . . the host of angels (is) among our numbered men, the mighty one of wa[r] (is) in our congregation and the host of his spirits (is) with our foot-soldiers and our horsemen" (1QM 12:7–9). Accordingly, 1QM 7:5–6 stipulates that Israel is to maintain cultic purity on account of the presence of angels among them: "Any man who is not purified from a (bodily) discharge on the day of the battle shall not go down with them, for the holy angels are together with their hosts."[44] Column 1 views the final conflict similarly. The Sons of Light and the Sons of Darkness in this column are also called, respectively, the *ʿdt ʾlym*, "congregation of divine beings," and the *qhlt ʾnšym*, "assembly of men" (1:10–11).[45] The Sons of Light are assisted by divine beings, while, it is implied, the Sons of Darkness have no such help.[46]

44. Crispin H. T. Fletcher-Louis, *All the Glory of Adam: Liturgical Anthropology in the Dead Sea Scrolls,* STDJ 42 (Leiden: Brill, 2002), 402, argues that many scholars overestimate the participation of angels in the conflict in the War Rule; he claims that angels do not appear in this passage as combatants, but "are present here because of the issue of purity." But the text itself leads one to conclude that the reverse is true: the issue of purity appears in the War Rule because of the presence of angels among the military camp. This purity requirement is also based on Deut 23:14, which stipulates that Israel's army must maintain its purity so that God will remain among the people, fighting on their behalf.

45. It is possible that "congregation of divine beings" refers not to the human Sons of Light but to the divine beings themselves, as opposed to the human participants in the battle, "the assembly of men." But the parallelism of these passages makes it more likely that this group is that of the human Sons of Light: "the congregation of divine beings and the assembly of men, the Sons of Light and the lot of darkness, shall fight each other" (1:10–11). In this interpretation the "congregation of divine beings" is the human congregation that is associated with divine beings. Compare this designation of God's people with "the people of the holy ones of the Most High" of Dan 7:27 (on the meaning of which see John J. Collins, *Daniel,* Hermeneia [Minneapolis: Fortress, 1993], 312–18, 322). Whether the "congregation of divine beings" is human or divine, the Sons of Light in this passage are associated with certain superhuman figures, who fight alongside them in battle. See also 1QM 1:11, which speaks of "the uproar of a large multitude and the war cry of divine beings and men." On the difficulty of deciphering the "angelic" terminology of the War Rule, see Fletcher-Louis, *All the Glory of Adam,* 395–402.

46. 1QM 1:15–16 also mentions certain "angels of his dominion" and "holy ones," but the poor condition of the text at this point conceals the precise identity of these figures and their part in whatever events transpire. It may be that the designation "angels of his

A significant portion of 1QM 2–9 is devoted to describing the banners and other equipment to be used in the battle against the Sons of Darkness. Slogans are to be written on these items that declare God's part in the battle. There are to be banners, for example, displaying the words "Battle of God," "Vengeance of God," "Strife of God," "From God a hand of war against all flesh of deceit," "Destruction by God of every nation of vanity," and "Victory of God" (1QM 4:2–3, 12–13). Four shields to be used in the war bear the names Michael, Gabriel, Sariel, and Raphael, signifying that these divine beings are also involved in the conflict (1QM 9:15–16).[47]

Interestingly, according to the words written on one of the banners, Belial is included among the objects of God's wrath: "Wrath of God in outburst towards Belial and against all the men of his lot without any remnant" (4:1–2). That God would oppose Belial is also assumed in 18:1, which says that "the great hand of God is [rai]sed against Belial." The idea that Belial, the leader of the Sons of Darkness, would be punished may be related to the biblical traditions in which deities are punished for their rebellion. In Ps 82, God judges the various gods of the nations, who had not governed their peoples with justice. Isaiah 14 compares the king of Babylon to a certain "Day Star, son of Dawn," who tries to make himself like the Most High but is brought down to the Pit.[48] That the Satan figure would be a recipient of God's wrath at the end of the age is an idea that will be picked up by early Christian writers (Matt 25:41; Rev 20:10).

A view of international strife in which the status of a nation was inextricably linked with the status of its divine patron among the gods is found in 1QM 17: "(This is) the day [God] has set to humiliate and to bring low the commander of the dominion of wickedness. . . . (He will set) the authority of Michael in everlasting light. He will cause the covenant of Israel to shine in joy! Peace and blessing to the lot of God! He will exalt over the divine beings the authority of Michael and the dominion of Israel over all flesh" (1QM 17:5–8). Here Michael's rise to supremacy among the divine beings is associated with Israel's ascendancy among the nations.

---

dominion" implies that there are angels under the dominion of another being. In this case, both God and Belial would have angels in their service. Unfortunately, the text is too fragmentary to be certain.

47. Cf. the four figures who come to the help of the righteous in 1 En. 9–11.

48. Another example of this motif is found in the oracle against the prince of Tyre in Ezek 28.

The divine beings (*'lym*) include the "commander [or 'prince,' Heb. *śr*] of the dominion of wickedness," which in the context of the War Rule must be another designation for Belial. The sentiment of this passage resembles that of Dan 10–12, where Michael, Israel's prince, fights the princes of other nations. As in Daniel, the notion of national deities has been subordinated to a monotheistic theology. Ultimately, Israel is the "lot of God," and God is the one who ensures that Michael, rather than Belial, will be preeminent among the divine beings, and that the people of Israel, rather than Israel's enemies, will be preeminent among all flesh.

The opposition between Michael and the prince of the dominion of wickedness is typical of much of the literature we have considered up to this point, in that the Satan figure stands opposite a good angelic figure. It can be compared to the conflict between the Satan and the angel of Yahweh in Zechariah, between the Prince of Mastema and the angel of the presence in Jubilees, or between the Angel of Darkness and the Prince of Lights in the Treatise on the Two Spirits. In 11QMelchizedek, the heavenly representative of righteousness who opposes Belial is named Melchizedek. This text interprets Ps 82, which speaks of God assuming control of the nations, taking authority over these nations away from their wicked gods.[49] 11QMelchizedek reads Ps 82 as a prophecy concerning the end of Belial's reign: "And Melchizedek will carry out the vengeance of Go[d]'s judgements, [and on that day he will f]r[ee them from the hand of] Belial and from the hand of all the s[pirits of his lot]" (11QMelch 2:13).

While Jewish literature from this period retains the notion of numerous heavenly beings who rule over the nations, whether spirits or angels, works such as Jubilees, the War Rule, and other writings from Qumran differ from Daniel and earlier biblical literature in that they have subordinated all of these beings to a single satanic ruler (cf. Luke 4:5–6). Beliefs about national gods and about the opposition between the Satan and the angel of Yahweh have been combined. In the War Rule Israel is led by Michael, and all the other nations of the world have Belial as their leader.

49. Florentino García Martínez, Eibert J. C. Tigchelaar, and Adam S. van der Woude, *Qumran Cave 11, II*, DJD 23 (Oxford: Clarendon, 1998), 223; J. J. M. Roberts, "Melchizedek," in *Pesharim, Other Commentaries, and Related Documents,* vol. 6B of *The Dead Sea Scrolls: Hebrew, Aramaic, and Greek Texts with English Translations,* ed. James H. Charlesworth, PTSDSSP (Tübingen: Mohr Siebeck; Louisville: Westminster John Knox, 2002), 264. 11QMelchizedek has been dated paleographically to the mid-first century BCE.

Belial versus God

Some passages in the War Rule identify the divine representatives of the conflict between the Sons of Light and the Sons of Darkness not as Michael and Belial, but as God and Belial. The Sons of Light and the Sons of Darkness are alternatively designated, respectively, as the "lot of God" and the "lot of Belial" (1:5; 13:4–5).[50] The juxtaposition of God and Belial, as opposed to Michael and Belial, may stem from the teaching of Deut 32:8–9 that Israel belongs to Yahweh, not to another divine being. This theology is adopted by the book of Jubilees, which says that God has caused spirits to rule over all the nations of the world, except for Israel (Jub. 15:31–32). In the War Rule, however, the lot of God and the lot of Belial are at war, and God's hand is raised in wrath against Belial (1QM 4:1–2; 18:1). One should not infer from this juxtaposition of God and Belial that Belial has risen to the level of God's equal in the theology of the War Rule. The War Rule is firmly grounded in Jewish monotheism, and God's superiority to Belial is never in question. Nevertheless, the War Rule represents an important step in the development of beliefs regarding the Satan. With Belial's troops arrayed against God's, and Belial destined to receive God's wrath, no longer does it suffice to speak of the Satan as one of God's servants. Belial has become something more akin to God's enemy.

Primarily, Belial in the War Rule is the leader of the nations against God's people. Column 1 introduces the work as a manual for the eschatological battle between the Sons of Light and the Sons of Darkness, the lot of God and the lot of Belial, and Belial occupies the role of leader of the Sons of Darkness throughout the work. Belial, however, is much more than the leader of the gentile nations. The War Rule combines various earlier traditions about the Satan figure more so than any work we have considered thus far. That an author might engage earlier texts in this eclectic fashion goes some way toward explaining how the Satan eventually becomes God's principal antagonist. When the various evils attributed to the Satan figure individually in earlier texts (leading the nations against the elect, leading the nations into sin, leading Israel into sin, etc.) are combined, the end result is a Satan figure who is responsible for all of these evils. Belial also continues to be depicted as a functionary of God in the War Rule. In a way that surpasses the others we have

50. Cf. the pairing of "lot of God" with "lot of Belial" in 1QS 2:2–5.

considered up to this point, however, this document leaves one with the impression that Belial is God's enemy and is behind all that is wrong in the world.

Etiologies of Maleficent Superhuman Beings

In the Book of the Watchers and in Jubilees, the story of the rebellious watchers serves an etiological function, explaining the origin of certain harmful superhuman beings, as well as the origin of a number of sinful practices. In the Dead Sea Scrolls we have discussed, by contrast, the story of the watchers does not figure as prominently. Of the major texts considered above, the story of the watchers and their children appears only in the Damascus Document. In CD 2:17–21, the story is put forward as an example of sinners who followed after their guilty inclination. Although this story occupies an important place as the first instance of such wickedness cited, the story is not presented as an etiology of sin, of demons, or of evil spirits. The most extensive discussion of the origin of evil and of evil superhuman entities is that offered by the Treatise on the Two Spirits. According to the Treatise's teaching, the spirit of falsehood was not bred into the world by rebellious angels. Rather, God created the spirits of truth and falsehood. This teaching resembles that of Jubilees, insofar as the distinction between the righteous and the wicked is based on the divinely created order. Jubilees claims only that God established Israel's election at creation, however; it says nothing about God's creation of evil beings.

This is not to say that the etiology of evil spirits based on Gen 6 is absent from the scrolls. In addition to the copies of the Book of the Watchers and Jubilees among the scrolls, several incantation texts refer or allude to the story. The Apocryphal Psalms mentions the hybrid origin of harmful spirits (11Q11 v 6). Some texts also speak of the "spirits of the bastards" (*rwḥwt mmzrym*), recalling the illegitimate parentage of the evil spirits as described in the Book of the Watchers. As mentioned in the previous chapter, the Songs of the Maskil mentions "spirits of the bastards" as one kind of being in a list of several different kinds of malevolent spirits: "spirits of the destroying angels, spirits of the bastards, demons, Lilith, howlers and [desert dwellers]" (4Q510 1 5). Although this passage alludes to the watcher etiology, "bastard spirits" are merely one kind of superhuman being among several that cause trouble for humans. This differs from the etiology of the Book of the Watchers, which seems to account for all of the various harmful spirits with a single etiology based on Gen 6.

While the watcher story and its etiology of malevolent spirits has a place in the theologies of the Dead Sea Scrolls, the significance of the story in this corpus as an explanation for the existence of evil and its superhuman proponents may be regarded as diminished in comparison with the Book of the Watchers and even Jubilees. This etiology accounts for only some of the harmful beings listed in the Songs of the Maskil. If there is a place for the watcher etiology in the theological system of the Treatise on the Two Spirits, it would be subordinate to the conflict between the spirits of truth and falsehood, whose origins are traced back to God's creative work.

The Question of Zoroastrian Influence

As noted above, some Dead Sea Scrolls have an impressive number of parallels with Iranian ideas; and from almost the very outset of Dead Sea Scrolls research, scholars have hypothesized that the theology of some of these Jewish documents was influenced by contact with the Iranian religion known as Zoroastrianism.[51] The possibility of Zoroastrian influence on early Jewish thought, of course, is not restricted to the scrolls. Many have speculated, for instance, that the demon Asmodeus in the book of Tobit is based on the Iranian Aeshma Daeva (Tob 3:8, 17).[52] Although it goes well beyond the scope of this study to deal fully with this question of Iranian influence, it is appropriate to take up the matter very briefly.

This question is complicated by several factors. One problem that scholars often note concerns the dating of the Zoroastrian texts with which the scrolls are typically compared. Although scholars agree that the Avesta (the collection of Zoroastrian sacred writings) preserves teachings from the first millennium BCE, the text itself is dated to the ninth century CE, nearly a thousand years after the period under consideration.[53] There is

51. Dupont-Sommer, "L'instruction sur les deux Esprits," 16–17, 21, 25, 28–30, 34; Kuhn, "Sektenschrift und die iranische Religion."

52. See M. Hutter, "Asmodeus," *DDD* 106–8. Other scholars are more skeptical that Asmodeus is derived from a Zoroastrian figure, e.g., James Barr, "The Question of Religious Influence: The Case of Zoroastrianism, Judaism, and Christianity," *JAAR* 53.2 (1985): 214–18.

53. Antonio Panaino, "Avesta," *Religion Past and Present: Encyclopedia of Theology and Religion*, ed. Hans Dieter Betz, Don S. Browning, Bernd Janowski, and Eberhard Jüngel, 14 vols. (Leiden: Brill, 2007–2013), 1:527–29.

also the difficult issue of identifying the channels through which Jewish theologians of this period would have come into contact with Iranian thought. Scholars further disagree as to the particular variety of Zoroastrianism that influenced the thinking of the authors of the Dead Sea Scrolls.[54] That very few scholars have expert command of both the early Jewish and the Iranian material means that most scholars are ill-qualified to deal with half of the puzzle.

Absolute confirmation one way or the other on this issue is very unlikely to be obtained. It will nearly always be possible to explain a doctrine in the Dead Sea Scrolls by positing a development within Jewish tradition, and it will nearly always be impossible to prove beyond a doubt that a doctrine was borrowed from a foreign source. Jewish theologians would not have found use for an idea that was entirely "foreign" to their way of thinking. The more compatible that a concept was with their own view, the more likely it is that they would have found a place for it in their theology. As a result, the sorts of concepts that are more easily "borrowed" are at the same time those that are more difficult to identify later as of foreign origin.

In favor of the hypothesis that the theology contained in certain Dead Sea Scrolls was influenced by Iranian religious thought is the lengthy list of ideas they share. Both these scrolls and Zoroastrian sources, for example, describe the world in terms of a polarity between light and darkness and between truth and deceit. And both speak of two warring, evenly matched superhuman figures, one representing good and the other evil.[55] Also, the

54. Some scholars maintain that it was not "normative" Zoroastrianism with which the scrolls have the most in common, but a "heretical" form of it known as Zurvanism; see, e.g., Charlesworth, "Critical Comparison," 87–89; Marc Philonenko, "La doctrine qoumrânienne des deux Esprits: Ses origins iraniennes et ses prolongements dans le judaïsme essénien et le christianisme antique," in *Apocalyptique iranienne et dualisme qoumrânien*, ed. Geo Widengren, Anders Hultgård, and Marc Philonenko; Recherches Intertestamentaires 2 (Paris: Adrien Maisonneuve, 1995), 161–211.

55. For a discussion of these parallels, see Paul J. Kobelski, *Melchizedek and Melchireša*, CBQMS 10 (Washington, DC: Catholica Biblical Association of America, 1981), 84–98; Davidson, *Angels at Qumran*, 232–34; Philonenko, "Doctrine qoumrânienne des deux Esprits"; Levison, "Two Spirits in Qumran Theology," 169–94; Collins, "Mythology of Holy War," 604–12; Collins, *Apocalypticism*, 41–51, 101–3. See also Klaus Koch, "History as a Battlefield of Two Antagonistic Powers in the Apocalypse of Weeks and in the Rule of the Community," in *Enoch and Qumran Origins: New Light on a Forgotten Connection*, ed. Gabriele Boccaccini (Grand Rapids: Eerdmans, 2005), 185–99, who argues that the Apocalypse of Weeks (1 En. 93:1–10; 91:11–17) and the Two Spirits Treatise describe history in terms of an opposition between *qušṭa* ("righteousness"/"truth") on the one hand and *šiqra* ("deceit") and *ḥamsa*

theology of these scrolls departs notably from early biblical and Jewish tradition. Although a polarity between light and darkness is attested in various places in earlier literature (e.g., Isa 45:7), this polarity is fundamental to the worldview of the War Rule and the Two Spirits discourse in a way that it is not in earlier Jewish writings. The resemblance between these documents' teachings and Zoroastrianism is not merely a matter of a handful of shared motifs, but is systemic.[56]

Those who are not persuaded of Iranian influence correctly point out that it is possible to account for many of the ideas in the scrolls based on Jewish tradition without recourse to Iranian texts.[57] The scrolls' teachings on the Satan figure are certainly among those with unmistakable antecedents in books like Jubilees. One need not infer from this observation, however, that continuity with Jewish tradition alone explains the particular doctrines of works like the War Rule and the Treatise. One finds in these scrolls a conspicuous convergence of a number of ideas that have striking parallels in the sacred texts of Zoroastrianism. Perhaps it is not simply a single idea that the authors of the Treatise on the Two Spirits or the War Rule borrowed from Zoroastrianism, but the thoroughgoing way in which they articulate their theology in terms of a conflict between light and darkness, good and evil.

While the hypothesis of Zoroastrian influence in the Dead Sea Scrolls has much to commend it, beliefs about the Satan figure also exhibit a great deal of continuity with earlier Jewish texts, as do many of the ideas in the scrolls. Those adaptations of the Satan tradition that are attested for the first time or exclusively in the scrolls (e.g., Belial as God's enemy, the Angel of Darkness as an instigator of all sorts of sin) may also be explained exegetically or otherwise as natural developments within the dynamic and multifaceted Satan tradition of early Judaism. On the other hand, al-

("violence") on the other. On the conflict between good and evil, compare esp. Plutarch, *On Isis and Osiris,* 47, with 1QM 1 and 15–19.

56. Albert de Jong, "Iranian Connections in the Dead Sea Scrolls," in *Oxford Handbook of the Dead Sea Scrolls,* ed. Timothy H. Lim and John J. Collins (Oxford: Oxford University Press, 2010), 479–500.

57. A recent example of an attempt to refute any connection between the theology of the Dead Sea Scrolls and Zoroastrianism is Paul Heger, "Another Look at Dualism in Qumran Writings," in *Dualism in Qumran,* ed. Xeravits, 39–101. See also the arguments of Barr, "Question of Religious Influence"; and the discussion of the current state of the question in Edwin M. Yamauchi, "Did Persian Zoroastrianism Influence Judaism?," in *Israel: Ancient Kingdom or Late Invention?,* ed. Daniel I. Block (Nashville: Broadman & Holman, 2008), 282–97, who finds the case for Zoroastrian influence dubious.

though it is not necessary to hypothesize Zoroastrian influence in order to explain these developments, neither is such influence implausible. The Zoroastrianism of the Gathas, should the authors of the War Rule or the Treatise on the Two Spirits have come into contact with such thinking, would have certainly provided a conceptual system very conducive to these developments.

The Satan as Leader of the Forces of Darkness

The Satan in the Treatise on the Two Spirits and the War Rule, whether he is called Belial or the Angel of Darkness, is undeniably an evil figure. To be sure, he is not depicted in entirely negative terms. The War Rule preserves some of the earlier notion of the Satan as a punishing figure. Even in the Treatise on the Two Spirits, since it is God who created the spirits of truth and falsehood, the Angel of Darkness apparently functions within the order established by God. Nevertheless, these texts, which depict reality in terms of a cosmic conflict between light and darkness, identify the Satan as the leader of the forces of darkness.

Both of these texts mark important steps in the development of the Satan tradition, each in its own way. The Treatise on the Two Spirits, like the texts considered in the previous chapter, focuses on the Satan's work of leading humankind into sin. The Treatise, however, surpasses the Damascus Document in its claims about this figure's involvement with sin. The Angel of Darkness in the Treatise is the leader of the superhuman forces of darkness and falsehood against the forces of light and truth in a conflict that can be traced all the way back to the creation of the world. He exercises influence over both the wicked and the righteous, causing them to sin. With regard to the scope of his activity, there is apparently no type of moral evil for which the Angel of Darkness is not responsible.

In the War Rule, Belial is the superhuman representative of the Sons of Darkness against the Sons of Light in the eschatological conflict. Belial's rival in some passages in the War Rule is Michael, the Prince of Lights. In other passages in the War Rule, Belial is presented as opposing not Michael or another angelic prince, but God. The War Rule depicts Belial not simply as a functionary of God, nor merely engaged in a conflict with an angelic figure who is subordinate to God, but as in conflict with God, as accursed, and as one who is destined to experience God's wrath.

CHAPTER 9

The Satan in the New Testament

In the preface I called attention to the contrast between the Satan as he is depicted in the book of Revelation and the Satan of the Hebrew scriptures. The Satan of Revelation is the deceiver of the whole world, the accuser of the comrades, the ancient serpent, and the leader of the forces of evil. The earliest texts that speak of superhuman satan figures, on the other hand, present these figures as functionaries of God who punish evildoers. Up to this point we have analyzed early Jewish texts that speak of the Satan and related figures, discerning the literary and theological process that gave rise to the ideas of the Satan that would have been current in Judaism around the time that the NT was composed. In the present chapter I discuss what the writings of the NT say (or assume) about the Satan.

Here I have two primary objectives. The first is to summarize how the NT authors conceive of the Satan, particularly in light of the preceding discussion of early Jewish notions of this figure. I include a brief consideration of the terminology and categories that the NT authors employ to speak of the Satan and related figures, as well as a discussion of the Satan's activity as depicted in the NT. The second objective is to consider two important developments within the Satan tradition to which the NT attests. One of these is the notion of the Satan as "the accuser of our comrades," as Rev 12:10 calls him. The other is the identification or association of the Satan with the serpent of Gen 3. Since a thorough, passage-by-passage or author-by-author analysis of NT texts pertaining to the Satan would require its own book-length study, here I proceed largely thematically. I try, nonetheless, to interpret each text in its own right and with proper attention both to the unity and the diversity among the NT writings.

Taxonomies, Terminology, and Titles for Harmful Superhuman Beings

The NT is rife with references to harmful superhuman figures. Demons and evil spirits appear especially frequently in the Synoptic Gospels, which use the designations "demon" and "spirit" interchangeably with reference to maleficent beings.[1] These Gospels mention demons/spirits primarily in the context of Jesus's healing ministry as those invisible beings that cause illness and disability (e.g., Mark 1:32–34; 3:1–12).[2] Other NT texts perhaps preserve the earlier distinction between "demons" and "spirits." Some passages refer to the (false) gods of the nations as "demons" (1 Cor 10:20–21; Rev 9:20).[3] Drawing on earlier texts, such as Isa 13:21, Rev 18:2 speaks of "demons" as those beings that inhabit areas that have been desolated by God's judgment.[4] There are "spirits," on the other hand, who inspire false or illegitimate prophecy and lead humans into error (e.g., Acts 16:16; 1 John 4:1).[5] Whether the authors of these texts distinguished spirits and demons or simply happen to preserve the earlier terminology is not clear.

Nor is it apparent whether the NT authors distinguish spirits or demons from angelic beings. Several passages in the NT mention angels who mete out death and destruction in the service of God. These include an "angel of the Lord" who strikes Herod Agrippa dead (Acts 12:23), "the angel of the bottomless pit/Abaddon/Apollyon" (Rev 9:11), and perhaps "the destroyer" (1 Cor 10:10; Heb 11:28).[6] The NT authors are also aware of traditions pertaining to sinful angels (1 Pet 3:18–22; 2 Pet 2:4; Jude 6).

1. *Daimonion* appears synonymously with *pneuma* (Luke 9:39–42), with *pneuma akatharton* (Mark 7:25–30; Luke 4:33–41; 8:27–38; 9:39–42; 11:14–26), and with *pneuma ponēron* (Luke 8:2; perhaps 11:14–26). *Daimonion* and *pneuma* are associated, perhaps synonymous, in 1 Tim 4:1 and Rev 18:2. See also the ambiguous expressions *pneuma daimoniou akathartou* (Luke 4:33–41) and *pneumata daimoniōn* (Rev 16:14).

2. A recent study on the topic of evil spirits in the Synoptic Gospels is Michael J. Morris, *Warding off Evil: Apotropaic Traditions in the Dead Sea Scrolls and Synoptic Gospels*, WUNT 2/451 (Tübingen: Mohr Siebeck, 2017). Morris's study focuses on preventative measures against evil spirits that are attested in the Synoptic Gospels rather than exorcisms.

3. Cf. Deut 32:17; Ps 106:37; 1 En. 19:1; 99:7.

4. Cf. also Isa 34:14; 4Q386 1 iii 4. According to Rev 18:2, both "demons" and "unclean spirits" inhabit fallen Babylon.

5. Cf. 1 En. 19:1.

6. Some scholars identify the "destroyer" in 1 Cor 10:10 and/or Heb 11:28 as an alternative designation for the Satan. See most recently Thomas J. Farrar and Guy J. Williams, "Diabolical Data: A Critical Inventory of New Testament Satanology," *JSNT* 39.1 (2016): 54–56, who deem both of these to be probable references to the Satan.

Some of these authors are clearly indebted to the Book of the Watchers and may assume a similar etiology and taxonomy for demons and spirits as found in the earlier Enochic work (1 En. 15:1–16:1; 19:1), but they do not say so explicitly. No NT book, for that matter, offers an etiology of these beings. Nor does any NT text explain the relationship between demons or spirits and rebellious angels. Further, given the diverse taxonomies of the superhuman realm in early Judaism, one cannot assume that the NT authors were completely uniform in their classification of divine beings.[7]

Of course, numerous texts also speak of the Satan. Precisely to what category of superhuman being the Satan belongs is never stated. Similar to Jubilees and several of the Dead Sea Scrolls, some NT texts identify him as the leader of maleficent superhuman forces. Some texts depict him as the prince of demons/spirits (e.g., Mark 3:22–30; Luke 13:10–17). Others say (or imply) that he has angelic beings at his disposal (Matt 25:41; 2 Cor 12:7; Rev 12:7–9). Presumably, the authors of these texts supposed that the Satan was himself an angel and/or a demon. That he is presumed to be among those angelic beings who harm or kill humans in the service of God would make sense of some NT texts (e.g., 1 Cor 5:1–5). In other texts, he appears to have more in common with the rebellious angels of 1 Enoch who are imprisoned and will eventually be judged (e.g., Rev 20:1–10).

The Satan appears under various titles and designations in the NT. The numerous appellatives applied to this figure include *ho satanas*, "(the) Satan," *ho diabolos*, "the adversary," *ho ponēros*, "the evil one," *ho peirazōn*, "the tester/tempter," *ho echthros*, "the enemy," *Beelzeboul*, "Beelzebul," *Beliar*, "Beliar," and *ho archōn tou kosmou toutou*, "the ruler of this world."[8] The variety of designations for the Satan reflects the variety of activities that the NT authors believed that the Satan was engaged in and the variety of traditions about this figure to which the NT authors were heirs.

By far the most common designations for the Satan in the NT are *ho satanas*, "(the) Satan," and *ho diabolos*, "the adversary" or "the devil." These two designations, therefore, merit special comment.

7. As mentioned above, the authors of 1–2 Peter and Jude may have presumed the etiology and taxonomy of angels, demons, and spirits found in 1 En. 15:1–16:1; 19:1. The author of Colossians, in contrast, alludes to the origin of superhuman powers in a passage laden with the language of Gen 1 and may presume an etiology and taxonomy more akin to those of the Treatise on the Two Spirits (1QS 3:13–4:26).

8. For a list of all the possible designations for the Satan in the NT and where they are located, see Farrar and Williams, "Diabolical Data," 42, 61.

Ho satanas, *"(the) Satan"*

Satanas is a transliteration of Heb. *śṭn*. This word occurs in the Greek translation of Sir 21:27, though its sense in this verse is uncertain. It could refer either to a human or to a superhuman being.[9] The related transliteration *satan* occurs in the LXX of 1 Kgs 11:14, 23, where it refers to the human opponents of Solomon and Israel.[10] In contrast to *satan* in the LXX, which refers to human opponents, *satanas* in the NT refers predominantly, perhaps exclusively, to a superhuman person.[11] Also, unlike *śṭn* in some early Jewish texts (e.g., Jub. 23:29; 4Q213[a] 1 i 17), *satanas* in the NT does not refer merely to a class of attacker, but denotes predominantly, perhaps exclusively, a particular individual, "(the) Satan."[12]

From a grammatical perspective, there is some question about how *satanas* should be translated in the NT. It typically appears with the definite article and is assumed by translators to be the name Satan. *Ho satanas* could just as easily, however, be taken as a title, "the Satan," corresponding to Heb. *hśṭn* of Zech 3 and Job 1–2. Since Greek uses the definite article under certain circumstances with personal names as well as to mark common nouns as definite, its presence does not indicate whether *satanas* is a name or a title.[13] Further, that the word is transliter-

9. Sir 21:27 says, "When an ungodly person curses an adversary [*ton satanan*], he curses himself." Although the original Hebrew of this passage has been lost, one can safely surmise that it had *(h)śṭn*. Alexander Di Lella reasons that this "satan" was a human adversary (Patrick W. Skehan and Alexander A. Di Lella, *The Wisdom of Ben Sira*, AB 39 [New York: Doubleday, 1987], 311–12). Cf. Sir 21:28, which contains a similar idea to that of 21:27 and pertains to a human being. Armin Lange, "Satanic Verses: The Adversary in the Qumran Manuscripts and Elsewhere," *RevQ* 24.1 (2009): 42–43, however, suggests that although Ben Sira seems to have had a human adversary in mind, the Greek translator mistook this satan for a superhuman satan.

10. Elsewhere, the LXX translates *śṭn* with *diabolos* (Job 1–2; 1 Chr 21:1; Zech 3:1–2 [2×]; Ps 108:6 [MT, Eng. 109:6]) or *epiboulos* (1 Sam 29:4; 2 Sam 19:23 [Eng. 19:22]).

11. The possible exception to this is Mark 8:33, where Jesus calls Peter *satanas*. Jesus's response to Peter's attempt to protect him may be modeled on David's rebuke of Abishai in 2 Sam 19:23 (Eng. 22). It is less likely that a human satan is intended in the parallel account in Matt 16:23, where, after calling Peter *satanas*, Jesus explains that Peter is a stumbling block to him. In Matthew, Jesus likely associates Peter with the Satan, who is the tempter par excellence.

12. See the possible exception of Mark 3:23, which, according to Jan Dochhorn, "The Devil in the Gospel of Mark," in *Evil and the Devil*, ed. Ida Fröhlich and Erkki Koskenniemi, LNTS 481 (London: Bloomsbury, 2013), 104, uses *satanas* to refer to a class of satan.

13. On the use and nonuse of the definite article with personal names in NT Greek,

ated or borrowed from Hebrew rather than translated with a previously known Greek word does little to resolve the matter. While one would expect Hebrew personal names to be transliterated into Greek, other sorts of words could be transliterated as well. As noted in the previous paragraph, the transliteration (or loanword) *satan* appears in the LXX rendering of 1 Kgs 11:14, 23. In this text, the word is not a name but merely a noun meaning "attacker." Hence, whether *ho satanas* in the NT is a title or a name is ambiguous.

Translators who interpret *ho satanas* as a name in the NT often do so on the assumption that *śṭn* had come to be used as a name in Judaism by the time that the NT was composed. While the noun *śṭn* eventually comes to function as a name in Judaism, it is not clear exactly when this transition takes place.[14] We have observed that some of the oft-cited examples of the name Satan in earlier literature are unlikely to be such (e.g., 1 Chr 21:1; Jub. 10:11). *Śṭn* could be a name in 11QPsalms[a] 19:15, though it could instead refer to a category of harmful being (cf. 4Q213[a] 1 i 17). First Enoch 53:3 and 54:6 may also have the name Satan, though it is impossible to judge from the Ethiopic translation whether the name Satan or "the Satan" appeared in the original, since Ethiopic has no definite article.[15] There are a small number of possible instances of *śṭn* as a name in early Jewish literature outside the NT, but no unambiguous instance.

There is more evidence, albeit sparse, that Jews continued to use the title *hśṭn*, "the Satan," during this period. The Dead Sea Scrolls do not use *hśṭn* for the Satan figure, but prefer *bly'l*, "Belial," and other designations. The title "the Satan" probably appeared in the original Hebrew of Jub. 10:11. As noted above, it is possible that the name also appeared in the original Hebrew or Aramaic of 1 En. 53:3 and 54:6, though it is impossible

---

see Herbert Weir Smyth, *Greek Grammar,* rev. Gordon M. Messing (Cambridge: Harvard University Press, 1956), 289–91; Daniel B. Wallace, *Greek Grammar beyond the Basics: An Exegetical Syntax of the New Testament* (Grand Rapids: Zondervan, 1996), 245–47.

14. "Satan" functions unambiguously as a name in rabbinic and Christian texts. According to Thomas J. Farrar, "New Testament Satanology and Leading Suprahuman Opponents in Second Temple Jewish Literature: A Religion-Historical Analysis," *JTS* (forthcoming), *śṭn* appears unambiguously as a name for the first time in t. Šabb. 17:23, and *satanas* in Justin, *Dialogue with Trypho* 103.5.

15. The Enochic Book of Parables is preserved only in Ethiopic. Whether the original language was Hebrew or Aramaic and whether the Ethiopic was translated directly from this language or mediated by a Greek translation are disputed. On these questions, see George W. E. Nickelsburg and James C. VanderKam, *1 Enoch 2*, Hermeneia (Minneapolis: Fortress, 2012), 30–34.

to judge from the Ethiopic translation. Since this title appears in the Hebrew scriptures, however, and resurfaces in early rabbinic texts, one may reasonably assume that it remained in use during the intervening centuries. Given the limited evidence, however, one cannot know how frequent and widespread the title "the Satan" was for the chief superhuman opponent in Jewish discourse around the time of the NT nor precisely when *śṭn* began to be used as a name for this figure.

In the NT, it is likely that many of the occurrences of *ho satanas* are intended to be the title "the Satan" rather than the name Satan. In this respect, the NT authors would have been among those Jews who maintained the terminology of Zech 3 and Job 1–2 with respect to the Satan figure. That *satanas* occurs in some NT texts without the definite article, on the other hand, suggests that in at least some instances we probably have the name Satan (e.g., Luke 22:3; 2 Cor 12:7).[16] In these texts, the noun *satanas* has made a transition similar to that of *bly'l*, "Belial," in the Dead Sea Scrolls, from common noun to name.[17] Determining which instances of *ho satanas* in the NT should be translated as the name Satan and which should be translated as the title "the Satan," unfortunately, may not ultimately be possible.[18]

16. As Farrar, "New Testament Satanology," observes, the absence of the article does not in every instance necessarily rule out the possibility that a title rather than a name is intended. He notes the expected absence of the article in the vocative case (e.g., Mark 8:33). He also dismisses the significance of *angelos satana*, "angel of Satan," in 2 Cor 12:7 on the basis of the parallel *angelos kyriou*, "angel of the Lord" (e.g., Matt 1:20). If, however, *angelos kyriou* has been influenced by Heb. *ml'k yhwh*, "angel of Yahweh/the Lord," then this example would not support the contention that *angelos satana* should be translated as "angel of the Satan."

17. Douglas L. Penney, "Finding the Devil in the Details: Onomastic Exegesis and the Naming of Evil in the World of the New Testament," in *New Testament Greek and Exegesis: Essays in Honor of Gerald F. Hawthorne*, ed. Amy M. Donaldson and Timothy B. Sailors (Grand Rapids: Eerdmans, 2003), 38, calls the interpretive process by which common nouns from the Hebrew scriptures, such as "satan" and "belial," came to function as names of particular figures "onomastic exegesis."

18. Farrar, "New Testament Satanology," cautions that one "should not conclude that ['satan'] has transitioned from *Funktionsbezeichnung* to name in any early Christian text without compelling exegetical reasons to do so," arguing that the burden of proof is on the interpreter who wishes to interpret "satan" as a name rather than a title in any NT text. If, as seems to be the case, however, the name Satan appears in some first-century Christian texts, then the burden of proof is equally on those who would translate *ho satanas* either as "Satan" or as "the Satan."

Ho diabolos, *"the Adversary"*

Diabolos, "adversary" or "devil," is the word with which the Greek translators of the Hebrew scriptures chose to render the noun *śāṭān* in Zech 3:1–2, 1 Chr 21:1, and Job 1–2. This word and related terms (*diabolē, diaballein*) can refer to opposition of various sorts. In some cases, they refer specifically to verbal opposition, such as "complaint," "slander," or "accusation."[19] It was probably not these specific connotations, however, that led translators to choose *diabolos* to render *śāṭān*, but rather its more generic sense of "adversary." This is indicated by the choice of *endiaballein* and *diabolē* to translate *śāṭān* in Num 22, where "slander" or "accusation" would not be appropriate (Num 22:22, 32).[20] That *antikeimai*, "to oppose," and *diabolos*, "adversary," appear together in Zech 3:1 as translations of the verb *śāṭan* and the noun *śāṭān*, respectively, also suggests that the translators were thinking primarily not of verbal attack but of opposition or attack more generally.[21] In this respect, *diabolos* and similar words were suitable translations of *śāṭān*, "attacker."[22] Although the specific connotations of verbal attack do not appear to have motivated the Greek translators' choice of *diabolos* to render *śāṭān*, such connotations likely would have been conducive to the later development of the idea that the Satan was an "accuser."

The NT employs *diabolos* to refer both to human and superhuman beings. It refers to human opponents or slanderers, for example, in John 6:70 and 1 Tim 3:11. More commonly, *ho diabolos*, "the adversary," in the

19. Werner Foerster, "διάβολος," *TDNT* 2:72; Madeleine Wieger, "'Celui qu'on appelle διάβολος' (Apocalypse 12,9): L'histoire du nom grec de l'Adversaire," in *L'adversaire de Dieu—Der Widersacher Gottes*, ed. Michael Tilly, Matthias Morgenstern, and Volker Henning Drecoll, WUNT 364 (Tübingen: Mohr Siebeck, 2016), 204.

20. See also the use of *endiaballein* to translate *śāṭan* in Ps 71:13 (LXX 70:13), where the word refers to "attack" rather than "slander" or "accusation."

21. Foerster, "διάβολος," 73. In addition, note that Greek translators use *diabolos* to render *ṣar*, "enemy," and *ṣārar*, "to treat with hostility, attack," with reference to Haman in Esth 7:4 and 8:1. Elsewhere, *epiboulos*, "one who plots against," renders *śāṭān* (e.g., 1 Sam 29:4; 2 Sam 19:23 [Eng. 22]). There is little evidence that Greek translators understood *śāṭān* as "verbal attack" or that they selected *diabolos* and related terms as translations for *śāṭān* with this connotation in mind.

22. Weiger's contention that *diabolos* carries a pejorative connotation absent from *śāṭān* may be correct ("Celui qu'on appelle διάβολος," 208). In this case, the use of *diabolos* with reference to the Satan may reflect a more negative view of this figure on the part of Greek translators than is found in the Hebrew scriptures. Cf., however, the related *endiaballein* in place of *śāṭān* in Num 22:22, where a negative connotation would not be appropriate.

NT refers to the Satan. In this usage, *ho diabolos* appears to have been interchangeable with *ho satanas* with no observable difference in referent or meaning.[23]

The Activity of the Satan

The Satan was clearly an important figure for the authors of the NT, a fact that scholars have increasingly recognized in the last decade or so.[24] The impressive frequency with which the Satan appears in the literature of the NT is one indicator of the Satan's significance in early Christian thought. He is mentioned in nineteen of the twenty-seven books of the NT.[25] This frequency differs markedly from that of the Hebrew scriptures, only two books of which, Job and Zechariah, mention the Satan.[26] In this respect, one can compare the NT writings with the sectarian Dead Sea Scrolls, a

23. Foerster, "διάβολος," 79. Cf., however, Jutta Leonhardt-Balzer, "Gestalten des Bösen im frühen Christentum," in *Apokalyptik und Qumran*, ed. Jörg Frey and Michael Becker (Paderborn: Bonifatius, 2007), 203–35, who distinguishes to some extent between the uses of *satanas* and *diabolos* in the NT writings.

24. Note the number of scholarly monographs on the topic of the Satan in the NT that have recently appeared, including Richard H. Bell, *Deliver Us from Evil: Interpreting the Redemption from the Power of Satan in New Testament Theology*, WUNT 216 (Tübingen: Mohr Siebeck, 2007); David Raymond Smith, *"Hand This Man over to Satan": Curse, Exclusion and Salvation in 1 Corinthians 5*, LNTS 386 (New York: T&T Clark, 2008); Derek R. Brown, *The God of This Age: Satan in the Churches and Letters of the Apostle Paul*, WUNT 2/409 (Tübingen: Mohr Siebeck, 2015); Florian Theobald, *Teufel, Tod, und Trauer: Der Satan im Johannesevangelium und seine Vorgeschichte*, NTOA, SUNT 109 (Göttingen: Vandenhoeck & Ruprecht, 2015). In addition to these studies, numerous articles and essays have been published on the topic of the Satan in the NT.

25. The following NT books mention the Satan: Matthew, Mark, Luke, John, Acts, Romans, 1–2 Corinthians, Ephesians, 1–2 Thessalonians, 1–2 Timothy, Hebrews, James, 1 Peter, 1 John, Jude, and Revelation. Farrar and Williams, "Diabolical Data," 40–71, count a total of 137 references to the Satan in the NT and 20 NT books that mention this figure. They arrive at this total by including the expression "power of darkness" in Col 1:13 among the probable references, albeit an implicit one (51–52). They discuss the implications of their statistical findings in Thomas J. Farrar and Guy J. Williams, "Talk of the Devil: Unpacking the Language of New Testament Satanology," *JSNT* 39.1 (2016): 72–96.

26. If one includes 1 Chron 21 among the references to the Satan in the Hebrew Scriptures, as this passage traditionally has been interpreted, this would bring the total to three. I argued in ch. 1, however, that the Chronicler's satan is far more likely a generic attacker, such as the satan of Num 22, rather than *the* Satan.

great number of which refer to Belial.[27] Thus the NT, along with the sectarian corpus from Qumran, attests to the theological prominence the Satan had attained in some Jewish circles by the first century CE. It is also clear that the Satan is not merely a symbol for social evils or other sorts of sin in the NT. The NT books that refer to the Satan, like the Jewish texts considered in previous chapters, assume that he is an actual, personal being whose nefarious influence was behind many of the churches' problems.[28]

The material in the NT pertaining to the Satan is in many respects what one would expect based on the Jewish literature surveyed in the previous chapters. Early Christian notions of the Satan, like the Jewish conceptions of this figure, are multifaceted, portraying a Satan who is engaged in a wide range of activities. Many of these maleficent works are the same ones that the Satan is up to in earlier literature (e.g., deception, attack). Also, as in the Jewish texts considered thus far, some NT depictions of the Satan stand in tension with one another, particularly with regard to the Satan's relationship to God. The Satan appears in many texts to be God's enemy, but also in several passages to be more of a functionary who willingly serves God's purposes.

Some of the ideas about the Satan found in the NT, in contrast, are previously unattested in Jewish literature. Some of these ideas would have circulated in Jewish circles outside Christianity but happen to be preserved for the first time in the NT. As we will discuss below, this may have been the case, for instance, with the association of the Satan with the serpent of Gen 3. Other ideas were more likely to have been unique to early Christian depictions of the Satan, such as the opposition between the Satan and Christ portrayed in several NT passages.[29] Even these previously unattested ideas of the Satan, nonetheless, have antecedents in earlier Jewish

27. According to Annette Steudel, "Der Teufel in den Texten aus Qumran," in *Apokalyptik und Qumran*, ed. Frey and Becker, 193, Belial appears in sixteen of the approximately forty Essene documents found at Qumran. Taking the fragmentary condition of the documents into consideration, she suspects that an even larger number of the documents would have mentioned Belial.

28. See the arguments of Farrar, "New Testament Satanology," that the NT authors had a "mythological" conception of the Satan, as opposed to a "rationalistic," "non-mythological" conception.

29. Gerd Theissen, "Monotheismus und Teufelsglaube: Entstehung und Psychologie des biblischen Satansmythos," in *Demons and the Devil in Ancient and Medieval Christianity*, ed. Nienke Vos and Willemien Otten, VCSup 108 (Leiden: Brill, 2011), 55–57, helpfully summarizes the various ways in which different NT authors conceive of Christ's defeat of the Satan.

literature. In the case of the Satan's opposition to Christ, one might compare this idea with the Prince of Mastema's opposition to Moses in Jub. 48 or Belial's opposition to Michael in the War Rule.

The Satan and Sin

Although the Satan of the Hebrew scriptures is primarily a figure who brings physical harm on his victims, he came to be regarded in early Judaism as one who leads humans into sin. By the time that the NT was written, his association with wickedness had become primary for many Jewish theologians. Numerous NT texts speak of the Satan's role in leading people into sin. They portray the Satan as a tempter/tester (e.g., Matt 4:1–11; 1 Cor 7:5; Rev 2:10) or as one who otherwise lures the unsuspecting into error (e.g., Mark 4:15; Acts 5:3; 2 Cor 4:4; 2 Tim 2:26; Rev 12:9). Sins that the NT credits the Satan with instigating (or attempting to instigate) include idolatry, sexual immorality, and unbelief. As in several earlier texts (e.g., Jub. 11:4-5; CD 4:12-19), the NT associates the Satan with idolatry and other traditional boundary-making sins.[30]

Further, according to some NT texts, the Satan is involved with a wide range of sins of various sorts. In Matthew and Luke's temptation accounts, the Satan tempts Jesus to violate the Torah by breaking his fast and by testing God (Matt 4:1–7; Luke 4:1–4, 9–12). James 4:1–10 attributes several sins to the devil's influence (e.g., disputes, conflicts, covetousness, pride, and "friendship with the world"). Behind such claims about the Satan's involvement in these sins may lie the belief that the Satan is a proponent of wickedness of any sort, not just a select few especially heinous or boundary-marking sins, such as idolatry. The NT clearly depicts the Satan as one who works delusion both within and outside the early Christian communities.[31]

Related to the Satan's role as deceiver, several NT passages also speak of the Satan as the one who is ultimately behind the religious and political

30. Susan R. Garrett, *The Demise of the Devil: Magic and the Demonic in Luke's Writings* (Minneapolis: Fortress, 1989), 40, probably correctly claims that Acts 26:18, which speaks of gentiles being under the authority of the Satan, implicitly associates the Satan with idolatry.

31. Cf. the Treatise on the Two Spirits (1QS 4:9–11), which implicitly associates the Angel of Darkness with all kinds of sin among both the Sons of Darkness and the Sons of Light.

opponents of Christ and the early Christians. Paul refers to those "false apostles" who create problems for his ministry as servants or "ministers" of Satan (2 Cor 11:14–15). In the Gospel of John, Jesus tells those who are seeking to kill him that they are children of the devil, the father of lies, and that they are doing what their father desires (John 8:39–47). Later in the Gospel of John, it is the devil who puts it into the heart of Judas to betray Jesus (13:2). The Satan is also at work in Judas's betrayal of Jesus in Luke 22:3. In Revelation, the Satan gives his power to the beast who makes war on the saints (Rev 13:1–10). He also deceives the nations, gathering them for battle against the saints (Rev 20:7–10).[32]

The Satan as Attacker

Despite the NT's emphasis on the Satan's involvement in moral evil, the earlier notion of the Satan as an attacker or executioner who brings about physical suffering and death remains an important part of the tradition. The Synoptic Gospels attribute illness to the Satan. As the chief of demons/spirits, the Satan is implicitly associated with the afflictions these beings cause. The connection between the Satan and physical suffering is explicit in Luke 13:10–17, where Jesus heals a disabled woman. Luke attributes the woman's condition to a spirit (13:11), but says also that it is a result of her having been bound by the Satan (13:16). Perhaps the most direct statement regarding the Satan's role as attacker or executioner is Heb 2:14: "Since, therefore, the children share flesh and blood, [Jesus] himself likewise shared the same things, so that through death he might destroy the one who has the power of death, that is, the devil."[33]

32. The portrayal of the Satan in Rev 20 probably has its closest parallel in Jub. 48. There the Prince of Mastema is bound as Israel begins its exodus from Egypt, but is released to lead the Egyptian army in one final attack on Israel. In Rev 20, the Satan is bound for a thousand years, but is released to lead the nations in one final attack on the saints.

33. Many commentators attempt to explain the devil's association with death in Heb 2:14 by citing the Satan's connection with the Gen 3 story in some Jewish and Christian literature (e.g., William L. Lane, *Hebrew 1–8*, WBC 47A [Dallas: Word, 1991], 61; Craig R. Koester, *Hebrews: A New Translation with Introduction and Commentary*, AB 36 [New York: Doubleday, 2001], 231). Harold W. Attridge, *The Epistle to the Hebrews*, Hermeneia (Minneapolis: Fortress, 1989), 92, is exceptional in that he acknowledges also the traditional link between the Satan or other superhuman emissaries and death in texts such as Jub. 49:2. The idea that the Satan is a superhuman agent of death, as in Zech 3, Jub. 48, and other texts, better accounts for the theology of Heb 2:14 than a nebulous association of the Satan with

In addition, the belief that part of the Satan's work was to attack a person's "flesh" is almost certainly the proper background for comprehending some of Paul's seemingly enigmatic statements. In 1 Cor 5, Paul instructs the church in Corinth to hand a sexually immoral member of their community over to (the) Satan. The purpose of this act, according to Paul, would be "for the destruction of the flesh, so that his spirit may be saved in the day of the Lord" (1 Cor 5:5).[34] Paul's vocabulary in this passage is indebted to Job 2, in which the Satan launches a vicious physical attack on Job.[35] Nevertheless, some commentators have argued that Paul did not envision the immoral man suffering physically at the hand of Satan, but that to hand the man over to Satan meant merely to "excommunicate" him, that is, to remove him from the church into the realm of Satan's dominion.[36] Another interpretation of this passage holds that handing the man over to Satan was to have a purely psychological (rather than a physical) effect.[37] Given Paul's indebtedness to Job and the widespread conception in early Judaism of the Satan as one who would harm and kill errant humans, however, it is unlikely that Paul believed that handing the man over to Satan would involve merely social or psychological suffering.[38] Like many of his contemporaries, Paul envisions the Satan as one who would chastise sinners physically (e.g., Jub. 10:8; CD 8:1–2).[39] In the case of the immoral

death via a theological exegesis of Gen 3. On the association of the Satan with the serpent and the events in the garden of Eden, see the discussion later in this chapter.

34. Cf. the similar statement in 1 Tim 1:20.

35. Note especially the similarity between 1 Cor 5:5 and LXX Job 2:5–6. Both texts speak of someone being "handed over" (*paradidōmi*) to the Satan, who is to attack that person's "flesh" (*sarx*).

36. E.g., James T. South, "A Critique of the 'Curse/Death' Interpretation of 1 Corinthians 5.1–8," *NTS* 39.4 (1993): 539–61.

37. Jerome Murphy-O'Connor, *1 Corinthians*, NTM 10 (Wilmington, DE: Glazier, 1979), 42, argues that, in Paul's mind, a person who had become accustomed to a loving Christian community would "suffer severe pain when cast out into the cold egocentricity of the 'world.'"

38. Interpreting "destruction of the flesh" in 1 Cor 5:5 as physical suffering does not necessarily exclude the possibility that handing the man over to Satan also involved the man being expelled from the community. It is possible that removal from the community of the faithful and physical attack by Satan go hand in hand in Paul's thought. Cf. Jubilees' teaching that the Prince of Mastema is free to deceive and attack all the nations of the world except for those who belong to the chosen line of Jacob. For a summary of the various approaches to 1 Cor 5:5, see D. Smith, *"Hand This Man over to Satan,"* who situates the verse within the context of Jewish and Greco-Roman cursing traditions.

39. Cf. 1QS 2:5–6, which speaks of the lot of Belial being destroyed by punishing angels.

man in 1 Cor 5, Paul hopes that this destructive work of the Satan will result in the man's salvation.[40]

Paul also associates the Satan with an affliction of the "flesh" in 2 Cor 12:7. In this verse, Paul says that he has been given a "thorn in the flesh" to prevent him from becoming too elated because of his revelatory experiences. Paul clarifies that his "thorn in the flesh" is an "angel of Satan" who torments him.[41] Paul does not reveal the precise nature of his suffering, and interpreters have identified Paul's affliction in various and creative ways. Some have even suggested nonphysical interpretations of Paul's "thorn," understanding "flesh" metaphorically and identifying Paul's problem as psychological or as external harassment by human opponents.[42] The belief that the Satan and his emissaries would attack an individual's body and would do so at times on behalf of God, however, best accounts for Paul's comments regarding his "thorn in the flesh" and its pedagogical purpose.

40. Certain elements of the destruction and salvation that Paul anticipates remain obscure. Did Paul expect the man to die, as in the case of those members of the Corinthian community mentioned in 1 Cor 11:27–32? Or did he expect the Satan to attack the man's flesh but stop short of killing the man, as in the case of Job? If the man were to die, then the salvation of the man's "spirit" would have to be in the form of resurrection (e.g., Rom 1:3–4; 1 Cor 15:35–50). If Paul expected the destruction of the man's flesh to stop short of death, then the anticipated salvation would involve the man's repentance and restoration. In support of this interpretation is 1 Tim 1:20, which appears to envision the restoration of Hymenaeus and Alexander, who are handed over to the Satan so that they will be taught not to blaspheme. Antecedents for the idea that satanic attack or the threat could be corrective, not merely punitive, can be found in Num 22:22–35 and 1 Chr 21:1–17. Perhaps Jub. 48:2–4 is also relevant, if Paul believed, as did many later Jewish interpreters, that the threat to Moses's life was the consequence of his not circumcising his son (e.g., m. Ned. 3:11). Adela Yarbro Collins, "The Function of 'Excommunication' in Paul," *HTR* 73.1–2 (1980): 259–61, suggests a different interpretation of "flesh" and "spirit" in 1 Cor 5:5. While she holds that Paul anticipated the man's death, the flesh that was to be destroyed, according to her reading, was "those elements and aspects of creation hostile to God." The "spirit" to be saved was not the man's own spirit, but the "Holy Spirit of God and Christ which dwells in the community" (259).

41. Some translations, including the NRSV, render *angelos* as "messenger" rather than "angel" (of Satan) in 2 Cor 12:7. In light of the numerous texts that speak of the Satan as leader of harmful superhuman beings who bring various sorts of physical harm on human beings, "angel" is the better translation.

42. For a succinct summary and evaluation of the major interpretations of Paul's "thorn in the flesh," see Margaret E. Thrall, *The Second Epistle to the Corinthians*, ICC, 2 vols. (London: T&T Clark, 1994, 2000), 2:809–18.

The Satan as God's Agent and as God's Enemy

First Corinthians 5:5 and 2 Cor 12:7, both of which presume that the Satan is a superhuman attacker, also raise questions about the relationship that Paul and other NT authors believed existed between the Satan and God. As argued earlier, the Satan and other satanic beings in the Hebrew scriptures are functionaries of God, agents of divine punishment bringing death and destruction upon humans. By the time that the NT was composed, however, some Jews, such as the author(s) of the War Rule, had come to regard the Satan more as the enemy of God than as God's functionary. That the Satan could be portrayed alternately as God's disciplinary emissary and as one who opposed God's plan, even within one and the same writing (e.g., Jubilees), indicates that thinking about the Satan was not as monolithic and simple as it eventually came to be in later Christian theology. The NT is not exceptional among Jewish literature from this period in this respect, but reflects the complexity of the Satan tradition as it existed in first-century Judaism.[43]

Numerous NT texts speak of the Satan as one who is opposed to God. God and the Satan are said to rule two opposing and competing kingdoms (Luke 11:18–21; Acts 26:18). First John 3:10 divides humankind into two camps, the children of God and the children of the devil. A number of texts speak similarly of an opposition between the Satan and Christ (Matt 13:38–39; 2 Cor 6:14–15; 1 John 3:8). From an eschatological perspective, a judgment befitting one who has rebelled against God awaits the Satan (Matt 25:41; Heb 2:14; Rev 20:10).

Other texts seem to presume that the Satan serves God. This understanding of the Satan is most obvious in texts associated with Paul. In 1 Cor 5:5, the Satan was to destroy the sexually immoral man's flesh "so that his spirit may be saved on the day of the Lord." In 2 Cor 12:7, Paul's "thorn in the flesh," an angel of Satan who tormented Paul, was given to him (pre-

43. Perhaps more than any other writer, Henry Ansgar Kelly has stressed that the NT depicts the Satan as an agent of God. See, e.g., *Satan: A Biography* (Cambridge: Cambridge University Press, 2006); and *Satan in the Bible, God's Minister of Justice* (Eugene, OR: Cascade, 2017). Kelly is to be commended for calling attention to a facet of NT beliefs about the Satan that many readers have overlooked. Kelly errs, however, in that he underestimates the extent to which the Satan came to be regarded as a rebel in early Judaism and is presented as such in the NT. Beliefs about the Satan as attested in many early Jewish writings, including some of the NT texts, were more complex than either that the Satan is merely a rebel or that he is merely a functionary of God.

sumably) by God to keep Paul from becoming overly elated. First Timothy 1:20 says that Paul handed Hymenaeus and Alexander over to the Satan in order that they would be taught not to blaspheme. These texts give no indication that the Satan is being manipulated and only unwittingly serves God's beneficent purposes. They presuppose that the Satan is God's agent of attack for the purpose of punishing or disciplining errant humans, much as the Satan of earlier literature.

This diversity or tension in early Christian views of the Satan perhaps explains the controversy that underlies Jude 8–10. In these verses, Jude criticizes those who "slander the glorious ones." As an example of how people are supposed to engage glorious ones, Jude refers to a story about a dispute between Michael and the devil about the body of Moses.[44] In this dispute, Jude points out, even the archangel Michael refrained from slandering the devil. It is impossible to know precisely how Jude's opponents "slandered the glorious ones." They may have engaged in a practice of cursing the Satan and his spirits resembling that attested in some of the Dead Sea Scrolls: "Cursed be Belial for the hostile plan and may he be denounced for his guilty authority! Cursed be all the spirits of his lot for their wicked plan and may they be denounced for all their service of impure uncleanliness! For they are the lot of darkness, but the lot of God is for [everlast]ing light!" (1QM 13:4–6).[45] This practice reflects the view that the Satan and the spirits in his service are more the opponents of God than they are God's agents. According to Jude, however, the Satan is one of the "glorious ones" in God's service. Jude contends that his opponents "slander whatever they do not understand." Since the Satan and those spirits who serve him are among God's glorious ones, it is inappropriate to slander them.

At least one NT text appears to address the ambiguous nature of the Satan's relationship to God. In Rev 12, the Satan and his angels are defeated in heavenly battle and are thrown down to the earth. Then a voice in heaven proclaims, "Now have come the salvation and the power and the

44. The story to which Jude refers, unfortunately, has not been preserved among the literary remains of early Judaism. Early Christian tradition attributes this story to a work called the Assumption of Moses. For a discussion of the story to which Jude refers and the Satan's role in it, see Ryan E. Stokes, "Not over Moses' Dead Body: Jude 9, 22–24 and the *Assumption of Moses* in Their Early Jewish Context," *JSNT* 40.2 (2017): 192–213.

45. Translation is that of Jean Duhaime, "War Scroll," in *Damascus Document, War Scroll, and Related Documents*, vol. 2 of *The Dead Sea Scrolls: Hebrew, Aramaic, and Greek Texts with English Translations*, ed. James H. Charlesworth, PTSDSSP (Tübingen: Mohr Siebeck; Louisville: Westminster John Knox, 1995), 123.

kingdom of our God and the authority of his Messiah, for the accuser of our comrades has been thrown down, who accuses them day and night before our God" (12:10). This text depicts the Satan not as a punishing attacker but as an "accuser." It assumes that the Satan possesses some official standing in heaven that allows him to create problems for the righteous, but that his appointment to this office is not permanent. John speaks of a time when, as a result of the death of Christ and of the faithful testimony of the saints, the Satan will no longer accuse the comrades before God.[46]

Numerous NT texts, similar to the sectarian Dead Sea Scrolls (e.g., Damascus Document, War Rule, Rule of the Community), depict the Satan as an evil figure. Given this emphasis in the NT and the trajectory of the tradition, it is understandable that later Christian theology would characterize the Satan as God's enemy, even to the exclusion of any notion of the Satan as a functionary of God. During the era of the NT, nonetheless, some Jews continued to regard the Satan as an agent of God. This conception of the Satan is not absent from the NT. Jude regards the devil as one of the "glorious ones." The belief that the Satan is an agent of God also surfaces in the Pauline tradition, though even Paul speaks of the Satan primarily in evil terms. The book of Revelation addresses the tension created by the diverse portrayals of the Satan and prophesies about a time when the Satan would forfeit his heavenly office.

The Accuser of the Comrades

Commenting on John's identification of the Satan as "the accuser of our comrades" in Rev 12:10, scholars typically assert that biblical and early Jewish literature depicts the Satan as one who functioned as an accuser in the heavenly court.[47] The accuracy of this claim depends on precisely

46. Additional NT texts that may assume that the Satan is a functionary of God include Luke 22:31 and Matt 6:13, in which the Satan works in conjunction with God to test humans. As I argue below, the designation "accuser of our comrades" in Rev 12 is probably to be understood within this context.

47. E.g., David E. Aune, *Revelation 6–16*, WBC 52B (Nashville: Nelson, 1998), 700–702; G. K. Beale, *The Book of Revelation*, NIGTC (Grand Rapids: Eerdmans, 1999), 661–63; Jan Dochhorn, *Schriftgelehrte Prophetie: Der eschatologische Teufelsfall in Apc Joh 12 und seine Bedeutung für das Verständnis der Johannesoffenbarung*, WUNT 268 (Tübingen: Mohr Siebeck, 2010), 368–70; Craig R. Koester, *Revelation: A New Translation with Introduction and Commentary*, AYB 38A (New Haven: Yale University Press, 2014), 551.

what one means by "accuser." Often scholars conflate two different notions in their discussions of the Satan as accuser. One of these is that of a prosecutor who brings charges against sinners in the heavenly courtroom. The other is that of an individual who persuades God to test the innocent with adversity. This individual could be a sort of "accuser," in that he might allege that the innocent person would not remain faithful to God in the midst of suffering. There is more evidence in Second Temple literature for the latter belief than there is for the former. Revelation also presents the Satan as one who would test the righteous.

With regard to the notion of the Satan as a prosecutor of sinners, the evidence prior to the second century CE is scant. Although several texts from the Hebrew scriptures and early Jewish literature often feature in scholarly discussions of the Satan as an accuser of the wicked, few, if any, of these actually portray him in this capacity. In chs. 1 and 2 of this book I contended that Heb. *śāṭān* denotes physical "attack" and that the satans of the Hebrew scriptures are attackers or executioners rather than accusers (e.g., Num 22; Zech 3). With respect to Jub. 1:20 and 48:15–19, in ch. 5 I demonstrated that the idea of attack best accounts for these passages as well. While the Ethiopic translator appears to have understood the Prince of Mastema's activity in these verses as "accusation," the original Hebrew likely spoke of physical attack. The same translation issue also likely accounts for an apparent reference to satanic accusation in the Enochic Book of Parables (1 En. 40:7).[48] Scholars have claimed that a small number of additional texts from the first century CE or earlier portray the Satan as this sort of accuser, but only on very tenuous grounds.[49]

Neither is the belief that the Satan would prosecute sinners before God clearly attested in the NT. A small number of texts possibly refer to the Satan occupying such a juridical office, but none is certain. First

48. For a discussion of this verse and others verses in the Book of Parables (1 En. 37–71) that mention satanic beings, see the excursus below.

49. See, e.g., 1QM 13:11, which says, "You have made Belial to corrupt [or 'destroy'], a hostile angel. In the darkne[ss] . . . his counsel is aimed towards wickedness and guiltiness [*lhršyʿ wlhʾšym*]." Miryam T. Brand, *Evil Within and Without: The Source of Sin and Its Nature as Portrayed in Second Temple Literature*, JSJSup 9 (Göttingen: Vandenhoeck & Ruprecht, 2013), 234, translates *lhršyʿ wlhʾšym* as "to cause wickedness and to accuse." This translation is far from certain. Indeed, the parallelism between the two infinitives suggests that they would be better rendered "to cause wickedness and to cause guilt." Another text that scholars have assumed refers to satanic accusation is 4Q225 2 i 9–10. See, however, the criticism of this interpretation of the text in ch. 5, n21.

Peter 5:8 says, "Like a roaring lion your adversary [*ho antidikos*] the devil prowls around looking for someone to devour." *Antidikos* can refer to an "opponent" in the context of a lawsuit, though it could just as easily denote an "enemy" or "opponent" in general (e.g., LXX 1 Sam 2:10; Sir 36:6 [Eng. 9]).[50] And the imagery of this passage, though clearly figurative, would lend itself more naturally to a depiction of physical attack than to a depiction of prosecution in a courtroom. First Timothy 5:14 advises younger widows to remarry so that they will not give *ho antikeimenos*, "the adversary," reason for *loidoria*, "abuse." It is not clear, however, either that the "adversary" of this verse is the Satan rather than a human adversary, or that the "abuse" envisioned is specifically that of legal accusation.[51]

Recognizing that the satanic role of accuser or prosecutor is largely absent from the NT, some scholars have recently expressed consternation over this absence. These scholars perceive the dearth of references to this particular role of the Satan in the NT as an aberration among early Jewish literature. Derek Brown, for instance, says that the notion of the Satan as an accuser appears "to have run aground in early Christian theology."[52] In actuality, that this role of the Satan does not figure prominently in the NT is consistent with other early Jewish writings of the late Second Temple period that also have very little to say about the Satan's work of accusing sinners. If Jews of this era believed that the Satan was one who stood before God to accuse the wicked of their transgressions, this belief left hardly a mark on the literature from this period.

In contrast, several texts from the first century CE and earlier speak of the Satan as one who would persuade God to test the righteous with suffering. In the book of Job, the Satan incites God against the blameless Job (Job 1:6–12; 2:1–6). The author of Jubilees, retelling the story of Isaac's binding according to the pattern of Job, attributes the faithful Abraham's ordeal to the instigation of the malevolent Prince of Mastema (Jub. 17:15–18:16). Pseudo-Jubilees portrays Abraham's test and Isaac's peril similarly to the way Jubilees does, as a threat prompted by the Prince of Mastema

50. BDAG 88.

51. According to some scholars, another verse that assumes that the Satan serves in the role of accuser is Jude 9, which refers to a dispute between Michael and the devil over Moses's body. See, however, the arguments against this interpretation in Stokes, "Not over Moses' Dead Body."

52. Brown, *God of This Age*, 201. See also the assessment of Farrar and Williams, "Talk of the Devil," 85n52, that the NT authors mention the Satan's role as prosecutor "rarely, and then usually to undermine it."

(4Q225 2 i 9–10). The notion of the Satan as one who would incite God to test the innocent with adversity explains a handful of NT passages as well. In Luke 22:31, Jesus informs Peter that the Satan has demanded to sift Peter and the other apostles like wheat. In Matt 6:13, Jesus instructs his followers to pray that God would not bring them into *peirasmos*, "trial," but would instead deliver them from the evil one.[53]

The belief that the Satan would malevolently incite God against the innocent is also that from which John's understanding of the Satan as the accuser arose. Appropriately, Rev 12 does not call the Satan the accuser of humankind or the accuser of sinners, but the accuser of *adelphoi hēmōn*, "our comrades" or "our brothers." That the Satan malevolently incites God to test the faithfulness of the innocent also comports well with other statements in the book. John warns the church in Smyrna, "Beware, the devil is about to throw some of you into prison so that you may be tested, and for ten days you will have affliction. Be faithful until death, and I will give you the crown of life" (Rev 2:10). In Rev 12:11, the accuser of the comrades is defeated, in part, by the faithfulness of the saints, "for they did not love their lives even in the face of death."[54]

This statement (Rev 12:11) echoes the stories mentioned above in which the Satan incites God against the righteous. The Satan contends before God in Job 2:4 that Job will be unfaithful to God in order to preserve his own life. In Jub. 17:15, the Satan questions whether Abraham will prove unfaithful to God out of his love for Isaac. When Abraham demonstrates that he is willing to sacrifice what he loves most for the sake of his faithfulness to God, Jubilees says, "the Prince of Mastema was put to shame" (Jub. 18:12).[55] Whether the comrades would be unfaithful to God in order to save their own lives is what the Satan tests in Revelation. The churches were to participate in the Satan's defeat by remaining faithful in the face of their trials and thus proving his allegations before God to be groundless.

53. The Satan and God also seem to work in conjunction in the test/temptation of Jesus in the Synoptic Gospels. In all three accounts, the Spirit leads Jesus into the wilderness, where he is tested/tempted by the devil (Matt 4:1–11; Mark 1:12–13; Luke 4:1–13). Matthew's version emphasizes this role of the Satan the most, indicating that the Spirit led Jesus into the wilderness "to be tested/tempted" (*peirasthēnai*) by the devil, whom Matthew also refers to as *ho peirazōn*, "the tester/tempter."

54. My translation. NRSV has "they did not cling to life even in the face of death."

55. Cf. also T. Job 27:1–5, in which the Satan admits that Job has defeated him by faithfully enduring his trials. Both Rev 12:11 and T. Job 27:5 use the verb *nikaō* to speak of the victory of the righteous over the Satan.

In addition to encouraging the churches to prove the Satan's accusations groundless by remaining faithful, it is possible that John believes that sins that the churches had already committed needed to be accounted for as well, in order to bring about the accuser's defeat. This would explain the role of the "blood of the lamb" in Michael's victory over the dragon (Rev 12:11; cf. 1:5; 7:14). If Rev 12 indeed presumes that the Satan would accuse the churches before God of sins they had committed, this would be the only passage in Revelation that does so. It is also potentially the earliest attestation of this idea in our literature.[56] What is more evident, however, is that the prophet John and other early Jewish writers regarded the Satan as one who would malevolently incite God to test the righteous with adversity.

Interestingly, Revelation goes beyond Job, Jubilees, and other Second Temple–era texts in its portrayal of the Satan's "accusation" of the faithful before God in at least one respect. While several texts speak of an occasion on which the Satan goes before God to create problems for the righteous, Revelation teaches that the Satan engages in this activity constantly "day and night" (12:10). This sort of accusation is the essence of the Satan's activity before God in Revelation. John prophesies, nonetheless, that the Satan would eventually be defeated and lose his standing in heaven, putting an end to the Satan's work of inciting God to test the faithful.

Excursus: Satans in the Book of Parables

One verse in the Enochic Book of Parables (1 En. 37–71) appears at first glance to refer to satanic accusation.[57] In 1 En. 40, Enoch sees an innu-

56. For the belief that the Satan would accuse the wicked, see Apoc. Zeph. 3:8–9, which Gerbern S. Oegema, "Zephaniah, Apocalypse of," *EDEJ* 1358–59, dates to the second or third century CE.

57. Scholars generally date the Book of Parables to sometime during the last half of the first century BCE or during the first century CE. Some have argued for a narrower range of possible dates, citing supposed historical allusions in the book. See, e.g., the argument of Nickelsburg and VanderKam, *1 Enoch 2*, 58–63, that the Book of Parables was written during the reign of Herod the Great (37–4 BCE), specifically "between the latter part of Herod's reign and the early decades of the first century CE, with some preference for the earlier part of this time span" (62–63). Ted M. Erho, "Historical-Allusion Dating and the Similitudes," *JBL* 130.3 (2011): 493–511, however, contends that scholars ought to adopt a broader, more secure range of 50 BCE–100 CE for the composition of the work, rather than a narrower and more disputable range of dates.

merable host standing in God's presence. Enoch also notices that Michael, Gabriel, Raphael, and Phanuel are among them and are speaking. With regard to the words of one of them, Enoch explains, "And the fourth voice I heard driving away the satans, and he did not let them come before the Lord of Spirits, to accuse [*'astawādaya*] those who dwell on the earth" (1 En. 40:7). This text seems to be based on Zech 3, where the Satan intends to *śṭn*, "attack" or "execute," Joshua. The angel of Yahweh, however, verbally rebukes the Satan and spares Joshua. The Book of Parables does differ somewhat from Zech 3; for our purposes, it is noteworthy that it is not *the* Satan, but a class of satans that is thwarted. Nonetheless, this text's apparent reference to satanic beings accusing those who dwell on the earth is relevant for our investigation of the development of the notion of the Satan as an accuser.

There are several indicators that this passage may have originally spoken of satans *attacking* those who dwell on the earth rather than accusing them. As we noted in ch. 5, *'astawādaya* is the word that the Ethiopic OT uses to render the Gk. *endiaballō* where this word corresponds to the Hebrew verb *śāṭan*. This passage's indebtedness to Zech 3 and its use of the noun "satan" (Eth. *sayṭān*) likewise suggest that the Hebrew verb *śāṭan*, "attack," lies behind Eth. *'astawādaya*, "accuse."[58]

While the context of 1 En. 40 alone may be insufficient for a firm conclusion regarding the activity of the satans in this text, other passages in the Parables corroborate our suspicion that these satans are supposed to be attackers rather than accusers. Satanic beings are mentioned in three additional passages in the Parables. None of the other three passages speaks of satanic figures accusing anyone.[59] One passage associates the rebellious watchers who led humankind into sin with the Satan (54:6).[60] The two remaining passages that mention satanic beings speak of them as attackers.

58. See the similar arguments regarding the translation of Jub. 1:20 and 48:15–19 in ch. 5 above. This observation in the case of the present passage may favor the hypothesis that the Ethiopic of the Book of Parables is a translation of a Greek translation of a Hebrew original, but it does not rule out the possibilities that the work was originally Aramaic or that the Ethiopic is a direct translation of the original, whether that was Hebrew or Aramaic.

59. As observed by Nickelsburg and VanderKam, *1 Enoch 2*, 132.

60. Second Enoch, which may date as early as the first century CE, also brings together the watcher and Satan traditions. Andrei A. Orlov, *Dark Mirrors: Azael and Satanel in Early Jewish Demonology* (Albany: State University of New York Press, 2011), 85–99, discusses how 2 Enoch merges the two traditions.

> For I saw all the angels of punishment dwelling (there) and preparing all the instruments of [the] Satan. And I asked the angel of peace who went with me, "These instruments—for whom are they preparing them?" And he said to me, "They are preparing these for the kings and the mighty of this earth, that they may perish thereby." (1 En. 53:3–5)[61]

In this passage, the instruments with which the punishing angels will execute the kings and the mighty of the earth are referred to as "instruments of (the) Satan."

A second passage also seems to connect such implements of death with satans:

> A command has gone forth from the presence of the Lord against the inhabitants of the earth, that their end is accomplished, for they have learned all the secrets of the angels and all the violence of the satans, and all their powers, the hidden secrets. (1 En. 65:6)

The "violence of the satans" that humans have learned, according to this passage, likely refers to those iron weapons that Asael showed humankind how to manufacture in the Book of the Watchers (1 En. 8:1). In this passage, as in 53:3–5, the Book of Parables associates satans or the Satan with instruments of death. Although the Ethiopic translation of 40:7 speaks of satanic accusation, it is unlikely that this verse did so in the original language. Rather, as in earlier literature and as elsewhere in the Book of Parables itself, 1 En. 40:7 very probably originally referred to satanic physical attack.

The Ancient Serpent

Although the book of Genesis does not associate the crafty serpent of Eden with the Satan, two NT books appear to mention the Satan in connection with this serpent (Rom 16:20; Rev 12:9; 20:2).[62] The process that led to

61. G. W. E. Nickelsburg and James C. VanderKam, *1 Enoch: The Hermeneia Translation* (Minneapolis: Fortress, 2012), 67, have the name Satan in 53:3. On the question of whether this is a name or a title, see the discussion earlier in this chapter.

62. Scholars agree that Rev 12:9 and 20:2 allude to the Gen 3 story. They disagree, however, regarding the nature of the allusion in Rom 16:20: "The God of peace will shortly crush Satan under your feet." Paul's statement is commonly regarded as an allusion to Gen 3:15, though the language of Rom 16:20 and that of Gen 3:15 differ significantly. See the discussion

the identification or association of the Satan with the serpent of Gen 3 is worthy of a study in its own right. To deal comprehensively with this development in the Satan tradition, which appears to have taken place during or just prior to the first century CE, would take us far afield from the present study.[63] Nevertheless, given the importance of the Satan's association with the serpent in later tradition, a few comments regarding this development and the NT texts that may reflect it are in order.

1. The identification or association of the Satan with the serpent of Gen 3 in early Judaism should be understood within the context of other early Jewish interpretive retellings of Israel's sacred narratives. In the process of retelling and expanding their sacred stories, Jews imported the Satan or related figures into narratives from which they were originally absent. This practice can be observed already in the Hebrew scriptures. Although no "satan" appears in the census story of 2 Sam 24, the Chronicler reworks the story so that it is a "satan" who incites David to take the disastrous census of Israel (1 Chr 21:1). Early on in this process, since the Satan was perceived to be one who would harm God's people, interpreters would write this

---

of Rom 16:20 and the bibliography in Brown, *God of This Age*, 104–9, who argues that Paul alludes not to Gen 3:15 in this verse but to Pss 110:1 and 8:7. Although the language of Rom 16:20 has little in common with Gen 3:15, the preceding verses that mention deception, wisdom, good, and evil evoke the Eden narrative. For this reason, I treat Rom 16:20 tentatively as an allusion to Gen 3 (perhaps among other passages from the Hebrew scriptures), in which the Satan corresponds to the serpent of the earlier story.

63. The earliest reference to Satan's activity in the garden of Eden may be Wis 2:24: "but through the devil's envy death entered the world." It is possible, however, that the *diabolos* of this verse does not refer to the serpent but to Cain, whose envy of Abel introduced death into the world. Another interpretation of this verse is that of Jason M. Zurawski, "Separating the Devil from the *Diabolos*: A Fresh Reading of Wisdom of Solomon 2.24," *JSP* 21.4 (2012): 366–99, who regards this verse not as an etiology of death (either through the serpent or through Cain), but as a description of the ongoing state of the cosmos. If the Wisdom of Solomon does not refer to the serpent, then the NT may contain our earliest references to the Satan's involvement in the events of Eden. Other works that associate the serpent with the Satan and that may date as early as the first century CE include the Apocalypse of Abraham (chs. 13 and 23) and 3 Baruch (9:7). Daniel C. Harlow ("Abraham, Apocalypse of," *EDEJ* 297; and "Baruch, Third Book of," *EDEJ* 429) dates both of these works to the late first or to the second century. The Life of Adam and Eve and Ezekiel the Tragedian, frag. 18, both of which connect the Satan with the serpent, are more difficult to date and very possibly come from a much later period. On the uncertain dating of the Life of Adam and Eve, see Jean-Pierre Pettorelli, "Adam and Eve, Life of," *EDEJ* 305–6. On the questionable attribution of frag. 18 to Ezekiel, see Carl R. Holladay, *Poets*, vol. 2 of *Fragments from Hellenistic Jewish Authors*, TT 30, Pseudepigrapha Series 12 (Atlanta: Scholars Press, 1989), 526–29.

figure into stories in which Israel is threatened, such as the binding of Isaac (Jub. 17:15–18:16) and the exodus (Jub. 48; CD 5:17–19). As the Satan eventually came to be regarded as one who would lead humans into moral error, interpreters began also to write him into stories of sin. The Book of Parables, for instance, says that the angels who led humankind astray just prior to the flood were servants of the Satan (1 En. 54:6; cf. 1 En. 6–11).[64] Likewise, 1 John 3:12 explains that Cain, who murdered his brother Abel, belonged to the Evil One (cf. John 8:44). The association of the Satan with the serpent who instigated humankind's initial lapse should be understood as another example of this interpretive practice.

2. The serpent of Gen 3 was one of several serpent traditions in the literature of early Judaism and was not the only serpent tradition with which NT authors connect the Satan.[65] A number of texts in the Hebrew scriptures speak of mythological primordial serpents/dragons. These include Leviathan (e.g., Isa 27:1; Job 3:8; Ps 104:26) and Rahab (e.g., Job 26:12–13; Ps 89:11 [Eng. 10]; Isa 51:9). Revelation's portrayal of the Satan as the "dragon" and the "ancient serpent" reflects such primordial serpent/dragon traditions.[66] Many texts also refer to serpents (along with scorpions

64. Interestingly, according to the Book of Parables, it is not the Satan but an angel named Gadre'el who receives the blame for Eve's transgression (1 En. 69:6). It is possible, nonetheless, that the Book of Parables implicates the Satan indirectly in Eve's sin. Since elsewhere the Book of Parables says that the watchers became servants of the Satan when they misled humankind prior to the flood (1 En. 54:6), it may be that the work's author regarded Gadre'el's act of leading Eve astray as similarly in the service of the Satan. Cf. Apoc. Ab. 13, 23, in which Azazel, the leader of the watchers who taught humans sinful crafts according to 1 En. 8:1–2, is credited with leading Eve astray. A different reading of 1 En. 69:6, one which does not relate Gadre'el to Eden, is also possible. It may be that the reference to leading "Eve" astray refers to Gadre'el teaching womankind how to produce makeup and jewelry, giving rise to sexual immorality (cf. 1 En. 8:1). This interpretation would suit its context in 1 En. 69:6, which pertains to the watchers' teachings just prior to the flood, better than a reference to the garden story.

65. On the varied uses of serpent symbolism in the ancient world and in biblical literature, see James H. Charlesworth, *The Good and Evil Serpent: How a Universal Symbol Became Christianized*, AYBRL (New Haven: Yale University Press, 2010).

66. That Gen 3 also serves as a background for the depiction of the Satan in Rev 12 is suggested by the enmity between the dragon and the woman's "seed" in v. 17 (cf. Gen 3:15) and perhaps also the dragon's role as deceiver (Rev 12:9). In addition to Gen 3 and other Jewish traditions, it is possible that John made use of serpent/dragon traditions from outside Judaism, such as the Greek Apollo-Python-Leto myth. For a comparison of this myth with Rev 12, see Adela Yarbro Collins, *The Combat Myth in the Book of Revelation* (1976; repr., Eugene, OR: Wipf & Stock, 2001), 63–67.

and lions) as typical of dangerous wild animals (e.g., Deut 8:15; Isa 11:6–9; Amos 5:18–19). Luke 10:18–20 says that serpents and scorpions are among the Satan's harmful forces. Luke does not appear to have Gen 3 in mind in this statement, but merely expresses the belief that harmful animals, including serpents, are the agents of the Satan. One can compare Luke's thinking with Jub. 11:11–13, where the Prince of Mastema commands birds to eat the seed that farmers would sow, inducing a famine. It may have been that Jewish thinkers associated the Satan with serpents in general, among other dangerous animals, before they associated him with *the* serpent.

3. New Testament authors who associate the Satan with the serpent of Gen 3 are more interested in using the image of this serpent to characterize the Satan than they are in using the figure of the Satan to explain the events of the garden. This is most obvious in Revelation. This image-laden prophetic work refers to Rome as "Babylon" (17:5) and to the false teacher in Thyatira as "Jezebel" (2:20). Revelation uses such figures from the biblical past to describe the threats that currently face the churches of Asia. Revelation is not claiming that Rome was responsible for Babylon's treatment of Jerusalem centuries earlier or that the teacher in Thyatira was responsible for the idolatrous policies of the wicked queen Jezebel in Israel. Similarly, neither are Revelation's references to the Satan as "the ancient serpent" an attempt to explain the story of Gen 3 or any other passage from the Hebrew scriptures that refers to a primordial serpent. Revelation appropriates these traditional images in order to portray the Satan. It may be that the prophet believed that the Satan was behind the events that took place in the garden, but this is not the point he makes when he refers to the Satan as "the ancient serpent" (Rev 12:9; 20:2).

The same is true for the other NT text that may draw a connection between the Satan and the serpent of Gen 3. Near the end of his letter to the church in Rome, Paul warns the church not to be deceived by false teachers and assures them, "The God of peace will shortly crush Satan under your feet" (Rom 16:20). Paul's concern here is not to explain what took place in the garden, but to evoke that story in order to encourage the Romans to adhere to proper teaching. Intriguingly, when Paul speaks more directly about the transgression of the first human beings, he makes no mention of the Satan (Rom 5:12; 1 Cor 15:21–22; 2 Cor 11:3; cf. 1 Tim 2:13–15). In 2 Cor 11:3, he mentions only "the serpent" who deceived Eve.

Paul and John may have been among the Jewish interpreters of their era who believed that the Satan was involved in the rebellion of the first human couple, but they express no interest in explaining this story in light of their doctrine of the Satan. Instead, they evoke the Eden story allusively in order to communicate their doctrine of the Satan, vividly portraying his nefarious work and his eventual judgment.

The Satan is one of the many harmful superhuman beings to which the NT refers. Some NT texts reflect the earlier notion of the Satan as one who attacks humans physically on behalf of God. More NT texts, however, depict the Satan as an evil figure. He is the chief of a host of evil beings. He leads humans into sin, and he opposes God and Christ. He also opposes God's people in various ways, one of which is by inciting God to subject them to severe tests of their faithfulness. In an effort to describe the threat that the Satan poses, some NT authors draw on the imagery of their scriptures, depicting the Satan as a deceptive serpent. They also encourage their communities to remain faithful to God in the face of satanic pressure to be unfaithful, promising that the Satan's days of troubling them will come to an end.

Conclusion

The first "satan" that one encounters in the literature of Israel is the angel of Yahweh, who comes to execute Balaam as the prophet travels to Moab to curse the Israelites (Num 22). One next encounters a superhuman satan in Zechariah's vision of Joshua the high priest (Zech 3). This satan is also an executioner, who intends to put Joshua to death for having approached the angel of Yahweh in an unworthy manner. A third satan threatens Israel, inciting David to take a census of the people that unleashes the destroying angel of Yahweh on them (1 Chr 21). These three texts are likely the earliest to speak of superhuman "satans," and they reveal much about the origin of the Satan tradition.

The tradition of the Satan had its beginning in the belief that certain superhuman executioners were responsible to bring capital judgment on transgressors. Numbers 22, Zech 3, and 1 Chr 21 all reflect this belief and refer to their respective superhuman agents of death as satans. These texts also exhibit significant diversity. Whereas Numbers and Chronicles each speaks of *a* satan, Zechariah's satan is *the* Satan. Futhermore, while the satan of Numbers is identical with the angel of Yahweh, Zechariah distinguishes and even contrasts these two figures. The creation of an officer who was distinct from the angel of Yahweh and whose job it was to punish sinners served to distance this figure's maleficent activity from the beneficent Deity. Beliefs about superhuman satan figures, nonetheless, did not develop in a simple, linear fashion. Multiple notions of satanic attackers seem to have existed simultaneously in this early period. The Chronicler, writing after the time of Zechariah, borrows the conception of a superhuman attacker from the earlier Num 22. The Chronicler speaks simply of *a* satan, rather than *the* Satan, and likely supposes that this figure is identical with the angel of Yahweh mentioned later in the same chapter.

The book of Job contains what is perhaps the latest reference to a superhuman satan in the Hebrew scriptures and reflects the most developed understanding of this figure. The Satan of Job was likely added to the story by an editor who wished to diminish God's role in the righteous Job's suffering. According to Job's prologue in its current form, it was the Satan, rather than God, who instigated Job's severe trial. Job's contribution to the development of thinking about the Satan is difficult to overestimate. In Job, for the first time, the Satan attacks an innocent person. While subsequent literature would continue to speak of the Satan as a functionary of God who punishes evildoers, writings of the Second Temple era would increasingly portray the Satan as the enemy of the faithful.

Thinking about demons, evil spirits, and "sons of God" also underwent a transformation during the Second Temple period. Traditions about these three kinds of beings come together in the third-century BCE Book of the Watchers to account for the origin of many of the world's problems. Most notably, this work credits evil spirits with leading humankind astray to worship demons as gods. In the next century, the book of Jubilees would link together demons, evil spirits, and the Satan in a systematic explanation of Israel's unique relationship with God among the nations of the world. In this work, evil spirits/demons lead the nations into idolatry, violence, and other sins. God sets Israel apart from the nations, however, by providing Israel with literature that protects the descendants of Jacob from these spirits' deceptions.

Jubilees' depiction of the Prince of Mastema is complex. On the one hand, Jubilees incorporates the prince into its systematic presentation of Israel's election. The prince functions within the order that God has established as a punisher of evildoers and as the chief of those spirits who mislead the nations. On the other hand, some passages in Jubilees depict the prince as the enemy of Israel who opposes God's plan for them. In these stories, God protects Israel from the prince not by means of revealed literature, but by means of the angels of the presence, who thwart the prince's attacks.

As the belief that evil superhuman beings were responsible for human sin grew in popularity, several Jewish theologians endeavored to counter such beliefs. Their writings maintain that humans, rather than forces external to them, are to blame for moral evil. Ben Sira insists that God does not lead humans to sin. The Epistle of Enoch contradicts the teaching of

Jubilees and the Book of the Watchers that evil spirits are responsible for human sin. Evil spirits, according to the Epistle, are worshiped by idolaters, but they do not lead humans into this error. Humans who worship idols have deceived themselves. Other texts that emphasize human responsibility for sin include Barkhi Nafshi and the Epistle of James, though the latter is able to reconcile its emphasis on human volition with the belief that the Satan is active in the world and leading humans into error.

The authors of several of the Dead Sea Scrolls did not share the misgivings expressed in the Epistle of Enoch and other texts about blaming superhuman forces for human sin. Indeed, some of these writings surpass earlier writings in the role they assign to superhuman beings in leading humankind into moral evil. Melchiresha, Belial, and the Angel of Darkness are the designations for the Satan in these documents, which emphasize the connection between this figure and wickedness. The Damascus Document blames Belial for the sins of those Jews who do not follow the stipulations of the Mosaic Torah, as interpreted by the Damascus sect. The Two Spirits Treatise and the War Rule teach that light and darkness are locked in cosmic conflict. In the Treatise, the Angel of Darkness has authority over the Sons of Darkness, but also misleads the Sons of Light. Belial in the War Rule is the leader of the Sons of Darkness in the eschatological war with Israel, the Sons of Light. Belial opposes God, is to be cursed by the Sons of Light, and is destined to receive God's wrath.

The NT has much to say about the Satan. The Satan, or "the devil" as he is also called in the NT, is depicted most frequently in evil terms. He leads humans into sin and is responsible for opposition to Christ and the churches. The Satan in these writings is a rebel who will eventually be judged. On the other hand, some NT texts preserve the earlier notion of the Satan as a functionary of God who physically attacks evildoers. Some NT authors also describe the Satan as one who persuades God to test the faithful with adversity. In an effort to characterize the threat that the Satan poses to churches, two NT authors (Paul and John of Patmos) appropriate the image of the serpent from Gen 3. The Satan, like the serpent, is the deceiver of the world who is out to harm God's people. Also like the serpent, however, the Satan is ultimately destined for judgment.

The Satan began as a punishing emissary of God, bringing death on those whose actions warranted such treatment. The notion of the Satan as an attacker or executioner would remain part of the tradition through the first century CE and later. Nevertheless, this notion would recede into the background as thinking about the Satan evolved. The Satan came to be regarded more fundamentally as one who created problems for the righteous than as one who troubled the wicked. The Satan became a deceiver, a tester, the enemy of God's people, and eventually even the enemy of God.

Beliefs about the Satan, of course, would continue to develop in the centuries that followed the composition of the NT. One could extend the project begun in the present volume, following the evolution of ideas about the Satan through the literature of the second century CE and beyond. The church fathers, for instance, would speak of the Satan as one who leads people into moral and theological error and as the one who is behind the persecution of the faithful.[1] Rabbinic literature would depict the Satan as an accuser, a tempter, an adversary, and the angel of death.[2] The Satan also features prominently in a number of pseudepigrapha, whose date and/or provenance are uncertain (e.g., Testaments of the Twelve Patriarchs, Testament of Job, and Ascension of Isaiah). Both Jewish and Christian authors would continue to retell their sacred stories, inserting the Satan into narratives from which he was originally absent.

Eventually, the question of the Satan's origin would arise. As long as the Satan was believed to be a functionary of God, there was no real need to account for his existence. As the balance shifted from understanding him as God's agent to regarding him as a superhuman rebel, however, an explanation for this evil figure's existence became more necessary. In order to provide such explanations, theologians created stories of the Satan's primordial fall (e.g., Irenaeus, *Against Heresies* 4.41; 5.24; 2 En. 31:2–6 [recension J]; LAE 12–17).[3]

The history of beliefs about the Satan is in actuality a history of beliefs about God. Whether the Satan is a functionary of God or God's enemy, from ancient times until the present this figure has served to explain the relationship between the Creator and the challenges of life as created hu-

1. On beliefs about the Satan in the early-second-century Christian texts, see Thomas J. Farrar, "The Intimate and Ultimate Adversary: Satanology in the Early-Second-Century Christian Literature," *JECS* (forthcoming).

2. Gottfried Reeg, "The Devil in Rabbinic Literature," in *Evil and the Devil,* ed. Ida Fröhlich and Erkki Koskenniemi, LNTS 481 (London: Bloomsbury, 2013), 71–83.

3. Jan Dochhorn, "The Motif of the Angels' Fall in Early Judaism," in *Angels: The Concept of Celestial Beings—Origins, Development and Reception,* ed. Friedrich V. Reiterer, Tobias Nicklas, and Karin Schöpflin; *DCLY* (Berlin: de Gruyter, 2007), 477–95; Jan Dochhorn, "Der Sturz des Teufels in der Urzeit: Eine traditionsgeschichtliche Skizze zu einem Motiv frühjüdischer und frühchristlicher Theologie mit besonderer Berücksichtigung des Luzifermythos," *ZTK* 109 (2012): 3–47, summarizes early traditions pertaining to the original fall of the Satan, helpfully distinguishing these stories from stories of the Satan's eschatological fall.

man beings experience it. Belief in the Satan has accounted especially for the various evils that exist in a world that is supposed to be governed by a God who is good and just. The Satan has served to account for God's just retribution of sinners as well as for the unjust suffering of those who are faithful to God. Belief in the Satan has explained the wickedness of the wicked. The Satan has also provided an explanation for the evil that taints even the hearts of those who consider themselves to be among God's people. It identifies the origin of these evils and offers hope that God will one day bring them to an end.

Bibliography

Abegg, Martin G., Jr., with James E. Bowley and Edward M. Cook, in consultation with Emanuel Tov. *The Non-Biblical Texts from Qumran*. Vol. 1 in 2 parts of Martin G. Abegg Jr., James E. Bowley, and Edward M. Cook, *The Dead Sea Scrolls Concordance*. 3 vols. Leiden: Brill, 2003–2016.

Adams, Samuel L. *Wisdom in Transition: Act and Consequence in Second Temple Instructions*. JSJSup 125. Leiden: Brill, 2008.

Albani, Matthias. "Horoscopes in the Qumran Scrolls." Pages 279–330 in vol. 2 of *The Dead Sea Scrolls after Fifty Years: A Comprehensive Assessment*. Edited by Peter W. Flint and James C. VanderKam. 2 vols. Leiden: Brill, 1999.

Alexander, Philip S. "The Demonology of the Dead Sea Scrolls." Pages 331–53 in vol. 2 of *The Dead Sea Scrolls after Fifty Years. A Comprehensive Assessment*. Edited by Peter W. Flint and James C. VanderKam. 2 vols. Leiden: Brill, 1999.

———. "The Redaction-History of *Serekh ha-Yaḥad*: A Proposal." *RevQ* 17.65–68 (1996): 437–56.

Alexander, Philip S., and Geza Vermes. *Qumran Cave 4, XIX: Serekh ha-Yaḥad and Two Related Texts*. DJD 26. Oxford: Clarendon, 1998.

Allegro, J. M., M. Baillet, F. M. Cross, C.-H. Hunzinger, J. T. Milik, P. Skehan, J. Starcky, and J. Strugnell. "Le travail d'édition des fragments manuscrits de Qumrân." *RB* 63.1 (1956): 49–67.

Alt, Albrecht. "Zur Vorgeschichte des Buches Hiob." *ZAW* 55.3–4 (1937): 265–68.

Andersen, Francis I. *Job: An Introduction and Commentary*. TOTC. Leicester: InterVarsity Press, 1976.

Anderson, A. A. "The Use of 'Ruaḥ' in 1QS, 1QH and 1QM." *JSS* 7 (1962): 293–303.

Anderson, Braden P. "The Story of Job and the Credibility of God." *HBT* 34.2 (2012): 103–17.

Argall, Randal A. 1 Enoch *and Sirach: A Comparative Literary and Conceptual Analysis of the Themes of Revelation, Creation, and Judgment*. EJL 8. Atlanta: Scholars Press, 1995.

Attridge, Harold W. *The Epistle to the Hebrews*. Hermeneia. Minneapolis: Fortress, 1989.

Aune, David E. "Lists, Ethical." *NIDB* 3:670–72.

———. *Revelation 6–16*. WBC 52B. Nashville: Nelson, 1998.

Baillet, Maurice. *Qumrân Grotte 4, III*. DJD 7. Oxford: Clarendon, 1982.

Baillet, M., J. T. Milik, and R. de Vaux. *Les "Petites Grottes" de Qumrân: Exploration de la falaise, les grottes 2Q, 3Q, 5Q, 6Q, 7Q, à 10Q, le rouleau de cuivre*. DJD 3. Oxford: Clarendon, 1962.

Barr, James. "The Question of Religious Influence: The Case of Zoroastrianism, Judaism, and Christianity." *JAAR* 53.2 (1985): 201–35.

Baumgarten, Joseph M. *Qumran Cave 4, XIII: The Damascus Document (4Q266–273)*. DJD 18. Oxford: Clarendon, 1996.

Baumgarten, Joseph M., and Daniel R. Schwartz. "Damascus Document." Pages 4–79 in *Damascus Document, War Scroll, and Related Documents*. Vol. 2 of *The Dead Sea Scrolls: Hebrew, Aramaic, and Greek Texts with English Translations*. Edited by James H. Charlesworth. PTSDSSP. Tübingen: Mohr Siebeck; Louisville: Westminster John Knox, 1995.

Bautch, Kelley Coblentz. "What Becomes of the Angels' 'Wives'? A Text-Critical Study of *1 Enoch* 19:2." *JBL* 125.4 (2006): 766–80.

Beale, G. K. *The Book of Revelation*. NIGTC. Grand Rapids: Eerdmans, 1999.

Beentjes, Pancratius C. "Satan, God, and the Angel(s) in 1 Chronicles 21." Pages 139–54 in *Angels: The Concept of Celestial Beings—Origins, Development and Reception*. Edited by Friedrich V. Reiterer, Tobias Nicklas, and Karin Schöpflin. *DCLY*. Berlin: de Gruyter, 2007.

———. "Theodicy in Wisdom of Ben Sira." Pages 509–24 in *Theodicy in the World of the Bible*. Edited by Antti Laato and Johannes C. de Moor. Leiden: Brill, 2003.

Bell, Richard H. *Deliver Us from Evil: Interpreting the Redemption from the Power of Satan in New Testament Theology*. WUNT 216. Tübingen: Mohr Siebeck, 2007.

Berg, Shane Alan. “Religious Epistemologies in the Dead Sea Scrolls: The Heritage and Transformation of the Wisdom Tradition.” PhD diss., Yale University, 2008.

Berger, Klaus. *Das Buch der Jubiläen*. Vol. 3 of *Unterweisung in erzählender Form*. JSHRZ 2. Gütersloh: Gütersloher Verlagshaus Gerd Mohn, 1981.

Bhayro, Siam. *The Shemihazah and Asael Narrative of 1 Enoch 6–11: Introduction, Text, Translation and Commentary with Reference to Ancient Near Eastern and Biblical Antecedents*. AOAT 322. Münster: Ugarit-Verlag, 2005.

Black, Matthew. *The Book of Enoch or 1 Enoch: A New English Edition with Commentary and Textual Notes*. SVTP 7. Leiden: Brill, 1985.

Blair, Judit M. *De-Demonising the Old Testament*. FAT 2/37. Tübingen: Mohr Siebeck, 2009.

Blenkinsopp, Joseph. *Isaiah 56–66*. AB 19B. New York: Doubleday, 2003.

Block, Daniel I. “Empowered by the Spirit of God: The Holy Spirit in the Histographic Writings of the Old Testament.” *Southern Baptist Journal of Theology* 1.1 (1997): 43–61.

Boccaccini, Gabriele. *Beyond the Essene Hypothesis: The Parting of the Ways Between Qumran and Enochic Judaism*. Grand Rapids: Eerdmans, 1998.

———. “Enoch, Qumran, and the Essenes: The Rediscovery of a Forgotten Connection: A Response to ‘The Epistle of Enoch and the Qumran Literature.’” Pages 123–32 in *George W. E. Nickelsburg in Perspective*. Edited by Jacob Neusner and Alan J. Avery-Peck. JSJSup 80. Leiden: Brill, 2003.

———. *Middle Judaism: Jewish Thought, 300 B.C.E. to 200 C.E.* Minneapolis: Fortress, 1991.

Boccaccini, Gabriele, ed. *Enoch and Qumran Origins: New Light on a Forgotten Connection*. Grand Rapids: Eerdmans, 2005.

Borisov, A. Ya. “Epigraphical Notes: Four Hermitage Aramaic Magic Bowls.” [In Russian.] *Epigrafika Vostoka* 19 (1969): 7.

Botterweck, G. Johannes, Helmer Ringgren, and Heinz-Josef Fabry, eds. *Theological Dictionary of the Old Testament*. Translated by John T. Willis, Geoffrey W. Bromiley, and David E. Green. 15 vols. Grand Rapids: Eerdmans, 1974–2006.

Brand, Miryam T. *Evil Within and Without: The Source of Sin and Its Nature as Portrayed in Second Temple Literature*. JAJSup 9. Göttingen: Vandenhoeck & Ruprecht, 2013.

Breytenbach, C., and P. L. Day. “Satan שׂטן Σατάν, Σατανᾶς.” *DDD* 726–32.

Braun, Roddy. *1 Chronicles*. WBC 14. Waco, TX: Word, 1986.

Broshi, Magen, ed. *The Damascus Document Reconsidered.* Jerusalem: Israel Exploration Society, 1992.

Brown, Derek R. "The Devil in the Details: A Survey of Research on Satan in Biblical Studies." *CurBR* 9.2 (2011): 200–227.

———. *The God of This Age: Satan in the Churches and Letters of the Apostle Paul.* WUNT 2/409. Tübingen: Mohr Siebeck, 2015.

Burney, C. F. *The Book of Judges with Introduction and Notes.* London: Rivingtons, 1918.

Burns, John Barclay. "Why Did the Besieging Army Withdraw?" *ZAW* 102.2 (1990): 187–94.

Charles, R. H., ed. *The Apocrypha and Pseudepigrapha of the Old Testament.* 2 vols. Oxford: Oxford University Press, 1913.

———. *The Book of Enoch or 1 Enoch: Translated from the Editor's Ethiopic Text and Edited with the Introduction, Notes and Indexes of the First Edition Wholly Recast, Enlarged and Rewritten Together with a Reprint from the Editor's Text of the Greek Fragments.* Oxford: Oxford University Press, 1912.

———. *The Book of Jubilees or The Little Genesis.* London: Black, 1902.

Charlesworth, James H. "A Critical Comparison of the Dualism in 1QS 3:13–4:26 and the 'Dualism' Contained in the Gospel of John." Pages 76–106 in *John and the Dead Sea Scrolls.* Edited by James H. Charlesworth. Christian Origins Library. New York: Crossroad, 1990.

———. *The Good and Evil Serpent: How a Universal Symbol Became Christianized.* AYBRL. New Haven: Yale University Press, 2010.

———. "A Rare Consensus among Enoch Specialists: The Date of the Earliest Enoch Books." *Hen* 24 (2002): 225–34.

Childs, Brevard S. *Exodus: A Commentary.* OTL. London: SCM, 1974.

Cho, Paul Kang-Kul. "The Integrity of Job 1 and 42:11–17." *CBQ* 76.2 (2014): 230–51.

Clines, David J. A. *Job 1–20.* WBC 17. Dallas: Word, 1989.

Cogan, Mordechai. *1 Kings: A New Translation with Introduction and Commentary.* AB 10. New York: Doubleday, 2001.

Coggins, Richard J. "Prophecy—True and False." Pages 80–94 in *Of Prophets' Visions and the Wisdom of the Sages: Essays in Honour of R. Norman Whybray on His Seventieth Birthday.* Edited by Heather A. McKay and David J. A. Clines. JSOTSup 162. Sheffield: Sheffield Academic Press, 1993.

Collins, John J. *The Apocalyptic Imagination: An Introduction to Jewish Apocalyptic Literature.* 3rd ed. Grand Rapids: Eerdmans, 2016.

———. *Apocalypticism in the Dead Sea Scrolls*. London: Routledge, 1997.
———. "Before the Fall: The Earliest Interpretations of Adam and Eve." Pages 293–308 in *The Idea of Biblical Interpretation: Essays in Honor of James L. Kugel*. Edited by H. Najman and J. H. Newman. Leiden: Brill, 2004.
———. *Beyond the Qumran Community: The Sectarian Movement of the Dead Sea Scrolls*. Grand Rapids: Eerdmans, 2010.
———. *Daniel*. Hermeneia. Minneapolis: Fortress, 1993.
———. "The Genre of the Book of *Jubilees*." Pages 737–55 in vol. 2 of *A Teacher for All Generations: Essays in Honor of James C. VanderKam*. Edited by Eric F. Mason et al. 2 vols. JSJSup 153. Leiden: Brill, 2012.
———. *Jewish Wisdom in the Hellenistic Age*. OTL. Louisville: Westminster John Knox, 1997.
———. "Methodological Issues in the Study of 1 Enoch: Reflections on the Articles of P. D. Hanson and G. W. Nickelsburg." Pages 315–22 in vol. 1 of the *Society of Biblical Literature 1978 Seminar Papers*. 2 vols. SBLSP 13. Missoula, MT: Scholars Press, 1978.
———. "The Mythology of Holy War in Daniel and the Qumran War Scroll: A Point of Transition in Jewish Apocalyptic." *VT* 25.3 (1975): 596–612.
———. "The Origin of Evil in Apocalyptic Literature." Pages 287–99 in *Seers, Sibyls and Sages in Hellenistic-Roman Judaism*. JSJSup 54. Leiden: Brill, 1997.
Conrad, Edgar W. *Zechariah*. RNBC. Sheffield: Sheffield Academic Press, 1999.
Crenshaw, James L. *Defending God: Biblical Responses to the Problem of Evil*. Oxford: Oxford University Press, 2005.
———. "The Problem of Theodicy in Sirach: On Human Bondage." *JBL* 94.1 (1975): 47–64.
Cross, F. M., D. W. Parry, and R. J. Saley. "4QSam[a]." Pages 1–216 in *Qumran Cave 4, XII: 1–2 Samuel*, by Frank Moore Cross, Donald W. Parry, Richard J. Saley, and Eugene Ulrich. DJD 17. Oxford: Clarendon, 2005.
Curtis, Edward Lewis, and Albert Alonzo Madsen. *A Critical and Exegetical Commentary on the Books of Chronicles*. ICC. New York: Scribner's Sons, 1910.
Danker, Frederick W., Walter Bauer, William F. Arndt, and F. Wilbur Gingrich. *Greek-English Lexicon of the New Testament and Other Early Christian Literature*. 3rd ed. Chicago: University of Chicago Press, 2000.

Davenport, Gene L. *The Eschatology of the Book of Jubilees*. StPB 20. Leiden: Brill, 1971.

Davidson, Maxwell J. *Angels at Qumran: A Comparative Study of 1 Enoch 1–36, 72–108 and Sectarian Writings from Qumran*. JSPSup 11. Sheffield: Sheffield Academic Press, 1992.

Davies, Philip R. *1QM, the War Scroll from Qumran: Its Structure and History*. BibOr 32. Rome: Biblical Institute Press, 1977.

———. "And Enoch Was Not, for Genesis Took Him." Pages 97–107 in *Biblical Traditions in Transmission: Essays in Honour of Michael A. Knibb*. Edited by Charlotte Hempel and Judith M. Lieu. Leiden: Brill, 2006.

———. *The Damascus Covenant: An Interpretation of the "Damascus Document."* JSOTSup 25. Sheffield: JSOT Press, 1982.

———. "Dualism and Eschatology in the Qumran War Scroll." *VT* 28.1 (1978): 28–36.

Day, Peggy L. "Abishai the *śāṭān* in 2 Sam 19:17–24." *CBQ* 49.4 (1987): 543–47.

———. *An Adversary in Heaven: śāṭān in the Hebrew Bible*. HSM 43. Atlanta: Scholars Press, 1988.

De La Torre, Miguel A., and Albert Hernández. *The Quest for the Historical Satan*. Minneapolis: Fortress, 2011.

De Vries, Simon J. *1 Kings*. WBC 12. Nashville: Nelson, 2003.

———. *Prophet against Prophet: The Role of the Micaiah Narrative (I Kings 22) in the Development of Early Prophetic Tradition*. Grand Rapids: Eerdmans, 1978.

Dimant, Devorah. "1 Enoch 6–11: A Methodological Perspective." Pages 323–39 in vol. 1 of *Society of Biblical Literature 1978 Seminar Papers*. 2 vols. SBLSP 13. Missoula, MT: Scholars Press, 1978.

———. "Between Qumran Sectarian and Non-Sectarian Texts: Belial and Mastema." Pages 235–56 in *The Dead Sea Scrolls and Contemporary Culture*. Edited by Adolfo Roitman. STDJ 93. Leiden: Brill, 2010.

———. "The Biography of Enoch and the Books of Enoch." *VT* 33.1 (1983): 14–29.

———. "'The Fallen Angels' in the Dead Sea Scrolls and in the Apocryphal and Pseudepigraphic Books Related to Them." [In Hebrew.] PhD diss., Hebrew University, 1974.

———. "The Qumran Aramaic Texts and the Qumran Community." Pages 197–205 in *Flores Florentino: Dead Sea Scrolls and Other Early Jewish Studies in Honour of Florentino García Martínez*. Edited by Anthony Hilhorst, Émile Puech, and Eibert Tigchelaar. JSJSup 122. Leiden: Brill, 2007.

———. *Qumran Cave 4, XXI: Parabiblical Texts, Part 4: Pseudo-Prophetic Texts.* DJD 30. Oxford: Clarendon, 2001.

———. "Qumran Sectarian Literature." Pages 483–550 in *Jewish Writings of the Second Temple Period: Apocrypha, Pseudepigrapha, Qumran Sectarian Writings, Josephus.* Edited by Michael E. Stone. Compendia Rerum Iudaicarum ad Novum Testamentum, Section Two. The Literature of the Jewish People in the Period of the Second Temple and the Talmud. Assen: Ban Gorcum; Philadelphia: Fortress, 1984.

Dion, Paul E. "The Angel with the Drawn Sword (II Chr 21, 16): An Exercise in Restoring the Balance of Text Criticism *and* Attention to Context." *ZAW* 97.1 (1985): 114–17.

Dirksen, Peter B. *1 Chronicles.* HCOT. Leuven-Dudley: Peeters, 2005.

Dochhorn, Jan. "The Devil in the Gospel of Mark." Pages 98–107 in *Evil and the Devil.* Edited by Ida Fröhlich and Erkki Koskenniemi. LNTS 481. London: Bloomsbury, 2013.

———. "The Motif of the Angels' Fall in Early Judaism." Pages 477–95 in *Angels: The Concept of Celestial Beings—Origins, Development and Reception.* Edited by Friedrich V. Reiterer, Tobias Nicklas, and Karin Schöpflin. *DCLY.* Berlin: de Gruyter, 2007.

———. *Schriftgelehrte Prophetie: Der eschatologische Teufelsfall in Apc Joh 12 und seine Bedeutung für das Verständnis der Johannesoffenbarung.* WUNT 268. Tübingen: Mohr Siebeck, 2010.

———. "Der Sturz des Teufels in der Urzeit: Eine traditionsgeschichtliche Skizze zu einem Motiv frühjüdischer und frühchristlicher Theologie mit besonderer Berücksichtigung des Luzifermythos." *ZTK* 109 (2012): 3–47.

Dochhorn, Jan, Susanne Rudnig-Zelt, and Benjamin Wold, eds. *Das Böse, der Teufel und Dämonen—Evil, the Devil, and Demons.* WUNT 2/412. Tübingen: Mohr Siebeck, 2016.

Driver, Samuel Rolles, and George Buchanan Gray. *A Critical and Exegetical Commentary on the Book of Job.* ICC. 2 vols. New York: Scribner's Sons, 1921.

Duhaime, Jean. "Dualistic Reworking in the Scrolls from Qumran." *CBQ* 49.1 (1987): 32–56.

———. "L'instruction sur les deux esprits et les interpolations dualistes à Qumrân." *RB* 84.4 (1977): 566–94.

———. "La rédaction de *1 QM* XIII et l'évolution du dualisme à Qumrân." *RB* 84.2 (1977): 210–38.

———. "War Scroll." Pages 80–141 in *Damascus Document, War Scroll, and Related Documents*. Vol. 2 of *The Dead Sea Scrolls: Hebrew, Aramaic, and Greek Texts with English Translations*. Edited by James H. Charlesworth. PTSDSSP. Tübingen: Mohr Siebeck; Louisville: Westminster John Knox, 1995.

———. "The *War Scroll* from Qumran and the Greco-Roman Tactical Treatises." *RevQ* 13 (1988): 133–51.

Duhm, Hans. *Die Bösen Geister im Alten Testament*. Tübingen: Mohr Siebeck, 1904.

Duke, Robert R. *The Social Location of the* Visions of Amram *(4Q543–547)*. StBibLit 135. New York: Lang, 2010.

Dupont-Sommer, A. "L'instruction sur les deux Esprits dans le 'Manuel de Discipline.'" *RHR* 142.1 (1952): 5–35.

Durham, John I. *Exodus*. WBC 3. Waco, TX: Word, 1987.

Ellis, Nicholas. *The Hermeneutics of Divine Testing: Cosmic Trials and Biblical Interpretation in the Epistle of James and Other Jewish Literature*. WUNT 2/396. Tübingen: Mohr Siebeck, 2015.

Erho, Ted M. "Historical-Allusion Dating and the Similitudes." *JBL* 130.3 (2011): 493–511.

Eshel, Esther. "Demonology in Palestine during the Second Temple Period." [In Hebrew.] PhD diss., Hebrew University, 1999.

Evans, Paul. "Divine Intermediaries in 1 Chronicles 21." *Bib* 85.4 (2004): 545–58.

Everling, Otto. *Die paulinische Angelologie and Dämonologie: Ein biblisch-theologischer Versuch*. Göttingen: Vandenhoeck & Ruprecht, 1888.

Fabry, Heinz-Josef. "'Satan'—Begriff und Wirklichkeit: Untersuchungen zur Dämonologie der alttestamentlichen Weisheitsliteratur." Pages 269–91 in *Die Dämonen: Die Dämonologie der israelitisch-jüdischen und frühchristlichen Literatur im Kontext ihrer Umwelt = Demons: The Demonology of Israelite-Jewish and Early Christian Literature in the Context of Their Environment*. Edited by Armin Lange, Hermann Lichtenberger, and K. F. Diethard Römheld. Tübingen: Mohr Siebeck, 2003.

Fabry, Heinz-Josef, and Ulrich Dahmen, eds. *Theologisches Wörterbuch zu den Qumrantexten*. 3 vols. Stuttgart: Kohlhammer, 2011.

Farrar, Thomas J. "The Intimate and Ultimate Adversary: Satanology in the Early-Second-Century Christian Literature." *JECS* (forthcoming).

———. "New Testament Satanology and Leading Suprahuman Opponents in Second Temple Jewish Literature: A Religion-Historical Analysis." *JTS* (forthcoming).

Farrar, Thomas J., and Guy J. Williams. "Diabolical Data: A Critical Inventory of New Testament Satanology." *JSNT* 39.1 (2016): 40–71.

———. "Talk of the Devil: Unpacking the Language of New Testament Satanology." *JSNT* 39.1 (2016): 72–96.

Finkelstein, Louis. *The Pharisees: The Sociological Background of Their Faith*. 2 vols. Philadelphia: Jewish Publication Society of America, 1938.

Fletcher-Louis, Crispin H. T. *All the Glory of Adam: Liturgical Anthropology in the Dead Sea Scrolls*. STDJ 42. Leiden: Brill, 2002.

Fohrer, G. "Zur Vorgeschichte und Komposition des Buches Hiob." *VT* 6.3 (1956): 249–67.

Forsyth, Neil. *The Old Enemy: Satan and the Combat Myth*. Princeton: Princeton University Press, 1987.

Frey, Jörg. "Different Patterns of Dualistic Thought in the Qumran Library: Reflections on Their Background and History." Pages 275–335 in *Legal Texts and Legal Issues: Proceedings of the Second Meeting of the International Organization for Qumran Studies, Cambridge 1995*. Edited by Moshe Bernstein, Florentino García Martínez, and John Kampen. STDJ 23. Leiden: Brill, 1997.

Frey-Anthes, Henrike. *Unheilsmächte und Schutzgenien, Antiwesen und Grenzgänger: Vorstellungen von "Dämonen" im alten Israel*. OBO 227. Fribourg: Academic Press; Göttingen: Vandenhoeck & Ruprecht, 2007.

Fritz, Volkmar. "Abimelech und Sichem in JDC. IX." *VT* 32.2 (1982): 129–44.

Fröhlich, Ida. "Evil in Second Temple Texts." Pages 23–50 in *Evil and the Devil*. Edited by Ida Fröhlich and Erkki Koskenniemi. LNTS 481. London: Bloomsbury, 2013.

———. "'Invoke at Any Time . . .': Apotropaic Texts and Belief in Demons in the Literature of the Qumran Community." *BN* 137 (2008): 41–74.

Fröhlich, Ida, and Erkki Koskenniemi, eds. *Evil and the Devil*. LNTS 481. London: Bloomsbury, 2013.

Gagnon, Robert A. J. "How Did the Rule of the Community Obtain Its Final Shape: A Review of Scholarly Research." Pages 67–85 in *Qumran Questions*. Edited by James H. Charlesworth. BibSem 36. Sheffield: Sheffield Academic Press, 1995.

García Martínez, Florentino. "Apocalypticism in the Dead Sea Scrolls." Pages 162–92 in *The Origins of Apocalypticism in Judaism and Christianity*. Edited by John J. Collins. Vol. 1 of *The Encyclopedia of Apoca-*

lypticism. Edited by John J. Collins, Bernard McGinn, and Stephen J. Stein. 3 vols. New York: Continuum, 1998.

———. *Qumran and Apocalyptic: Studies on the Aramaic Texts from Qumran*. STDJ 9. Leiden: Brill, 1992.

García Martínez, Florentino, and Eibert J. C. Tigchelaar. *Dead Sea Scrolls: Study Edition*. 2 vols. Leiden: Brill; Grand Rapids: Eerdmans, 1997–1998.

García Martínez, Florentino, Eibert J. C. Tigchelaar, and Adam S. van der Woude. *Qumran Cave 11, II*. DJD 23. Oxford: Clarendon, 1998.

Garrett, Susan R. *The Demise of the Devil: Magic and the Demonic in Luke's Writings*. Minneapolis: Fortress, 1989.

Gaster, T. H. "Satan." *IDB* 4:224–28.

Geller, Markham J. *Evil Demons: Canonical Utukkū Lemnūtu Incantations*. SAACT 5. Helsinki: Neo-Assyrian Text Corpus Project, 2007.

Glasson, T. F. *Greek Influence in Jewish Eschatology: With Special Reference to the Apocalypses and Pseudepigraphs*. London: SPCK, 1961.

Goldman, Liora. "Dualism in the *Visions of Amram*." *RevQ* 24.3 (2010): 421–32.

Goldmann, Moshe. "The Book of Jubilees." [In Hebrew.] Pages 217–313 in vol. 1 of *The Apocryphal Books*. Edited by Abraham Kahana. 2 vols. Tel Aviv: Masada, 1956.

Goldstein, Jonathan A. "The Date of the Book of Jubilees." *PAAJR* 50 (1983): 63–86.

Good, Edwin M. "The Problem of Evil in the Book of Job." Pages 50–69 in *The Voice from the Whirlwind: Interpreting the Book of Job*. Edited by Leo G. Perdue and W. Clark Gilpin. Nashville: Abingdon, 1992.

Habel, Norman C. *The Book of Job: A Commentary*. OTL. Philadelphia: Westminster, 1985.

Halpern-Amaru, Betsy. *The Perspective from Mt. Sinai: The Book of Jubilees and Exodus*. JSJSup 21. Göttingen: Vandenhoeck & Ruprecht, 2015.

Hamilton, Victor P. "Satan." *ABD* 5:985–89.

Hamori, Esther J. "The Spirit of Falsehood." *CBQ* 72.1 (2010): 15–30.

Hanneken, Todd Russell. "Angels and Demons in the Book of Jubilees and Contemporary Apocalypses." *Hen* 28.1 (2006): 11–25.

———. *The Subversion of the Apocalypses in the Book of Jubilees*. EJL 34. Atlanta: Society of Biblical Literature, 2012.

———. "The Watchers in Rewritten Scripture: The Use of the Book of the Watchers in Jubilees." Pages 25–68 in *The Fallen Angels Traditions: Second Temple Developments and Reception History*. Edited by Angela

Kim Harkins, Kelley Coblentz Bautch, and John C. Endres. CBQMS 53. Washington, DC: Catholic Biblical Association of America, 2014.

Hanson, Paul D. "Rebellion in Heaven, Azazel, and Euhemeristic Heroes in 1 Enoch 6–11." *JBL* 96.2 (1977): 195–233.

Harlow, Daniel C. "Abraham, Apocalypse of." *EDEJ* 295–98.

———. "Baruch, Third Book of." *EDEJ* 428–30.

Hartley, John E. *The Book of Job*. NICOT. Grand Rapids: Eerdmans, 1988.

Heckl, Raik. *Hiob—vom Gottesfürchtigen zum Repräsentanten Israel: Studien zur Buchwerdung des Hiobbuches und zu seinen Quellen*. FAT 70. Tübingen: Mohr Siebeck, 2010.

Heger, Paul. "Another Look at Dualism in Qumran Writings." Pages 39–101 in *Dualism in Qumran*. Edited by Géza G. Xeravits. LSTS 76. New York: T&T Clark, 2010.

Heiligstedt, Augustus. *Commentarius Grammaticus Historicus Criticus in Jobum*. Leipzig: Sumptibus Librariae Rengerianae, 1847.

Hempel, Charlotte. "Community Origins in the *Damascus Document* in the Light of Recent Scholarship." Pages 316–29 in *The Provo International Conference on the Dead Sea Scrolls: Technological Innovations, New Texts, and Reformulated Issues*. Edited by Donald W. Parry and Eugene Ulrich. STDJ 30. Leiden: Brill, 1999.

———. *The Damascus Texts*. Companion to the Scrolls 1. Sheffield: Sheffield Academic Press, 2000.

———. "The Teaching on the Two Spirits and the Literary History of the Community Rule." Pages 102–20 in *Dualism in Qumran*. Edited by Géza G. Xeravits. LSTS 76. London: T&T Clark, 2010.

Henten, J. W. van. "Mastema." *DDD* 553–54.

Himmelfarb, Martha. *A Kingdom of Priests: Ancestry and Merit in Ancient Judaism*. Philadelphia: University of Pennsylvania Press, 2006.

Hoffman, Yair. *A Blemished Perfection: The Book of Job in Context*. JSOTSup 213. Sheffield: Sheffield Academic Press, 1996.

Hoftijzer, Jacob. "Some Remarks on the Semantics of the Root *bʿt* in Classical Hebrew." Pages 777–83 in *Pomegranates and Golden Bells: Studies in Biblical, Jewish, and Near Eastern Ritual, Law and Literature in Honor of Jacob Milgrom*. Edited by David P. Wright, David Noel Freedman, and Avi Hurvitz. Winona Lake, IN: Eisenbrauns, 1995.

Holladay, Carl R. *Poets*. Vol. 2 of *Fragments from Hellenistic Jewish Authors*. TT 30. Pseudepigrapha Series 12. Atlanta: Scholars Press, 1989.

Horst, Friedrich. *Hiob 1–19*. BKAT 16.1. Neukirchen-Vluyn: Neukirchener Verlag, 1968.

Hultgren, Stephen. *From the Damascus Covenant to the Covenant of the Community: Literary, Historical, and Theological Studies in the Dead Sea Scrolls*. STDJ 66. Leiden: Brill, 2007.

Hutter, M. "Asmodeus." *DDD* 106–8.

Isbell, Charles D. *Corpus of the Aramaic Incantation Bowls*. SBLDS 17. Missoula, MT: Society of Biblical Literature, 1975.

Jacobsen, Thorkild. *The Treasures of Darkness: A History of Mesopotamian Religion*. New Haven: Yale University Press, 1976.

Japhet, Sara. *1 Chronik*. HThKAT. Freiburg: Herder, 2002.

———. *I & II Chronicles: A Commentary*. OTL. Louisville: Westminster John Knox, 1993.

———. *The Ideology of the Book of Chronicles and Its Place in Biblical Thought*. Translated by Anna Barber. 2nd ed. BEATAJ 9. Frankfurt am Main: Lang, 1989.

Jarick, John. *1 Chronicles*. RNBC. London: Sheffield Academic Press, 2002.

Jastrow, Morris, Jr. "Dust, Earth, and Ashes as Symbols of Mourning among the Ancient Hebrews." *JAOS* 20 (1899): 133–50.

Jenni, Ernst, ed., with assistance from Claus Westermann. *Theological Lexicon of the Old Testament*. Translated by Mark E. Biddle. 3 vols. Peabody: Hendrickson, 1997.

Jeremias, Christian. *Die Nachtgesichte des Sacharja*. Göttingen: Vandenhoeck & Ruprecht, 1977.

Jong, Albert de. "Iranian Connections in the Dead Sea Scrolls." Pages 479–500 in the *Oxford Handbook of the Dead Sea Scrolls*. Edited by Timothy H. Lim and John J. Collins. Oxford: Oxford University Press, 2010.

Josephus. Translated by H. St. John Thackeray et al. 10 vols. LCL. Cambridge: Harvard University Press, 1926–1965.

Jurgens, Blake Alan. "Reassessing the Dream-Vision of the *Vision of Amram* (4Q543–547)." *JSP* 24.1 (2014): 3–42.

Kautzsch, Karl. *Das sogenannte Volksbuch von Hiob und der Ursprung von Hiob Cap I. II. XLII, 7–17: Ein Beitrag zur Frage nach der Integrität des Buches Hiob*. Leipzig: Drugulin, 1900.

Keith, Chris, and Loren T. Stuckenbruck, eds. *Evil in Second Temple Judaism and Early Christianity*. WUNT 2/417. Tübingen: Mohr Siebeck, 2016.

Kelly, Henry Ansgar. *Satan: A Biography*. Cambridge: Cambridge University Press, 2006.

———. *Satan in the Bible, God's Minister of Justice*. Eugene, OR: Cascade, 2017.

Kister, Menahem. "The Yetzer of Man's Heart, the Body and Purification from Evil: Between Prayer Terminologies and Worldviews." Pages 241-82 in *Meghillot: Studies in the Dead Sea Scrolls VIII*. Edited by M. Bar-Asher and D. Dimant. Jerusalem: Bialik Institute and Haifa University Press, 2010. Hebrew.

Kittel, Gerhard, and Gerhard Friedrich, eds. *Theological Dictionary of the New Testament*. Translated by Geoffrey W. Bromiley. 10 vols. Grand Rapids: Eerdmans, 1964–1976.

Klein, Ralph W. *1 Chronicles: A Commentary*. Hermeneia. Minneapolis: Fortress, 2006.

———. *1 Samuel*. WBC 10. Waco, TX: Word, 1983.

Kluger, Rivkah Schärf. *Satan in the Old Testament*. Translated by Hildegard Nagel. Studies in Jungian Thought. Evanston, IL: Northwestern University Press, 1967.

Knibb, Michael A. *The Ethiopic Book of Enoch: A New Edition in the Light of the Aramaic Dead Sea Fragments*. 2 vols. Oxford: Oxford University Press, 1978.

———. "*Jubilees* and the Origins of the Qumran Community." Pages 232–54 in *Essays on the Book of Enoch and Other Early Jewish Texts and Tradition*. SVTP 22. Leiden: Brill, 2009.

———. *The Qumran Community*. CCWJCW 2. Cambridge: Cambridge University Press, 1987.

———. "Rule of the Community." *EDSS* 2:793–97.

Knoppers, Gary N. *I Chronicles 10–29: A New Translation with Introduction and Commentary*. AB 12A. New York: Doubleday, 2004.

Kobelski, Paul J. *Melchizedek and Melchireša'*. CBQMS 10. Washington, DC: Catholic Biblical Association of America, 1981.

Koch, Klaus. "History as a Battlefield of Two Antagonistic Powers in the Apocalypse of Weeks and in the Rule of the Community." Pages 185–99 in *Enoch and Qumran Origins: New Light on a Forgotten Connection*. Edited by Gabriele Boccaccini. Grand Rapids: Eerdmans, 2005.

Koehler, Ludwig, Walter Baumgartner, and Johann J. Stamm. *The Hebrew and Aramaic Lexicon of the Old Testament*. Translated and edited under the supervision of Mervyn E. J. Richardson. 5 vols. Leiden: Brill, 1994–2000.

Koester, Craig R. *Hebrews: A New Translation with Introduction and Commentary*. AB 36. New York: Doubleday, 2001.

———. *Revelation: A New Translation with Introduction and Commentary*. AB 38A. New Haven: Yale University Press, 2014.

König, Eduard. *Einleitung in das Alte Testament mit Einschluss der Apokryphen und der Pseudepigraphen Alten Testaments*. Bonn: Weber, 1893.

Kugel, James. "On the Interpolations in the *Book of Jubilees*." *RevQ* 24.2 (2009): 215–72.

———. *A Walk through Jubilees: Studies in the Book of Jubilees and the World of Its Creation*. JSJSup 156. Leiden: Brill, 2012.

Kuhn, Karl Georg. "Die Sektenschrift und die iranische Religion." *ZTK* 49.3 (1952): 296–316.

Kvanvig, Helge S. "Jubilees—Read as a Narrative." Pages 75–83 in *Enoch and Qumran Origins: New Light on a Forgotten Connection*. Edited by Gabriele Boccaccini. Grand Rapids: Eerdmans, 2005.

———. *Primeval History: Babylonian, Biblical, and Enochic: An Intertextual Reading*. JSJSup 149. Leiden: Brill, 2011.

Lane, William L. *Hebrew 1–8*. WBC 47A. Dallas: Word, 1991.

Lange, Armin. "Considerations Concerning the 'Spirit of Impurity' in Zech 13:2." Pages 254–68 in *Die Dämonen: Die Dämonologie der israelitisch-jüdischen und frühchristlichen Literatur im Kontext ihrer Umwelt = Demons: The Demonology of Israelite-Jewish and Early Christian Literature in Context of Their Environment*. Edited by Armin Lange, Hermann Lichtenberger, and K. F. Diethard Römheld. Tübingen: Mohr Siebeck, 2003.

———. "Satanic Verses: The Adversary in the Qumran Manuscripts and Elsewhere." *RevQ* 24.1 (2009): 35–48.

———. *Weisheit und Prädestination: Weisheitliche Urordnung und Prädestination in den Textfunden von Qumran*. STDJ 18. Leiden: Brill, 1995.

———. "Wisdom and Predestination in the Dead Sea Scrolls." *DSD* 2.3 (1995): 340–54.

Lange, Armin, Hermann Lichtenberger, and K. F. Diethard Römheld, eds. *Die Dämonen: Die Dämonologie der israelitisch-jüdischen und frühchristlichen Literatur im Kontext ihrer Umwelt = Demons: The Demonology of Israelite-Jewish and Early Christian Literature in Context of Their Environment*. Tübingen: Mohr Siebeck, 2003.

Langton, Edward. *Essentials of Demonology: A Study of Jewish and Christian Doctrine, Its Origin and Development*. London: Epworth, 1949.

———. *Satan: A Portrait: A Study of the Character of Satan through All the Ages*. London: Skeffington & Son, 1946.

Lemke, Werner E. "Synoptic Studies in the Chronicler's History." ThD thesis, Harvard University, 1963.

Leonhardt-Balzer, Jutta. "Gestalten des Bösen im frühen Christentum." Pages 203–35 in *Apokalyptik und Qumran*. Edited by Jörg Frey and Michael Becker. Paderborn: Bonifatius, 2007.

Leslau, Wolf. *Comparative Dictionary of Geʿez*. Wiesbaden: Harrassowitz, 1991.

Levine, Baruch A. *Numbers 21–36: A New Translation with Introduction and Commentary*. AB 4A. New York: Doubleday, 2000.

Levison, John R. "The Two Spirits in Qumran Theology." Pages 169–94 in *The Dead Sea Scrolls and the Qumran Community*. Vol. 2 of *The Bible and the Dead Sea Scrolls*. Edited by James H. Charlesworth. Waco, TX: Baylor University Press, 2006.

Lewis, Theodore J. "Belial." *ABD* 1:654–56.

Liddell, Henry George, Robert Scott, and Henry Stuart Jones. *A Greek-English Lexicon*. 9th ed. with revised supplement. Oxford: Clarendon, 1996.

Lincicum, David. "Scripture and Apotropaism in the Second Temple Period." *BN* 138 (2008): 63–87.

Lindblom, Joh. *La composition du livre de Job*. Lund: Gleerup, 1945.

Lindström, Fredrik. *God and the Origin of Evil: A Contextual Analysis of Alleged Monistic Evidence in the Old Testament*. Translated by Frederick H. Cryer. ConBOT 21. Lund: Gleerup, 1983.

Ludolf, Hiob, ed. *Psalterium Davidis Aethiopice et Latine*. Frankfurt: Zunner, 1701.

Magdalene, F. Rachel. *On the Scales of Righteousness: Neo-Babylonian Trial Law and the Book of Job*. BJS 348. Providence: Brown University Press, 2007.

Marböck, Johannes. "Gesetz und Weisheit: Zum Verständnis des Gesetzes bei Jesus Ben Sira." *BZ* n.s. 20.1 (1976): 1–21.

———. *Weisheit im Wandel: Untersuchungen zur Weisheitstheologie bei Ben Sira*. BZAW 272. Berlin: de Gruyter, 1999.

Martin, Dale Basil. "When Did Angels Become Demons?" *JBL* 129.4 (2010): 657–77.

Martone, Corrado. "Evil or Devil? Belial from the Bible to Qumran." *Hen* 26.2 (2004): 115–27.

McCarter, P. Kyle, Jr. *I Samuel: A New Translation with Introduction, Notes, and Commentary*. AB 8. Garden City, NY: Doubleday, 1980.

———. "Evil Spirit of God." *DDD* 319–20.

McConville, J. G. *I & II Chronicles*. DSB. Philadelphia: Westminster, 1984.

McKenzie, Steven L. *1–2 Chronicles*. AOTC. Nashville: Abingdon, 2004.
———. *The Chronicler's Use of the Deuteronomistic History*. HSM 33. Atlanta: Scholars Press, 1985.
Meier, Samuel A. "Angel of Yahweh." *DDD* 53–59.
Mendels, Doron. *The Land of Israel as a Political Concept in Hasmonean Literature: Recourse to History in Second Century B.C. Claims to the Holy Land*. TSAJ. Tübingen: Mohr Siebeck, 1987.
Metso, Sarianna. *The Textual Development of the Qumran Community Rule*. STDJ 21. Leiden: Brill, 1997.
Meyers, Carol L., and Eric M. Meyers. *Haggai, Zechariah 1–8*. AB 25B. Garden City, NY: Doubleday, 1987.
Milgrom, Jacob. *Numbers*. JPSTC. Philadelphia: Jewish Publication Society, 1990.
Milik, J. T. *The Books of Enoch: Aramaic Fragments of Qumrân Cave 4*. Oxford: Oxford University Press, 1976.
Mitchell, Hinckley G., John Merlin Powis Smith, and Julius A. Bewer. *A Criticial and Exegetical Commentary on Haggai, Zechariah, Malachi and Jonah*. ICC. Edinburgh: T&T Clark, 1912.
Monger, Matthew Phillip. "4Q216 and the State of Jubilees at Qumran." *RevQ* 26.4 (2014): 595–612.
Morris, Michael J. *Warding off Evil: Apotropaic Traditions in the Dead Sea Scrolls and Synoptic Gospels*. WUNT 2/451. Tübingen: Mohr Siebeck, 2017.
Moses, Robert. "'The *satan*' in Light of the Creation Theology of Job." *HBT* 34.1 (2012): 19–34.
Murphy-O'Connor, Jerome. *1 Corinthians*. NTM 10. Wilmington, DE: Glazier, 1979.
———. "An Essene Missionary Document? CD II, 14–VI, 1." *RB* 77.2 (1970): 201–29.
———. "La genèse littéraire de la *Règle de la Communauté*." *RB* 76.4 (1969): 528–49.
Najman, Hindy. "Interpretation as Primordial Writing: Jubilees and Its Authority Conferring Strategies." *JSJ* 30.4 (1999): 379–410.
Naveh, Joseph, and Shaul Shaked. *Amulets and Magic Bowls: Aramaic Incantations of Late Antiquity*. 3rd ed. Jerusalem: Magnes, 1998.
———. *Magic Spells and Formulae: Aramaic Incantations of Late Antiquity*. Jerusalem: Magnes, 1993.
Newsom, Carol A. *The Book of Job: A Contest of Moral Imaginations*. Oxford: Oxford University Press, 2003.

———. "The Book of Job: Introduction, Commentary, and Reflections." *NIB* 4:317–637.

———. "The Development of *1 Enoch* 6–19: Cosmology and Judgment." *CBQ* 42.3 (1980): 310–29.

———. *The Self as Symbolic Space: Constructing Identity and Community at Qumran*. STDJ 52. Atlanta: Society of Biblical Literature, 2004.

Nickelsburg, George W. E. *1 Enoch 1: A Commentary on the Book of 1 Enoch Chapters 1–36; 81–108*. Hermeneia. Minneapolis: Fortress, 2001.

———. "Apocalyptic and Myth in 1 Enoch 6–11." *JBL* 96.3 (1977): 383–405.

———. "Enoch 97–104: A Study of the Greek and Ethiopic Texts." Pages 90–156 in *Armenian and Biblical Studies*. Edited by Michael E. Stone. Jerusalem: St. James, 1976.

———. "The Epistle of Enoch and the Qumran Literature." *JJS* 33.1–2 (1982): 333–48.

———. "Reflections upon Reflections: A Response to John Collins' 'Methodological Issues in the Study of 1 Enoch.'" Pages 311–14 in vol. 1 of the *Society of Biblical Literature 1978 Seminar Papers*. 2 vols. SBLSP 13. Missoula, MT: Scholars Press, 1978.

Nickelsburg, George W. E., and James C. VanderKam. *1 Enoch 2*. Hermeneia. Minneapolis: Fortress, 2012.

———. *1 Enoch: The Hermeneia Translation*. Minneapolis: Fortress, 2012.

Nielsen, Kirsten. *Satan: The Prodigal Son? A Family Problem in the Bible*. BibSem 50. Sheffield: Sheffield Academic Press, 1998.

Oegema, Gerbern S. "Zephaniah, Apocalypse of." *EDEJ* 1358–59.

Oppenheim, A. L. "The Eyes of the Lord." *JAOS* 88.1 (1968): 173–80.

Orlov, Andrei A. *Dark Mirrors: Azael and Satanel in Early Jewish Demonology*. Albany: State University of New York Press, 2011.

Osten-Sacken, Peter von der. *Gott und Belial: Traditionsgeschichtliche Untersuchungen zum Dualismus in den Texten aus Qumran*. SUNT 6. Göttingen: Vandenhoeck & Ruprecht, 1969.

Page, Sydney H. T. *Powers of Evil: A Biblical Study of Satan and Demons*. Grand Rapids: Baker, 1995.

Pagels, Elaine. *The Origin of Satan*. New York: Vintage, 1995.

———. "The Social History of Satan, the 'Intimate Enemy': A Preliminary Sketch." *HTR* 84.2 (1991): 105–28.

Panaino, Antonio. "Avesta." Pages 527–9 in vol. 1 of *Religion Past and Present: Encyclopedia of Theology and Religion*. Edited by Hans Dieter Betz, Don S. Browning, Bernd Janowski, and Eberhard Jüngel. 6 vols. Leiden: Brill, 2007.

Parker, Simon B. "Sons of (the) God(s)." *DDD* 794–800.

Parry, Donald W., and Emanuel Tov, in association with Geraldine I. Clements. *The Dead Sea Scrolls Reader*. 2nd ed. 2 vols. Leiden: Brill, 2014.

Pascale, Ronald Anthony. "The Demonic Cosmic Powers of Destruction in 1 Enoch 15:3–16:1 and Jubilees 10:5, and the Demonizing of the Avenging Angels." PhD diss., Harvard University, 1980.

Penney, Douglas L. "Finding the Devil in the Details: Onomastic Exegesis and the Naming of Evil in the World of the New Testament." Pages 37–52 in *New Testament Greek and Exegesis: Essays in Honor of Gerald F. Hawthorne*. Edited by Amy M. Donaldson and Timothy B. Sailors. Grand Rapids: Eerdmans, 2003.

Perrin, Andrew B. "Another Look at Dualism in *4QVisions of Amram*." *Hen* 36.1 (2014): 106–17.

Petersen, David L. *Haggai and Zechariah 1–8: A Commentary*. OTL. London: SCM, 1984.

Pettorelli, Jean-Pierre. "Adam and Eve, Life of." *EDEJ* 302–6.

Pfeiffer, Robert H. *Introduction to the Old Testament*. New York: Harper & Brothers, 1941.

Philonenko, Marc. "La doctrine qoumrânienne des deux Esprits: Ses origins iraniennes et ses prolongements dans le judaïsme essénien et le christianisme antique." Pages 161–211 in *Apocalyptique iranienne et dualisme qoumrânien*. Edited by Geo Widengren, Anders Hultgård, and Marc Philonenko. Recherches Intertestamentaires 2. Paris: Adrien Maisonneuve, 1995.

Pierce, Chad T. "Satan and Related Figures." *EDEJ* 1196–2000.

Pope, Marvin H. *Job: Introduction, Translation, and Notes*. AB 15. Garden City, NY: Doubleday, 1965.

Popović, Mladen. "Anthropology, Pneumatology and Demonology in Early Judaism: The *Two Spirits Treatise* (1QS 3:13–4:26) and Other Texts from the Dead Sea Scrolls." Pages 1029–67 in vol. 2 of *Sibyls, Scriptures, and Scrolls: John Collins at Seventy*. Edited by Joel Baden, Hindy Najman, and Eibert Tigchelaar with the assistance of Laura Carlson, James Nati, Olivia Stewart, and Shlomo Zuckier. JSJSup 175. Leiden: Brill, 2017.

———. "Light and Darkness in the *Treatise on the Two Spirits* (1QS III 13 –IV 26) and in 4Q186." Pages 148–65 in *Dualism in Qumran*. Edited by Géza G. Xeravits. LSTS 76. New York: T&T Clark, 2010.

———. *Reading the Human Body: Physiognomics and Astrology in the*

Dead Sea Scrolls and Hellenistic–Early Roman Period Judaism. STDJ 67. Leiden: Brill, 2007.

Pouilly, J. *La règle de la communauté de Qumran: Son evolution littéraire.* CahRB 17. Paris: Gabalda, 1976.

Prato, Gian Luigi. *Il Problema della Teodicea in Ben Sira.* AnBib 65. Rome: Pontifical Biblical Institute, 1975.

Propp, William H. C. *Exodus 1–18: A New Translation with Introduction and Commentary.* AB 2. New York: Doubleday, 1999.

Puech, Émile. "4Q543–4Q549. 4QVisions de 'Amram^{a-g} ar." Pages 283–405 in *Qumrân Grotte 4, XII: Textes araméens, première partie: 4Q529–549.* DJD 31. Oxford: Oxford University Press, 2001.

Qimron, Elisha, and James H. Charlesworth. "Rule of the Community." Pages 1–51 in *Rule of the Community and Related Documents.* Vol. 1 of *The Dead Sea Scrolls: Hebrew, Aramaic, and Greek Texts with English Translations.* Edited by James H. Charlesworth. PTSDSSP. Tübingen: Mohr Siebeck; Louisville: Westminster John Knox, 1994.

Reed, Annette Yoshiko. "Enochic and Mosaic Traditions in Jubilees: The Evidence of Angelology and Demonology." Pages 353–68 in *Enoch and the Mosaic Torah: The Evidence of Jubilees.* Edited by Gabrielle Boccaccini and Giovanni Ibba. Grand Rapids: Eerdmans, 2009.

———. *Fallen Angels and the History of Judaism and Christianity: The Reception of Enochic Literature.* New York: Cambridge University Press, 2005.

Reeg, Gottfried. "The Devil in Rabbinic Literature." Pages 71–83 in *Evil and the Devil.* Edited by Ida Fröhlich and Erkki Koskenniemi. LNTS 481. London: Bloomsbury, 2013.

Reiner, Erica. *Šurpu: A Collection of Sumerian and Akkadian Incantations.* AfOB 11. Graz: Biblio, 1958.

Reiterer, Friedrich V., Tobias Nicklas, and Karin Schöpflin, eds. *Angels: The Concept of Celestial Beings—Origins, Development and Reception. DCLY.* Berlin: de Gruyter, 2007.

Roberts, J. J. M. "Job and the Israelite Religious Tradition." *ZAW* 89.1 (1977): 107–14.

———. "Melchizedek." Pages 264–73 in *Pesharim, Other Commentaries, and Related Documents.* Volume 6B of *The Dead Sea Scrolls: Hebrew, Aramaic, and Greek Texts with English Translations.* Edited by James H. Charlesworth. PTSDSSP. Tübingen: Mohr Siebeck; Louisville: Westminster John Knox, 2002.

Rogland, Max. *Haggai and Zechariah 1–8: A Handbook on the Hebrew Text*. BHHB. Waco, TX: Baylor University Press, 2016.

Rollston, Christopher A. "An Ur-History of the New Testament Devil: The Celestial שׂטן (*śāṭān*) in Zechariah and Job." Pages 1–16 in *Evil in Second Temple Judaism and Early Christianity*. Edited by Chris Keith and Loren T. Stuckenbruck. WUNT 2/417. Tübingen: Mohr Siebeck, 2016.

Rosen-Zvi, Ishay. *Demonic Desires: "Yetzer Hara" and the Problem of Evil in Late Antiquity*. Philadelphia: University of Pennsylvania Press, 2011.

Rudman, Dominic. "Zechariah and the Satan Tradition in the Hebrew Bible." Pages 191–209 in *Tradition in Transition: Haggai and Zechariah 1–8 in the Trajectory of Hebrew Theology*. Edited by Mark J. Boda and Michael H. Floyd. LHBOTS 475. New York: T&T Clark, 2008.

Ruiten, Jacques T. A. G. M. van. *Abraham in the Book of Jubilees: The Rewriting of Genesis 11:26–25:10 in the Book of Jubilees 11:14–23:8*. JSJSup 161. Leiden: Brill, 2012.

———. "Abraham, Job and the Book of *Jubilees*: The Intertextual Relationship of Genesis 22:1–19, Job 1:1–2:13 and *Jubilees* 17:15–18:19." Pages 58–85 in *The Sacrifice of Isaac: The Aqedah (Genesis 22) and Its Interpretations*. Edited by Ed Noort and Eibert Tigchelaar. TBN 4. Leiden: Brill, 2002.

Russell, Jeffrey Burton. *The Devil: Perceptions of Evil from Antiquity to Primitive Christianity*. Ithaca, NY: Cornell University Press, 1977.

———. *Lucifer: The Devil in the Middle Ages*. Ithaca, NY: Cornell University Press, 1984.

———. *Mephistopheles: The Devil in the Modern World*. Ithaca, NY: Cornell University Press, 1986.

———. *Satan: The Early Christian Tradition*. Ithaca, NY: Cornell University Press, 1981.

Sacchi, Paolo. *Jewish Apocalyptic and Its History*. Translated by William J. Short. JSPSup 20. Sheffield: Sheffield Academic Press, 1990.

Sailhamer, John H. "1 Chronicles 21:1—A Study in Inter-Biblical Interpretation." *TJ* n.s. 10.1 (1989): 33–48.

Schechter, Solomon. *Documents of Jewish Sectaries Edited from Hebrew Manuscripts in the Cairo Genizah Collection Now in the Possession of the University Library, Cambridge*. Cambridge: Cambridge University Press, 1910.

Schmidt, Anne-Sarah. "Die biblische Satansvorstellung—eine Entwicklungsgeschichte: Altes Testament und zwischentestamentliche Texte." *BN* 166 (2015): 109–41.

Schnabel, Eckhard J. *Law and Wisdom from Ben Sira to Paul: A Tradition Historical Enquiry into the Relations of Law, Wisdom, Ethics*. WUNT 16. Tübingen: Mohr Siebeck, 1985.

Schodde, George H. *The Book of Jubilees Translated from the Ethiopic*. Oberlin, OH: Goodrich, 1888.

Schöpflin, Karin. "YHWH's Agents of Doom: The Punishing Function of Angels in Post-Exilic Writings of the Old Testament." Pages 127–37 in *Angels: The Concept of Celestial Beings—Origins, Development and Reception*. Edited by Friedrich V. Reiterer, Tobias Nicklas, and Karin Schöpflin. *DCLY*. Berlin: de Gruyter, 2007.

Schreiber, Stefan. "The Great Opponent: The Devil in Early Jewish and Formative Christian Literature." Pages 437–57 in *Angels: The Concept of Celestial Beings—Origins, Development and Reception*. Edited by Friedrich V. Reiterer, Tobias Nicklas, and Karin Schöpflin. *Deuterocanonical and Cognate Literature Yearbook*. Berlin: de Gruyter, 2007.

Schultz, Brian. *Conquering the World: The War Scroll (1QM) Reconsidered*. STDJ 76. Leiden: Brill, 2009.

Schwienhorst-Schönberger, Ludger, and Georg Steins. "Zur Entstehung, Gestalt und Bedeutung der Ijob-Erzählung (Ijob 1f; 42)." *Biblische Zeitschrift* 33 (1989): 1-24.

Segal, Michael. *The Book of Jubilees: Rewritten Bible, Redaction, Ideology and Theology*. JSJSup 117. Leiden: Brill, 2007.

———. "The Dynamics of Composition and Rewriting in Jubilees and Pseudo-Jubilees." *RevQ* 26.4 (2014): 555–77.

Seitz, Oscar J. F. "Two Spirits in Man: An Essay in Biblical Exegesis." *NTS* 6.1 (1959): 82–95.

Sekki, Arthur Everett. *The Meaning of Ruaḥ at Qumran*. SBLDS 110. Atlanta: Scholars Press, 1989.

Seow, C. L. *Job 1–21: Interpretation and Commentary*. Illuminations. Grand Rapids: Eerdmans, 2013.

Skehan, Patrick W., and Alexander A. Di Lella. *The Wisdom of Ben Sira*. AB 39. New York: Doubleday, 1987.

Smith, David Raymond. *"Hand This Man over to Satan": Curse, Exclusion and Salvation in 1 Corinthians 5*. LNTS 386. New York: T&T Clark, 2008.

Smith, Henry Preserved. *A Critical and Exegetical Commentary on the Books of Samuel*. ICC. New York: Scribner's Sons, 1899.

Smith, Ralph L. *Micah–Malachi*. WBC 32. Waco, TX: Word, 1984.
Smyth, Herbert Weir. *Greek Grammar*. Revised by Gordon M. Messing. Cambridge: Harvard University Press, 1956.
Soggin, J. Alberto. *Judges: A Commentary*. Translated by John Bowden. OTL. Philadelphia: Westminster, 1981.
South, James T. "A Critique of the 'Curse/Death' Interpretation of 1 Corinthians 5.1–8." *NTS* 39.4 (1993): 539–61.
Stegemann, Hartmut. *The Library of Qumran: On the Essenes, Qumran, John the Baptist, and Jesus*. Leiden: Brill. Grand Rapids: Eerdmans, 1998.
Steudel, Annette. "God and Belial." Pages 332–40 in *The Dead Sea Scrolls Fifty Years after Their Discovery*. Edited by Lawrence H. Schiffman, Emanuel Tov, and James C. VanderKam. Jerusalem: Israel Exploration Society, 2000.
———. "Der Teufel in den Texten aus Qumran." Pages 191–200 in *Apokalyptik und Qumran*. Edited by Jörg Frey and Michael Becker. Paderborn: Bonifatius, 2007.
Stokes, Ryan E. "Airing the High Priest's Dirty Laundry: Understanding the Imagery and Message of Zechariah 3:1–7." Pages 1247–64 in vol. 2 of *Sibyls, Scriptures, and Scrolls: John Collins at Seventy*. Edited by Joel Baden, Hindy Najman, and Eibert Tigchelaar with the assistance of Laura Carlson, James Nati, Olivia Stewart, and Shlomo Zuckier. JSJSup 175. Leiden: Brill, 2017.
———. "Belial." *EDEJ* 435–36.
———. "The Devil Made David Do It . . . Or *Did* He? The Nature, Identity, and Literary Origins of the *Satan* in 1 Chronicles 21:1." *JBL* 128.1 (2009): 91–106.
———. "Not over Moses' Dead Body: Jude 9, 22–24 and the *Assumption of Moses* in Their Early Jewish Context." *JSNT* 40.2 (2017): 192–213.
———. "Satan, YHWH's Executioner." *JBL* 133.2 (2014): 251–70.
———. "Sons of God." *EDEJ* 1251–52.
Stol, Marten. "Psychosomatic Suffering in Ancient Mesopotamia." Pages 57–68 in *Mesopotamian Magic: Textual, Historical, and Interpretative Perspectives*. Edited by Tzvi Abusch and Karel van der Toorn. Ancient Magic and Divination 1. Groningen: Styx, 1999.
Stuckenbruck, Loren T. *1 Enoch 91–108*. CEJL. Berlin: de Gruyter, 2007.
———. "The Book of Jubilees and the Origin of Evil." Pages 294–308 in *Enoch and the Mosaic Torah: The Evidence of Jubilees*. Edited by Gabriele Boccaccini and Giovanni Ibba. Grand Rapids: Eerdmans, 2009.

———. "The Demonic World of the Dead Sea Scrolls." Pages 51–70 in in *Evil and the Devil*. Edited by Ida Fröhlich and Erkki Koskenniemi. LNTS 481. London: Bloomsbury, 2013.

———. *The Myth of Rebellious Angels: Studies in Second Temple Judaism and New Testament Texts*. WUNT 335. Tübingen: Mohr Siebeck, 2014.

Sullivan, Kevin. "The Watchers Traditions in *1 Enoch* 6–16: The Fall of the Angels and the Rise of Demons." Pages 91–103 in *The Watchers in Jewish and Christian Traditions*. Edited by Angela Kim Harkins, Kelley Coblentz Bautch, and John C. Endres. Minneapolis: Fortress, 2014.

Tate, Marvin E. "Satan in the Old Testament." *RevExp* 89.4 (1992): 461–74.

Tcherikover, Victor. *Hellenistic Civilization and the Jews*. Peabody, MA: Hendrickson, 1999.

Terrien, Samuel. "The Book of Job: Introduction." *IB* 3:877–905.

———. *Job*. CAT 13. 2nd ed. Geneva: Labor et Fides, 2005.

Theobald, Florian. *Teufel, Tod, und Trauer: Der Satan im Johannesevangelium und seine Vorgeschichte*. NTOA, SUNT 109. Göttingen: Vandenhoeck & Ruprecht, 2015.

Theissen, Gerd. "Monotheismus und Teufelsglaube: Entstehung und Psychologie des biblischen Satansmythos." Pages 37–70 in *Demons and the Devil in Ancient and Medieval Christianity*. Edited by Nienke Vos and Willemien Otten. VCSup 108. Leiden: Brill, 2011.

Thompson, R. Campbell. *The Devils and Evil Spirits of Babylonia, Being Babylonian and Assyrian Incantations against the Demons, Ghouls, Vampires, Hobgoblins, Ghosts, and Kindred Evil Spirits, Which Attack Mankind: Translated from the Original Cuneiform Texts, with Transliterations, Vocabulary, Notes, etc.* 2 vols. London: Luzac, 1903.

Thrall, Margaret E. *The Second Epistle to the Corinthians*. ICC. London: T&T Clark, 2004.

Tigchelaar, Eibert J. C. "The Evil Inclination in the Dead Sea Scrolls, with a Re-edition of 4Q468I (4QSectarian Text?)." Pages 347–57 in *Empsychoi Logoi: Religious Innovations in Antiquity: Studies in Honour of Pieter Willem van der Horst*. Edited by Alberdina Houtman, Albert de Jong, and Magda Misset-van de Weg. AJEC 73. Leiden: Brill, 2008.

———. "Evil Spirits in the Dead Sea Scrolls: A Brief Survey and Some Perspectives." In *Dualismus, Dämonologie und diabolische Figuren: Religionshistorische Beobachtungen und theologische Reflexionen*. Edited by Jörg Frey and Enno Edzard Popkes with the assistance of Stefanie Christine Hertel-Holst. Tübingen: Mohr Siebeck, forthcoming.

———. *Prophets of Old and the Day of the End: Zechariah, the Book of Watchers and Apocalyptic*. OTS 35. Leiden: Brill, 1996.

———. "The Qumran *Jubilees* Manuscripts as Evidence for the Literary Growth of the Book." *RevQ* 26.4 (2014): 579–94.

———. "'These Are the Names of the Spirits of . . .': *4QCatalogue of Spirits* (*4Q230*) and New Manuscript Evidence for the *Two Spirits Treatise*." *RevQ* 84.4 (2004): 529–47.

Toorn, Karel van der. "The Theology of Demons in Mesopotamia and Israel: Popular Belief and Scholarly Speculation." Pages 61–83 in *Die Dämonen: Die Dämonologie der israelitisch-jüdischen und frühchristlichen Literatur im Kontext ihrer Umwelt = Demons: The Demonology of Israelite-Jewish and Early Christian Literature in Context of Their Environment*. Edited by Armin Lange, Hermann Lichtenberger, and K. F. Diethard Römheld. Tübingen: Mohr Siebeck, 2003.

Toorn, Karel van der, Bob Becking, and Pieter W. van der Horst, eds. *Dictionary of Deities and Demons in the Bible*. 2nd ed. Leiden: Brill; Grand Rapids: Eerdmans, 1999.

Tov, Emanuel. *Textual Criticism of the Hebrew Bible*. 2nd ed. Minneapolis: Fortress; Assen: Van Gorcum, 1992.

Treves, Marco. "The Two Spirits of the Rule of the Community." *RevQ* 3.3 (1961): 449–52.

Tsumura, David Toshio. *The First Book of Samuel*. NICOT. Grand Rapids: Eerdmans, 2007.

Tur-Sinai, N. H. *The Book of Job: A New Commentary*. Jerusalem: Kiryath Sepher, 1957.

Ulrich, Eugene Charles, Jr. *The Qumran Text of Samuel and Josephus*. HSM 19. Missoula, MT: Scholars Press, 1978.

VanderKam, James C. "The Angel Story in the Book of Jubilees." Pages 151–70 in *Pseudepigraphic Perspectives: The Apocrypha and Pseudepigrapha in Light of the Dead Sea Scrolls*. Edited by Esther G. Chazon and Michael Stone. STDJ 31. Leiden: Brill, 1999.

———. *The Book of Jubilees*. 2 vols. CSCO 510–511. Leuven: Peeters, 1989.

———. *The Book of Jubilees*. Guides to the Apocrypha and Pseudepigrapha. Sheffield: Sheffield Academic Press, 2001.

———. *Enoch: A Man for All Generations*. Columbia, SC: University of South Carolina Press, 1995.

———. *Enoch and the Growth of an Apocalyptic Tradition*. CBQMS 16. Washington: Catholic Biblical Association of America, 1984.

———. "Enoch Traditions in Jubilees and Other Second-Century

Sources." Pages 229–51 in vol. 1 of the *Society of Biblical Literature 1978 Seminar Papers*. 2 vols. SBLSP 13. Missoula, MT: Scholars Press, 1978.

———. "Jubilees 46:6–47:1 and 4QVisions of Amram." *DSD* 17.2 (2010): 141–58.

———. "Jubilees as the Composition of One Author?" *RevQ* 26.4 (2014): 501–16.

———. "Jubilees, Book of." *EDSS* 1:434–38.

———. "The Jubilees Fragments from Qumran Cave 4." Pages 635–48 in vol. 2 of *The Madrid Qumran Congress: Proceedings of the International Congress on the Dead Sea Scrolls, Madrid, 18–21 March 1991*. Edited by Julio Trebolle Barrera and Luis Vegas Montaner. Leiden: Brill, 1992.

———. *Textual and Historical Studies in the Book of Jubilees*. HSM 14. Missoula, MT: Scholars Press, 1977.

VanderKam, J. C., and J. T. Milik. "Jubilees." Pages 1–185 in *Qumran Cave 4, VIII: Parabiblical Texts, Part 1*, by Harold Attridge et al. DJD 13. Oxford: Clarendon, 1994.

VanGemeren, Willem A., ed. *New International Dictionary of Old Testament Theology and Exegesis*. 5 vols. Grand Rapids: Zondervan, 2012.

Vermes, Geza. *The Complete Dead Sea Scrolls in English*. New York: Allen Lane/Penguin, 1997.

Wallace, Daniel B. *Greek Grammar Beyond the Basics: An Exegetical Syntax of the New Testament*. Grand Rapids: Zondervan, 1996.

Walton, John H. "Satan." Pages 714–17 in *Dictionary of the Old Testament Wisdom Poetry and Writings*. Edited by Tremper Longman III and Peter Enns. Downers Grove, IL: InterVarsity Press, 2008.

Walton, John H., and Tremper Longman III. *How to Read Job*. Downers Grove, IL: InterVarsity Press, 2015.

Weinfeld, Moshe, and David Seeley. "4QBarkhi Nafshi[a-e]." Pages 255–334 in *Qumran Cave 4, XX: Poetical and Liturgical Texts, Part 2*, by Esther Chazon et al. DJD 29. Oxford: Clarendon, 1999.

Wernberg-Moller, P. *The Manual of Discipline: Translated and Annotated with an Introduction*. STDJ 1. Leiden: Brill; Grand Rapids: Eerdmans, 1957.

———. "A Reconsideration of the Two Spirits in the Rule of the Community (1 Q Serek III,13–IV,26)." *RevQ* 3.3 (1961): 413–41.

Wieger, Madeleine. "'Celui qu'on appelle διάβολος' (Apocalypse 12,9): L'histoire du nom grec de l'Adversaire." Pages 201–18 in *L'adversaire de Dieu—Der Widersacher Gottes*. Edited by Michael Tilly, Matthias Morgenstern, and Volker Henning Drecoll. WUNT 364. Tübingen: Mohr Siebeck, 2016.

Wilson, Robert R. *Prophecy and Society in Ancient Israel*. Philadelphia: Fortress, 1980.

Winston, David. "Theodicy in Ben Sira and Stoic Philosophy." Pages 239–49 in *Of Scholars, Savants, and Their Texts: Studies in Philosophy and Religious Thought*. Edited by R. Link-Salinger. New York: Lang, 1989.

Wintermute. O. S. "Jubilees: A New Translation and Introduction." Pages 35–142 in *Expansions of the "Old Testament" and Legends, Wisdom and Philosophical Literature, and Odes, Fragments of Lost Judeo-Hellenistic Works*. Vol. 2 of *The Old Testament Pseudepigrapha*. Edited by James H. Charlesworth. New York: Doubleday, 1985.

Wise, Michael, Martin Abegg, and Edward Cook. *The Dead Sea Scrolls: A New Translation*. New York: HarperCollins, 1996.

Wray, T. J. and Gregory Mobley, *The Birth of Satan: Tracing the Devil's Biblical Roots*. New York: Palgrave Macmillan, 2005.

Wright, Archie T. "Evil Spirits in Second Temple Judaism: The *Watcher Tradition* as Background to the Demonic Pericopes in the Gospels." *Hen* 28.1 (2006): 141–59.

———. *The Origin of Evil Spirits: The Reception of Genesis 6.1–4 in Early Jewish Literature*. WUNT 198. Tübingen: Mohr Siebeck, 2005.

Wright, Benjamin G., III. "Putting the Puzzle Together: Some Suggestions concerning the Social Location of the Wisdom of Ben Sira." Pages 89–112 in *Conflicted Boundaries in Wisdom and Apocalypticism*. Edited by Benjamin G. Wright III and Lawrence M. Wills. SymS 35. Leiden: Brill, 2006.

Wright, John W. "Beyond Transcendence and Immanence: The Characterization of the Presence and Activity of God in the Book of Chronicles." Pages 240–67 in *The Chronicler as Theologian: Essays in Honor of Ralph W. Klein*. Edited by M. Patrick Graham, Steven L. McKenzie, and Gary N. Knoppers. JSOTSup 371. London: T&T Clark International, 2003.

———. "The Innocence of David in 1 Chronicles 21." *JSOT* 60 (1993): 87–105.

Wright, R. B. "Psalms of Solomon." Pages 639–70 in *Expansions of the "Old Testament" and Legends, Wisdom and Philosophical Literature, and Odes, Fragments of Lost Judeo-Hellenistic Works*. Vol. 2 of *The Old*

Testament Pseudepigrapha. Edited by James H. Charlesworth. New York: Doubleday, 1985.

Yadin, Yigael. *The Scroll of the War of the Sons of Light against the Sons of Darkness*. Translated by Batya and Chaim Rabin. Oxford: Oxford University Press, 1962.

Yamauchi, Edwin M. "Did Persian Zoroastrianism Influence Judaism?" Pages 282–97 in *Israel: Ancient Kingdom or Late Invention?* Edited by Daniel I. Block. Nashville: Broadman & Holman, 2008.

Yarbro Collins, Adela. *The Combat Myth in the Book of Revelation*. 1976. Repr., Eugene, OR: Wipf & Stock, 2001.

———. "The Function of 'Excommunication' in Paul." *HTR* 73.1–2 (1980): 251–63.

Zurawski, Jason M. "Separating the Devil from the *Diabolos*: A Fresh Reading of Wisdom of Solomon 2.24." *JSP* 21.4 (2012): 366–99.

Index of Authors

Abegg, Martin G., Jr., 144n3, 147n13
Adams, Samuel L., 121n3, 122n4, 124n7
Albani, Matthias, 177n26
Alexander, Philip S., 144n2, 163n50, 163n51, 168n4
Alt, Albrecht, 36n14
Andersen, Francis I., 41n21
Anderson, A. A., 169n7
Anderson, Braden P., 39n19
Argall, Randal A., 124n7
Attridge, Harold W., 205n33
Aune, David E., 178n26, 210n47

Baillet, Maurice, 152n29, 181n30
Baloian, Bruce, 7n8
Barr, James, 191n52, 193n57
Baumgarten, Joseph M., 152n29, 153n30, 153n32, 159n44
Bautch, Kelley Coblentz, 69n42, 69n43
Beale, G. K., 210n47
Beentjes, Pancratius C., 19n32, 125n11
Bell, Richard H., 3n4, 202n24
Berg, Shane Alan, 173n19
Berger, Klaus, 108n14
Bewer, Julius A., 14n23
Bhayro, Siam, 62n30
Black, Matthew, 69n42
Blair, Judit M., 52n9
Block, Daniel I., 53n11
Boccaccini, Gabriele, 116n23, 121n3, 126n13, 132n30
Borisov, A. Ya., 72n52
Bowley, James E., 144n3
Brand, Miryam T., xx, 113n19, 123n5, 124n10, 131n28, 139n47, 147n15, 164n52, 164n54, 165n56, 211n49
Braun, Roddy, 19n30
Breytenbach, Cilliers, 7n8
Broshi, Magen, 152n28
Brown, Derek R., 3n4, 3n5, 202n24, 212, 216n62
Burney, C. F., 58n22
Burns, John Barclay, 1

Charles, R. H., 66n35, 83n16, 84n21, 86n26, 86n28, 128n20, 157n40
Charlesworth, James H., 61n28, 163n51, 170n10, 172n14, 192n54, 218n65
Childs, Brevard S., 105n8
Cho, Paul Kang-Kul, 36n14
Clines, David J. A., 31n6, 36n12
Cogan, Mordechai, 56n18
Coggins, Richard J., 57n20
Collins, John J., 62n30, 75n1, 93n36, 122n4, 123n6, 125n11, 126n12, 130n25, 131n26, 153n30, 171n12, 181n34, 185, 186n45, 192n55
Conrad, Edgar W., 12n20
Cook, Edward M., 144n3, 147n13

Crenshaw, James L., 125n11
Cross, F. M., 24n40, 24n41
Curtis, Edward Lewis, 19n30

Davenport, Gene L., 83n16, 84n21, 84n23
Davidson, Maxwell J., 130n25, 150n22, 169n7, 170n10, 192n55
Davies, Philip R., 61n29, 153n33, 154n34, 159n44, 182n35, 182n36
Day, Peggy L., xx, 5, 7n8, 9n11, 9n12, 10n15, 12n19, 13n22, 19, 41n22, 42n24, 45n27
De La Torre, Miguel A., xix n5
De Vries, Simon J., 56n18
Di Lella, Alexander A., 121n2, 198n9
Dimant, Devorah, 61n28, 62n30, 64n32, 148n17, 151n27, 154n34, 156n36, 156n38, 161–62
Dion, Paul E., 24n40
Dirksen, Peter B., 19n30, 21n37
Dochhorn, Jan, xviii n4, 198n12, 210n47, 224n3
Driver, Samuel Rolles, 13n21, 36n12
Duhaime, Jean, 157n40, 176n23, 181n31, 182n35, 182n36, 183n40, 184n41, 209n45
Duhm, Hans, 19n30
Duke, Robert R., 150n24
Dupont-Sommer, A., 169n8, 191n51
Durham, John I., 105n8

Ellis, Nicholas, 140n45
Erho, Ted M., 214n57
Eshel, Esther, 64n32
Evans, Paul, 21n37
Everling, Otto, 3n5

Fabry, Heinz-Josef, 31n6, 32n9, 32n10, 32n11, 58n23
Farrar, Thomas J., 84n23, 196n6, 197n8, 199n14, 200n16, 200n18, 202n25, 203n28, 212n52, 224n1
Finkelstein, Louis, 31n4
Fletcher-Louis, Crispin H. T., 186n44, 186n45
Foerster, Werner, 201n19, 201n21, 202n23
Fohrer, G., 31n4, 32n7
Forsyth, Neil, xix–xx, 13n21, 19n30, 84n23
Frey, Jörg, 180n29
Frey-Anthes, Henrike, 49n5, 52n7, 52n9, 145n6
Fritz, Volkmar, 58n22
Fröhlich, Ida, xviii n4, 144n2, 145n5

Gagnon, Robert A. J., 163n50
García Martínez, Florentino, 131, 188n49
Garrett, Susan R., 204n30
Gaster, T. H., 7n8, 13n22
Geller, Markham J., 52n8, 54n12, 67n37, 68n40
Glasson, T. F., 65n33
Goldman, Liora, 151n26
Goldmann, Moshe, 108n14
Goldstein, Jonathan A., 77n3
Good, Edwin M., 45n26
Gray, George Buchanan, 13n21, 36n12

Habel, Norman C., 13n21
Halpern-Amaru, Betsy, 78n7, 108n14
Hamilton, Victor P., 7n8
Hamori, Esther J., 53n10
Hanneken, Todd Russell, 78n7, 79n9, 84n23, 116n24
Hanson, Paul D., 62n30
Harlow, Daniel C., 217n63
Hartley, John E., 13n21
Heckl, Raik, 31n5, 36n14
Heger, Paul, 193n57
Heiligstedt, Augustus, 37n15
Hempel, Charlotte, 152n29, 153n31, 154n34, 168n3, 168n4
Henten, J. W. van, 81n12
Hernández, Albert, xix n5
Himmelfarb, Martha, 77n3
Hoffman, Yair, 31n3, 32n7
Hoftijzer, Jacob, 55n16
Holladay, Carl R., 217n63
Horst, Friedrich, 7n8, 36n14

Hultgren, Stephen, 153n31, 157n40
Hutter, M., 191n52

Isbell, Charles D., 72n51

Jacobsen, Thorkild, 53n11
Japhet, Sara, 4–5, 19–20, 20n33, 22n38
Jarick, John, 20n33
Jastrow, Morris, Jr., 38n16
Jeremias, Christian, 12n19
Jong, Albert de, 193n56
Jurgens, Blake Alan, 150n24

Kautzsch, Karl, 32n8
Keith, Chris, xviii n4
Kelly, Henry Ansgar, xix n5, 208n43
Kister, Menahem, 124n9
Klein, Ralph W., 19n30, 19n31, 21n37, 24n40, 54n13, 55n17
Kluger, Rivkah Schärf, 11n17, 19n30
Knibb, Michael A., 66n35, 154n34, 157n40, 163n50, 173n20
Knoppers, Gary N., 19n32, 20n36, 24n40
Kobelski, Paul J., 192n55
Koch, Klaus, 192n55
Koester, Craig R., 205n33, 210n47
König, Eduard, 31n4, 40n20
Koskenniemi, Erkki, xviii n4
Kugel, James, 78–79, 97n46, 101n1, 105n7, 110n16
Kuhn, Karl Georg, 169n8, 191n51
Kvanvig, Helge S., 61n29, 116n23

Lane, William L., 205n33
Lange, Armin, 72n49, 81n12, 115n21, 147n11, 147n15, 175n22, 198n9
Langton, Edward, 13n21, 19n30, 52n9
Lemke, Werner E., 24n40
Leonhardt-Balzer, Jutta, 202n23
Leslau, Wolf, 112
Levine, Baruch A., 10n15
Levison, John R., 169n5, 192n55
Lewis, Theodore J., 161n46
Lincicum, David, 144n2
Lindblom, Johannes, 32n10, 36n13, 40n20
Lindström, Fredrik, 53n11, 56n18, 58n22, 58n23
Longman, Tremper, III, 45n27
Ludolf, Hiob, 112n18

Madsen, Albert Alonzo, 19n30
Magdalene, F. Rachel, 45n27
Marböck, Johannes, 122n4
Marcus, Ralph, 168n2
Martin, Dale Basil, 49n5, 71n48
Martone, Corrado, 156n36
McCarter, P. Kyle, Jr., 53n11, 54n13, 55n17
McConville, J. G., 19n30
McKenzie, Steven L., 19n32, 24n40
Meier, Samuel A., 11n17, 26n44
Mendels, Doron, 77n3
Metso, Sarianna, 163n50, 168n4
Meyers, Carol L., 12n19, 13n21, 14n23
Meyers, Eric M., 12n19, 13n21, 14n23
Milgrom, Jacob, 10n15
Milik, J. T., 61n28, 61n29, 102n3, 115n21, 127n15, 128n20, 131n26, 152n29, 161–62, 163n51
Mitchell, Hinckley G., 14n23
Mobley, Gregory, 19n30
Monger, Matthew Phillip, 77n3, 80n10
Morris, Michael J., 196n2
Moses, Robert, 39n19
Murphy-O'Connor, Jerome, 157n40, 163n50, 206n37

Najman, Hindy, 76n2
Naveh, Joseph, 17n26, 68n38, 72n51, 72n52, 84n19
Newsom, Carol A., 30n2, 39n18, 62n30, 179n28
Nickelsburg, George W. E., 62n30, 64, 65n33, 66n34, 66n35, 67n36, 69n43, 70n44, 73, 121n1, 126n13, 127n14, 128n20, 129n22, 130n25, 133n32, 136n38, 137–38, 199n15, 214n57, 215n59, 216n61

Nielsen, Kirsten, 7n8, 19n30, 21n37

Oegema, Gerbern S., 214n56
Oppenheim, A. L., 42n24
Orlov, Andrei A., 215n60
Osten-Sacken, Peter von der, 154n34, 176n23, 182n36

Page, Sydney H. T., 13n21, 19n30
Pagels, Elaine, xx
Panaino, Antonio, 191n53
Parker, Simon B., 59n25
Parry, Donald W., 24n40, 24n41
Pascale, Ronald Anthony, 64n32, 68n40, 83n16, 86n26, 96n42
Penney, Douglas L., 200n17
Perrin, Andrew B., 149n21, 151n26
Petersen, David L., 12n19, 14n23
Pettorelli, Jean-Pierre, 217n63
Pfeiffer, Robert H., 31n4
Philonenko, Marc, 192n54, 192n55
Pierce, Chad T., 7n8, 161n46
Pope, Marvin H., 13n21, 31n6, 36n12, 45n26
Popović, Mladen, 169n5, 177n26
Pouilly, J., 163n50
Prato, Gian Luigi, 125n11
Propp, William H. C., 105n8
Puech, Émile, 149n19, 149n21, 150n25

Qimron, Elisha, 152n28, 163n51, 172n14

Rad, Gerhard von, 7n8, 8n10
Reed, Annette Yoshiko, 116n24, 131n26
Reeg, Gottfried, 224n2
Reiner, Erica, 53n11
Roberts, J. J. M., 29n1, 188n49
Rogland, Max, 12n20
Rollston, Christopher A., 27n46
Rosen-Zvi, Ishay, 155n35
Rudman, Dominic, 14n23, 19n29
Rudnig-Zelt, Susanne, xviii n4
Ruiten, Jacques T. A. G. M. van, 81n13, 102n2, 104n6
Russell, Jeffrey Burton, xix n5

Sacchi, Paolo, 131n26
Sailhamer, John H., 19n32
Saley, R. J., 24n40, 24n41
Schechter, Solomon, 152n28, 157n40
Schmidt, Anne-Sarah, xviii n4
Schnabel, Eckhard J., 122n4
Schodde, George H., 84n21
Schöpflin, Karin, 14n23
Schreiber, Stefan, xviii n4, 19n30, 19n31
Schultz, Brian, 181n32, 182n35
Schwartz, Daniel R., 152n29, 153n30, 159n44
Schwienhorst-Schönberger, Ludger, 32n9
Seeley, David, 138n44, 139n45
Segal, Michael, 64n32, 77–79, 92n35, 93n36, 97n46, 98n47, 101n1, 104n6, 105n7, 106n11, 108n14, 109n15, 110n16, 116–17, 162n49
Seitz, Oscar J. F., 172n17
Sekki, Arthur Everett, 169n7
Seow, C. L., 29n1, 30n2
Shaked, Shaul, 17n26, 68n38, 72n51, 72n52, 84n19
Skehan, Patrick W., 121n2, 198n9
Smith, David Raymond, 202n24, 206n38
Smith, Henry Preserved, 54n13
Smith, John Merlin Powis, 14n23
Smith, Ralph L., 13n21, 14n23
Smyth, Herbert Weir, 198n13
Soggin, J. Alberto, 58n22
South, James T., 206n36
Stegemann, Hartmut, 163n50, 175n22
Steins, Georg, 32n9
Steudel, Annette, 156n36, 161n47, 203n27
Stokes, Ryan E., 7n9, 9n12, 9n13, 12n20, 15n24, 20n34, 22n38, 60n27, 161n46, 209n44, 212n51
Stol, Marten, 55n16
Stuckenbruck, Loren T., xviii n4, 116n22, 126n13, 127n14, 128n19, 131n26, 131n29, 137n39, 144n2, 147n13, 156n38
Sullivan, Kevin, 71n48

Tate, Marvin E., 13n21, 19n31
Tengström, S., 58n23
Terrien, Samuel, 32n8, 41n21
Theissen, Gerd, xviii n4, 203n29
Theobald, Florian, 202n24
Thomas, Samuel, 156n36
Thompson, R. Campbell, 53n11
Thrall, Margaret E., 207n42
Tigchelaar, Eibert J. C., 62n30, 77n3, 80n10, 139, 144n2, 146n10, 167n1, 188n49
Toorn, Karel van der, 52n9
Tov, Emanuel, 70n46
Treves, Marco, 170n9, 170n10
Tsumura, David Toshio, 53n11, 55n15, 55n17
Tur-Sinai, N. H., 20n33, 42, 42n24

Ulrich, Eugene Charles, Jr., 24n40

VanderKam, James C., 61n28, 64, 77n3, 78n7, 80n10, 80n11, 83n17, 84n21, 86n26, 86n27, 86n28, 89n32, 91n33, 92n35, 102n3, 108n14, 115n21, 116n24, 121n1, 126n13, 127n17, 128n19, 130n25, 150n25, 161–62, 173n18, 199n15, 214n57, 215n59, 216n61
Vaux, R. de, 152n29
Vermes, Geza, 159n44, 163n51

Wallace, Daniel B., 198n13
Walton, John H., 7n8, 45n27
Wanke, G., 7n8
Weinfeld, Moshe, 138n44, 139n45
Wernberg-Moller, P., 170n9, 170n10, 173n19
Wieger, Madeleine, 200n19, 201n22
Williams, Guy J., 196n6, 197n8, 202n25, 212n52
Wilson, Robert R., 57n21
Winston, David, 125n11
Wintermute, O. S., 83n16, 84n21, 86n26, 86n28, 92n35
Wise, Michael, 147n13
Wold, Benjamin, xviii n4
Woude, Adam S. van der, 188n49
Wray, T. J., 19n30
Wright, Archie T., 64n32
Wright, Benjamin G., III, 124n7
Wright, John W., 19n32, 26n45
Wright, R. B., 130n23

Yadin, Yigael, 181n33
Yamauchi, Edwin M., 193n57
Yarbro Collins, Adela, 207n40, 218n66

Zurawski, Jason M., 217n63

Index of Subjects

Abraham, 94–95, 101–4, 114–15, 212–13
accuser: in book of Jubilees, 111–15; in Book of Parables, 214–16; in Hebrew scriptures, 4–7, 9n12, 14–15, 19, 25, 45–46; in New Testament, 201, 210–14
Adam and Eve, 116n22, 117, 173n19, 179; Life of Adam and Eve, 217n63. *See also* Eve
adversary, xx, 3–8, 9n11, 10n16, 13n21, 19n32, 41n23, 83, 197, 198n9, 201, 212, 224
agent of God, Satan as: in the book of Jubilees, 91–92, 118; in the Hebrew scriptures, 3–4, 4, 13, 16–17, 17–19, 27; in the New Testament, 203, 208–10; in the War Rule, 187. *See also* enemy of God, Satan as
Amram, Visions of, 149–51, 174–75, 184
angels: of Darkness, xiii, xxii, 144, 148, 167, 169, 170–71, 173–81; of death, 224; of destruction, 25, 146, 148, 149, 157–58, 183–184; of light, 73, 174; of Mastema/obstruction, 81n12, 156, 158; of the Satan, 158, 188, 197, 207, 209, 215, 218, 220. *See also* angel of the LORD/Yahweh; angels of the presence; destroyer; Lights, Prince of; Michael; watchers
angel of the LORD/Yahweh: as executioner, 10–11, 18, 22–26, 27, 105, 196, 221–22; opposes the Satan, 12–17, 27–28, 43, 103, 150, 188, 215, 221
angels of the presence: reveal literature 76, 80–81, 98; oppose the Prince of Mastema, 91, 96n41, 102–6, 110, 112, 113n19, 119, 157, 188, 222
apotropaism, 98, 124n9, 144n2, 147, 158, 185, 196n2
Asael, 63, 81, 84n23, 216
attacker/executioner: in the book of Jubilees, 91–93, 105–6, 112–15; in the Dead Sea Scrolls, 151n26, 157–58, 176, 183–85; in the Hebrew scriptures, 8–10, 11–12, 15–16, 25, 27, 40–46, 221–22; in the New Testament, 203, 204, 205–7, 208, 220, 223
Azazel, 52n9, 218n64

Balaam, 10–11, 21–25
Barkhi Nafshi, 138–39, 141, 223
Beelzebul, 68n38, 197
Belial/Beliar: dominion of, 143, 164–66, 184–85; lot of, 164–65, 187, 188, 189, 206n39; name, 85–86, 144, 148, 155–56; nets of, 159–60, 165; same as Mastema, 160–63; spirits of, 146, 158, 183–84, 188, 209

Cain, 116n22, 117, 179, 217n63, 218
Chronicles, book of: relationship to book of Job, 21–22, 43–44; relationship to book of Numbers, 21–25; rela-

tionship to books of Samuel, 4, 17–18, 21–26; *śāṭān* in Chronicles, 17–26
church fathers, 224
combat myth, xix–xxi, 218n66
Community Rule. *See* Rule of the Community

Damascus Document, 133n31, 152–63, 164–165, 177–79
David: census, 4, 10, 17–26, 27–28, 43, 46, 93, 124, 217, 221; rebukes Abishai, 8–9, 11, 15–16, 198n11; and Saul's spirit, 54–55, 89
Dead Sea Scrolls, 138–39, 142–94
death: origin of, 126, 205n33, 217n63; personified, 151n26; sin as the cause of, 123, 126, 140, 173. *See also* attacker/executioner
deceiver, 73, 92–93, 99, 110, 203, 204–5, 218n66. *See also* sin, Satan's role in; tempter; tester
demons: and evil spirits, 48–50, 69–72, 87, 134–35, 145, 196–97, 222; origin of, 70–71, 197; protection from, 98, 124n9, 144n2, 147, 158, 185, 196n2; and the Satan, 88, 90–94, 133; and sin, 87, 124n9, 140; terminology for, 48–50, 85–86, 143–46; types of, 144–45; worship of, 51–52, 69–74, 87, 134–38, 145, 196. *See also* evil spirits; Satan, chief of demons/evil spirits/angels
destroyer, 26–27, 46, 110n16, 144, 147, 148, 184, 196. *See also* angels of death; angels of destruction
devil. *See* Satan, names/titles for devil
dragon, xv, xvi, 214, 218
dualism, 154n34, 182n36

Eden, 73n56, 126, 205n33, 216–20
enemy of God, Satan as: in the book of Jubilees, 103, 108–9; 118; in the New Testament, 203, 208–10; in the War Rule, 167, 183–84, 187, 189–90, 193–94. *See also* Satan, names/titles for; agent of God, Satan as
Enoch, book of (1 Enoch): Book of Parables, 214–16; Book of the Watchers, 61–74; Epistle of Enoch, 126–38
Eve, 73, 116n22, 117, 125–26, 179, 218n64, 219
evil, God's responsibility for: God is not responsible for human sin, 120–21, 123–26, 133–34, 140; God is responsible for human sin, 97, 155, 160, 171–73, 177–79, 181; God is responsible for human suffering, 2, 23, 39, 43; God plays a diminished role or no role in the suffering of Israel/the righteous, 17, 25–26, 28, 44–45, 100, 104, 106–9, 115, 225
evil, human responsibility for, 120–41, 222–23
evil inclination, 123, 138–39, 155, 170, 176
evil one. *See* Satan, names/titles for
evil, origin of: in the Book of the Watchers, 62–74, 222; in the Epistle of Enoch, 130–34; in the book of Jubilees, 93, 115–18, 177; in Sirach (Ben Sira), 125; in the Treatise on the Two Spirits, 171–73, 177, 181; in the War Rule, 182. *See also* demons; evil, God's responsibility for; evil spirits
evil spirits: deception, 53, 56–58; and demons, 48–50, 69–72, 87, 134–35, 145, 196–97, 222; from God, 54–59, 172; and illness, 52, 66–67, 69, 73, 88, 90–91, 196; and Israel, 94; origin of, 63–74, 116, 143, 146, 170–73, 177, 189–90, 194, 197; and prophecy, 55–58, 71–72, 136, 196; protection from, 98, 124n9, 144n2, 147, 158, 185, 196n2; as psychological dispositions, 58–59; and sin (spirits lead humans into sin), 69–74, 98–99, 116, 146, 158, 183, 196; and sin (spirits do not lead humans into sin), 133–35, 138, 141; terminology for, 48–50, 85–86, 143–46; two spirits, 168–73; types of, 52–59, 145–46. *See also* demons; Satan, chief of demons/evil spirits/angels
executioner. *See* attacker/executioner

exorcism, 17n26, 54

fall/defeat of the Satan, 209–10, 213–14
free will, 123, 125, 155, 222. *See also* evil, human responsibility for

Gabriel, 187, 215
Gadre'el, 218n64
Gentiles, 46–47, 158, 183, 188, 189

illness: caused by the Satan, 84, 205; caused by spirits, 52, 66–67, 69, 73, 88, 90–91, 196
Israel: deceived by the Satan/spirits, 158–60, 165, 177; not deceived by spirits, 94–98, 118; opposed by the Satan 100–111, 185–88

James, Epistle of, 139–40, 204
Jesus: as healer, 196, 205; defeats the Satan, 205, 214; opposed by the Satan, 205, 208; possessed by Beelzebul, 68n38; statements concerning the Satan, 198n11, 205, 213; temptation of, 204, 213n53
Job, book of, 29–47: composition of, 30–40; contribution to the Satan tradition, 6, 46–47; relationship to Chronicles, 21–22, 43–44
Joshua, the high priest, 12–17, 27, 43, 45n27, 47, 103, 215, 221
Jubilees, book of, 75–119: composition of, 75–79; unity and diversity of, 79, 109–11, 118–19

Leviathan, 218. *See also* dragon
light and darkness: opposition characteristic of several Dead Sea Scrolls, 143, 151, 165–66; in Treatise on Two Spirits, 169, 171–73, 176, 192–94, 223; in Visions of Amram, 151; in War Rule, 167, 181, 182–83, 192–94, 223; in Zoroastrianism, 192–94. *See also* Lights, Prince of
Lights, Prince of: opposes Angel of Darkness, 170–71, 174–76, 180, 188; opposes Belial, 162, 184n41, 194; opposes Moses 157, 177n25. *See also* angels
Lilith, 52n9, 144, 149, 190

Mastema, Angel of, 81n12, 156, 158
Mastema: and Belial, 160–63; deceives nations through the agency of evil spirits, 88, 90–94, 98–99, 133; name/title for the Satan, 81–82; opposes angel of the presence, 91, 96n41, 102–6, 110, 112, 113n19, 119, 157, 188, 222; opposes Israel, 100–114, 118–19, 156
Melchiresha, 144, 148, 149–51, 161n47, 165–66, 223
Melchizedek, 150, 151, 156, 188
Michael: corresponds to the angel of the presence, 81; with Gabriel, Raphael, Phanuel, and/or Sariel, 187, 215; as prince of Israel, 2, 96, 167, 185, 187, 188; as Prince of Lights, 194; versus the Satan, 17n25, 187–89, 204, 209, 212n51, 214. *See also* angels; Lights, Prince of
Moses: angel of the presence speaks with, 80, 85, 98, 102; and Egyptian magicians, 106, 157, 161, 177; law of, 76, 100, 156, 158; prays for protection from deceptive spirits, 86–90, 98, 112, 113–14, 150; prince of Mastema attempts to kill, 105–6, 107, 113, 115, 204, 207n40

Noah, 73n55, 81, 88–91, 98, 114, 136
Numbers, book of, 10–11, 21–25

Paul: calls opponents ministers of the Satan, 205; on the Satan as an angel of light, 73; on the Satan as an attacker, 206–7; on the Satan as God's agent, 208–9, 210; on the Satan as serpent, 216n62, 219, 223
possession, 57n21, 67n36, 68n38
Pseudo-Jubilees, 85n24, 102n3, 115, 161–62, 212–13

rabbinic literature: on good and bad inclination, 155, 170, 176; on the Satan, 147n12, 199n14, 200, 224
Rahab, 218. *See also* dragon
Raphael, 70n45, 81, 187, 215
Revelation, book of, 47, 195, 205, 210–14, 218–19
Rule of the Community, 163–65; Treatise on the Two Spirits, 167–81
Rule of the War between the Sons of Light and the Sons of Darkness. *See* War Rule/War Scroll

śāṭān: meaning of, 3–4, 5, 6–10, 13–15, 20n33, 82–84; title *haśśāṭān*, xviii, 4, 5, 13, 19, 44, 45, 84; title/name *ho satanas*, 197–200
Satan, chief of demons/evil spirits/angels: chief of punishing angels, 158, 188, 197, 207, 209, 215, 218, 220; demons/spirits of Mastema, 88, 90–94, 133; demons/spirits of the Satan in the New Testament, 197, 205, 209, 220; spirits of the Angel of Darkness, 169, 174; spirits of Belial, 146, 183–84, 188
Satan, fall/defeat of, 205, 208, 209–10, 213–14, 220
Satan, names/titles for: Angel of Darkness, 174; Beelzebul, 197; Belial/Beliar, 85–86, 142, 155–56, 160–63, 165–66; 197; devil, 197, 201–2; enemy, 197; evil one, 197; Mastema, 81–82, 156, 160–62; Melchiresha, 150–51, 165–66; tempter/tester, 197, 213n53. *See also śāṭān*
Satan, origin of, 93–94, 224. *See also* fall/defeat of the Satan
Satan, roles of. *See* accuser; attacker/executioner; deceiver; tempter; tester
satans (generic): class of human attacker, 5, 7–9, 19–21, 83, 146–47, 198; class of superhuman attacker, 83–84, 146–47, 198, 199, 215
Saul, king of Israel, 53–55, 58n23, 65
serpent, 203, 205n33, 216–20, 223
Shemihazah, 63, 81
sin: conception of, 177–79; human responsibility for, 120–41, 129–31, 133, 139, 141, 222–23
sin, Satan as instigator of: in the book of Jubilees, 92–93, 109–10; in the Damascus Document, 158–60; in the Dead Sea Scrolls (in general), 142, 156, 163, 165; in the Hebrew scriptures, 4; in Melchizedek, 151; in the New Testament, 140, 204–5, 218; in Rule of the Community, 165; in Treatise on the Two Spirits, 174, 175, 177, 179–80, 183, 193; in War Rule, 189–90
Sirach (Ben Sira), 121–26
sons of God, 40–41, 50, 59–61, 65, 70, 94, 95–97
spirits. *See* evil spirits
suffering. *See* evil, God's responsibility for

tempter, 25, 197, 198n11, 204–5. *See also* tester
tester: concept in New Testament, 204, 210n46; Prince of Mastema tests Abraham, 82–83, 101–4, 114–15; the Satan sifts Peter and apostles as wheat, 213; the Satan tests Jesus, 213n53; the Satan tests Job, 10n14, 42, 43; the Satan tests the righteous, 211–14; title for the Satan, 197
temptation/test of Jesus, 204, 213n53
Treatise on the Two Spirits, 167–81

Visions of Amram, 149–51, 174–75, 184

War Rule/War Scroll, 181–90
watchers, 62–63, 69, 73, 116–17, 132, 137, 146, 155, 190, 215, 218n64

Zechariah, book of: the Satan in, 4–5, 12–17, 27–28; reception of, 103, 150, 215
Zoroastrianism, 169–70, 181n34, 191–94

Index of Ancient Sources

Hebrew Scriptures

Genesis 75–76, 155, 216
1 171–73, 197n7
1–5 179
1:1–2:4a 171n13
1:2 172–73
1:3–5 172
1:11–12 173n19
1:21 173n19
1:24–25 173n19
1:26–27 173n19
1:27–30 173n19
2–3 73n56, 173n19
2:4 172
3 xxii, 125–26, 171, 195, 203, 205n33, 216–20, 223
3:15 216n62, 218n66
6 171, 190–91
6:1–4 50, 60–62, 65, 70, 94, 96
6:5 123, 139, 155
8:21 123, 139, 155
16:7–14 26n43
17 94–95
22 101–4, 115
22:1 104n5
22:11–12 26n43
22:12 104n6
27:41 82, 115n21
49:23 82n14, 115n21
50:15 82n14, 115n21

Exodus 75–76
4 105
4:24 105
4:24–26 105n8
4:25–26 105
12:23 27, 148
12:23a 110n16
12:23b 110n16
12:35–36 108
14:4 106–7
14:8 106–7
14:17 106–7
23:22 14n23
28:43 15
30:12–16 18n28

Leviticus
17:7 52n7
20:27 159n43

Numbers
5:14 59
5:30 59
22 xii, 3–4, 9–11, 13, 15–16, 21–22, 25, 27–28, 42, 47, 201, 202n26, 211, 221
22:20 10n15, 11n17
22:20–22 23
22:22 10, 22, 41n23, 82, 112n18, 201
22:22–30 22
22:22–35 10n15, 207n40
22:31 23
22:32 10n16, 41n23, 82, 201
22:32–33 11
22:32–35 25
22:34 22
22:35 11n17, 23

Deuteronomy
4:5–6 122n4
8:15 218–19
13:1–3 71
13:5 71
13:7 [Eng. 13:6] 20n35
13:14 85, 86n26, 156
23:14 185n43, 186n44

32:8 59, 70, 94, 95n39, 96–97
32:8–9 95–96, 189
32:16–17 51–52, 97n45
32:17 49–50, 52n7, 69–70, 196n3

Joshua
5:13–15 24n41
15:18 20n35

Judges
1:14 20n35
5 185
9 53, 58–59, 89
9:23 65–66, 135, 171
9:23–24 53n10, 58
13:2–23 26n43
19:22 86n26
20:13 86n26

1 Samuel
1:16 85, 86n26
2:10 212
2:12 86n26
10:5 55
10:6 55, 72
10:10 55, 72
10:27 86n26
16 53–54
16–19 53–55, 58
16:14 53, 55n16, 172–73
16:14–23 53n10, 65–68, 71, 135
16:23 54n14, 55n16
18:10 55, 65–68, 71–72
18:10–11 54, 89n31, 135
18:10–12 53n10
19:9 65–68, 71
19:9–10 53n10, 89n31
19:19–24 55
19:20 55
25:17 86n26
26:7–11 9n12
26:19 20n35
29:4 8, 41n23, 82, 198n10, 201n21

2 Samuel
3:17–39 9n12
8:10 14n23
16:9 9n12
18:5–33 9n12
20:4–10 9n12
24 4,
19 8–9, 11, 15
19:22 [Eng. 19:21] 8
19:23 [Eng. 19:22] 8–9, 41n23, 198n10, 198n11, 201n21
22:5 85, 156
24 17–18, 21–24, 26–27, 43, 44n25, 46, 124, 217
24:1 18, 20n35, 22–23, 25n42
24:10 18n28
24:12–14 46
24:15–16 22
24:17 18n28, 22
24:18–19 24, 26
24:18–25 23
24:19 24, 25n42

1 Kings
2:5–6 9n12
3 1
5 8, 83, 146–47
5:18 [Eng. 5:4] 8, 82–83, 84n19, 147n11
11 19
11:14 8, 198–99
11:23 8, 198–99
11:25 8
21:10 86n26
21:13 86n26
21:25 20n35
22 21, 53, 56–58, 72, 89n31
22:19–23 53n10, 56–57
22:28 57n21

2 Kings
18:32 20n35
19:7 53, 59
19:35 26n44, 27

Isaiah
5:20 172n15
6 16
6:7 16
11:6–9 218–19
13:21 49, 52n7, 145, 196
14 187
19:13–14 53n10
24:17 159
24:21–22 70n47
27:1 218
29:10 53, 59, 171
34:14 49n3, 145n7, 196n4
36:18 20n35
37:7 53, 59
37:36 27
44:18–20 136
44:20 135–36
45:6b–7 2,
45:7 172, 193
47:1 38n16
51:9 218
58:5 38n16
59:9 172n15
63 106n9
63:9 106n9
65:11 49n4
65:14 58n23

Jeremiah
6:26 38n16
13:16 172n15
23:9–40 72n50
28:8–9 57
32:42–44 36n14

38:22 20n35
43:3 20n35
44 1–2

Ezekiel
9 27
27:30 38n16
28 187n48
38–39 185

Hosea
9:7–8 82n14, 82n15

Amos
3:6b 2
5:18 172n15
5:18–19 218–19
5:20 172n15
9:14 36n14

Jonah
3:6 38n16

Micah
3:5–8 57

Zechariah 4–5, 7, 12n19, 13n22, 19, 25, 27n46, 47, 79, 143, 148, 151, 174, 188, 202
3 xvi, 9–10, 12–17, 21–22, 27–28, 41–43, 91–92, 102n2, 102n3, 103, 111, 139, 150–51, 198, 200, 205n33, 211, 215, 221
3:1 14n23, 21, 45n27, 102–3, 201
3:1–2 13n21, 82, 198n10, 201
3:1–7 12–13
3:2 16–17, 103, 147
3:4 16
4:10 42n24
13:2 57n21, 72

Psalms
8:7 216n62
18:5 [Eng. 18:4] 85, 156
29:1 59
38:21 [Eng. 38:20; LXX 37:21] 9, 112n18
41:9 [Eng. 41:8] 85
51:12 [Eng. 51:10] 58n23
51:19 [Eng. 51:17] 58n23
55:4 [Eng. 55:3] 82n14, 115n21
71:13 [LXX 70:13] 9, 112n18, 201n20
78:49 110n16, 157
82 59, 70, 95, 187–88
89:7 [Eng. 89:6] 59
89:11 [Eng. 89:10] 218
96:5 [LXX 95:5] 49, 52, 70
104:26 218
106:34–38 51
106:37 [LXX 105:37] 49–52, 69–70, 196n3
106:37–38 89n31
109 22, 97n45
109:4 [LXX 108:4] 9, 112n18
109:6 [LXX 108:6] 14–15, 21–22, 198n10
109:6–9 14–15
109:8–9 15
109:20 [LXX 108:20] 9, 112n18
109:29 [LXX 108:29] 9, 112n18
110:1 216n62

Job xvi, xxi, 4–7, 13n22, 19, 20n34, 25, 27n46, 29–47, 79, 81, 102, 104n5, 111, 114–15, 118, 121, 143, 148, 174, 202, 212, 214, 222
1 36n14
1–2 xvi, 4, 9–10, 13n21, 21–22, 30–47, 38n17, 45n27, 59, 81n13, 82, 91, 92n34, 94, 102n2, 102n3, 103, 111, 198, 200–201, 222
1:1–5 32n9, 32n10, 33, 36
1:4–5 37
1:5 37
1:6 37, 40, 94
1:6–12 31, 32, 33, 37n15, 40, 46, 212
1:7 41
1:8 41, 101–2, 104n5
1:9–11 102
1:11 44, 114
1:12 37, 42
1:13 37
1:13–19 36, 38
1:13–22 32n9, 32n10, 34
1:14–15 46
1:15 185
1:17 46, 185
1:20 38
1:20–22 38
1:21 45
1:21–22 38n17
2 36n14, 206
2:1 37, 40, 94
2:1–6 31–32, 212
2:1–7 31n6, 32n9
2:1–8 34–35, 40, 46
2:1–10 32n9
2:2 41
2:3 20n35, 41, 43, 101–3, 104n5
2:4 213
2:4–5 36, 102
2:5 44, 114
2:5–6 206n35
2:6 36n14, 42
2:7 32, 37–38

2:7–8 32
2:8 38
2:9 38
2:9–10 38n17
2:9–13 35
2:11–13 31n6, 32n10
2:12 38
3:1–42:6 (or dialogues) 30–31, 39–40
3:8 218
7:5 39
7:11 58n23
11:15 39n18
16:9 82n14, 82n15, 115n21
18:13 39n18
19:20 39
26:12–13 218
28 31
30:21 82, 115n21
30:26 172n15
30:30 39
32–37 31
33:2 39n18
33:25 39n18
34:18 85
36:16 20n35
36:18 20n35
38 59
38:1–42:6 31
42 36n14
42:2–17 32n9
42:7–9a 31n6
42:7–9 36n14
42:7–17 30–31, 36, 38
42:10a 36n14
42:10aα 31n6
42:10b–17 36n14
42:12–17 36n14

Proverbs 121
4:11–19 173
14:29 58n23
17:27 58n23
19:28 85

Ecclesiastes 121
2:13 172n15
9:1–3 121n3

Esther
7:4 201n21
8:1 201n21
8:11 14n23

Daniel 96n41, 188
3 60
3:25 60
3:25–28 94n38, 96n43
3:28 60
7:27 186n45
10–12 188
10:13 2, 95, 185–86
10:20–21 2, 95, 185–86
10:21 80–81, 95–96
12:1 2, 80–81, 95–96

1 Chronicles 7–8, 19n29, 22, 24, 44, 143
21 4–6, 11n18, 17–22, 25–28, 42, 44n25, 46–47, 92–93, 124, 202n26, 221–22
21:1 10, 17–19, 20n34, 20n35, 21–22, 25n42, 43–44, 84n22, 147, 184n41, 198n10, 199, 201, 217
21:1–17 207n40
21:8 18n28
21:9 26n45
21:10–13 46
21:12 147, 184n41
21:15 26n44, 147, 184n41
21:16 23, 24n41
21:17 18n28
21:18 25n42, 26
21:18–19 24

2 Chronicles
11:15 52n7
13:7 86n26
16:9 42, 42n24
18 21
18:2 20n35
18:18–22 57n19
18:31 20n35
32:11 20n35
32:15 20n35
32:21 26n44

New Testament

Matthew 202n25, 213n53
1:20 200n16
4:1–7 204
4:1–11 204, 213n53
6:13 210n46, 213
13:38–39 208
16:23 198n11
25:41 187, 197, 208

Mark 202n25
1:12–13 213n53
1:32–34 196
3:1–12 196
3:20–22 67–68, 68n38
3:22–30 197
3:23 198n12
4:15 204
7:25–30 196n1
8:33 198n11, 200n16

Luke 202n25, 219
4:1–4 204
4:1–13 213n53
4:5–6 188
4:9–12 204
4:33–41 196n1
8:2 196n1
8:27–38 196n1
9:39–42 49, 196n1

10:18–20 219
11:14–26 196n1
11:18–21 208
13:10–17 197, 205
13:11 205
13:16 205
22:3 200, 205
22:31 210n46, 213

John 202n25
6:70 201
8:39–47 205
8:44 218
13:2 205

Acts 202n25
5:3 204
12:23 196
16:16 196
26:18 204n30, 208

Romans 202n25
1:3–4 207n40
5:12 219
16:20 216, 219

1 Corinthians 202n25
5 206–7
5:1–5 197
5:5 206–8
7:5 204
10:10 196
10:20 69–70
10:20–21 196
11:27–32 207n40
15:21–22 219
15:35–50 207n40

2 Corinthians 202n25
4:4 204
6:14–15 208
6:15 85n25, 156
11:3 219
11:14 73
11:14–15 205
12:7 197, 200, 207–9

Galatians
5:19–23 178

Ephesians 202n25

Colossians 197n7
1:13 202n25

1 Thessalonians 202n25

2 Thessalonians 202n25

1 Timothy 202n25
1:20 206n34, 207n40, 209
2:13–15 219
3:11 201
4:1 196n1
5:14 212

2 Timothy 202n25
2:22–23 178
2:26 204
3:8 157

Hebrews 202n25
2:14 205, 208
7:1–2 150n23
11:28 196

James xxii, 121, 139–41, 202n25, 223
1:13 129–30
1:13–15 139–40
3:14–15 140
3:15 140
4:1–10 204
4:7 158n42
4:7–8a 140

1 Peter 197n7, 202n25
3:18–22 196
5:8 211–12

2 Peter 197n7
2:4 196

1 John 202n25
3:8 208
3:10 208
3:12 218
4:1 72n51, 196

Jude 197n7, 202n25, 210
6 196
8–10 209
9 17n25, 212n51

Revelation 47, 195, 210–11, 213–14, 219
1:5 214
2:10 204, 213
2:20 219
7:14 214
9:11 196
9:20 196
12 xxii, 7, 209, 210n46, 213–14, 218n66
12:7–9 197
12:9 204, 216, 218n66, 219
12:9–10 xv
12:10 7, 47, 195, 209–10, 214
12:11 213–14
12:17 218n66
13:1–10 205
16:14 196n1
17:5 219
18:2 196
20 205n32
20:1-10 197
20:2 216, 219
20:7–10 205
20:10 187, 208

Apocrypha

Baruch
4:7 69–70

Sirach 120–26, 130, 139, 155, 222
Prologue 121n2
6:18–37 122
7:19 122
7:24–26 122
10:30–31 122
11:26–27 121n3
13:13 125
15 124–25, 173–74
15:11 120, 123, 130, 180
15:11–15 155
15:11–20 122–25, 129–30, 139–40, 173
17:1–7 126
17:17 95n40
21:27 198, 198n9
21:28 198n9
22:27–23:6 124n9
24:1–31 122
25:13–26:18 122
25:24 125–26
30:14–17 122
33:14–15 125
36:6 [Eng. 36:9] 212
37:26 121n3
38:16–23 122
38:21 121n3
42:14 126
44:1–50:21 122
50:1–21 121n2
50:27 121

Tobit 67n36, 70n45, 144n3, 145, 145n5, 191
3:8 191
3:16–17 81
3:17 191
6:7 67n36, 70n45, 87n29, 135n34, 145
6:14–18 145

Wisdom of Solomon 121, 217n63
2:24 217n63

Pseudepigrapha

1 Enoch xix, 62, 94, 124n7, 144–45, 154n34, 197
1–36 (Book of the Watchers) xxi, 48, 50, 52, 61–76, 87–89, 92, 96, 116–17, 120, 123–24, 127, 129–32, 134–37, 141, 143, 146, 171, 178–79, 190–91, 197, 216, 222–23
6–11 61–63, 64n32, 65, 68, 81, 137, 218
7:1 63
7:1–2 63
7:3–5 63
8:1 216, 218n64
8:1–2 63, 218n64
9–11 187n47
10:4–8 81
10:11 80–81
10:14 121n3
10:15 65n32
12–16 67n36
15–16 63–69
15:1–16:1 146, 197, 197n7
15:7b–16:1 64n32, 69
15:8 64n32
15:8–10 64–66, 69
15:8–16:1 69, 71, 74, 89
15:9a 64n32
15:11 66n34, 66n35, 67n36, 73
15:11–16:1 66–67
16:1 64n32
17–19 67n36, 69
19 69–70, 124
19:1 60, 67n36, 69–74, 89, 97n45, 134–37, 196n3, 196n5, 197, 197n7
24:2–25 73n56
25:3–7 121n3
32:3–6 73n56
37–71 (Book of Parables) 211, 214–16, 218
40 214–15
40:7 211, 215–16
53:3 199–200, 216n61
53:3–5 215–16
54:6 199–200, 215, 218
65:6 215–16
69:6 218n64
72–82 (Astronomical Book) 127
83–90 (Book of Dreams) 77n3, 127
85–90 (Animal Apocalypse) 96n41
89:59–90:19 96n41
91–108 (Epistle of Enoch) xxi–xxii, 72, 120–21, 126–38, 141, 143, 159–60, 171, 173, 222–23
91:1–94:2 127n16
91:11–17 126n13
92–105 126n13
92:1–5 126n13
93:1–10 126n13
93:1–10+91:11–17 (Apocalypse of Weeks) 126n13, 128, 137, 192n55
93:10–11 126n13
93:11–105:2 126n13
94:6–104:6 126n13, 132n30
94:6–104:8 126n13
96:4–8 127
97:8–10 127
98:4 132n30, 133, 135, 160
98:4b 120–21, 130, 133

98:4–5 129–34, 137, 139–40
98:15–16 127
99:2 127
99:6–9 134
99:7 69–70, 129, 134n33, 136, 196n3
99:7–9 134–37
99:8 72, 136
100:6 137–38
101:1 138
104–7 127n16
104:9–11 127
105:1–2 138n42

2 Enoch 215n60
31:2–6 [recension J] 224

3 Baruch
9:7 217n63

4 Ezra
3:20–26 155
4:30 155
7:92 155

Apocalypse of Abraham
13 217n63, 218n64
23 217n63, 218n64

Apocalypse of Moses
17:1 73

Apocalypse of Zephaniah
3:8–9 214n56

Ascension of Isaiah 224

Assumption of Moses 209n44

Jubilees xix, xxi, 47, 61n28, 68n41, 74–120, 124, 127–29, 132–38, 141–43, 148, 150–51, 153–54, 156–62, 165, 171, 176–79, 184, 188–91, 193, 197, 206n38, 208, 212–14, 222–23
1:11 87
1:19–28 98, 98n47
1:20 85–87, 89, 107n13, 112–114, 137, 150, 156, 211, 215n58
1:20–21 86
2:1 80–81
2:2 80, 93, 94n37, 172, 173n18
2:17–24 137
2:19–20 94
2:19–33 117
3:8–31 116n22
3:17–25 117
4:1–6 116n22, 117
4:9 116n22
4:16–26 127–28
4:17 128n19
4:18 128n19
4:18–19 128
4:31–32 116n22
5:1 94, 96n43
5:1–11 81
5:1–19 116n22
6:7–14 153n33
7:7–15 116n22
7:20–39 79n8, 116n22
7:21 94, 96n43
7:26–27 89–90
7:27 67n36, 87–88, 90
7:29 128n19
8:1–4 116n22
10 18, 88, 90–93, 93n36, 110, 184
10:1 87, 135
10:1–2 136
10:1–13 106, 133–34
10:1–14 68n41, 96n42, 109–11, 116n22, 158
10:2 67n36, 87
10:2–3 87
10:3 87–88, 91n33, 114, 147n14
10:3–6 90–91
10:5 87, 89n30, 184n41
10:6 91, 147n14
10:7–9 174
10:8 81–82, 87, 91, 206
10:8–9 84n23
10:8–11 84n23, 108n14
10:8–12 161
10:8–14 92n35
10:9 91
10:10 81, 98n47
10:10–14 98
10:11 80, 81–82, 84, 87, 91, 94, 199
10:12 73n55, 98n47
10:13 87
10:14–17 79n8
10:17 128n19
10:18–11:6 116n22
11 92–93
11:1–6 132–33
11:4 87
11:4–5 87, 158, 204
11:5 59n24, 81, 87–88, 92, 108n14, 109–11, 133, 137, 160, 174
11:11 81, 174
11:11–13 101, 219
11:11–24 101
11:18–24 101
12:19–27 98
12:20 87, 147n14
15 94–98, 124
15:25–32 137
15:25–34 97n46
15:31 97
15:31–32 87, 92n35, 94–98, 111, 133–34, 136, 151, 189
15:32 94n37
15:33 85–86, 156

17 81–82, 102n2
17:15 101–2, 213
17:15–18:12 174
17:15–18:16 84n23, 101–4, 107, 109–11, 114–15, 118–19, 212, 217–18
17:15–18:17 101n1
17:16 81, 102, 114
17:17–18 96n41, 103
18:9 80–81, 102–3
18:9–11 103
18:12 81, 103, 109, 213
18:18–19 101n1
19:28 86–87
22:17 87
22:17–18 136
23 83
23:28–29 83–84, 147n11
23:29 82–83, 84n23, 87, 94, 198
40:9 82–83, 84n23
46:2 82–83, 84n23, 147n11
48 105–11, 113, 115, 118–19, 184–85, 204, 205n32, 205n33, 217–18
48:2 81, 106n11, 174
48:2–4 96n41, 105, 107, 157, 207n40
48:4 80–81
48:9 81, 106–7, 157, 161
48:9–10 106
48:9–12 177n25
48:12 81, 106, 109
48:13 106
48:14 107n12, 109n15
48:15 81, 108n14
48:15–17 107
48:15–19 107–8, 112–13, 211, 215n58
48:16 108n14, 109n15
48:17 106–9
48:18 113n19
48:18–19 107–8, 113n19
49 105n7
49:2 81n12, 87, 110–11, 157, 205n33
49:2–17 105n7
49:4 87
49:20–22 105n7
50:5 82–83, 84n23, 147n11

Liber antiquitatum biblicarum (Pseudo-Philo)
32:1–2 103n4

Life of Adam and Eve 217n63
12–17 224

Psalms of Solomon
9:4–5 130n23

Sibylline Oracles 156
3:63–74 156n37

Testament of Abraham 151n26

Testament of Job 224
27:1–5 213n55
27:5 213n55

Testament of Moses (Assumption of Moses)
10:1 83n16

Testaments of the Twelve Patriarchs 156, 172n17, 224

Testament of Dan
5:1 156n37

Testament of Issachar
6:1 156n37

Testament of Joseph
20:2 106n10

Testament of Judah
25:3 156n37

Testament of Levi
3:3 156n37
19:1 156n37

Testament of Reuben
4:11 156n37
5:6 73
6:3 156n37

DEAD SEA SCROLLS

CD (Damascus Document) xxii, 133n31, 142, 152–60, 162, 164–65, 177–80, 184–85, 190, 194, 210, 223

CD [MS A] 152n29
1 154n34
2:5–6 157–58
2:7 155
2:7–13 154
2:13 155
2:14–4:12b 153n33
2:16 154–55
2:17–21 155, 190
4:12–13 159–60
4:12–18 174
4:12–19 85n24, 159–60, 185, 204
4:12–21 164
4:13 155–56
4:13–18 161
4:15 155–56
5:17–18 174
5:17–19 85n24, 157, 161, 176–77, 218
5:17c–19 157n40
5:18 155–56, 184

5:18–19 177n25
5:20–6:1 157n40
6:5 152n28
6:19 152n28
7:15 152n28
7:19 152n28
8:1–2 156–158, 161, 206
8:2 155–56
8:21 152n28
12:2 146, 155–56, 161
12:2–3 158–59, 174
16:1–5 158, 185
16:3–4 153
16:4–5 174
16:5 81n12, 156, 184
19:4 155–56
19:13–14 157n41

1Q17 (1QJubilees[a]) 80n10

1Q18 (1QJubilees[b]) 80n10

1QapGen[ar] (Genesis Apocryphon)
20:16 59n24
20:16–17 146
20:26 146

1QS (Rule of the Community) 153n30, 154, 156, 163–65, 167–68, 174, 175n22, 179n28, 185, 210
1:17–18 164
1:18 164, 185
1:22–24 164
1:23–24 164, 185
2:2–5 189
2:4–18 164
2:5 164
2:5–6 206n39
2:19 164, 185
3:13 172n16
3:13–14 176n24
3:13–4:26 (Treatise on Two Spirits) xxii, 143, 151, 154, 167–81, 184, 188, 190–91, 192n55, 193–94, 197n7, 204n31, 223
3:14 169n6, 173n19
3:15–16 168n2
3:17–18 173n19
3:17–19 168–69, 171–72
3:18 170n10
3:19 172
3:20 184
3:20–21 174
3:21–23 175, 177, 180
3:23 174
3:23–25 176–77
3:24 169, 174, 175n22
3:25 169
4:3–6 178
4:9–11 178, 204n31
4:10 169n6
4:15 172n16
4:18–21 180
4:23 173n19
4:23–25 170, 175
4:24 180n29
4:26 173n19
5:20–24 176, 176n24
10:21 164n53

1QSb (1Q28b)
1:8 148n16

1Q29[a] (=1Q29 frags. 13–17) 167n1

1QM (War Rule, 1Q33, see also 4Q494, 11Q14) xxii, 47, 151, 156, 164, 167, 177n25, 181–90, 193–94, 204, 208, 210
1 181–82, 183n37, 186, 189, 192n55, 223
1–9 182n35
1:1 161
1:5 164, 183n38, 189
1:10 183n37
1:10–11 183n39, 186
1:11 186n45
1:13 183n38
1:15–16 186n46
2 181
2–9 182, 187
3:6 183n37
3:9 183n37
4:1–2 183n38, 187, 189
4:2 164
4:2–3 187
4:12–13 187
7:5–6 183n39, 186
9:14–15 183n39
9:15–16 187
10–12 182n35
10–14 182–83
10–19 182n35
11:8 183n38
12:7–9 186
12:7–13 183n39
13 182n35, 183
13:2 183n38
13:4 161
13:4–5 184, 189
13:4–6 183, 209
13:4–12 184
13:9 183n37
13:9–12 183–84
13:10–11 147n12, 156
13:10–12 85n24
13:11 81n12, 161, 184n41, 211n49
13:11–12 146n9, 158
13:12 148–49
13:16 183n37
14 182n35, 184
14:9 161, 164, 183n38
14:9–10 164, 184–85
14:17 183n37

15–19 182, 192n55
16:11 183n37
17 187
17:5–8 187–88
17:6–8 183n39
18:1 183n38, 187, 189
18:3 183n38

1QH[a]
4:6 148n16
11:30 156
11:33 156
14:20 172n14
22:25 147, 184n41
24:23 147, 184n41
25:8 146
45:3 148n16

2Q19 (2QJubilees[a]) 80n10

2Q20 (2QJubilees[b]) 80n10

3Q5 frags. 3, 1 (3QJubilees) 80n10

4QDeut[j] (4Q37)
32:8 59n26, 70n46, 95n39

4QSam[a] (4Q51) 23–24, 44n25
frag. 164, 1–3 23, 24n41

4Q174
4 4 115n21, 161

4Q176[a] frags. 19–21 (=Jubilees) 80n10

4Q186 (4QZodiacal Physiognomy) 177n26

4Q196 (4QpapTobit[a])
14 i 5 144n3, 145
14 i 12 144n3, 145

4Q197 (4QTobit[b])
4 i 13 144n3
4 ii 9 144n3, 145
4 ii 13 144n3, 145

4Q201 (4QEnoch[a]) 61n28, 127n15

4Q202 (4QEnoch[b]) 127n15

4Q204 (4QEnoch[c]) 127n16

4Q212 (4QEnoch[g]) 127n16

4Q213[a] (Aramaic Levi Document)
1 i 17 84n20, 147, 148n16, 198–99

4Q216 (4QJubilees[a]) 77n3, 80n10

4Q218 (4QJubilees[c]) 80n10

4Q219 (4QJubilees[d]) 80n10

4Q220 (4QJubilees[e]) 80n10

4Q221 (4QJubilees[f]) 80n10

4Q222 (4QJubilees[g]) 80n10

4Q223–224 (4QpapJubilees[h]) 80n10

Pseudo-Jubilees (see also 4Q225–226) 85n24, 161–62, 212–13

4Q225 (4QPseudo-Jubilees[a]) 162
2 i–ii 102n3
2 ii 162
2 i 9–10 115, 211n49, 212–13

4Q226 (4QPseudo-Jubilees[b]) 162
frag. 7 162

Pseudo-Daniel (see also 4Q243–4Q244) 144–45

4Q243 (4QPseudo-Daniel[b])
13 2 145

4Q244 (4QPseudo-Daniel[c])
12 2 145

4QSc (4Q257) 167n1, 168n4

4Q280 (or 4QCurses) 150n22, 151

4Q286–4Q287 (or 4QBerakhot) 164n55

4Q286 (4QBerakhot[a])
frag. 7a 164n55
7 ii 2 161

4Q287 (4QBerakhot[b])
frag. 6 164n55

4Q386 (or Pseudo-Ezekiel)
1 iii 4 — 145, 196n4

4Q387
2 iii 4 — 81n12, 96n41, 148

4Q390
1:11 — 81n12
2 i 7 — 81n12, 96n41

4Q417 (or 4QInstruction[c])
1 ii 12 — 139

Barkhi Nafshi (see also 4Q434, 4Q436–4Q438) — xxii, 138–39, 141, 223

4Q434 (4QBarkhi Nafshi[a]) — 121

4Q436 (4QBarkhi Nafshi[c])
1 i–ii — 139n46
1 i 10–ii 4 — 138–39

4Q437 (4QBarkhi Nafshi[d])
4 — 139n46

4Q438 (4QBarkhi Nafshi[e]) — 138n44
4 ii — 139n46

4Q444
1–4 i + 5 8 — 146
2 i 4 — 149n18

4Q494 (4QM[d]) — 181n32

4Q504 (Words of the Luminaries)
17:13–14 — 83n18, 146–47

Songs of the Maskil (see also 4Q510–4Q511) — 144–45, 191

4Q510 (4QSongs of the Maskil[a])
1 5 — 144–46, 190–91
1 5–6 — 148–49

4Q511 (4QSongs of the Maskil[b])
1 6 — 146, 148
1 6–7 — 144
43 6 — 146

Visions of Amram (see also 4Q543–4Q544, 4Q547) — 149–51, 165, 174–75, 175n22, 184

4Q543 (4QVisions of Amram[a]) — 149n19, 149n21
frags. 5–9 — 149n20, 175n21

4Q544 (4QVisions of Amram[b]) — 149n19, 149n21
frag. 1 — 149n20, 175n21
frag. 3 — 150n22

4Q547 (4QVisions of Amram[e]) — 149n19, 149n21
1–2 iii — 149n20, 175n21
3 1 — 145n4

7Q4
1 4 — 145n8

11Q5 (11QPsalms[a])
19:14 — 147n15
19:15 — 146–48, 199

11Q11 (Apocryphal Psalms)
i 10 — 144n3
ii 3 — 144n3, 145
ii 4 — 144n3
v 6 — 68n40, 190
v 12 — 144n3

11Q12 (11QJubilees) — 80n10

11QMelchizedek (11Q13) — 150–51, 156, 188
2:13 — 188

11Q14 (=War Rule) — 181n32

Hellenistic Jewish Sources

Ezekiel the Tragedian
frag. 18 — 217n63

Josephus
Jewish Antiquities
1.180 — 150n23
13.172–73 — 168n2
Jewish War
6.438 — 150n23

Philo
Allegorical Interpretation
3.79 — 150n23
De fuga et inventione
79 — 130n23

Christian Sources

Barnabas
18–21 — 173n20

Didache
1–6 173n20

Irenaeus
Against Heresies
4.41 224
5.24 224

Justin
Dialogue with Trypho
103.5 199n14

Sherpherd of Hermas
Mandate 172n17

Rabbinic Sources

b. Berakhot
16b 147n12

b. Sanhedrin
89b 103n4

Book of Asaph the Physician 84n23

m. Berakhot
9:5 155, 170, 176

m. Nedarim
3:11 207n40

t. Šabbat
17:23 199n14

Classical Sources

Hesiod
Works and Days
110–127 65n33

Plato
Apology
15 (27B–E) 65n33

Plutarch
On Isis and Osiris
47 181n34, 192n55

Sumerian and Akkadian Sources

Gilgamesh and Huwawa xx

Utukkū Lemnūtu incantations 52n8, 54n12, 65n33, 67–68
tablet 4, ll. 139–49 68n39
tablet 4, ll. 158–75 68n38
tablet 5, l. 10 68n30
tablet 6, ll. 40–90 73n54
tablet 6, ll. 55–90 67n37
tablets 13–15, ll. 220–30 67n37

Jewish/Aramaic Amulets and Magic Bowls

Isbell 1975
text 11.10 72n51
text 19.8 72n51

Naveh/Shaked 1993
bowl 22 84n19

Naveh/Shaked 1998
amulet 7, ll. 16–22 68n38
amulet 12, ll. 12–13 72n52
bowl 13, ll. 11–13 72n51, 72n52
bowl 18, ll. 1–2 72n52
bowl 25, ll. 9–10 72n52

Persian Sources

Gathas/Avesta 169–70, 191, 194

Yasna
30:3–5 170